MODERN STUDIE

RYLE

Oscar P. Wood is a Student of Christ
Church, Oxford

George Pitcher is a Professor of
Philosophy, Princeton University

MODERN STUDIES IN PHILOSOPHY
Edited by Amelie Rorty

Modern Studies in Philosophy is a series of anthologies presenting contemporary interpretations and evaluations of the works of major philosophers. The editors have selected articles designed to show the systematic structure of the thought of these philosophers, and to reveal the relevance of their views to the problems of current interest. These volumes are intended to be contributions to contemporary debates as well as to the history of philosophy; they not only trace the origins of many problems important to modern philosophy, but also introduce major philosophers as interlocutors in current discussions.

Titles in the Series

Other titles in preparation

MODERN STUDIES IN PHILOSOPHY

RYLE

EDITED BY OSCAR P. WOOD
AND GEORGE PITCHER

Introduction by Gilbert Ryle

MACMILLAN

© Doubleday & Co. Inc. 1970

First published in the United States of America 1970
First published in Great Britain 1971

Published by
MACMILLAN AND CO LTD
London and Basingstoke
Associated companies in New York Toronto
Dublin Melbourne Johannesburg and Madras

SBN 333 12263 1 (hard cover)

Printed in Great Britain by
RICHARD CLAY (THE CHAUCER PRESS), LTD
Bungay, Suffolk

CONTENTS

Gilbert Ryle's writings over the last forty years have established him as the most fertile British philosopher of the middle of the century. Few philosophers have been unaffected by his views and almost all have at some time made use of his extensive additions to the battery of philosophical tools. The essays in this volume, most of which were written specially for it, are eloquent evidence of the stimulus he continues to provide to fruitful explorations over a wide area of philosophical concerns.

O. P. W.
G. P.

AUTOBIOGRAPHICAL

GILBERT RYLE

I

My father was a general practitioner, with two deep extrinsic interests. He was an amateur astronomer and a philosopher. He contributed two papers to the Aristotelian Society in its very early days. I do not recollect him talking much in the home on philosophical matters, but his large and variegated library contained many philosophical and semi-philosophical works—and I was an omnivorous reader.

When he was a young man he had migrated into agnosticism from the Evangelicalism in which his father, eventually the first Bishop of Liverpool, had raised him.

We ten children were brought up unchurched and non-church-going. I fancy that I was stimulated in my teens to think defensive heretical thoughts by our exemption from the orthodoxies that naturally prevailed at school. But I cannot claim to have been persecuted there, or even vexatiously teased for our godlessness. My schooldays coincided with the First World War and this preoccupied us all. I remember a young schoolmaster, recently down from Oxford, asking us in the Sixth Form "What is colour?" I gave a Lockean sort of answer, and laughed knowingly at the expense of a boy who declared that colour was paint. I scored five marks for my sapience. I remember another master saying, "Ryle, you are very good on theories, but you are very bad on facts." My attempts to repair this latter weakness were short-lived and unsuccessful.

In 1919 I went up to Oxford, where for the first five terms I was working rather half-heartedly for Classical Honour Moderations. I lacked the ear, the nostrils, the palate, and the toes that are needed for excellence in linguistic and literary studies. However I took greedily to the off-centre subject of Logic. It felt to me like a grown-up subject, in which there were still unsolved problems. This was not my impression of the Classics in general, as they were then taught. However I gladly learned from Aristophanes and from an Aristophanic tutor that Ancient Greece had not been wholly populated by the stately, cultured, and liberal-minded sages whom Alma Tadema depicted and in whom eminent Hellenists encouraged us to believe.

For my next seven terms I was working for Greats in ancient and modern philosophy, and in Greek and Roman history. I do not recall being at all worried by the non-integration of our Roman history with our modern philosophy; or even of our Greek history with our Greek philosophy, which happened to belong to different curricular "periods." But I did think that the Academy mattered more than the Peloponnesian War.

I was from the start philosophically eager. I became a member of the undergraduates' Jowett Society fairly early and I read a lot of self-discovered things that surprised my philosophy tutor to hear about. I disappointed him by failing to appreciate the bulk of Plato's *Republic*. This tepidness was not due to any comparisons between it and other, philosophically superior dialogues. I had not read any of these, any more than had, apparently, most of the Plato-venerating philosophy tutors of that era. They treated the *Republic* like the Bible, and to me most of it seemed, philosophically, no better.

H. J. Paton was my tutor. Some of my fellow students found him too unforthcoming, but for me his untiring "Now, Ryle, what *exactly* do you mean by . . . ?" was an admirable spur. He was an unfanatical Crocean, which, at the time, was the main alternative to being a Cook Wilsonian. His evolution into a wholehearted Kant-scholar and expositor had begun before I ceased to be *in statu pupillari.* In 1924 I spent some time acquiring a reading knowledge of Italian and a modest grasp of Italian philosophy by reading some Croce, but more Gentile, with the text under my nose and a dictionary in my hand. The chief thing that I now remember having learned from Croce was this quite unintended lesson. Croce seemed to divide the Spirit, whatever that was, into two houses, each of which was divided into two floors. Spirit, *qua* theoretical, split into Philosophical and Scientific thinkings, *qua* practical into moral and economic doings. The philosophical top-floor of the theoretical half enjoyed some sort of zenith-standing. I remember drawing the startling conclusion, though not in these words, "Then, since philosophical thinking is a Good Thing, Bertrand Russell's thinking, in so far as it is philosophical, cannot be a Bad Thing, yet that is what Oxford philosophers ostracise it for being. So, despite them, I ought to look at it, lest I miss something that ought not to be missed." I did look at it. I dare say that this hop from a book by Croce to Russell's *Principles of Mathematics* was partly powered by some native recalcitrance towards the official line.

In my fifth year I worked for the new school of Modern Greats. Though my time was short and heavily preempted by unacademic avocations, I managed, without over-industry, not only to accumulate an adequate stock of Economics and Politics, but also to teach myself a smattering of scholastic philosophy. I did this partly from inquisitiveness and partly as a strategic move against my examiners-to-be, who would get from the other candidates nothing but post-Cartesian pabulum. I believe I did in fact refresh them with my uncovenanted Greek and mediaeval philosophy. In October 1924 I became a lecturer in philosophy at Christ Church, and began teaching at once. The senior philosophy tutor was then H. W. Blunt. He soon retired, and I was joined by M. B. Foster.

II

During my time as an undergraduate and during my
first few years as a teacher, the philosophic kettle in Oxford was barely lukewarm. I think that it would have been
stone cold but for Prichard, who did bring into his chosen
and rather narrow arenas vehemence, tenacity, uncere-
moniousness, and a perverse consistency that made our
hackles rise, as nothing else at that time did. The Bradleians were not yet extinct, but they did not come out
into the open. I cannot recollect hearing one referring
mention of the Absolute. The Cook Wilsonians were
hankering to gainsay the Bradleians and the Croceans,
but were given few openings. Pragmatism was still represented by F. C. S. Schiller, but as his tasteless jocosities
beat vainly against the snubbing primnesses of his colleagues, even this puny spark was effectually quenched.

Logic, save for Aristotelian scholarship, was in the
doldrums. Little was heard now even of the semi-
psychological topics discussed in Bradley's mis-titled *Principles of Logic*. Russell's *Principles of Mathematics* had
been published when I was three; twenty-five years later
it and *Principia Mathematica* were still only the objects
of Oxonian pleasantries. The names of Boole, De Mor-
gan, Venn, Jevons, McColl, Frege, Peano, Johnson, and
J. M. Keynes did not yet crop up in lectures or discussions. In the bibliography of the Kneales' *The Development of Logic* no Oxford entries, save contributions to
scholarship, belonged to the half century from Lewis Car-
roll (1896).

The two branches of philosophy in which there was
some life were ethics and the theory of sense-perception.
It was from a consuming interest in sense-perception that
Henry Price, with heroic sangfroid, migrated for a post-
graduate spell to the university of Moore, Russell, and
Broad. He thus made himself our first personal and doc-
trinal link with "the other place," and launched the idea

that young Oxford could and should learn from Cambridge. Soon Oxford's hermetically conserved atmosphere began to smell stuffy even to ourselves.

Two other major ventilators were opened in the second half of the 1920s.

1). Some of us junior philosophy tutors began to attend the annual Joint Sessions of the Mind Association and the Aristotelian Society. We thus got to know, and to exchange ideas with our colleagues, senior and junior, from Cambridge, London, Scotland, Ireland, Wales, and the provincial universities, and occasionally also with visitors from overseas. Moore was always there; and even by itself, his to us surprising willingness to listen, combined with his impartial readiness to explode at our sillinesses and to explode at his own, would have made the week-end a heart-warming and hair-raising experience. It was at the Joint Session of 1929 that I struck up a friendship with Wittgenstein, of whose *Tractatus Logico-Philosophicus* I had for some time been a mystified admirer. I had already realized that it was centrally concerned with Russell's antithesis of the nonsensical to the true-or-false, an antithesis which mattered a lot to me then and has mattered ever since.

2). Before the end of the 1920s some of us junior philosophers started the "Wee Teas." This was an informal dining-club of six members that met once a fortnight during term, with the host of the evening providing a discussion-opening paper after dinner. The club, which we wound up in the middle 1960s, took its name "the Wee Teas" by parody from the famous Scots sect; but it also signalised a contrast with a current Oxford institution known as "the Thursday Teas." This was a weekly *omnium gatherum* of teachers of philosophy, at which a short philosophical discussion ensued upon tea and buns. These meetings tended to be crowded and hurried. They were dominated, quite properly, by our seniors, too few of whom, owing to the 1914–18 massacres, were much less than a generation older than our juvenile selves. We did not secede from this semi-routine philosophical tea-party. But our tongues wagged more freely and our wits moved less deferentially in our own evening sessions. The members of the "Wee Teas" were, not all synchronously, Cox, Franks, Hardie, Kneale, C. S. Lewis, Mabbott, Maclagan, Price and Ryle. The club was not, either academically or philosophically, a cabal or a crusade. We never aimed at unanimity or achieved it; but we could try out anything on one another without anyone being shocked or rude or polite. Each of us had five friends and no allies. Without our noticing it at the time, hustings-words ending in "ism" and "ist" faded out of our use. In this and other ways we were outgrowing some then prevalent attitudes towards philosophical issues. We discovered that it was possible to be at once in earnest and happy.

III

I must have been near my middle twenties when good-humoured fraternal scepticisms about the existence of my subject showed me that it really was part of my business to be able to tell people, including myself, what philosophy is. Perhaps it was this brotherly tail-twisting that awakened me rather early to the plot of Wittgenstein's *Tractatus*. Anyhow, probably over-influenced by Socrates' fruitless hunts for definitions, I was soon declaring, vaguely enough but not yet modishly, that what philosophers examine is the meanings of expressions. In the discussion that followed my, I suppose, first paper to the Jowett Society, Paton asked, "Ah, Ryle, how *exactly* do you distinguish between philosophy and lexicography?" I am sure that it was only much later than this that I was prepared to reply that the philosopher's proprietary question is not "What does this or that expression mean?", but "Why does this or that expression make nonsense? and

what *sort* of nonsense does it make?". By this time, I expect, I would have flourished the grand phrases "logical
syntax" and "logical grammar."

It was, I suppose, at about this same time and partly in
reaction to the same tail-twistings, that I got the idea,
which I have retained, that philosophising essentially incorporates argumentation; and so incorporates it that,
whereas a weak or faulty inference might by luck put
Sherlock Holmes on the track of the murderer, a weak or
faulty philosopher's argument is itself a philosophical
blind alley. In this field there is no detachment of the
conclusion from its premisses, if indeed the idiom of
premisses and conclusions is appropriate here at all.

If, for whatever reasons and in whatever way, philosophy involves reasoning, then, I argued, the theory and
technology of reasoning needed to be studied by a
would-be philosopher. It was from this interest, and not
from Price's interest in sense-perception, that I "went all
Cambridge." It was Russell and not Moore whom I
studied, and it was Russell the logician and not Russell
the epistemologist. Having no mathematical ability,
equipment, or interest, I did not make myself even competent in the algebra of logic; nor did the problem of the
foundations of mathematics become a question that
burned in my belly. My interest was in the theory of
Meanings—horrid substantive!—and quite soon, I am
glad to say, in the theory of its senior partner, Nonsense.
I laboured upon the doublets:—Sense and Reference, In-
tension and Extension, Concept and Object, Propositions
and Constituents, Objectives and Objects, Facts and
Things, Formal Concepts and Real Concepts, Proper
Names and Descriptions, and Subjects and Predicates. It
was in Russell's *Principles of Mathematics* and not his
Principia Mathematica, in his Meinong articles and his
"On Denoting" and not his epistemology that I found the
pack-ice of logical theory cracking. It was up these cracks
that Wittgenstein steered his *Tractatus.*

IV

At about the time that I became a don, I started to
teach myself German, partly by travel and partly by
dictionary-aided reading. It may have been on a suggestion from Paton that I quite soon embarked on Husserl's *Logische Untersuchungen*; before long I was reading this alongside of Meinong, Brentano, Bolzano, and
Frege. My interest was at first in the strengths, and then
in the endemic weaknesses of Platonistic, because anti-
psychologistic theories of Meaning, i.e. of concepts and
propositions. I even offered an unwanted course of lectures, entitled "Logical Objectivism: Bolzano, Brentano,
Husserl and Meinong." These characters were soon
known in Oxford as "Ryle's three Austrian railway-
stations and one Chinese game of chance." I was right in
thinking that their Meaning-theories would reflect some
light on and borrow some light from the partly parallel
doctrines of Frege and of Moore and Russell in their early
Edwardian days. Because Mill was wrong, Heaven had to
be stocked with Logical Objects. But could the Angel
Gabriel admit Illogical Objects? or must even Heaven
kowtow to what Husserl, like Wittgenstein after him,
called "the rules of logical grammar" or "logical syntax?"
When, if ever, is an *Ens Rationis* qualified to be an Entity? Of what class of Objects can logic be the science, if
disqualified Objects have to be amongst them? Although
Husserl, unlike Meinong and like Russell, interested me
by taking very seriously the opposition between Sense
and Nonsense, he failed to make very much of it. Unlike
Russell, he did not adduce ensnaring, and so challenging,
specimens of breaches of logical syntax. He did not hit
upon the paradox-generators and therefore did not try to
build up any general diagnostic or preventive theory. I
suppose that there was no one around him to keep him
on the *qui vive* with logicians' teasers. It was a pity, but
not a very great pity that his *Logische Untersuchungen*

was not, as projected, reviewed for *Mind* by Russell during his period of incarceration in the First World War.

It is sometimes suggested that in my well or ill spent youth I had been for a while a disciple of Husserl's phenomenology. There is not much truth in this. A good deal of phenomenology does indeed get into the second edition of Husserl's *Logische Untersuchungen*, which is what I was reading alongside of Meinong, Frege, Bolzano, Moore and Russell. So I did duly try to make out what this new "-ology" was, and why it was there. This involved me in reading things that Husserl and others contributed to the *Jahrbuch für Philosophie und Phänomenologische Forschung*. One of these, by R. Ingarden, I reviewed in *Mind* in 1927. I realized pretty soon that Husserl's intentionalist, anti-psychologistic theory of Meaning/Nonsense, which was what interested me, owed nothing to his posterior Phenomenology, and bequeathed too little to it. I consolidated what I had moderately industriously made out of Husserl's generous promises for Phenomenology and out of his slenderer performances in it in three or four only partly sympathetic things that were published in *Mind*, 1927 and 1929, in the *Aristotelian Society Proceedings* (1932), and *Philosophy*, 1946; and finally in "*La Phenomenologie contre 'The Concept of Mind,'*" 1962. In 1929 I had in *Mind* a long notice of Heidegger's *Sein und Zeit*. I wrote this in ignorance of the existence of Kierkegaard, and with no thought of distinguishing Husserlian Phenomenology from something to be called "Existentialism." Fairly soon in the 1930s I dropped my rather solitary studies of Husserl's *Logische Untersuchungen* and of his phenomenology. I was amused to find the latter, together with Heidegger's Existentialism, becoming the *dernier cri* in France after the Second World War.

v

In the 1930s the Vienna Circle made a big impact on my generation and the next generation of philosophers.

Most of us took fairly untragically its demolition of Metaphysics. After all we never met anyone engaged in committing any metaphysics; our copies of *Appearance and Reality* were dusty; and most of us had never seen a copy of *Sein und Zeit*. On the other hand there was obviously something very important, though still disordered, in the Principle of Verifiability (and Falsifiability), quite apart from its Augean applications. We were not yet talking in the obsessive lingo of "criteria." But its cash-equivalents were already entering into our purchases and sales.

There was a second quite unintended result of Logical Positivism. For by jointly equating Metaphysics with Nonsense and Sense with Science, it raised the awkward question "Where then do we anti-nonsense philosophers belong? Are the sentences of which *Erkenntnis* itself is composed Metaphysics? Then are they Physics or Astronomy or Zoology? What of the sentences and formulae of which *Principia Mathematica* consists?" We were facing what was in effect the double central challenge of Wittgenstein's *Tractatus Logico-Philosophicus* and the single central challenge of his future *Philosophical Investigations*. Neurath, Schlick, Carnap, Waismann, and for us, above all others, Ayer had undeliberately raised a problem the solution to which was neither in the *Logical Syntax of Language* nor yet in the *Tractatus*. We philosophers were in for a near-lifetime of enquiry into our own title to be enquirers. Had we any answerable questions, including this one?

The conviction that the Viennese dichotomy "Either Science or Nonsense" had too few "ors" in it led some of us, including myself, to harbour and to work on a derivative suspicion. If, after all, logicians and even philosophers can say significant things, then perhaps some logicians and philosophers of the past, even the remote past, had, despite their unenlightenment, sometimes said significant things. "Conceptual analysis" seems to denote a permissible, even meritorious exercise, so maybe some of our forefathers had had their Cantabrigian moments. If we are careful to winnow off their vacuously speculative tares from their analytical wheat, we may find that some of them sometimes did quite promising work in our own line of business. Naturally we began, in a patronising mood, by looking for and finding in the Stoics, say, or Locke, primitive adumbrations of our own most prized thoughts. But before long some of them seemed to move more like pioneers than like toddlers, and to talk to us across the ages more like colleagues than like pupils; and then we forgot our pails of whitewash.

In my own case this reaction was strengthened by my occasional visits to the Moral Sciences Club at Cambridge. At its meetings veneration for Wittgenstein was so incontinent that mentions, for example my mentions, of other philosophers were greeted with jeers. Wittgenstein himself not only properly distinguished philosophical from exegetic problems but also, less properly, gave the impressions, first, that he himself was proud not to have studied other philosophers—which he had done, though not much—and second, that he thought that people who did study them were academic and therefore unauthentic philosophers, which was often but not always true. This contempt for thoughts other than Wittgenstein's seemed to me pedagogically disastrous for the students and unhealthy for Wittgenstein himself. It made me resolve, not indeed to be a philosophical polyglot, but to avoid being a monoglot; and most of all to avoid being one monoglot's echo, even though he was a genius and a friend. This resolve was all the easier to keep because, for local curricular reasons, I and my colleagues had as students had to study, and had now as teachers to teach in considerable detail some of the thoughts of, *inter alios*, Plato, Aristotle, Descartes, Hume, and Kant. Some of these thoughts were potent enough to make comparison of their author with, say, Wittgenstein, honorific to both, and, what matters much more, elucidatory of both.

VI

Quite soon after I doffed my khaki in 1945, Paton, as Editor of the new series, Hutchinson's *Philosophical Library,* invited me to contribute to it. I agreed, without yet having a clear mind about the future book's theme. I did know, however, that I wanted to apply, and be seen to be applying to some large-scale philosophical crux the answer to the question that had preoccupied us in the 1920s, and especially in the 1930s, the question namely "What constitutes a philosophical problem; and what is the way to solve it?" Lots of us had delivered and replied to papers on this theme; lots of us had published articles and discussion-notes bearing directly or indirectly on it; and our useful little discussion-journal *Analysis* had for its title the noun that was prevalently used to identify the thing, or one of the things, that non-metaphysical philosophers were permitted carefully to do. But by the later 1940s it was time, I thought, to exhibit a sustained piece of analytical hatchet-work being directed upon some notorious and large-sized Gordian Knot. After a long spell of enlightened methodological talk, what was needed now was an example of the method really working, in breadth and depth and where it was really needed.

For a time I thought of the problem of the Freedom of the Will as the most suitable Gordian Knot; but in the end I opted for the Concept of Mind—though the book's actual title did not occur to me until the printers were hankering to begin printing the first proofs. *The Concept of Mind* was a philosophical book written with a meta-philosophical purpose. Five years later my Tarner Lectures, entitled "Dilemmas," were fairly explicitly dedicated to the consolidation and diversification of what had been the meta-theme of the *Concept of Mind.*

VII

About the last twenty years of my professorial-*cum*-editorial existence nothing genetically informative remains to be said. However, for the sake of the record, I give two negative things in reply to questions that have been asked and will be asked.

1). R. G. Collingwood, despite the great, but belatedly recognized merits of some of his philosophical writings, had no influence at all on me, or I think on most of my contemporaries, either in our student days or after we had become his colleagues. That I did not attend his lectures shows little, since I was unassiduous as a lecture-goer. But I do not think that they were attended much even by other philosophically lively undergraduates. When we became philosophy tutors we saw a little more of him at Sub-Faculty Committee meetings and at those "Thursday Teas" of which he was host. He was completely conscientious, though cheerless, in the performance of his academic duties. I think he was as unhappy in the company of his philosophical colleagues as he was, I gather, happy in that of archaeologists and musicians. I surmise that he had quite early been lacerated by the Joseph-Prichard treatment, but lacked the resilience to retaliate; and that he then, very unwisely, deemed all philosophical colleagues to be unworthy. When, in 1935, I launched in *Mind* an unconciliatory criticism of the version of the Ontological Argument in his *Essay on Philosophical Method*, I had never heard him say a word on this or any contiguous matter; and though my article resulted in some correspondence between us, I am pretty sure that we never met to reduce or to liquidate our differences. If I knew his Christian name, it certainly never tripped off my tongue, even behind his back. I think, in retrospect, that my generation was at fault in not even trying to cultivate our remote senior; but he missed a golden opportunity by keeping himself aloof from the post-war recruits into the Sub-Faculty of Philosophy. Philosophy got moving at Oxford without his participation.

2). John Austin and I had a good deal to do with one another in administrative matters, especially after he became my brother-professor. There were many routine contingencies and one or two rows in which we were allies. On the other hand I did not see or hear very much of him as a philosopher. He was not a member of the "Wee Teas"; and we who were senior to him were wisely made ineligible for his "Saturday Mornings." By cultivating hearsay I did get to know something of what had passed in these Saturday discussions, but until Urmson and Warnock published his ideas after his tragically early death, I did not realize their range and depth. Many of them were completely new to me. Naturally I heard his formal and informal contributions to our Philosophical Society; but not his contributions to the undergraduates' Jowett Society, since I had for a long time kept away from its meetings in the belief that it was being suffocated by over-patronage from dons and graduates. A paper of mine entitled "Ordinary Language," which came out in the *Philosophical Review* in 1953, touches, I now think, only peripherally on the features of language in which Austin had been chiefly interested, though at the time I was almost unaware of this.

In any case I doubt if there would have been very much overlap between his thoughts and mine—or much conflict either. My chief, though not sole, interest in linguistic matters focussed on such dictions as were, (or else by contrast were not) in breach of "logical syntax"; and of the outcasts it focussed especially on the trouble-makers and the paradox-generators. For these enquiries written or printed specimens are more convenient than those which are vocally uttered, very much as the anatomist of fallacies prefers, if possible, to have his specimens on paper or on the blackboard.

Austin's main interests, however, were in the dictions which constitute communications between persons, with

spoken communications having preference over even
epistolary communications. It is almost true to say that
he was out to classify and describe all the kinds of our
sayings *other* than that one kind of saying that logicians
care about, namely delivering a premiss or a conclusion.
What the blackboard is for is not what the voice is for.

An examiner might pose two questions:—

1) Why cannot a traveller reach London gradually?
2) Why is "I warn you . . ." the beginning of a warning, but "I insult you . . ." not the beginning of an
insult?

On six days out of seven Question 1 would be Ryle's favourite; Question 2, Austin's. Each of us would think—
wrongly—that there is not much real meat in the un-
favoured question. But their meats are of such entirely
disparate kinds that the epithet "linguistic" would apply
in totally different ways 1) to the answer-sketch "Adverbs
like 'gradually' won't go with verbs like 'reach' for the
following reason . . ."; 2) to the answer-sketch "To
insult is to say to someone else pejorative things with
such and such an intention, while to warn is to say. . . ."
Anti-nonsense rules govern impartially sayings of all
types. "Reach gradually" will not do in questions, commands, counsels, requests, warnings, complaints, promises, insults, or apologies, any more than it will do in
statements. Epimenides can tease us in any grammatical
mood. To an enquiry into categorial requirements, references to differences of saying-type are irrelevant; to an
enquiry into differences between saying-types, references
to category-requirements are irrelevant. Infelicities and
absurdities are not even congeners.

CRITICAL REVIEW OF
THE CONCEPT OF MIND

This is probably one of the two or three most important and original works of general philosophy which have been published in English in the last twenty years. Both its main thesis and the mass of its detailed observations will certainly be a focus of discussion among philosophers for many years to come; and it has the distinction of style and the large simplicity of purpose which have always made the best philosophical writing a part of general literature. The avoidance of technical jargon, and the disdain of footnote and historical allusion, are evidently parts of a design to restore philosophy to common sense in the manner of the eighteenth century; as in Hume, the accepted distinctions of the Schools are very rarely introduced except as subjects for derision, though the derision is generally of a more robust, and sometimes even knockabout, character than was natural to Hume. The thought and the style are indissolubly linked in a manner which constitutes both the strength and, as it seems to me, also the weakness of the book; its strength, in that the reader is carried from beginning to end by a single sustained impetus; its weakness, in that its argument seems somehow to fade and to lose some of its force when, laying the book down, one probes it again in some other and less powerful idiom. There is only one property which I can discover to be common to Professor Ryle and Immanuel Kant; in both cases the style is the philosopher—as Kant thought and wrote in dichotomies, Professor Ryle writes in epigrams. There are many passages in which the argu-

Mind, Vol. LIX, 1950, pp. 237–55. Reprinted with permission of the author and the Editor of *Mind*.

ment simply consists of a succession of epigrams, which
do indeed effectively explode on impact, shattering conventional trains of thought, but which, like most epigrams, leave behind among the debris in the reader's
mind a trail of timid doubts and qualifications. The book
is avowedly a recantation; the ghost which has haunted
the author is being publicly exorcised; and so the false
doctrine is assailed with that intimate savagery which is
peculiar to recantations. The case is admittedly presented in a forensic manner and with many devices of
rhetoric. What is presented as a case and polemically asks
to be examined as a case and polemically; for out of such
definite statement and counter-statement may emerge
some outline of what is in general tenable and untenable.
Therefore this review will be one-sidedly critical.

Professor Ryle's argument is not merely that previous
philosophers have made a number of particular mistakes
in the characterisation of particular points of ordinary
usage and ways of thought; they have been wrong in detail because they have been wrong in principle. His brilliant exposures of particular misinterpretations is designed to replace one general principle of interpretation
by another; the slogan is—not Two Worlds, but One
World. It is for this reason that the book must serve as a
catalyst in contemporary philosophy, causing half-defined
views and methods to separate and crystallise by its own
original energy. There have been so many guarded adumbrations and esoteric hints in British philosophy in the
last fifteen years; here at last is a book which actually uses
the now rapidly changing methods of linguistic analysis
to cut the root of a large metaphysical problem. Methods
perpetually refined but never applied become a new form
of scholasticism. The old high metaphysical philosophy,
the tradition of Plato and Spinoza, claiming access to
special truths not vulgarly expressible, could reasonably
be recondite; but if analytical philosophy really is what it
claims to be, it must ultimately issue in plain and pointed

prose, with most of the workshop apparatus of technical distinction left in the background; this, in the tradition of Locke and Berkeley, Mill and Russell, Professor Ryle supremely achieves, though perhaps with the plainness sometimes rather heavily emphasised.

I shall argue that "The Concept of Mind" has the radical incoherences natural to a book written in transition, the transition being from one conception of logic and philosophical method to another. Not Two-Worlds, but One World; not a Ghost, but a Body; (people are not) Occult but Obvious. Professor Ryle has been betrayed into using the weapons of his enemy; it appears that the arguments which are fatal to the assertion in each case must be no less fatal to the counter-assertion: for they are *logical* arguments directed against the form and generality of such philosophical statements, irrespective of whether they are affirmed or denied; and these logical arguments are often used and implied by Professor Ryle himself as part of his attack, only to be neglected again in the polemical form of his conclusions. Thus there is (I think) an ambiguity of purpose confusing the argument from its beginning.

I shall assume that almost every reader of *Mind* will be a reader of this book, and that therefore a detailed summary of its argument would be a waste of space. I cannot even mention the less radically controversial and more purely analytical parts of the book, although they are among its most original contributions. In particular, I cannot discuss the detailed analysis of skills, competences, learnings, knowing how, which are parts of a general Aristotelian theory of παιδεία re-introduced into philosophy as one of the rightful heirs of the condemned pseudo-science of epistemology (pp. 317–18); for I believe that this valuable analysis becomes open to challenge only when it is made the type to which the analysis of all mental concepts must be assimilated.

2. *The Myth; its Nature and Origins.*

A polemic requires an enemy. The difficulty is to pick out the Enemy in actual historical shape; it is Cartesianism (not simply and solely Descartes himself (p. 23)), also "the official doctrine" and "the para-mechanical hypothesis." But precise historical identification, and even more the historical order of responsibility, are not relevant to Professor Ryle's purposes. He holds it enough that the false doctrine is known to have been held by at least one person (the author) in order that by its public destruction the true may be imparted. But the first cardinal mistake pervading the book is just this assumption that the *origin* of the conception of the mind as a ghost within a machine is of purely historical and of no philosophical interest. Had Professor Ryle pressed the inquiry into the origins of the conception (there is a half-page Historical Note on p. 23, which is particularly inadequate on the Greeks, who are here all-important), he must have realised that, so far from being imposed on the plain man by philosophical theorists, and even less by seventeenth century theorists, the myth of the mind as a ghost within the body is one of the most primitive and natural of all the innumerable myths which are deeply imbedded in the vocabulary and structure of our languages. The plain fact is that in many (perhaps most) European languages the words for mind, soul or spirit are the same as, or have the same roots as, the words for ghost, and were the same long before Descartes or modern mechanics were conceived. Apart altogether from the actual myth of detachable minds surviving as ghosts, which extends continuously from early epic into Christian literature, there is the traceable history of such words as ψυχη, πνεῦμα, *anima*, and many others, from which our vulgar concept of mind is descended. Such a philosophically relevant word-history would show the ghost and the two-substance conception of persons as the natural, vernacular mode of description existing before, and developing in part independently of, the attempts of Plato and of Christian theorists to systematise it as self-conscious doctrine. Professor Ryle throughout represents philosophers as corrupting the literal innocence of common sense speech with alien metaphors. In this he not only greatly exaggerates the influence of philosophers, and particularly of Descartes, on the forms of common speech, but (more seriously) neglects the fact, or rather the necessity, that the forms of common speech and its modes of description should be permeated with such metaphors, most of which can ultimately be traced back to underlying myths and imaginative pictures. In his suspicion of metaphor and of graphic representations in language he is himself a follower of Descartes. It is characteristically a philosopher's complaint (*e.g.* Bradley, Bergson and many others) that we normally describe mental processes and conditions in terms which have been transferred from an original use in application to physical objects. As transferred terms are, by definition and etymology, metaphors, most commonplace psychological descriptions may therefore be said to be ultimately metaphorical. How otherwise can language develop?

Professor Ryle is here protesting not (as he believes) against a *philosophical theory* of mind, but against a universal feature of ordinary language itself—namely, that most of its forms of description have been and are being evolved by the constant transfer of terms from application in one kind of context to application in another, and in particular by the transfer of what were originally physical descriptions (*e.g.* "wires and pulleys," "impulses," "pushes and pulls," "agitations," etc.) into psychological descriptions. A typical instance of this Fallacy of Literalness comes in the discussion of the common and ancient phrase "In my head" (p. 35); the underlying assumption is that the "primary" or "real" sense of the word "in" is the spatial sense, and that other senses or uses must be metaphorical. In fact there are tens and perhaps hundreds of established uses of "in" in a non-spatial sense which can no longer be described as metaphorical (e.g. "In the English constitution," "In the spirit of the Act"). Even if some of these uses ultimately originated as spatial metaphors, their significance does not now depend on their being given any spatial or physical interpretation. Again, Professor Ryle distinguishes (p. 37) the tune which is only metaphorically in my head from noises which are *literally* in my head *by the use of a very significant criterion;* the *"real"* head-borne noises are those "which the doctor could hear through his stethoscope"—(*cf.* p. 199, "A special sense of 'in,' since the surgeon will not find it (*sc,* a sensation) under the person's epidermis"). These are only two instances of a fallacy which largely vitiates the discussion of impulses, motives, volitions, and mental conflicts, and to a less extent, of images and sense-impressions (consider the history of the words εἴδωλον, φάντασμα "species," "idea" and many others). It seemed as natural to the Greeks and Romans as it still does to us to describe the experience of mental conflict in terms of pushes and pulls, to describe themselves as *moved* to action, and to speak of images as mental pictures. The so-called para-mechanical hypothesis is no more than the very general fact that we naturally think and describe diagrammatically (*e.g.* about God, Time, and the English constitution), even when we are not talking about objects in space, or (the same fact differently expressed) we transfer terms originally used to describe visual or other sense-experience into other contexts, unconnected with sense-perception (most cognitive verbs are so derived). Another example—un-philosophical man had naturally talked of "the inward eye" (in the Bible for instance) hundreds of years before introspection became "a term of art" (p. 163); the inner-outer "metaphor" was incorporated in the verbs and adjectives of ordinary speech long before it was formulated as explicit theory by modern epistemologists. Lastly, common-sense language is in fact, for better or for worse, firmly dualistic, in the sense that we do operate—and have operated since the earliest known literature—a distinction, or rather a whole set of distinctions, involving various and shifting criteria, between mental and physical states and events. We constantly ask, and are beginning to answer, various more or less general questions about the relation between a person's body and his mind, questions which cannot therefore be dismissed as "improper" (p. 168) if ordinary usage is to be authoritative; it is Professor Ryle, and not only Descartes, who displays an *a priori* theory of language involving a conflict with established usage, when he rejects (p. 22) the dogma that "there occur physical processes and mental processes; that there are mechanical causes of corporeal movements, and mental causes of corporeal movements" and argues that "these and other analogous conjunctions are absurd," his cryptic reason being "that the phrase 'there occur mental processes' does not *mean the same sort of thing** as 'there occur physical processes' and therefore that it makes no sense to conjoin or disjoin the two" (p. 22). Certainly when, outside philosophy, we habitually distinguish between the mental and physical causes of bodily conditions or movements, we are often confused, and would almost always find difficulty in formulating the very various and also historically changing criteria of distinction which we apply in different contexts; and certainly Descartes in his rigid formulation deliberately over-simplified the distinction in the interests of his programme of science (p. 21). But, just because Professor Ryle has from the beginning confused a general feature of common language with a particular metaphysical theory, it is never clear precisely whom he is attacking when he attacks the Ghost and therefore what weapons are appropriate. His own explanations of his method (pp. 8, 16, 17, 21–23) unfortunately involve such notoriously obscure expressions as

---

* The asterisk throughout indicates that the italics are my own.

"logical category," "logical type" and "the sort of thing
which is meant by . . ."; obscure, because they at first
look like distinctions in actual grammar (see p. 101) but,
where attacked with counter-examples, turn into some
ideal, "Logical Grammar" (p. 244); in fact behind this
ideal grammar there is implied this literalist theory of
language, which betrays itself in many of the arguments
used.

3. *What do our principal mental concepts stand for?*

This is the fatal question in terms of which much of
the argument proceeds; take any psychological verb, and
ask whether it "stands for," "names," "denotes," "signi-
fies," or "designates," either an occurrence (episode) or
a disposition, two processes or one process, a relation
("such transitive verbs do not signify relations" p. 209),
a thing ("the phrase 'my twinge' does not stand for any
sort of thing or 'term,'" p. 209) ("the objects proper to
such verbs are things and episodes"), a performance or
a manner of performance. "Liking and disliking, joy and
grief, desire and aversion are not. . . . episodes, and so
are not *the sorts of things** which can be witnessed or
un-witnessed" (p. 109). "The verb and its accusative
('Feel a tickle') are two expressions *for the same thing**"
(p. 101). Do such verbs as "minding" and "migrating"
stand for single processes or for a complex of processes?
(pp. 136–38). Many of the arguments in the book seem
to turn on these Categorial distinctions descried in reality, so reminiscent of earlier philosophers' distinctions
between Substances, Qualities and Relations, as though
there were *natural* or real accusatives and adverbs to be
found behind the vagaries of actual grammar. On what
grounds does Professor Ryle decide that there are no acts
"answering to" such verbs as "see," "hear," "taste," "deduce," and "recall" in the way in which familiar acts and
operations do answer to such verbs as "kick," "run,"
"look," "listen," "wrangle" and "tell"? (p. 151). The

grounds suggested in this particular passage are insufficient, namely, that certain adverbs which can in English be combined with the second class cannot be combined with the first; for it is always easy to find many exceptions to such generalisations about English idioms, even apart from the idioms of other equally adequate languages. Yet the counter examples will always be dismissed as special cases (*e.g.* as not "the dominant sense" of the word) precisely because Professor Ryle, in common with all other serious philosophers, here lays emphasis on a particular English idiom, only as a *pointer* to something other than itself, namely, to necessary *logical* distinctions. Words such as "act," "event," "performance," "episode," "occurrence," "disposition," "achievement" and, derivatively, such words as "mood" and "agitation," function in this book mainly (but not consistently) as logical words, in the special sense that to say that an English verb is the name of an achievement or a disposition, and not of an episode, is *primarily* to say something about the kind of evidence or argument which is relevant to any statement in which it occurs. So on p. 83—"The word 'emotion' is used to designate at least *three or four kinds of different things*,* which I shall call 'inclinations' (or 'motives'), 'moods,' 'agitations' (or 'commotions') and 'feelings,'" and "feelings are occurrences"—but—"Inclinations and moods are not occurrences. They are propensities, not acts or states."—These sentences can be understood when taken together with later statements such as (p. 244) "Words like 'distress,' 'distaste,' 'grief' and 'annoyance' are names of moods." To say of a particular word that it is the name of, or designates, a mood and that moods are not occurrences, amounts to saying (misleadingly) something about the kind of evidence or tests of truth which are appropriate to any statement in which this word occurs. But the non-logical terminology of "different kinds of things designated" sometimes leads Professor Ryle into uses which are inappropriate to such category-terms. He asks (p. 138) whether the same verb "minding" stands

for two processes or one—and this is a form of argument
which occurs repeatedly. If "process" is here marking a
logical distinction, and is a logical or category word and
not a descriptive expression, the question as it stands
must be meaningless. It is surely only this naive correspondence theory of language which leads to the remark
(p. 142) that only one thing need be going on when a
bird is described either as "migrating" or as "flying south."
Is it to be expected that there should be a visibly separate process corresponding to each verb, each perceptible process being uniquely named by its own verb?
Because words like "activity" and "process" are category-
words, it is equally meaningless to say (p. 139) that minding or the brow-knitting associated with it are the same
activities or that they are different activities, unless this
is a question about the conventional rules of use of the
two verbs, that is, the question whether any statement
containing the second entails, or is entailed by, some
statement containing the first; the answer to the question
so interpreted is simple—"No." But for Professor Ryle
the answer is difficult (pp. 138–41) because his terminology of "standing for," "designating," and "naming,"
here leads him to write as if there were a real answer,
independent of the conventions of a particular language,
to such questions as "Does the verb 'mind' or 'try' designate a single, distinct activity or a complex of activities?"
—as though the world consisted of just so many distinguishable Activities (or Facts (p. 140) or States or
Things) waiting to be counted and named.

In this crucial passage (pp. 138–41) the underlying
confusion in the use of these category-terms emerges on
the surface; for it suddenly becomes clear that there must
be many verbs (e.g. "concentrating," "dying," "being
anaesthetised" and countless others) which stand for
an occurrence as opposed to a disposition in some of the
many senses given of this central distinction, namely, that
they name incidents which can be significantly dated or
clocked, or that certain adverbs are applicable to them,

but which in another and predominant sense of the distinction are dispositional verbs, namely, that any statement containing them can be accepted as true only if some testable hypothetical statements about the future are accepted as true. Yet the *general* thesis of the book—that there are no such things as "mental happenings" (p. 161), that to speak of a person's mind is to speak "of certain ways in which some of the incidents of his one life are ordered" (p. 167)—largely hinges on this distinction between occurrences and dispositions. The core of the argument is that to talk of a person's mind is "to talk of the person's abilities, liabilities and inclinations to do and undergo certain sorts of things, and of the doing and undergoing of these things in the ordinary world" (p. 199). So the original plan of the book seems to have been to re-interpret most of the statements which have generally been construed as categorical statements about "ghostly" (= invisible, intangible, inaudible) events, as hypothetical statements about events in the so-called "ordinary" world, where "ordinary" strangely means (literalism or correspondence theory again) whatever can be perceived by anyone (not "Privileged Access") by the use of one or more of five senses (also stethoscopes, cameras, gramophones, and other accredited instruments). So putative statements, whether biographical or autobiographical, about immaterial and imperceptible occurrences must in each representative case be exhibited as disguised hypothetical statements about perceptible behaviour.

The argument about occurrences and dispositions, therefore, at first looks like one further application of the old high empiricist Hume-and-Russell method of "analysis," the logical construction method, whereby impalpable and oppressive substances, the Mind no less than the State, are shown to be logically reducible to less pretentious material. But such a simple design is never in fact executed, Professor Ryle himself indicating (*e.g.* p. 117), not only where in particular such reductions or rules of translation cannot be provided (*e.g.* for statements about emotional agitations, hankerings, pangs and thrills, silent calculations and imaginings), but also hinting in various places that to look for translations of categorical statements about mental states and activities into hypothetical statements about perceptible behaviour is, as a matter of logic, a pure mistake. The double distinction, occurrence versus disposition, categorical versus hypothetical, in fact breaks down in application in that almost any statement, even the most evidently simple, may be said to be, in Professor Ryle's confusion of senses, *both* categorical *and* hypothetical (*e.g.* p. 228 " 'He espied the thimble' has a considerable logical complexity," p. 141 "Most of the examples ordinarily adduced of categorical statements are mongrel categoricals" and see p. 220 on the logical complexity of "The field is green" or "This bicycle cost £12"). But if this distinction is shown to be unworkable, and cannot be clearly formulated, the whole account of the relation between mind and body— "Overt intelligent performances are not clues to the workings of minds; they *are* those workings" (p. 58)—collapses with it. It must be re-formulated.

4. *Occurrence versus Disposition as a pseudo-logical distinction.*

There are three traditional enquiries which issue in distinctions between types of expression in a language; grammar, logic in the strict or text-book sense, and theory of knowledge, sometimes called logic in a loose sense. In grammar individual words may be classified into types by the forms which they may assume, or the positions which they may occupy, in various typical sentences of a particular language. In logic *sentences* are classified into types by the positions which they may occupy in typical formal or deductive arguments and, derivatively from this, certain individual words (*e.g.* "all," "if," "or," etc.) may be singled out as logical words because of their formal inference-grounding functions. A sentence is classified as hypothetical in text-book logic if and only if it is explicitly of a form which indicates that certain deductive inferences or transformations are allowed in respect of it, irrespective of the topic discussed in the sentence or the particular occasion of its use. Clearly Professor Ryle's occurrence—disposition distinction is wholly different from a strictly logical distinction in at least two all-important respects: (*a*) it is generally applied (the analogy of grammar here misleads him) to *individual words* or *phrases* (*e.g.* "believing," "understanding," "knowing," "trying," "thinking"), taken apart from the various forms of sentence in which they may occur: (*b*) it is designed to mark, not solely or primarily the *deductive* inferences arising from the rules of use of particular expressions, but chiefly the *tests* that are appropriate to the sentences in which the expressions occur. "To rectify the logic of mental conduct concepts" (p. 16), Professor Ryle's own description of his aim, is to correct what other philosophers have said about the *methods of verification* of statements involving mental concepts (*i.e.* not Introspection, not Privileged Access); "roughly, the mind is not the topic of sets of *untestable** categorical propositions, but the topic of sets of *testable** hypothetical and semi-hypothetical propositions" (p. 46). He is throughout trying to show, taking each of the main mental concepts in turn, that any statement involving these concepts can be impartially tested, its truth or falsity decided, solely or primarily, or at least in part, by reference to the overt and perceptible performance and reactions of the person concerned. So the "logic of a description" (p. 104) or sentence here means "the standard tests appropriate to" or "the method of verification associated with"— which is logic in the wider sense, also sometimes called epistemology, that is, characterising in very general terms the kind of reasons which we normally give in accepting or rejecting statements about the mental activities of persons. I suspect that one of the main confusions of the book comes from the use of distinctions, such as the hypothetical-categorical distinctions, which are borrowed from logic in the strict sense, in order to mark distinctions which (I shall argue) cannot be strictly logical.

Professor Ryle is not really arguing that all or most statements involving mental concepts are (or are expressible as) hypothetical statements about overt behaviour, but (and it is very different) that to give reasons for accepting or rejecting such statements must always involve making some hypothetical statements about overt behaviour. Typical mental concepts are called dispositional and typical statements in which they occur are called "law-like propositions" (pp. 167 and 169) only because it is claimed that their application or assertion must in general be supported by observation of patterns of overt behaviour. See particularly pp. 167 *et seq.* "The *test** of whether you understood it. . . ." "How we *establish** and apply certain law-like propositions about the overt and silent behaviour of persons. . . ." "I *discover** my or your motives in much, though not quite the same way as I discover my or your abilities. . . ." (See also p. 136 on "minding".) So the force of this analysis of the main mental concepts in terms of the distinction between disposition and occurrence is that almost all statements about mental states and activities are confirmed or rejected as tenable or untenable *interpretations* of overt behaviour. They are denied the status of reports or of narrative of incidents (p. 125) (and therefore misleadingly denied the status of categorical propositions) only because evidence drawn from a variety of overt behaviour is always, or generally, relevant in deciding whether they are true or false.

5. *Proving too much.*

But Professor Ryle himself indicates (pp. 239 and 317) the fallacy which undermines any attempt so to generalise epistemological ("How do we test?" "How do we discover?") distinctions and to convert them into distinctions of logic. He suggests that for any given statement, whether involving mental or other concepts, there are an indefinite number of possible answers to the questions "How do you know?" or "What are the reasons for saying?", *depending on who made the statement, when and in what circumstances.* Such epistemological distinctions— ("what kind of test is appropriate?") can never be applied to any sentence or class of sentences *without specification of the particular occasion of use of the sentence in question.* If one takes either the sentence "I am in a state of panic" or the sentence "He was in a panic" apart from any particular context or occasion of their use (see p. 97), and considers them simply as *sentences of the English language,* one can only explain their meaning and use in the language by bringing out their strictly logical relations to other sentences in the language, that is, by showing what they entail or what else *must* be true if they are true. But unless a particular occasion of use is specified, one cannot answer, *a priori and in general,* the epistemologist's question "How can these statements be tested and their truth established?"; for, as Professor Ryle self-destructively says (p. 239), there are any number of ways in which we may legitimately confirm or refute the statements conveyed on different occasions of the use of these sentences, and a great variety of different kinds of reason may in different circumstances be accepted as sufficient justification of them. The answer to the question will generally be altogether different in kind if I am testing my own statement about my panic and not someone else's statement about theirs, and very different again if I am making the statement contemporaneously with the experience which it describes. Professor Ryle's *general* thesis, no less than its rival, rests on this confusion between (*a*) showing the truth-conditions of a given sentence, that is, what is entailed by the sentence as part of the rules of its use as a sentence of the language: this can be shown quite generally and without mentioning

particular contexts of use,[1] and (b) describing a range of
typical conditions under which someone (not anyone, but
someone in a particular situation) might properly claim
to know, or to have established beyond reasonable doubt,
that the statement in question is true. This is the confusion which either comes from, or leads to, 'identifying the
meaning of a statement with *the* method of its verification, and therefore identifying the statement itself with
what would (in some specified conditions of use) be
taken as sufficient evidence for it. Because overt behaviour
often constitutes for most people the best, and, in some
conditions of utterance, the sole available evidence for
statements about mental activities and states of mind,
such statements come to be *identified* with hypothetical
statements about behaviour—*e.g.* "Even to be for a brief
moment scandalised or in a panic is, for that moment, to
be liable to do some such things as stiffen or shriek"
(p. 97); sometimes, but not *necessarily* and always. Again,
"In ascribing a specific motive to a person we are describing the sorts of things that he tends to try to do"
(p. 112); usually, but again not *necessarily:* we might discover from his diary or by overhearing a soliloquy exactly
what moved him to action on this single and quite exceptional occasion. Again (p. 136) we *usually* test a child's
concentration by testing his performance, but we do not
identify the performance and the concentration, precisely
because although the first may often (not always or necessarily) be properly accepted as sufficient evidence for the
other, it is not a *necessary* condition in the sense of being
in *all* circumstances the *only* kind of relevant evidence
available, either to the child himself or to the teacher.
But it is the mark of dispositional terms in the *strictly logical sense* of the word—*e.g.* of things "brittle," of persons

---

[1] Analysis in this sense of what is necessarily involved in being in
a panic must of course disregard the words (pronouns, demonstra-
tives, proper names, etc.) which can only be interpreted in a particular context of use: it only elucidates the open sentence "*x* is in a
panic." The case of tenses is more complicated.

"irritable"—that *any* statement involving them, whatever may be the occasion of its utterance, can (as a matter of correct English) be accepted as true only if some hypothetical statements about the perceptible actions or reactions of the thing or person concerned are accepted as true. Thus "He is an irritable man but never shows it in his behaviour" is (as normally used) a contradiction in terms, while "He often feels irritable but never shows it" (see p. 203 for sentences of this pattern) is not self-contradictory or meaningless, although often to observers other than the subject himself no means may be available of testing the truth of the statement; whether any test is possible, and what kind of test, must depend on the particular circumstances. A statement only becomes void, if it is *logically* precluded, by the rules of use of the words involved, that *anyone* should *ever* under *any* conditions establish its truth or falsity beyond reasonable doubt.

It follows that the *same* logical mistake is involved whatever *general* account is given of the logic of statements containing mental concepts, where "the logic" means "*the* method of establishing the truth of . . ."; the too-general thesis of the solipsist (Privileged Access)—"I know about my own states of mind directly or by introspection, but I must always infer what your state of mind is and I can never in principle check my inference"— Professor Ryle effectively undermines by showing that conditions can always be described in which the observable behaviour of the subject would properly be quoted as sufficient reason for rejecting any autobiographical statement, whatever the statement may be; the possibility of obtaining relevant behavioural evidence is never excluded, *as a matter of logic or of the meaning of the words involved,* although on *many occasions of the use of such sentences* as, "I was thinking of . . . ," "I dreamt of . . . ," "I felt . . . ," no such tests of the truth of the particular statement made may be available to the audience.

But Professor Ryle, at the same time proves too much

by proving, apparently as a *general* thesis of logic, that
(p. 155) "The sorts of things that I can find out about
myself are the same as the sorts of things that I can find
out about other people, and the methods are much the
same": and again the odd but revealing statement
(p. 114) "In fact they (people) are relatively tractable
and relatively easy to understand" (see also p. 172 about
"familiar techniques of assessing").[2] This is open paradox
because (if any general statement is to be made) people
notoriously *are* occult in at least one very important
sense, namely, that in comparison with animals and inanimate things, it is difficult to establish the truth about
them, if only because there is more to be known with
more sources of information. They are occult and are said
to have inner lives, just because, and in the sense that, in
establishing the truth of many kinds of statements about
them (about their thoughts, feelings, day dreams, night
dreams, stifled impulses, imaginings, concealed hopes and
plans), I am often (but not always) concerned in weigh-
ing and comparing two different kinds of evidence—what
they themselves confess or report and what I can observe
independently of their avowal. Just because they alone
of natural objects are language-users and therefore are
potential reporters, they are (unlike stones and dogs)
liars, hypocrites, and suppressors of the truth about themselves. It is just this conflict between what they report
(and fail to report) and how they behave which distinguishes them as occult relatively to animals and even
infants who, because they make no disclosures, allow no
contrast between inner and outer life. Most "mental" concepts therefore are used in application to animals (and

[2] In fact all the familiar techniques of assessing people are constantly questioned even by the most philosophically innocent; the
criteria of assessment are disputed in a way which has no parallel in
the assessment of the properties of physical things; about moods,
motives, desires, fears and ambitions we feel a general and constant
dissatisfaction with our methods, however complacent we may be
about skills and competences. We are always ready for new suggestions, *e.g.* from Freud.

hesitantly to infants) *solely* and always as interpretations of observable behaviour.[3] We peer at people and wonder what is going on "inside" them occultly, the wonder having point and significance just because there is always a possibility of disclosure and therefore always a possibility of non-disclosure or lies. It is this puzzlement, peculiar to the description of the states and activities of human minds, which is paradoxically omitted in Professor Ryle's polemic. His counter-theory leads him to say, what is certainly false (p. 168) "Where logical candour is required from us, we ought to follow the example set by novelists, biographers and diarists, *who speak only of persons doing and undergoing things*."* In fact, very many, perhaps the majority of novelists and diarists, and some biographers, find comedy or tragedy precisely in the contrast between the narrative description which an observer reasonably gives of a person's life, with no data other than his own and other people's observations, and the missing confession or avowal which the person himself, if suitably gifted, may supply; and some novelists, and even more diarists, have been exclusively concerned with the provision of the missing data, that is, with that uncommon kind of autobiographical description which, in a universal and natural metaphor, is called the description of inner life. Professor Ryle himself admits (p. 58) that Boswell's description of Johnson's mind was incomplete, "since there were notoriously some thoughts which *Johnson kept carefully to himself** and there must have been many dreams, day dreams and silent babblings,[4] which only *Johnson could have recorded** and only a James Joyce would wish him to have recorded." But here lies no less the novelists' than

[3] Do dogs dream? We hesitate as to what kind of question this is, because we are uncertain whether we may not one day obtain better evidence; the possibility of evidence beyond their visible twitchings is not definitely and finally excluded.

[4] Surely "silent babblings" (*cf.* "silent colloquies" on p. 182) is metaphorical in Professor Ryle's sense if anything is: also "operations" with propositions (p. 30). Yet such phrases (*e.g.* "silent monologues") enter into his analysis of thinking.

the philosophers' problem; for we ask—since the story *must* always be incomplete unless told in the first person singular, with the hero also the narrator, must each character be his own centre of narration in order to construct the complete story involving them all? Or is there no such single story, but as many stories as there are characters?

6. *Privileged Access.*

On this crux of the use of mental concepts with the first person singular Professor Ryle again approaches, but (I think) falls short of, a solution (see pp. 60–61); there is the same ambiguity of purpose (pp. 183–84). Will he say that first person reports of mental activities are reducible to statements about perceptible behaviour? Nearly, but not quite. "We eavesdrop on our own voiced utterances and our own silent monologues. On noticing these we are preparing ourselves to do something new, namely to describe the frames of mind which these utterances disclose. . . . I can pay heed to what I overhear you saying as well as to what I overhear myself saying, though I cannot overhear your silent colloquies with yourself. Nor can I read your diary, if you write in a cipher, or keep it under lock and key." The impossibility (logical) of my hearing you think (silent colloquies), if you refuse to utter or even whisper your thoughts[5] is radically unlike an unfortunate incapacity to decipher and unlock (empirical); I often fail simply because there is nothing to hear, even with a stethoscope. I may *see* you thinking—"I saw him sitting in the corner thinking." But if I am asked "How do you know that he was thinking?" the answer "I saw him" is by itself insufficient, while it is normally a sufficient answer to a similar question about

[5] Compare "He cannot think without talking to himself" with "He cannot think without pencil and paper." If talking to oneself is a way of thinking, as drawing diagrams or writing are ways of thinking, then it ought not to be identified with thinking.

your sitting or your talking,[6] and this (an epistemological or "How-do-you-know" distinction) leads us to say
that I always have to *infer* that you are thinking, and also
that thinking, unlike sitting and talking, is ("strictly")
invisible (= ghostly). But you yourself always know both
whether you are thinking and also of what you are thinking, and never have any need of inference in the matter;
that is, if you declare "I am thinking of climbing
Helvellyn," it is pointless and silly to ask "How do you
know?" or "Are you certain?"; and these questions seem
equally inapplicable when you avow your sensations
(p. 209), or a momentary mood or frame of mind, which
leads Professor Ryle desperately to assimilate avowals of
the last kind to gestures and mere expressions of mood
rather than to statements (p. 103). But an avowal, unlike a yawn, may be false and may be discovered to be a lie
or mis-description by a careful collection of evidence.
There is no *logical* difference between your avowal ("I am
thinking of . . .") and my diagnosis, interpretation or
guess ("You are thinking of . . ."); two people have
made the same categorical statement; but my justification
for making it, if any, is naturally very different from yours
in these circumstances. The point becomes clearer as
soon as it is noticed that the challenges "How do you
know?" or "What is your evidence?" are inapplicable to
avowals of thoughts and sensations (*e.g.* "I am in pain"),
only when these are expressed in the present tense. If you
make the statement about your thoughts or sensations a
year later, or an hour before, you, no less than I, might
reasonably be required to produce evidence that these
were or will be your thoughts and sensations; but who-
ever makes it and whenever it is made, the possibility of

[6] But would Professor Ryle as a literalist say that I only "strictly"
hear the sounds of the words, and not what you say, your statements?
Do I "strictly" see only the movement of your pen, and not the sign-
ing of the cheque? And are these two processes or one? At the cinema
I really literally see only an illuminated sheet of linen: the prairies
are "a certain sort of dreaming" (p. 255).

finding sufficient evidence against it is never in principle,
though often in practice, excluded. For any avowal,
whether of thoughts, feelings, even dreams,[7] conditions
can always be described in which it would generally be
withdrawn, in the face of further evidence, even by the
subject himself, however rare such conditions may be
("You could not have been in pain; you were anaesthetised." "You did not dream of peacocks: you were awake
at the time and read about them in this book"). Privileged Access ("Only I can ever know about my own
states of mind") *cannot* be true, generalised as a point of
logic: nor, for precisely the same reasons, can Professor
Ryle's Open Access.

7. *Avowals versus Behaviour as Evidence.*

But of course there are great and also subtle differences, to some of which Professor Ryle alludes, between
(*a*) *pure descriptions* of sensations (p. 209), also of
dreams, of momentary moods, and impulses (p. 103), of
mental distresses, thrills, qualms and agitations, in which
the autobiographer generally exposes himself to the few-
est possibilities of correction, by describing in a way
which is essentially figurative, indefinite and imprecise;
and (*b*) the official diagnoses in standard terms of emotions, attitudes, intellectual efforts and achievements, inclinations, and motives, diagnoses which are sometimes in
part based upon such subjective descriptions of symptoms,
but which are themselves relatively definite and therefore
more precisely testable. But because his theory leads him
to deny in general the peculiar occultness of persons, that
is, the characteristic conflict between what people say of

[7] Dreams, about which Professor Ryle says little, are important
(*e.g.* in Descartes) because they are the archetype of ghostly occult
experiences: they admit no avowals in the present tense; I cannot
normally ask you what you are dreaming about and you cannot say—
almost logically cannot. But some trance mediums and other seers
try to make the best of both worlds.

themselves (their avowals) and how they behave, Professor Ryle neglects the all-important and revealing function of the word "really" in combination with mental concepts. "You do not *really* enjoy gardening (avowal), because when it rains . . ." (behaviour). "He does not *really* believe in the coming Revolution (as he declares) because . . ." "His *real* fears, hopes, and ambitions (as opposed to his declared) motive. . . ." "He was not *really* in love (though he said he was), because. . . ." The force of the word is generally to impose more than normally stringent conditions for the use of the mental concept by stressing one kind of evidence at the expense of another, namely, the subject's behaviour in contrast to his avowals, the implied opposition being "He declares this, and there is no reason to suppose that he is lying, but he behaves. . . ." So "He does not *really* believe in life after death" has a different use, and (in one sense) therefore a different meaning, from simply "He does not believe in life after death," the implied antithesis, what is denied, being different in the two uses; and to assess one's own or somebody else's *real* motives, fears, desires, ambitions etc. is to make a statement which has a different purpose, and which generally involves attending to a different kind and quantity of evidence, than is involved in the corresponding straightforward and unqualified assessment; the "really" statements, even when they are autobiographical, are always intended more as interpretative diagnoses in the sense that they draw attention away from declared symptoms to a wider range of patterns of behaviour. Because a wider range of evidence is involved, there are more occasions for saying "I think this is my *real* attitude, motive or feeling, but I am not certain," than there are for saying "I think this is my attitude or motive or feeling but I am not certain"; since his thesis compels him to overstress the evidence of perceptible behaviour Professor Ryle is often—*e.g.* pp. 107-9 on "enjoyment," and pp. 135-45 on "belief"—in fact describing how we generally test statements about what someone really enjoys or really believes, when he claims to be describing the tests we apply to the corresponding straight-forward statements. Having (p. 182) included "unstudied talk" or self-expression under the heading of behaviour, he has destroyed the characteristic opposition (avowal versus behaviour, words versus deeds) which constitutes the peculiarity and the difficulty of assessments of people —even autobiographical assessments.[8]

8. Will, Sensations and Images.

It has been my argument that Professor Ryle has not decided whether he is saying (a) that no mental concepts "stand for" imperceptible (= ghostly) processes or states: all "designate" some perceptible or nearly-perceptible (e.g. "silent colloquies") pattern of behaviour: or less drastically (b) that all statements involving mental concepts are in principle testable, directly or indirectly and in various degrees, by observation of the behaviour of the person concerned. The mountaineer (p. 42), may pause to think what to do next, the chess-player (p. 29) to plan his moves; someone asks, "What are you doing?" "I am planning my next move." In every sense these are incidents in the narrative of the day, clockable episodes, acts ("You ought to have planned your next move"), and such a report of them is logically independent of any hypothetical statements about overt behaviour. But they are worrying to Professor Ryle—they are not *strictly* visible (although one can sometimes see people thinking) or audible incidents; so he tries to convert them either into just-not-audible incidents ("the trick" of thinking so

[8] Professor Ryle takes simulation and hypocrisy (p. 173) in addition to deliberate lying (miscalled insincerity on p. 102) and deliberate reticence, as the primary forms of human deceit or occultness. But there are more complicated cases—e.g. of *general* insincerity, self-dramatisation and self-deceit, the analysis of which would (I think) involve this important contrast between "feeling" and "really feeling," "believing" and "really believing," etc.

quietly that no one except the subject can eavesdrop) or
into dispositions to climb or play thoughtfully and in a
planned manner. Equally "resolving or making up our
minds" (p. 68), "making an effort of will" (p. 72), "trying" (p. 134), "concentrating" (p. 133) are recognisable
and dateable activities, but not *strictly* visible, audible or
otherwise open to inspection by witnesses, who must
therefore guess or infer their occurrence or simply wait to
be told. Professor Ryle admits that these peculiarly human and mental occurrences do occur (pp. 68–69), although he also mistakenly thinks that if he can show, as
of course he can, that observation of behaviour may provide evidence of such an occurrence, he has thereby
shown that it is not really or wholly an occurrence, but
also a propensity to behave in certain ways (p. 72 and pp.
138 *et seq.*). But having admitted the irreducible concepts of "trying" or "deciding," which many philosophers
would take as the defining activities of the human mind
(see p. 129), it is odd to dismiss "the will" as a myth
(pp. 63 *et seq.*) because of the Kantian theories associated with it; and it is both historically and logically untrue that the problem of free-will arises wholly or mainly
from Mechanism. Briefly, we are not prepared to say "He
ought not to have done it" unless we are also prepared to
say "He could have avoided doing it if he had tried or if
he had made an effort." "He could not have helped doing
it, however hard he tried" is normally a conclusive rejection of the moral imputation "He ought not. . . ." Everyone seems to know the difference between making an
effort to stifle (physical metaphor) an impulse and not
making an effort, and we sometimes even attach meaning
to degrees of effort. The dipsomaniac may be held to be
blameless because helpless, where "helpless" means "no effort of will would make any difference," while the culpable
drunkard is culpable because he fails to make the effort
of will which would make the difference. It is therefore
not true (p. 76) that the perplexity arises solely or even
mainly from asking whether volitions are the effects of

mechanical causes, although it is true that "He could have avoided it if he had tried" has often been confused by philosophers with "There is no causal explanation of his action," particularly, in the unfortunate formula "Ought implies can" (= "In his power") (see p. 129). The perplexity arises rather from the effects of increasing scientific (and particularly physiological) knowledge on our readiness (reasonably or unreasonably) to say "He could have avoided it if he had tried." What Professor Ryle with the aid of parody dismisses (p. 80) as the "silly view" of moral philosophers—that increasing scientific knowledge diminishes the field within which moral terms are applicable—so far from being a silly philosophical theory, is a plainly observable fact about common usage. As knowledge advances, sin, crime and wickedness become maladjustment, delinquency and disease ("You cannot blame them: they cannot help it: it is a matter of glands, alterable states of the brain, complexes and neuroses, conditions producing juvenile delinquency," etc.). It was just this revolution of thought and language, this gradual restriction in the use of moral terms as scientific knowledge advances, which Kant anxiously and Spinoza calmly anticipated.

(b) *Sensations.* The same ambiguity of purpose, the conflict between general thesis and particular instance produces contradictions. "An oculist who cannot speak my language is without the best source of information about my visual sensations" (p. 209). This is plainly true, but also plainly incompatible with "Secondary quality adjectives are used and used only for the reporting of publicly ascertainable facts about common objects" (p. 220). It is also incompatible with questioning the propriety of this non-technical, centuries-old use of the word "sensation" (pp. 200 and 243). Again, "He espied the thimble" has a considerable logical complexity but does not therefore report a considerable complication of processes" (p. 230), "The field is green" entails (hypothetical) propositions about observers" (p. 200)—these two propositions (which I consider false) might be taken to define Phenomenalism, the theory which Professor Ryle thinks he has refuted. His two main reasons for rejecting the theory are (*a*) that there are no such things or *objects* as sensations (p. 214, p. 236), the implication being that nouns ought to stand for things or objects, as verbs for processes; (*b*) that "in its dominant sense" (p. 238), "see" is an achievement word like "solve" and so can only be used "in its primary sense" of perception of physical objects which actually exist (p. 238). The justification given for this revision of ordinary usage is that we cannot be said to "see incorrectly." The confusion in this surprising argument is between seeing and *describing* what we see; of course we cannot see either correctly or incorrectly; we can only *describe* what we see correctly or incorrectly; and of course we withdraw a claim to have seen a linnet when we have been convinced that in fact there was no linnet (p. 238.); but this does not necessarily involve us in admitting that we did not see anything, or that it was not a case of seeing, but only that it was not a linnet which we saw. We may see spots in front of the eyes, reflections in the water, rainbows, houses in the distance in a picture—there are hundreds of (for some purposes usefully) distinguishable contexts in which "see" is used, but there is no one achievement or performance which the verb "denotes." "Gate-posts" is a specimen of the sorts of complements which alone can be significantly given to such expressions as "John Doe is looking at a so and so" (p. 238); but when he looks at the gate-post in the picture, or at the sky, or at his own reflection, are these the same sorts of complements?

(*c*) *Imagination*—The same ambiguity. First, the sweeping general thesis "There are just things and events, people witnessing some of these things and events, and people fancying themselves witnessing things and events that they are not witnessing" (p. 249). But Professor Ryle does not really cling to this programme: it is plainly false, since we may imagine things without fancying ourselves witnessing them. The lesser thesis is—"Roughly, imaging occurs, but images are not seen" (p. 247). The arguments are the same: (*a*) restriction of "seeing" to "literally seeing" with "the eyes open," and under conditions in which other people could also see what the subject claims to be seeing; so the drunkard does not literally see snakes, nor do we literally see (presumably) mirror-images, afterimages and eidetic images, nor do we literally smell obsessional smells. And this is to prove that "There are no such *objects** as mental pictures"—as though it were wrong to use the noun unless there are solid objects (gate-posts and grit) to correspond to it. To enforce this principle would be allowing the fear of ghosts to drive us into pidgin English—which might be the ultimately literal language.

9. Professor Ryle writes with Aristotelian pregnancy, and almost every paragraph contains observations which require, and will certainly be given, many thousands of words of discussion; for example, the section on "The Systematic Elusiveness of 'I'" would alone require almost as much space for adequate discussion as is available for this review, and a sentence on p. 189 on the conception of a person as body and non-body in itself provides the clue to the Cartesian myth. It is the mark of enduring philosophical works that by their force and originality they both provoke and endlessly sustain such piecemeal nibbling as this, without their content being within sight of exhaustion; and, like most permanently interesting philosophies, together with a peculiar theory of language "The Concept of Mind" conveys a sharply personal and definite view of the world: a world of solid and manageable objects, without hidden recesses, each ibly functioning in its own appropriate pattern.

INTELLIGENT BEHAVIOUR
A Critical Review of *The Concept of Mind*

J. L. AUSTIN

Even to the undergraduate, plain thinking and plain living as the work of the past fifty years has made him, Professor Ryle's first book, long awaited, will seem one that he cannot afford not to possess and that he can afford to possess. This is a very considerable achievement on the part of both author and publisher. Not only is the book stimulating, enjoyable and original, but a quite unusually high percentage of it is true, the remainder at least false. In short, it stands head and shoulders above its contemporaries; it will deservedly enjoy a success, and even a vogue. Because this is so certain, and after emphasizing that it is to be welcomed most warmly as a voice which speaks, where too many are mute, for the genuine work being done at present in philosophy, the risk may be taken of referring freely to points of criticism.

Professor Ryle is at pains to put his points not merely honestly but fairly. But he is by nature a *philosophe terrible*, and has chosen therefore to cast his work in the form almost of a manifesto. His interest lies in the words we use when we speak—or think we do—of the qualities, faculties and performances of men's minds, and in the persistent misunderstanding of such words by theorists: but he develops his theme as a sustained series of skirmishes against what he calls, "with deliberate abusiveness," the official philosopher's myth of "the ghost in the machine."

This myth he describes in the form given to it by Descartes. Every man has both a *body* (the machine), which

The *Times Literary Supplement*, April 7, 1950. Reprinted with permission of Mrs. J. L. Austin and the Editor of the *Times Literary Supplement*.

is in space, is rigidly governed by physical laws, and leads
a public career of movement; and also a *mind* (the
ghost), which is not in space, is not governed by physical
laws, and leads a private career of thinking, sensing, willing, feeling and so on, activities of which the self alone is
aware through introspection. Both bodies and minds
"exist"; but how they interact is a mystery—especially for
Cartesians, who hold the ghost itself to be rigidly governed by para-mechanical laws of its own.

According to Professor Ryle, this myth is "not merely
an assemblage of particular mistakes. It is one big mistake,
and a mistake of a special kind. It is, namely, a category-
mistake. It represents the facts of mental life as if they
belonged to one logical type or category . . . when actually they belong to another." He proceeds to deal in suc-
cessive chapters with Intelligence, Will, Emotion, Self-
Knowledge, Sensation, Imagination and Intellect. In the
middle (for no very apparent reason) is a chapter in
which he expounds some of his principal techniques, more
particularly the logic of "dispositional" words and of
"achievement" words; and a concluding chapter discusses
the roles, actual, possible and impossible, of psychology.

Disarmingly, Professor Ryle admits at the start that he
will "probably be taken to be denying well-known facts
about the mental life of human beings," and unfortunately few readers will escape an uneasy feeling that this
is at times the case. In spite of the conviction carried by
many of the acute and illuminating discussions in the
body of the book, it is impossible not to feel that he is
misguided, as a strategist, both in his choice of objective
and in his appreciation of his own forces. What he has
produced is a quiverful of miscellaneous and original arguments, all either sound or not without substance, tending
to show that many "mental" words do not describe the
"mind" and its "activities" in the simple way in which
they are commonly thought to do: but the idea that these
arguments add up to a single logical method and tend to

a single clear-cut conclusion looks like an afterthought and seems an illusion.

To take first the objective. There can be no doubt that, though Professor Ryle does genuinely attack the myth as a whole, his fire is directed primarily against the "ghost." He is, of course, entirely convinced that the body is not a "machine," and argues forcibly to that effect, especially in his chapter on the Will. Yet the very term "ghost" is in one way more deliberately abusive than "machine"; for a ghost does not really exist at all. Professor Ryle holds that we should contrast not mind with body but intelligent behaviour with unintelligent behaviour: behaviour is intelligent when executed "in certain frames of mind" or "from certain dispositions," by which phrases we introduce a reference, not to entities and episodes different in kind from behaviour, but to past and future and possible behaviour in addition to actual present behaviour. But behaviour by what? Officially, Professor Ryle would answer: By the *man* (not merely by his body). Yet he seems to take it that all behaviour "by the man" must be *bodily* behaviour (as indeed the term "behaviour" itself implies). Thus he expresses again and again, but especially in the last chapter, views sympathetic to Behaviourism, in spite of his disapproval of its "mechanistic" bias; and he would apparently like, though he does not quite dare, to endorse the James-Lange theory of feelings and the view that thinking *is* just sub-audible utterance (in a certain frame of mind, of course). Undoubtedly he does persuade himself that what he has to show is that "occult" episodes "in the mind," which are "private" to one person, simply do not occur at all—not merely that they are never mysterious causes, themselves mysteriously caused, of our physical movements, nor merely that their numbers and varieties have been exaggerated.

Those who, like Professor Ryle, revolt against a dichotomy to which they have been once addicted, commonly go over to maintain that only one of the alleged pair of opposites really exists at all. And so he, though he does not believe the body is a machine, does believe that it alone, and not the "ghost," exists: he preaches with the fervour of a proselyte a doctrine of "one world." Yet what has ever been gained by this favourite philosophical pastime of counting worlds? And why does the answer always turn out to be one or two, or some similar small, well-rounded, philosophically acceptable number? Why, if there are nineteen of any thing, is it not philosophy?

Then, for Professor Ryle's methods. He claims to expose the myth as "one big category-mistake." Yet what he says in explanation of this term will hardly suffice to show that there is here a single clear type of mistake at all. If there is, it is something so very general as misunderstanding the ways in which words are intended to be, and normally are, used, and so wrongly inferring that they can be made to behave like other, very different, words, and that what they "stand for" (dangerous phrase) is "like" what those other words stand for. But this, broad as it is, is not the only basis of Descartes' myth; nor is it a mistake peculiar to him—it lies behind other, quite different, theories of the mind also. Nor, surely, is it a mistake which is in any clear or special sense "logical." Where Professor Ryle says that something has been wrongly taken to belong to a certain "logical" category or to be of a certain logical type, it is not easy to see why "logical" might not be omitted without loss. It may be time that we stopped talking of "logical" grammar and "logical" syntax, when all we mean is grammar and syntax, or perhaps even nothing in sufficient particular. For the author, "logic" still has a mystique, which leads him, for example, regularly to express a preference, in clinching his arguments, for some rather unconvincing appeal to an "infinite regress," rather than for his own convincing elucidations of the correct meanings and usages of words, about which he is inclined, in his preface, to be unnecessarily apologetic.

The fact is that Professor Ryle does not confine himself to any single technique or method of argument, nor is the book one whit the worse for that. He has a number of regular, and most effective, stand-bys. He shows repeatedly that we are inclined to suppose that words which stand for dispositions stand for episodes, which then, since they are clearly not episodes of the ordinary observable kind, are taken to be "occult" episodes "in the mind"; or again, he shows that we often wrongly take words which describe "achievements," like winning or curing, to describe the exercise of mysteriously infallible faculties; or again, he shows that we mistake for categorical descriptions of unobservable facts statements which really, in spite of their grammatical form, are hypothetical or at most "mongrel-categorical." But elsewhere he as commonly invokes doctrines which are quite peculiar to the particular topic concerned. To "debunk" self-knowledge he calls on the theories of "index-words" and "second-order processes"; sensation he shows to be simply quite different from observation; imagining and willing are said just not to occur, and so on.

These two errors in strategy—the belief that he has to show that only one world exists, that of bodily behaviour, actual *cum* hypothetical, and the belief that he has ready to his hand a single Excalibur, clothed in the name of Logic—combine to produce in Professor Ryle what amounts to a genuine, if surely temporary, delusion. He seems successfully to conceal from himself, at essential moments, both the actual occurrence of numbers of experiences which, it seems obvious, do occur and which he himself, when not immediately concerned to eliminate them, does admit to occur; and, further, that many of his arguments, among them some which are thoroughly sound and important, are from the point of view of eliminating the "ghost" quite beside the mark.

To take some examples. Imagination is commonly supposed to be or to include the "seeing" of "mental pictures." Professor Ryle argues that there is no such thing; he explains imagining as being, roughly, like pretending. Yet though, no doubt, the extent to which people do genuinely "see images" is often grossly exaggerated, surely they do sometimes see images. To take an obvious example, they do see after-images. The author seems to argue that because a man seeing Helvellyn in his mind's eye does not see Helvellyn but only "sees" it, therefore he "sees" nothing; but he may "see" something.* To "see" may be a metaphor; but not all metaphors should be assumed to be misleading. And even in the same chapter, when Professor Ryle discusses memory, he speaks of "visual imagery" as something which obviously occurs. Again, in dealing with sensation, he rightly points out that this is constantly confused with observation, which is quite different, including as it does the watching, recognizing, naming, &c., of what we sense. Yet however true this is, how could it tend to disprove that the experience of sensation ("glimpsing" or what not) does actually occur, or that it is not a "private" or "occult" experience? Similarly, in the chapter on Intellect, although the distinction drawn at some length between a man's performance in expounding a theory and his performance in inventing it ("pondering") is a useful one, and although it may well be true that the attention of philosophers has been too exclusively directed to the former, to which their terminology is alone appropriate, how can this justify an omission to notice that "ponderings" are in fact "internal episodes"? "Ponderings," like "feelings," once firmly distinguished from what they are not, are thenceforward left in the air, where they are surely not more happily located than "in the mind."

Professor Ryle is admirably sensitive to the nuances of

* This sentence is printed as in the original but it looks as though it should read:

The author seems to argue that because a man seeing Helvellyn in his mind's eye does not see Helvellyn but only "sees" it, therefore he sees nothing; but he may see something.

In this and the next sentence quotation marks would then always indicate a metaphorical use of the word "see" whereas in the preceding sentences they are used to draw attention to a particular phrase without implying a special sense. [Eds.]

words: a good example is his thorough and expert analysis of the various meanings of the word "can." He is, however, capable of abusing his own favourites, such as the word "disposition" itself, and even of an occasional surprising looseness of expression in the formulation of critical points in his own doctrine.

Such looseness, however, is only the defect of the very great virtues of Professor Ryle's chosen manner of writing, which is racy, untechnical and idiosyncratic, and which will make his book readable and intelligible to many outside the fold of philosophy who will benefit from it. Close-packed though the thought is, it is so firmly expressed that it can be followed with the greatest of ease. The simple syntax is enlivened by a refreshingly wide choice of words, especially of polysyllables, often surprisingly and tellingly apt, only rarely archaic or pedantic. The abundant examples are both striking and helpful, and Professor Ryle's wholehearted faith in the deliverances of his own personal experience, which prompts him to assure us now that beggar-my-neighbour is a more intellectual game than snap, now that men are relatively easy to understand, cannot but endear him to his readers. All, too, save those who have never learned to suspect solemnity, will join in his enjoyment of his numerous jokes, for the most part shrewd and spontaneous, only occasionally straying over the borderline into facetiousness. The jokes of a clown, says the professor, *are* the workings of his mind; and certainly his own wisecracks and epigrams (though far from clowning) go to bear out his theory in his own case. *Le style, c'est Ryle.*

AN HONEST GHOST?

A. J. AYER

How radical is the central thesis of Ryle's *The Concept of Mind*? Would it be true to say that it denied the very existence of minds, insofar as their existence is understood to imply that there are "inner" states or processes, or objects or events? There is, indeed, a great deal of evidence in the book that this is what Ryle intends. "It is being maintained," he says, "throughout this book that when we characterise people by mental predicates, we are not making untestable inferences to any ghostly processes occurring in streams of consciousness which we are debarred from visiting: we are describing the ways in which these people conduct parts of their predominantly public behaviour."[1] Or again: "The radical objection to the theory that minds must know what they are about, because mental happenings are by definition conscious, or metaphorically self-luminous, is that there are no such happenings: there are no occurrences taking place in a second-status world, since there is no such status and no such world and consequently no need for special modes of acquainting ourselves with the denizens of such a world."[2] Or again: "It has been argued from a number of directions that when we speak of a person's mind, we are not speaking of a second theatre of special-status incidents, but of certain ways in which some of the incidents of his one life are ordered. His life is not a double series of events taking place in different kinds of stuff: it is one concatenation of events, the differences between some and other classes of which largely consist in the applicability or inapplicability to them of logically different types of law-propositions and lawlike propositions. . . . So

[1] Gilbert Ryle, *The Concept of Mind*, p. 51.
[2] p. 161.

questions about the relations between a person and his mind, like those about the relations between a person's body and his mind are improper questions. They are improper in much the same way as is the question 'What transactions go on between the House of Commons and the British Constitution?' "[3]

It is in the same spirit that Ryle maintains that to explain an action is not to "infer to occult causes" but to "subsume under hypothetical and semi-hypothetical propositions," that "the imputation of a motive for a particular action is not a causal inference to an unwitnessed event but the subsumption of an episode proposition under a law-like proposition";[4] that "consciousness and introspection cannot be what they are officially described as being, since their supposed objects are myths";[5] and that while "the concept of picturing, visualising or 'seeing' is a proper and useful concept . . . its use does not entail the existence of pictures which we contemplate or the existence of a gallery in which such pictures are ephemerally suspended."[6] All these and many similar passages suggest very strongly that the doctrine which Ryle is putting forward is a version of what is technically known as logical behaviourism. This is borne out by the fact that when he briefly discusses behaviourism in the concluding section of his book, the only serious fault that he finds with psychologists of this school is their tendency to combine a meritorious denial of "'inner-life' occurrences" with what he regards as a mistaken addiction to Hobbist mechanism.

Nevertheless a closer reading of the book may make us wonder whether Ryle's position is quite so straightforward. For the programme of logical behaviourism to succeed, it has to be shown that all our talk about mental states and processes can be reformulated in such a way as

[3] p. 167–68.
[4] p. 90.
[5] p. 155.
[6] p. 247.

to eliminate any reference to an inner life. In the version of the programme which we might attribute to Ryle, what would remain would be a set of dispositional statements about people's overt behaviour. "To talk of a person's mind . . . is to talk of the person's abilities, liabilities and inclinations to do and undergo certain sorts of things, and of the doing and undergoing of these things in the ordinary world."[7] The reasons for taking a view of this kind are commonly not that it is semantically plausible, but rather that it offers a way of escape from philosophical perplexities. It saves us from the difficulty, to which all dualistic theories are exposed, of explaining how mental and physical processes are related or how one person can ever come to know what goes on in the mind of another. This is, indeed, a great advantage, but it has to be earned. The elimination of all the ostensible references that we make to inner occurrences has to be carried through.

Ryle does take it quite a long distance. He has arguments to show that displays of intelligence, whether in speech or action, do not entail private planning, that to exercise the will is not to engage in mental acts of volition, that motives are not "ghostly thrusts," that neither perceiving nor imagining entails the awareness of private objects. He does not, however, take it all the way. There are many passages in his book in which a reference to what would appear to be inner occurrences is still permitted to remain. Thus, in the course of making out his distinction between knowing how and knowing that, he remarks that much of our ordinary thinking is conducted in internal monologue or silent soliloquy, usually accompanied by an internal cinematograph-show of visual imagery"[8] and he says of the exercises of knowing how that they "can be overt or covert, deeds performed or deeds imagined, words spoken aloud or words heard in one's head, pictures painted on canvas or pictures in the mind's

[7] p. 199.
[8] p. 27.

eye."[9] He recognizes a special sense of the words "mental" and "mind," in which "a boy is said to be doing mental arithmetic" when he says numerical symbols to himself "performing his calculations in silent soliloquy," or "a person is said to be reading the mind of another when he describes truly what the other is saying or picturing to himself in auditory or visual images."[10] He does, indeed, go on to say that "this special use of 'mental' and 'mind' in which they signify what is done 'in one's head' cannot be used as evidence for the dogma of the ghost in the machine."[11] The secrecy which we secure for our thinking by conducting it in auditory word-images "is not the secrecy ascribed to the postulated episodes of the ghostly shadow-world. It is merely the convenient privacy which characterises the tunes that run in my head and the things that I see in my mind's eye."[12] But, whatever may be the differences between these sorts of secrecy, the existence of inner processes appears in any case to be conceded.

In one significant passage, an admission of this kind immediately follows what might otherwise be taken to be its denial. Ryle has been arguing that the assumption made by historians and scholars that the qualities of people's minds are reflected in the things they say and do is only "on the edge of the truth." The truth is that "the styles and procedures of people's activities *are* the way their minds work"; they are not reflections of any "postulated secret processes." So "Boswell described Johnson's mind when he described how he wrote, talked, ate, fidgeted and fumed." But it would seem not entirely, for Ryle immediately goes on: "His description was, of course, incomplete, since there were notoriously some thoughts which Johnson kept carefully to himself and there must have been many dreams, day-dreams and

[9] p. 47.
[10] p. 34.
[11] p. 35.
[12] *Ibid.*

silent babblings which only Johnson could have recorded and only a James Joyce would wish him to have recorded."[13] Whatever we may think of the implication that the stream of consciousness which Joyce attempted to reproduce is not worth transcribing, there is also the implication that it is there to be transcribed.

A further admission is that of the existence of feelings, which Ryle equates with "the sorts of things which people often describe as thrills, twinges, pangs, throbs, wrenches, itches, prickings, chills, glows, loads, qualms, hankerings, curdlings, sinkings, tensions, gnawings and shocks."[14] As his choice of language indicates, he comes near to identifying feelings with bodily sensations, though he thinks that our descriptions of feelings may be metaphorical in a way that our descriptions of bodily sensations are not. He maintains that there are some feelings which we are ready to locate in particular parts of the body, as, for example, "the sinking feeling of despair in the pit of the stomach" and of others, like glows of pride, which are not specifically located, he says that they "seem to pervade the whole body in much the same way as do glows of warmth."[15] All this is no doubt intended to take away from the "mentality" of feelings, but the fact remains that they are allowed to be felt. There is no suggestion that talk of what a person feels, in this sense, can be translated into talk of the ways in which he is disposed to behave.

It may be unfair to add visual, auditory and other perceptual sensations to the list of inner occurrences which Ryle apparently admits, since it would appear from the postscript to his chapter on "Sensation and Observation" that he came to think that he had been mistaken in accepting the conventional view that perceiving entailed having sensations of these sorts. In the same way, the references to visual and auditory images, which we have found him making in the earlier part of his book, ought

13 pp. 58–59.
14 pp. 83–84.
15 p. 84.

perhaps to be discounted on the ground that when at a
later stage he writes about Imagination, he argues that
"seeing things in one's mind's eye does not involve either
the existence of things seen or the occurrence of acts of
seeing them."[16] Even so, we are still left with what Ryle
describes as fancying that one sees or hears things, as well
as with seeing, hearing and the other forms of perception
themselves. Ryle does not explain what he takes fancying
to be, apart from its not consisting in observing images,
but if it is to do the work that he assigns to it, it would
seem that it must be a mental state or process of some
sort, and one for which no analysis is given in behavioural
terms. Admittedly, Ryle argues that the various forms of
sense-perception are not mental states or processes,
since they are not states or processes at all. His ground for
this is that verbs like "see" and "hear" are what he calls
achievement words: like the words "win" or "cure" or
"discover" they are not used to describe any activity but
rather to state that something has been brought off, some
task accomplished, some process carried to fulfillment.
I am not entirely convinced that this is so, but even if it
were so, it would make little difference to the present
argument. For now we have to ask what are supposed to
be the processes of which seeing and hearing and the
other modes of perception are the fulfillment. In the case
of sight and hearing, the words "looking" and "listening"
can be called into play: when it comes to the other senses,
we shall probably be forced into circumlocution, unless
words like "touching," "smelling," and "tasting" are made
to do double duty. But whatever words we use to stand
for them, these processes cannot on the face of it be taken
to be purely physical. If it is to be related to seeing as
running in a race is related to winning it, looking at an
object must imply more than having one's eyes in such
and such a physical relation to it. In old-fashioned terms,
looking and listening must be conscious processes. At

[16] p. 245.

any rate Ryle gives us no reason to think otherwise. He does not take the desperate course, which has been followed by some contemporary materialists, of trying to identify seeing and hearing with the acquisition of true beliefs, themselves reduced to behavioural dispositions, in consequence of the stimulation of the relevant sense-organs. However dissatisfied he may be with the standard philosophical accounts of sense-perception, he does not go to the length of dispensing altogether with any form of sentience.

What then are we to make of these mental residues: the silent soliloquies, the itches, pangs, and gnawings, the dreams and day-dreams, the processes of fancying and those of which the various modes of perception are the achievements? Taken together, do they not furnish quite a robust inner life? How can Ryle admit them and yet not be haunted by "the ghost in the machine"?

Though he would not care to have it put in these terms, the answer may be that he believes his ghost to be an honest ghost. It would, therefore, have to differ in some vital respect from the ghost which represents "the official doctrine"; and the way in which he may think that it differs is that it does not command the stage of a private theatre. The inner occurrences which he is prepared to tolerate are not "proprietary" in the way that the denizens of the mind have commonly been thought to be.

One difficulty at this point is that Ryle does not go into the question of privacy in any detail. There are, however, indications that the type of privacy to which he objects is that which is ascribed to occurrences, or objects, or states, or processes, of which it is held to be characteristic that the person to whom they are private observes them and that it is logically impossible that they should be observed by anyone else. He wishes to say that nothing is private in this sense.

Does he succeed in showing that the inner life to which I have argued that he is still committed does not have this forbidden type of privacy? In the case of sensations and feelings, the argument on which he relies is that, so far as the power of observation goes, there is no asymmetry between oneself and other people. "It is true," he says, "that the cobbler cannot witness the tweaks that I feel when the shoe pinches. But it is false that I witness them. The reason why my tweaks cannot be witnessed by him is not that some Iron Curtain prevents them from being witnessed by anyone save myself, but that they are not the sorts of things of which it makes sense to say that they are witnessed or unwitnessed at all, even by me. I feel or have the tweaks, but I do not discover or peer at them; they are not things that I find out about by watching them, listening to them, or savouring them. In the sense in which a person may be said to have had a robin under observation, it would be nonsense to say that he has had a twinge under observation. There may be one or several witnesses of a road-accident: there cannot be several witnesses, or even one witness, of a qualm."[17] Of course there is still the difference that I feel this particular twinge and the cobbler cannot, but Ryle maintains that this is no more than a trivial point of logic. Another person cannot feel my twinges for the same reason that he cannot smile my smile or run my races or die my death. It is just that we are concerned here with cognate accusatives.

I am not convinced by this argument. The only reason which Ryle gives for saying that one cannot observe or witness one's sensations is that epithets which can be coupled with words like "observing" and "witnessing," when these are construed as task-words, cannot be applied to having sensations. We can be more or less successful at observing but not at having sensations, we can be said to observe, but not to have sensations, carefully or systematically, we can have motives for observing but not for having sensations, we can make mistakes of observation,

[17] p. 205.

but not of sensation, and so forth.[18] But the most that this proves is that having sensations is not engaging in a task. It is not doing research, though research may lead to it. But, if we are to believe Ryle, exactly the same is true of seeing, hearing, touching and the other modes of perception. All his grammatical points apply just as well to them. Yet surely he would not wish to say that we do not observe or witness what we see.

The truth is that verbs like "observe" and "witness" are commonly used both as task words and as achievement words. If Ryle is to capitalize on the fact that not everything that can be said about observing can also be said about having sensations, he will therefore have to maintain that it is only when construed as a task that observing is cognitive. But then he will be mistaken. The parallel case of seeing is a sufficient counter-example.

There remains the point that sensations are cognate to feeling, whereas the objects which we perceive are not cognate to our perceiving them: from which it is inferred that the difference between perceiving and having sensations is not that one is acquainted with public objects in the one case and private objects in the other, but that while we can properly speak of there being objects of perception, to have a sensation is not to be acquainted with any object at all. My own view, about which I shall say a little more later on, is that this is a matter of policy. We are not bound to treat sensations, or feelings, or for that matter images, as private objects, but there is no compelling reason why we should not do so if we wish. But, however this may be, even if we rule out private objects, it still will not follow, as Ryle assumes, that feeling is not a privileged source of information. The sense in which it is privileged can be illustrated by returning to Ryle's example of the ill-fitting shoe. No doubt the cobbler has ways of knowing that I feel the tweaks, although the sceptical arguments which put this assumption in

18 *Vide* p. 204.

question still have to be met: but only I know that the
tweaks are being felt, on the basis of feeling them. It is
for this reason and not, as has sometimes been suggested,
because it is improper to credit a person with knowledge
of his own sensations, that the question how I know that
I feel the tweaks is not appropriate, though it would be
appropriate to ask any other person how he knew that I
felt them. This point is in fact conceded by Ryle, when
he sanctions the dialogue "How do you know that the
pain is in your leg and not in your shoulder?" "They are
my leg and shoulder, aren't they?"[19] This need not imply
that I cannot be mistaken with regard to such things as
the location of my pains, but surely it is a claim, and a
valid claim, to the possession of what Ryle calls "privileged
access."

Much the same considerations apply to the cases of
imagining and perceiving. It is not enough for Ryle's purposes to do away with mental images and sense-data. The
fact that I am imagining or ostensibly perceiving whatever it may be will still be known to me in a way that it
cannot be known to other people. On the assumption
that the objects of sense-perception are public, if they
exist at all, I am not in a privileged position with respect
to the identification of what I perceive: there are, however, the same reasons as in the case of my sensations for
holding that I am in a privileged position with respect to
knowing what it seems to me that I perceive, and my use
a moment ago of the artificial expression "ostensibly perceiving" was intended to make this qualification. In the
case of imagining, the parallel with having sensations is
obvious and Ryle indeed concedes it when, in a passage
which I have already quoted, he speaks of Dr. Johnson's
day-dreams as something that only Johnson could record.

A point to which Ryle attaches some importance is that
such records are retrospective. He rejects the theory according to which "mental processes are conscious, not in

[19] p. 239.

the sense that we do or could report on them *post mortem*, but in the sense that their intimations of their own occurrences are properties of those occurrences and so are not posterior to them."[20] He denies not only that mental processes, if they existed, could be self-luminous but also that there could be such a thing as introspection, if this is taken to be a species of perception which has internal rather than external objects. His main argument against the view that mental processes are self-luminous is that the consciousness of a mental process cannot be identical with the mental process itself. For example, if the process is one of carrying out an inference, then "my consciousness is of a process of inferring, but my inferring is, perhaps, of a geometrical conclusion from geometrical premisses. The verbal expression of my inference might be, 'because this is an equilateral triangle, therefore each angle is 60 degrees,' but the verbal expression of what I am conscious of might be 'Here I am deducing such and such from so and so.' "[21] In the same way, my consciousness of my consciousness of my process of inferring must be differentiated from my consciousness of the process. But then, if we take every mental process to be self-luminous we are led into an infinite regress. One might have expected Ryle to argue that a similar regress would arise on the assumption that every mental process was introspective, but he contents himself instead with the empirical arguments that there must be "some limit to the number of possible synchronous acts of attention"[22] and that, as Hume pointed out, there are some states of mind which put us into too much agitation for it to be possible for us to scrutinize them coolly. These last objections do not apply to retrospection which, in Ryle's opinion, achieves all the legitimate ends for which introspection was thought to be required. Of course, retrospection is not infallible, as introspection has sometimes

[20] p. 160.
[21] p. 162.
[22] p. 165.

been taken to be: but the quest for infallibility is anyhow mistaken.

These arguments are not very easy to evaluate. What they seem to me to prove is first that the metaphor of the inner searchlight is not felicitous and, secondly, that it cannot rightly be assumed that we always in fact know what our mental processes are. On the other hand, they do not prove that there are any mental processes which are such that we are not in a position to know that they are occurring: and, what is more important, they do not prove that we do not obtain this knowledge, when we have it, in a way that is not available to anybody else. Neither does it seem to me to matter very much whether the knowledge is acquired concurrently with the mental process to which it relates or a little subsequently to it. I should have thought that in some cases it was concurrent and in others not. The important point, in either case, is that, although the knowledge can be shared with others, we alone obtain it on the basis of actually undergoing, or having just previously undergone, the experience in question.

Ryle admits it to be true and important that "the objects of my retrospection are items in my autobiography,"[23] but will not allow that there is anything "intrinsically ghostly" about them. "In the same way that I can catch myself day-dreaming, I can catch myself scratching: in the same way that I can catch myself engaged in a piece of silent soliloquy, I can catch myself saying something aloud."[24] But this is to miss the point. The fact that I can "catch myself" in the performance of physical as well as mental activities does not entail that when the object of retrospection is mental, my access to it is not privileged. All that it entails is that this does not follow merely from the fact that it is retrospective.

In general, Ryle's strategy is not so much to deny the

[23] p. 167.
[24] p. 166.

existence of "privileged access" as to represent it as marking a difference of degree and not a difference of kind. "The superiority of the speaker's knowledge of what he is doing over that of the listener does not indicate that he has Privileged Access to facts of a type inevitably inaccessible to the listener, but only that he is in a very good position to know what the listener is often in a very poor position to know."[25] So, when Ryle speaks of thinking as silent soliloquy, the suggestion is that what makes it impossible for others to eavesdrop on my unspoken thoughts is that they are pitched in too low a key: thinking without saying what we think is like whispering very softly; so softly that no one else can overhear you. And then one wonders whether there could not be some device by which these whisperings could be magnified. For example, if, like the behaviourist Dr. Watson, one were to identify thoughts with movements of the larynx, one could look forward to the time when all such movements would be capable of being recorded and the thoughts which they represented read off from them. But this is not Ryle's position. He nowhere suggests that his silent soliloquies are to be equated with physiological states or processes: nor does he make any attempt to translate them into behavioural dispositions. But if they are not transmutable into physical terms, it may not be a contingent fact that only their author overhears them. It is, indeed, contingent that I keep certain thoughts to myself, instead of expressing them in writing or in speech: but given that I do keep them to myself, it is arguable that the possibility of any other person's listening in to them is logically excluded, since there is nothing that would count as his listening in.

To this it may be objected that while such an argument may conform to our current usage, it still takes too narrow a view of the empirical possibilities. Whatever the technical difficulties, it is surely not inconceivable that a

[25] p. 179.

portion of my brain should be transplanted into another person's body: and if that were to happen, he might come to remember my thoughts in just the way that I myself remember them. Indeed, one might go further: it is imaginable that my brain should be so connected to another person's that he currently caught on to my mental processes in just the way that I do. Admittedly, such examples put a strain on our concept of personal identity. There could be circumstances in which we should find it more natural to say that I had been translated into another body than that another person shared my memories, let alone my present consciousness. On the other hand, there could be circumstances in which we should find it more natural to abandon the rule that the experiences which one can remember, or even those of which one can be currently aware, are necessarily one's own.

I think that these possibilities have to be admitted; and if we admit them we may have to allow that it is only a contingent fact that my experiences are accessible to me in a way that they are not accessible to anyone else. Nevertheless, there will still be a distinction between knowing about an experience on the basis of having it, or recollecting it, and knowing about it only on the basis of observing the bodily states or behaviour of the person whose experience it is; and there will still be grounds for holding that a claim to knowledge which is based on having the experience in question is authoritative in a way that a claim which is based only on observation cannot be.[26] Moreover, some at least of the sceptical arguments concerning the possibility of our having any knowledge of this kind on the basis of "external" observation will still need to be met. I do not say that there is no way of meeting them, although I do not think that any satisfactory way has yet been found. This is a problem that is almost ignored by Ryle, no doubt because he sees himself as hav-

[26] Cf. my essay on "Privacy" in *The Concept of a Person*, especially pp. 68–73.

ing undercut it. He would, indeed, be justified in this assumption if he had made good the thesis of logical behaviourism. I have, however, tried to show not only that he has not made it good, but that it is doubtful even if he holds it in any rigorous form.

In fact, I think that there are three general theses in *The Concept of Mind* which Ryle does not explicitly distinguish. The thesis which I have just suggested that he probably does not hold, though his programmatic statements often imply that he does, is that all our talk about the mind is translatable into talk about behaviour. If he does hold this thesis, the least that one can say is that he has left himself a great deal of work to do: we have seen that he makes a number of admissions, which appear to be inconsistent with it. There is, however, a weaker thesis which is consistently held throughout the book. This is the thesis that, whether or not the programme of logical behaviourism can be carried through in its entirety, it does give a correct account of a great deal of what is ordinarily classified as talk about the mind. In a great many instances in which a person is said to satisfy a "mental" predicate, what is being said of him is not only, and perhaps not at all, that he is undergoing some inner process, but rather that he is exhibiting or disposed to exhibit a certain pattern of behaviour. This can apply to the ascription of intelligence, of motives and purposes, of voluntary actions, of emotions and moods, and of thoughts when they are overtly expressed.

This thesis is weaker than the other, in that it does not do away with inner processes altogether. What it does is to minimize their rôle. When someone acts intelligently, his movements may be preceded or accompanied by some inner planning, but they need not be; the silent thought is not necessary for the performance to be intelligent. Similarly, when I utter a meaningful sentence, it is possible, but not necessary, that I have already run through the sentence "in my head"; even if no such inner process has taken place, the utterance will still be the expression of my thought. In the case of the will, Ryle takes the stronger line of denying that there are any inner acts to which "willing" could be taken to refer; but his main point, here again, is that even if such acts of volition were to occur, their occurrence could not be necessary to make an action voluntary; for one thing, the assumption that they were necessary would lead to an infinite regress, since it would make sense to ask whether these acts were voluntary themselves. When it comes to motives Ryle is on less sure ground, since his theory that "the imputation of a motive . . . is the subsumption of an episode proposition under a law-like proposition"[27] applies only to standing motives, like vanity or ambition, to which, indeed, he confines his examples: it does not apply to the occurrent motives that one may have for doing particular actions, like leaving early to catch a train. He could, however, have argued that even when one is acting from an occurrent motive, one need not, though one may, avow it oneself: and even if one does avow it, the avowal may take the form of an overt utterance. Finally, the case of emotions is different from the others, since here the occurrence of some inner feeling, or at least a bodily sensation, does seem to be essential: even so it can be argued that the feeling plays a relatively minor part in the complex state of affairs in which the emotion consists: the attendant behaviour and, still more, the behavioural dispositions are what really count.

I am doubtful whether this is true of all emotions—it applies, for example, to anger better than it does to sorrow—but even if the emphasis is wrong in this case, the general thesis seems to me true and important. There has been a tendency among philosophers to assume that everything that commonly passes for the work of mind consists in, or at least essentially involves, some inner process, and it is useful to have this tendency corrected. It needed to be shown that such things as intending, willing,

[27] Loc. cit.

understanding, desiring, exercising intelligence, even thinking, may, in concrete instances, consist in nothing more than the fact that the person of whom they are predicated is behaving or is disposed to behave in such and such a fashion. Nevertheless the scope of the thesis should not be over-estimated. In the areas which it covers, it establishes for the most part only that the occurrence of inner processes is not essential for the application of a given mental predicate, not that they do not occur at all; and there are important areas of mental activity which it does not cover. As a result, no doubt, of his flirtation with the more radical thesis of logical behaviourism, Ryle gives the impression of thinking that all the mental operations that really matter are overt operations. For any ordinary purpose, the residue is negligible. Only a James Joyce would bother with it. But, as we have seen, the residue is far from negligible. It includes a considerable part of the exercise of memory and of the imagination, and it includes every form of sentience. Until it is shown that perceiving can be analysed in behavioural terms, the erosion of the inner life, to which this second thesis tends, will remain seriously incomplete. As I said before, attempts have been made to bring perception into line, but I do not myself think that they have been, or are likely to be, successful.

The third thesis which I find in *The Concept of Mind* is weaker still. It is that our ordinary talk about the mind is open to what Quine calls regimentation.[28] We do not have to conceive of minds as substances, or indeed as entities of any kind. We do not have to admit thoughts, or feelings, or sensations, or mental images, or sense-data as objects. The only subjects to which mental predicates need to be ascribed are persons, and any particular mental object, like an image or a sense-datum, can be transformed into a way in which a person is affected, that is, into a state or process which is adjectival to him. So

[28] *Vide* W. V. Quine, *Word and Object*, Ch. V.

thought will be replaced by thinking, images by imagining, feelings by feeling, and sense-data by perceiving or
seeming to perceive.

But what of the accusatives of these words? Ryle does
not enter into the question in any detail but I think that
his policy, except in the case of perception and feeling,
would be to make them propositional. Not all thinking is
straightforwardly "thinking that," but with a little adjustment, such activities as wondering, musing, speculat-
ing, doubting, pondering, even dreaming, can be represented as being directed on to propositions. Without too
much strain, the same can be made true of optative activities like wishing, hoping, fearing, desiring, seeking, and
regretting: their object will be the proposition that such
and such a state of affairs obtains or does not obtain. In
spite of Ryle's efforts, the case of imagining remains more
difficult. It is not easy to see how having an after-image
can be represented as fancying that something is the case.
To this extent, imagining comes closer to perceiving, in
cases where the perception is delusive. In the cases where
it is veridical, there is no problem. The objects which are
perceived are physical entities, in the broad sense in
which anything counts as physical if it is a real constituent of the external world. These objects will serve also in
the delusive cases in which the infidelity of the perception
consists in its making them appear other than they are.
But what is to be said when the delusive perception is a
total hallucination? This does not force the admission of
sense-data. We can talk of our seeming to perceive, or
thinking that we perceive, physical entities which do not
in fact exist. But what sort of objects are these?

The case of feeling, except in the sense, which is not
here in question, in which "feeling" is roughly equivalent
to "touching," is different in that it is not possible to
divide its objects into those which do and those which do
not exist. The pang which is felt in a phantom limb has
the same status, as an entity, as the pang which is felt in
any actual part of the body. If this status is not to be that

of an object, it seems that expressions which refer to feelings will have to be treated as cognate accusatives of the verbs which govern them. What this amounts to is that one refuses to license the existential inference from a proposition of the form "A has the feeling *f*" to a proposition of the form "There is a feeling *f*, which A has." I do not know that any good reason can be given for this prohibition, except that on grounds of economy or a taste for neatness, one decides to have only physical entities in one's ontology, but neither do I see any strong objection to it. The objection that one might raise would be epistemological. It might be argued that since "feelings are first," in the sense that they are epistemologically prior to the persons to whom they are attributed, they have the better title to existence. I accept the premiss of this argument and have in the past accepted its conclusion, but I now think, for reasons which I have developed elsewhere,[29] that epistemological and ontological priority do not have to go together.

The same technique can be applied to images and to the objects of hallucinatory perception. One can simply refuse to license the inference from "A is having an image" to "There is an image which A is having" and from "A perceives a non-existent physical entity" to "There is a non-existent physical entity which A perceives." But here there is more reason for disquiet. Even as the designates of cognate accusatives, non-existent physical entities have a disreputable air. A better course, it seems to me, would be to admit sense-data and treat them as cognate to perceptual acts. But if we admit sense-data at all, how can we resist admitting them in other cases of perception, including those that are veridical? The answer is that there is no call to resist. That a perceptual act always has a cognate object does not preclude its also having a real one: and the real object, when it exists, will be a physical entity.

[29] *Vide The Origins of Pragmatism*, pp. 329 ff.

Since this technique could also be applied to thoughts and to the possibly non-existent objects of optative acts, one may wonder what is gained by bringing in propositional accusatives. A motive for doing so might be that propositions are at least not mental objects, but this is not enough to make them respectable. We can indeed refuse to treat them as entities, but then it is not clear why they are to be preferred to the non-entities which they replace. There would, however, be a reason for preferring them if they were thought to be eliminable. The introduction of propositional accusatives would then be a stage in the process of getting rid of intentionality. Propositions would be replaced in their turn by sentences: and an account of the use and understanding of sentences would be given in behavioural terms. I am attracted by this programme, and think that it ought to be successful, but it meets with difficulties which have not, in my view, as yet been overcome.[30]

Failing the completion of a programme of this sort, the regimentation of mental discourse does not amount to very much. It comes down to little more than a decision not to say that such things as feelings, images and sense-data exist, or at any rate not to allow them the status of entities. No doubt Ryle intended more than this. When he denied the existence of images or sense-data, he wanted to show not only that we were not bound to include such things in our ontology, but that we were not entitled to. This could be achieved either by deduction from some ontological theory, which would itself then need to be justified, or by showing that the concept of the type of entity in question was such that nothing answered to it. Though Ryle has a physicalist ontology in the background, and sometimes proceeds as though he had established it, the course which he mainly follows is the second. The argument on which he relies is that neither imagining nor sensing, as this term is used by

[30] Vide *The Origins of Pragmatism*, pp. 173 ff.

sense-datum theorists, is a sort of observing; in the case
of sensing, this is backed by the argument that if perceiving entailed sensing, and sensing were itself a sort of
perceiving, the admission of sense-data would involve a
vicious infinite regress. If "observing" is taken here as a
task word, the main argument holds; but then, as we have
seen, it proves nothing to the purpose. If, in accordance
with the infinite regress argument, observing is equated
with perceiving, the grounds for saying that imagining
and sensing are not sorts of observing would be either
that they are not the completion of activities like looking
and listening, or that they do not have physical entities
as their objects. But even on the dubious assumption
that perceiving is always the completion of an activity,
there is no good reason why this should be made a necessary condition for any conscious state to have an existent
object: and the point that the objects of imaging and
sensing would not be physical entities plainly begs the
question. Neither is there anything in the infinite regress
argument. The ground for bringing in sense-data is that
our ordinary judgments of perception commit us to more
than is contained in the experiences on which they are
based.[31] The invocation of sense-data is intended to provide us with a way of describing the contents of the experiences, without incurring any further commitments. It
is not universally agreed that it succeeds in this, but if,
as I believe, it does succeed, it clearly does not entail that
we have to go on reducing our commitments *ad infinitum*.
There is no foothold here for the regress to begin.

I conclude that Ryle has not shown that we are not entitled to admit even sense-data as entities, but at most
that we are not bound to do so. The decision not to
admit them, together with other "private" entities like
images and feelings, does not require a denial of their
legitimacy. I think it can be shown that even if one starts;

[31] Cf. my article "Has Austin Refuted the Sense-Datum Theory?"
Synthese 17 (1967).

epistemologically, from the neutral monist basis of sense-data, images and feelings, it is still possible and indeed desirable to have a physicalist ontology.[32] This is, indeed, a much weaker result than one would get if one were able to prove that all mental states or processes were logically or even factually identical with physical ones, but here I doubt if anything better is obtainable. If there are any hopes for physicalism, they must lie in the attempt to establish factual identity. The belief in a logical identity is simpler and bolder, but I think it has become clear that it is false.

This is not necessarily a reproach to Ryle since we have seen that he does not attempt to carry the logical thesis all the way. In fact, I believe that he takes it about as far as it can legitimately go. Of the three theses that I have extracted from *The Concept of Mind*, it is only the second that yields a substantial result, the third, in the form in which it is true, being too weak to be of very much interest. In short, what Ryle has succeeded in doing is to reduce the empire of the mind over a considerable area. This is an important achievement, and one that is brilliantly effected, but it does not fulfill Ryle's professed intention of entirely exorcizing the ghost in the machine. The movements of the ghost have been curtailed but it still walks, and some of us are still haunted by it.

[32] Vide *The Origins of Pragmatism*, pp. 173 ff.

RYLE AND THINKING

F. N. SIBLEY

I

This article is concerned mainly with views about thinking put forward by Ryle in a series of papers[1] published since the discussion in Chapter IX of *The Concept of Mind*. He regularly distinguishes thinking, where this refers to "such activities as pondering, musing and calculating," from thinking "that something is the case" (*TL* 65), and in most of these papers he deals with the former notion. I shall concentrate on this too.

Ryle does not always draw the boundaries of thinking in the same way. He always includes (1) activities, either theoretical or practical, like excogitating, multiplying, trying to solve problems and translating, that end in a solution, conclusion, or result; he usually includes (2) activities, like following an argument or going over something in one's head, where no solving is attempted; and he sometimes includes (3) daydreams and undirected reverie ("A man in a daydream is thinking," *T* 195). Sometimes, within one article, he shifts back and forth between broader and narrower senses. Such shifts accord with our ordinary uses of "thoughts" and "thinking." I

---

[1] "Thinking and Language," *Proceedings of the Aristotelian Society*, Supplementary Volume 25, 1951, pp. 65–82.

"Thinking," *Acta Psychologica*, Volume 9, 1953, pp. 189–96.

"A Puzzling Element in the Notion of Thinking," *Proceedings of the British Academy*, Volume 44, 1958, pp. 129–44.

"Thinking and Reflecting" in *The Human Agent*, Royal Institute of Philosophy Lectures, Volume I, 1966–67.

"The Thinking of Thoughts," *University of Saskatchewan University Lectures*, No. 18, 1968.

I abbreviate these respectively to *TL, T, PE, TR,* and *TT,* and *The Concept of Mind*, 1949, to *CM*.

shall follow the main gist of Ryle's discussions by confining my attention to categories (1) and (2).

Ryle's primary question throughout is what thinking is, what constitutes it, what it essentially consists in, though not all he says is directly relevant to this. His main negative task is to reject accounts which find thinking to consist in any single ingredient or unitary activity. In different papers this negative aim takes various shapes. In some the stress is on arguing that thinking comprises a collection of activities with no common strand of importance. In the latest papers (*TR* and *TT*), however, he argues that thinking is not a separate activity (or even group of activities) at all. Verbs of thinking are really "adverbial"; they do not themselves denote activities, but ways or manners in which other, often overt, activities are performed. In making these various attacks on the essential ingredient view, Ryle sometimes seems to be putting forward incompatible accounts of thinking. I want first to separate these different strands so that they can be seen not to be incompatible.

The first line of argument to deny the "natural supposition" that "'thinking' stands for a specific process or activity" is familiar: "words like 'gardening,' 'working' and 'housekeeping' cover a great number of widely different things" and the same, he says, is true of "thinking." "The word 'thinking' covers some activities which are attempts to reach the answers to questions, as well as others which are not; some activities in which there is scope for originality and insight, as well as others where there is not; some activities which incorporate ratiocination, as well as others which do not; some activities, like multiplication and translation, which require special training, as well as others, like reverie, which do not. To look for some common and peculiar ingredients of all thinking is like looking for an ingredient common and peculiar to cats-cradle, hide-and-seek, billiards, Snap and all the other things which we call 'games'" (*T* 191–93). The many things the *Penseur*, for instance, may be doing—trying to construct a philosophical theory, solve a chess problem, recollect a telephone number, compose an after-dinner speech, translate a poem, or run through the Kings of England—refute "our vain presumption" that thinking is "one uniform and nominatable X-ing" (*TR* 219). The account offered in some of these passages seems clearly to be a "multiple-activity" or "family" account (though he *also* says (*TR* 219), where he is developing the different ("adverbial") line of thought, that he is not going "to resort to the now over-hallowed 'family likeness' device so long before reaching, what it is for, the last resort").

The second distinguishable explanation Ryle gives for rejecting a single-activity account of thinking is that thinking is "polymorphous." This second explanation is not explicitly distinguished from the multiple-activity explanation; indeed they are usually given side by side as if parts of one account. But they should be distinguished; for while both claim that thinking involves not one, but any of a diverse range of activities, the examples of these diverse activities must be different ones. The two accounts must operate on different levels with different examples.

I interpret the polymorphous view as different from the multiple-activity view (whether or not Ryle intended a distinction) for this reason: according to the polymorphous view, the activities a thinker may perform are not only heterogeneous, but are also activities that might be performed without the performer thinking. In introducing the notion, Ryle says, for instance, "There need be no action, inner or overt, performed by the policeman on his beat, which he may not also perform when strolling round the same streets when his work is over" (*TL* 68 and similarly elsewhere). But if so, the examples Ryle gave earlier, calculating, composing poems, trying to solve chess problems and so on, to illustrate the heterogeneity of thinking activities, cannot also be examples of the heterogeneous X-ings that make thinking polymorphous. For calculating or trying to compose a poem are, *ipso facto*, instances of thinking. Ryle, however, does not always make this plain; immediately after explaining that thinking is polymorphous (*TL* 68–69), for instance, he gives examples of what he calls "proper specimens" of thinking, which illustrate not polymorphousness but multiple-activity. The two can easily be confused, because thinking, with which Ryle introduces polymorphousness, involves two distinct elements: (*a*) thinking always involves an X-ing which is non-constitutive of thinking and (*b*) thinking involves any of a heterogeneous group of such X-ings. The first point, which I take as the more important, is independent of the second; an activity could involve necessarily only one kind of X-ing which nevertheless is not constitutive of that activity, as in Ryle's later example of winking (*TT*). Winking involves always and only the contraction of one eyelid, though not all such contractions are winkings. This point, however, for which "polymorphous" is strictly a misnomer, I shall retain as the key element in that notion.

The third account of thinking that Ryle offers is the "adverbial" account, first put forward under this label in *TR*, and modified or developed in *TT*. This view, that thinking is not itself an activity, but the way or circumstances in which other activities are performed, he illustrates first by the tennis-player. The latter is certainly thinking while playing tennis. But this is to be construed adverbially; he is doing various things intelligently, with his wits about him, warily. Since the force of "thinking" is the force of these adverbs, thinking cannot occur on its own; one must be doing something to do it intelligently and warily, or stupidly and carelessly. "Thinking" means "with thought," as "hurrying" means "with speed." I cannot continue to hurry, as I can continue to talk, if I cease to walk. The doctrine, but not the label, is familiar from *CM*.

Ryle is quite explicit that the adverbially qualified activity cannot itself be an activity of thinking; obviously so, or the adverbial account would have failed. "The notions of being pensive and having thoughts do not explain, but need to be explained via the notion of intelligently X-ing, *where 'X' is not a verb of thinking*" (TR 216–17, my italics). The mentality of activities resides in the adverbial element, not in the activity, or X-ing, itself. I shall comment briefly on this programme.

First, within this theory, mental adverbs, like "carefully," "attentively" and "purposefully," will not qualify the verbs they most commonly qualify. Ordinarily we apply them to verbs like "pondering," "counting," "planning," "calculating," etc., and these are verbs of thinking. Pondering, etc. are already necessarily impregnated with some degree of some of Ryle's thought-adverbs. They can be done with greater or less care, attention, etc., but not with a zero degree, mindlessly—or, as Ryle himself puts it, "absentmindedly or deliriously." Whatever counts as a proper specimen of thinking (excluding category (3)) is of this kind. But the X-ings Ryle needs must not be. Nor, it must be noted also, may Ryle's X-ings be positively *non*-mental either. It would be easy, but mistaken, to suppose that, with the tennis-player for instance, Ryle has dissolved the player's thinking into a set of adverbs qualifying various purely physical doings or movements. Any exclusively *non*-mental X-ing would, by that token, be incapable of qualification by mental adverbs; Ryle's adverbs cannot qualify physical processes like sweating or twitching. (Equally, they cannot even qualify those mental occurrences, like daydreaming, that constitute category (3) of my tripartite division of thinking.) So Ryle's X-ings must be neutral *vis-à-vis* thought. They must be qualifiable *either* as careful, careless, attentive, etc., *or* as mindless, absent-minded, involuntary, etc. Indeed, they are the same X-ings that the polymorphous account required.

On the whole, in the later articles, Ryle provides the right sort of examples. With the tennis player, he gives X-ings like moving his feet, making eye and arm movements, and swinging his racquet. With other activities, including those of the *Penseur*, he mentions such inward doings as picturing numbers, saying words to oneself and manipulating imaginary chessmen, together with such overt X-ings as writing numbers on paper, uttering words aloud and manipulating real chessmen. All these can be qualified both by thought-adverbs and also by adverbs, like "absently," "randomly" and "without attention," that exclude thought.

Ryle, then, seems to deny, earlier on, an *essential* activity, by opposing to it both a *multiple*-activity account and the *polymorphous* account; and to deny, later, *any* activity, by opposing to it an *adverbial* account. But the three accounts are not incompatible, even if Ryle's presentation and examples occasionally obscure the fact. Proper specimens of thinking, like anagram-solving and composing sonatas, might have no common ingredient; each might also involve different neutral X-ings, like manipulating letters and striking piano keys; and thinking might be not an activity additional to these X-ings, but the manner of X-ing.

II

The three accounts that occur in Ryle's papers on thinking are compatible. But are they true? Or, at least, has he any cogent arguments for them? His denial of an essential activity proceeds, I have indicated, first by proposing that the proper specimens of thinking comprise a family, more recently, and for him more importantly, by proposing the adverbial theory. I want to ask, first, whether he offers any cogent arguments, aside from the adverbial account, against an essential ingredient view; secondly, whether any of his arguments establish the adverbial account.

The answer to the first question, I think, is that in the papers prior to *TR*, where the adverbial view is developed, Ryle gives no argument at all to refute the essential activity view, though he certainly claims to be rejecting it. The arguments he does use are not relevant to this question. Those, especially in *PE* and *TR*, to which he devotes much space (and which I discuss in III below), attacking the view that thinking requires images or words as a necessary "vehicle" do not bear on ingredient *activities* at all. Those about polymorphousness *are* about activities. But since the X-ings relevant here must be neutral as between mental and non-mental, no essential ingredient of thinking *could* come to light in the investigation of them. So their obvious heterogeneity, which may seem to prove his point, is irrelevant, and does not establish the absence of a common feature at the other level, among proper specimens of thinking. It may seem *likely* that there is also no important common ingredient among these very varied proper specimen activities too; but nothing has shown this. Simply citing the varieties of thinking, like citing varieties of games, does not yet establish the point. Ryle himself regards the "family resemblance" device as a last resort; and in the articles before *TR* he has hardly attempted to reach this. It may be that the adverbial argument, when it appears in *TR*, will establish what he has claimed throughout. But even before looking at that, it could do no harm, even if it did no good, to *look* for a common ingredient in all thinking. It is not clear that we must fail to find one, any more than it is clear that we can succeed. Unless the adverbial, or some other argument against the very possibility is successful, the only course is to look and see. This Ryle does not attempt.

I shall just mention one possibility (there may be others) that *prima facie* might be worth examining. It seems indisputable that, with the *Penseur*, the tennis-player and any other kind of thinking, some more than zero degree of attention is necessarily involved. The composer must attend to the notes he plays or imagines, the man trying to recall a telephone number to the numbers that pass through his head, and the architect or

mathematician to the bricks or numbers that he moves
about on his actual or mental table or sheet of paper. If
not, they are thoughtlessly doodling. But if attending is
necessary to make activities involving it cases of thinking,
is it also *sufficient?*

There seems one obvious objection to saying so. The
man doodling may be attending to the random and purposeless way his hand traces marks on paper, in the
minimal sense that he may see and be able to report
later how his hand moved: that he began with swirling
lines on the left and ended with squares on the right. He
was not unaware of what he was doing, but he was not
thinking either. Again, a man listening, even attentively,
to a lecturer's words need not be thinking. He might
register perfectly the lecturer's words, without taking in,
thinking about, accepting, or rejecting his argument. One
might therefore suggest, as a not unplausible sufficient
condition of thinking, that one must be attending to or
watching for considerations of a certain kind, namely,
those of relevance or appropriateness. There is no objection, in defining an activity, to specifying the kind of
object the defining verb requires, just as "bibbing" has to
be defined as excessive drinking, not just of water, but
of alcohol.

Relevance and appropriateness, of course, are themselves broad notions, open to various interpretations. Just
as the objects or activities attended to are heterogeneous,
so will be the kinds of relevance and appropriateness also.
If I try to run through the list of Kings, or assess the list
someone else produces, I shall expect and accept only
names of kings, and I shall reject Pitt or Lloyd George
if they come to mind or are mentioned. If I am composing
a sonata, I may reject note sequences that do not develop the first subject, and so on. But whether this is an
objection would itself need discussion.

Obviously, I am not seriously arguing for this suggestion about attention to relevance here. My point is that
Ryle asserts his view without looking for, or arguing

against, *any prima facie* candidates. So, unless he has other arguments that are telling, his claim, even if true, has not been made out. But another reason for not pursuing the suggestion here is that, even if it were correct, it is unclear whether it would refute Ryle's claims. For while he sometimes argues only against an essential *ingredient* in all thinking, he is usually arguing against an essential ingredient *activity*. So even if attending to relevance were essential, he might deny that it is an activity. He would presumably dissolve it, by the adverbial account, into an adverbial parasite upon non-mental X-ings. I leave these questions unresolved, therefore, and turn to the argument about adverbial verbs.

The adverbial account, if true, would exclude any essential activity; the only activities involved in thinking would be neutral X-ings. My inquiry again is less into whether the account is wrong, than into whether (as some seem to assume) Ryle has established it. If not, it remains at best *sub judice*.

Ryle links his distinction between "activity" and "adverbial" verbs with a distinction between "autonomous" and "non-autonomous" activities. A person thinking (Y-ing) is necessarily engaged in an activity (X-ing). The latter activity is autonomous in the sense that X-ing could occur without Y-ing; whereas Y-ing, which cannot occur without some X-ing, is non-autonomous. Singing is autonomous *vis-à-vis* walking; hurrying is not.

I consider, first, two things Ryle says in making the distinction. He says (TR 212–13), "If told that someone is hurrying, we have not been told what he is doing, but only that he is doing whatever he is doing at an abnormally high speed." Secondly, "The command 'Hurry' is only the beginning of a command; it cannot yet, context apart, be obeyed or disobeyed." By contrast, "The command . . . 'eat' is an obeyable command, and not the less so for being pretty unspecific. If I then eat lobster or bread or shoe-leather, I am obeying the command." But these tests are inconclusive. Indeed, it seems correct to say, if told that someone is thinking, that we *are* told what he is doing, though not very specifically, and *not* merely that he is doing whatever he is doing in some manner or other. Again, we might say that the command "think," like the command "eat," *is* obeyable, though pretty unspecific, and that if I then think about my income tax or a philosophical problem, I am obeying the command. Nothing in these examples shows that thinking is less an activity, more adverbial, or less autonomous, than running or eating; indeed *prima facie* they suggest the opposite.

Next, Ryle strongly suggests that the only true or genuine activities are autonomous ones. This sounds like a statement about "what there is." Indeed, he implies that autonomous, non-adverbial verbs are "verbs for separately do-able, lowest-level doings" (*TT* 11). Taken ontologically, so to speak, this suggests a category of genuine or basic activities which could occur on their own (and to which adverbial notions are applied), the only real goings-on of the world. But in the ontological sense of "autonomous" suggested here, it turns out that Ryle's X-ings are largely *not* autonomous, and that his Y-ings (like thinking) *are*. Take his example (*TT* 5) of the swift contraction of the right eyelid, which may be a twitch or a conspiratorial wink, or the shuffling of bricks on a table, which may be a scarcely noticed sort of doodling or a piece of architect's planning. For Ryle, the X-ings or autonomous doings in the two cases are, respectively, contracting the eyelid and moving bricks about. And, as I argued earlier, these X-ings must be neutral; they must no more be twitching or doodling (which are necessarily involuntary or purposeless) than they can be winking or planning (which are necessarily not). But that being so, the eyelid-contracting and the brick-moving seem *not* to be examples of activities that could occur alone. For it seems reasonable to argue that the eyelid contraction is either involuntary, in which case what occurred was a twitch, or not involuntary, in which case what occurred was a wink, or a practice wink, or any of a number of other things. What can occur on its own is one or other of *these* things, not a contraction which is neither involuntary nor not involuntary, but neutral; any more than the man in the next room can be neither white nor non-white. In this sense, neutral X-ings are not autonomous activities. What may be neutral is not the occurrence, but the description of the occurrence. What we have is, indeed, what Ryle also comes to call it, a "thin *description*." And to give something "the thinnest possible description" (*TT* 8) is not to find a simplest or basic or "separately do-able" doing. Real activities that occur occur *with* their adverbial features, whether we describe them fully or not. Anything may be more or less thinly described, but this does not entail that something corresponding merely to the thin description can occur separately, autonomously and on its own.

I have indicated that certain interpretations of autonomousness suggested by things Ryle says are unsatisfactory. So presumably the relevant sense involves taking activities in pairs: "Y-ing is not autonomous" means, for Ryle, that a man cannot engage in Y-ing (thinking) without doing something describable as "X-ing," whereas he can do something describable as "X-ing" without Y-ing (thinking); in which case, that element of the latter activity which "X-ing" describes is autonomous with respect to Y-ing.

However, if this is what is meant by saying that thinking is not an autonomous activity, it will not, even if true, make the case Ryle wants. The argument against thinking being an activity (and, *a fortiori*, the argument for it being adverbial) must establish more than that it is non-autonomous. Ryle must establish that thinking is not, or does not also include, some activity *additional* to X-ing which is nevertheless non-autonomous in the sense that it requires X-ing and ceases if X-ing ceases. There are plenty of at least *prima facie* activities that are non-autonomous in this sense, those for instance that require

another activity as their object or result. Refereeing, tim-
ing, controlling, trundling, propelling, listening to and
watching would all seem, unless Ryle can show otherwise,
to be activities requiring other activities as, in a broad
sense, their objects, and consequently not related to the
latter adverbially as hurrying is to running. So although
Ryle's denial that thinking involves any activity besides
neutral X-ing *may* be correct, it needs support by other
means. I postpone considering what other facts or assumptions Ryle relies on. Instead, I mention first a possible difficulty for the adverbial view and some considerations that seem to favour an activity view.

The difficulty is this. For thinking, attending, etc., to
be analysable adverbially, there must, on Ryle's own
terms, be an autonomous and neutral X-ing that the
thinker is doing and that the adverbs qualify. Ryle con-
centrates on examples like the tennis-player and the
Penseur, men thinking what they themselves are doing.
He scarcely discusses, in terms of this theory, the thought-
ful listener at the philosophy lecture or the mathematical
demonstration. The latter is certainly thinking, following
the speaker's argument, monitoring, trying to accept or
reject it as it occurs. But there seems to be no neutral
X-ing that he need be doing at all, and hence none to be
adverbially qualified. The X-ing, or at least the relevant
X-ing, the one he checks, rejects, accepts, etc., is not
something *he* is doing. He is not necessarily manipulating
images himself, nor need he be repeating the argument
under his breath. At least, Ryle would presumably not
want to say so, any more than he says that the man talking aloud or planning with real bricks need be silently
imagining words or picturing bricks as well. The man at
the lecture is just listening; though if he is listening
thoughtfully, he will be considering the *speaker's* X-ings,
the speaker's manipulations of spoken words or figures,
and perhaps silently approving some and rejecting others.
So what is the neutral X-ing that he is doing? Not the
silent approving or rejecting, since these are neither ac-

tivities nor neutral. Not nodding or shaking his head, since, like the *Penseur*, he may do nothing overt. Perhaps, it might be suggested, what he is doing attentively is listening to the argument. But this will not do. If "listening" is interpreted neutrally, as a verb of perception, not of thinking, then "listening attentively" may mean that he misses nothing said, can repeat the argument *verbatim* afterwards, but need not have thought about, or followed the steps of it at all. With a good auditory memory he could repeat a short argument delivered in a language he does not even understand. He was listening attentively, but not thinking or following. If we attempt a stronger interpretation, "listening" becomes what it must not become, a verb of thinking, *e.g.*, listening for implications and non-sequiturs.

There seems to be no third way, *viz.*, listening in the neutral, auditory sense, with the mental element packed into a lengthy and hyphenated adverbial phrase, *e.g.*, "attentively-to-actual-or-possible-irrelevances, non-sequiturs, etc.," since in this perceptual sense of "listening" you cannot be attentive to these things. Non-sequiturs have no characteristic sound, as sopranos or glockenspiels do. To speak of "listening thinkingly," in Ryle's manner, does not *show* that thinking is adverbial, but rather that we can provide an alternative and rather unnatural adverbial locution.

In short, it might seem an artificial move, adopted only to save the theory, to suppose that, besides listening to and following the argument, there is any neutral X-ing that the listener must be doing. In which case, there is nothing to be qualified adverbially. Listening *for* is of necessity purposeful; but it may not involve X-ing purposefully. Indeed, precisely what it may require is *no* X-ing, but various non-doings, not stamping, not shouting, etc. So even if this difficulty occurs only in the "spectator" cases, Ryle's adverbial account, taken at all literally, presumably fails, since it was intended at the outset to apply to the widest range of cases of thinking. A theory concerned with the manner of performing non-X-ings, which allowed us to do nothing in particular but do it very well, would be Gilbertian as well as Rylean, and the vanishing point of the adverbial theory.[2]

Perhaps these difficulties are either not genuine or not insuperable. Probably, the label "adverbial" must be taken, as Ryle said in introducing it, metaphorically and not very seriously (though he repeatedly says (TR 213 and elsewhere) that "there must be an X-ing"). But then it becomes unhelpful, if not misleading, and the literal interpretation of the doctrine becomes shadowy: perhaps simply that, whether X-ing occurs or not, thinking is not an additional activity. But we have still been offered no proof of this.

I shall mention therefore some considerations that seem to favour the view that thinking does involve something, perhaps activities, additional to the X-ings, and not merely the manner of those X-ings (though I do not regard them as more conclusive on this side than I regard Ryle's on the other).

These points can be made, in different ways, about either the listener or the active thinker. For brevity I consider mainly the latter. He has to try to call up, provide for himself, names, hypotheses, possible objections, etc., not merely, like the listener, to try to assess those presented to him. He does not try to call up anything at random, and then set to to assess its relevance. He tries to originate a controlled production of what is relevant or helpful. So his successes will in part show in what images, sentences, etc. he produces and in what sequence, and in their not being ones he has to dismiss out of hand.

[2] Ryle even offers a similar case himself: waiting for a train involves "no X-ing in particular that I must positively be doing" (TR 233). Here again, "adverbial" seems, on any strict interpretation, a misnomer; though, as an account of *waiting*, "abstaining from doings that conflict with the objective" may be correct. But here the absence of any activity does not sound strange, since few would suppose waiting, unlike thinking, to involve activity anyway.

Even so, having produced possible solutions, he may still have to ponder and assess them much as if another thinker had produced them, and sometimes he may be unable to decide on their acceptability or relevance. So his job overlaps with the listener's.

The first point is that the verbs used here all have the features by which, in CM, Ryle marked out activities or tasks. I may try for some time, or with intermissions, to think up suitable gestures, words, or hypotheses. I may try carefully or hard, or find it easy; there may be a successful outcome, or an unsuccessful outcome if I have to reject my productions as incorrect or irrelevant, or no outcome if I just keep trying till I give up. And so with pondering, considering, controlling, directing, vetting, monitoring and assessing the items of which my X-ings consist.

Secondly, these apparent candidates for activity status are used to indicate something responsible for, and explanatory of our X-ings, at least when we are successful. One may, indeed, try hard without anything relevant coming to mind. So the X-ings of the unsuccessful thinker may sometimes be indistinguishable from those of the man who is not trying to think. But when they are relevant, we explain the sequences of items that occur, the manner of their occurrence, and our acceptance, rejection, or reordering of them by reference to these tryings, efforts, and "activities." We say that, had we not been thinking, those items would not have come to mind in that way just then.

In short, the occurrence, and manner of occurrence, of my relevant and sequential X-ings seem to be the *outcome* of my trying, controlling and guiding; and the continuance or dismissal of my X-ings is the *result* of my assessings of what I call up. It therefore sounds decidedly odd to try to equate or identify these tryings and controllings, which are responsible for and explanatory of the manner of X-ing in certain circumstances, with the manner of X-ing in those circumstances. It does not follow, of course, that what is responsible for the manner of X-ing is a guiding *activity*. Nor, if there were such explanatory activities, could they be autonomous in the sense that they could continue when their objects, the X-ings, ceased; any more than one could go on guiding a horse or propelling a barrow if it stopped moving. But though I shall suggest in a moment that Ryle has a place for something that serves an explanatory-responsible role, it is certain that he denies the existence of explanatory activities.

It is time to ask why anyone should reject explanatory activities of the sort I have sketched. I assume that an advance *parti pris* against mental activities, were one operative, would not count as a reason. So I shall mention three factors that might be operating, and consider them in relation to Ryle. The first, a desire to wield Occam's Razor, would be justifiable only if explanatory activities are unnecessary, and if a more economical account will do everything as well. A second might be the implicit acceptance of an unduly narrow conception of an activity. A third might be the supposition that an activity account implies doctrines which are untenable or internally inconsistent.

With regard to Occam's Razor, the question is not so much whether Ryle's replacement of activities by adverbs is a legitimate, rather than an unjustifiably drastic use of the Razor, as whether it is a use of the Razor at all. This is far from clear and hinges on the interpretation of the adverbial account. Consider one doctrine that might be called "adverbial." Adverbial qualifications may have to do with time, place, order, manner, circumstances, etc. One sort of adverbial, *i.e.*, manner-cum-circumstance account which has been found satisfactory with other philosophical topics is roughly this. If someone X-es in a certain way and in certain surroundings, his X-ing thereby *is*, counts as, cannot but be, a case of Y-ing. X-ing in that manner is *called* "Y-ing." Nothing further needs to be said about, or true of, the doer, his wishes, efforts, intentions, etc. Doing certain things at home is not, but in a public place is, committing a nuisance. In these cases the manner and surroundings that make up the "adverbial" element concern simply the order of words uttered, the time, occasion, setting, etc.; that is, the adverbs are not mental adverbs. One might, and some have, put forward this kind of adverbial account of thinking. If a man produces, say, a particular and relevant string of sentences at a certain moment (*e.g.*, a question has just been asked in his hearing), this, and similar things, constitute a full account of what is involved in the fact that he was thinking. This would be a reductionist account in this sense, that thought-adverbs have disappeared entirely from the analysis. Whether or not this kind of account of thinking is tenable, it is not clear that it is Ryle's account. At least, he explicitly holds that the adverbial qualifiers must be thought-adverbs like "carefully," "attentively," or "purposefully," and it is not obvious that he regards these as reducible to adverbs of time, place, relevance, and order. There is room for a multitude of distinctions at this point which cannot be undertaken here. But it is not easy to decide, from Ryle's writings, what exactly he does hold as between, roughly, the reductionist view that thinking just *is* the occurrence of ordered and relevant X-ings (and the readiness to produce others) appropriate to time, place and circumstances, and the view that the occurrence of such relevant X-ings is normally the outcome of, and explained by, one's being on the *qui vive* and attentive (to put it "adverbially") or one's thinking (to put it "verbally"). Some of his examples suggest the reductionist view (according to which the X-ings of the thinker *must* differ from those of the non-thinker) as in the analogy of golfer and practice golfer, the second of whom picks the ball up and does not sink his putts. But elsewhere Ryle himself seems to stress, what is *prima facie* incompatible with a reductionist view, that, mental adverbs apart, the X-ings of the thinker and the non-thinker might happen to be identical in identical circumstances.

Certainly, from the fact that a man X-es in an adverbially correct way, in the manner-cum-circumstance sense, it need not follow that he is thinking; it could sometimes (though doubtless only sometimes) be coincidence. This lack of identity between thinking and X-ing adverbially in this sense is most notable when the thinking is stumbling or unsuccessful. The man who produces the wrong words at the wrong time because, though thinking hard, he is thinking unsuccessfully, may, in this sense, X in a manner indistinguishable from that of the man who is not really thinking at all. Indeed, the only X-ing a man who is trying to think hard, but for the moment stuck, does may be of the marking-time kind, repeating the question over and over like the man who, in identical circumstances, is not trying to think.

In any event, if, as seems likely, Ryle's thought-adverbs are not to be reducible in the end to the content, time, place and *de facto* relevance of X-ings, such X-ings being sequences of thought simply in virtue of these characteristics, it would seem that what the thought-adverbs add to the fact that X-ing is going on in this manner is an *explanation* of this manner of X-ing in those circumstances. But if a man X-es as he does because he is, and as the outcome of being, on the *qui vive*, it is not yet obvious why this explanation of the manner and aptness of his X-ing is to be preferred to saying that he is thinking, actively controlling and directing his X-ing. If Ryle's adverbs, "thinkingly," etc., serve the same function, to explain the what, how and when of X-ing, as the verbs "to think," etc., he is operating with explanatory adverbs where we commonly use verbs. But this raises the question whether there is anything positive and substantial in the adverbial view, or whether there is just a switch of labels and locutions. Certainly Ryle's opposition to thinking as an activity and his endorsement of adverbiality have a substantial and ontological ring, and seem to carry promise of different logical features. But what do they come to? Why not call the tryings, attendings, directings, and controllings that occur in thinking "activities," rather than, as Ryle calls them (TR 219), "adverbial things"?

I suspect that one main operative reason why Ryle rejects an activity view is that, by doing so, he rules out certain untenable views that a popular but restrictive concept of an activity encourages. Ryle is, apparently, committed to this concept or sense himself, and so, in that sense, is right to deny that thinking is an activity additional to the neutral X-ings. I shall call it the *procession* or *process* concept of an activity. The basic argument for that element in thinking which is additional to X-ing not being itself an activity seems to be this. For an activity to go on between t_1 and t_n there must be some procession of items, some sequence of changes, describable and datable. If between two times there are no such datable occurrences, no activity is going on. If thinking goes on from t_1 to t_n, this period will be occupied by a series of episodes, timeable at t_2, t_3, etc., comings and goings of words, changes or replacements of images, etc. These are the X-ings. Such series of events may occur when there is no thinking, and the neutral term "X-ing" may be used to describe them "thinly." What Ryle's view comes to, I think, is that when thinking goes on there are no describable or timeable processions of items and changes between t_1 and t_n *beyond* those that can be mentioned in the neutral "X-ing" description. This, as far as I can see, is a main ground for his anti-activity view; it is a direct outcome of a certain conception of an activity.

I think it reasonably clear that this is Ryle's conception. The reason he gives for a wink and a twitch involving only one and the same activity is that photographically they are alike (TT 5), and he says, of a man talking sensibly, that "a tape-recording would reproduce just what he was doing in this thinnest sense of 'doing'" (TT 9). Roughly, if no occurrences can be recorded, no activity is going on (though, since Ryle's account is not purely overt or "physicalist," what occurs between t_1 and t_n, when the *Penseur* thinks in silence, is a sequence of roughly describable and datable items which this time are subvocal or imagined). Given this conception of an activity, it follows immediately that thinking cannot be, or include, an additional explanatory activity; and for precisely the reasons it could not previously be identified with the X-ing. Thinking cannot consist in any procession of items or changes, since any such sequence could occur in mindless reverie. Hence, by a characteristically Rylean argument, the calling up, directing, controlling, and, in short, the explanation of a sequence of items cannot itself be sensibly regarded as an additional sequence of items, tangible, introspectible or "ghostly," beyond the X-ing.

Granting, however, that thinking cannot be an activity in this sense, the question remains whether this is the only permissible sense of "activity." Is an adverbial view, in some loose sense, forced on us? I believe that there is no reason to employ "activity" only in this way, nor is it the only use sanctioned by common speech. Ryle's is a philosopher's restriction. We use "activity" to cover many different though partly similar concepts; we are notoriously ill-equipped with specific category words, and elsewhere Ryle himself has invented many ("achievements," "tasks," "mongrel-categoricals"). Plenty of durational happenings that we might naturally call activities do not consist in processions of events and changes. The weight-lifter who for several seconds holds a heavy weight perfectly still above his head is not for those seconds doing nothing, though his activity is not of the same sort as when raising or lowering the weight. Photographically he may look just like the astronaut in flight who "holds" a similar weight above his head. While the weight-lifter holds the weight, no activity, in one sense, is going on. But in another he is certainly engaged in an activity, and a strenuous and taxing one. So with a man holding chest-expanders apart, or keeping up a steady pressure on something, etc. All these doings, to use Ryle's tests, may last a while, require effort, involve care, and may be tiring.

They are episodes, and of the "task," not the "achievement" sort. Of course, unlike such "process activities" as lifting the weight, they cannot be done fast or slowly; so too with such activities (if we may call them such) as watching, listening for irrelevances, or attending. But even some of Ryle's activities, like angling, to which we might add floating, sea-bathing and diving, which do involve episodes and changes, cannot be fast or slow. I see no reason, therefore, from our ordinary labelling tendencies or from the adverbial tests Ryle elsewhere employs, to deny that many verbs which are not verbs for "process activities" are verbs for activities. All that has been shown positively, I believe, is that thinking and pondering are not in *one* sense activities.

Ryle's denial of an activity account of thinking doubtless has important negative value. It excludes those objectionable suppositions already exposed in *CM*—that tennis-playing or conversing must be interspersed with or controlled by bursts of silent word or image manipulating, that the *Penseur's* sequences of subvocal talk must be controlled by similar but more hidden sequences. But these views result only from holding that thinking is an activity in the restricted "process" sense. If there is no reason to deny, and some to assert, that thinking is an activity in a less restricted sense, there may be little, other than labels and locutions, to choose between my non-process activities and Ryle's adverbiality except that "activity," misinterpreted, can encourage errors, whereas adverbiality is a departure from established usage. If Ryle meant something more substantial by his rejection of activities, I have not found a case made out. Nor have I found anything in these articles to recommend an "adverbial" view in any substantial sense. The label has to be taken, Ryle admits, in a metaphorical way. At most this seems to mean that the thinker is in a certain frame of mind or disposition *vis-à-vis* his own or others' X-ings, which still leaves a distinction to be made between kinds of dispositions. The spectator attentive to follow the lec-

ture shortly to begin and the would-be active thinker
ready for the conundrum to be put to him differ respectively from the spectator actively attending during the
lecture and the thinker actively on the *qui vive* about
his own X-ings while solving the conundrum. The former
pair, ready to think but not yet thinking, are ready in a
straight-forwardly dispositional sense. The latter pair, already actively exercising this disposition, are on the *qui
vive* in a different sense, respectively, listening for errors,
relevances and non-sequiturs, or trying to originate non-
errors and sequiturs. Whatever Ryle's reasons for calling
their states of mind adverbial or dispositional, they are
certainly states we normally call "thinking" and for which
we ordinarily and correctly employ the notion of activity.
The logic of this category of "active dispositions" will be
that of these "activities." It is hard to dispose of such
active notions as trying; and, despite the new set of
labels and the positive-sounding pronouncements in these
later papers on thinking, Ryle seems not to advance much
in elucidating these so-called dispositions beyond *CM*. In
fact in the two most recent papers he has pursued the
different topic, how the thinking of the originating and
experimental *Penseur* differs from that of *other* sorts of
thinkers. This involves his accounts of the pyramiding of
adverbs and implications, all of which would apply
equally to an "activity" or a "dispositional" labelling of
thinking. I have not attempted to discuss this question
(though it is worth noticing that the adverbial differences that characterize the *Penseur*, like "experimentally,"
"tentatively" and "suspiciously," are ones by which Ryle
qualifies, not neutral X-ings, but pondering, considering,
examining, etc.); for this is no longer to discuss the differences between thought-concepts (like examining, trying to find out, attending and considering) and mere
neutral X-ings (like uttering and muttering) in connection with which the labels "adverbial" and "non-autonomous" were introduced.

I have not discussed, in the foregoing, the characteristically valuable detail of Ryle's papers, but have concentrated on his more important-sounding and programmatic pronouncements, which do not always connect obviously with that detail. Nor have I argued for an activity view of thinking, but rather that, since it is unclear what refuting such a view amounts to, it is doubtful whether Ryle has done it. If the cash-value of the metaphor "adverbial" is really a dispositional account, it is not obvious that, with those "active dispositions" that we call "thinking," these papers of Ryle's have forwarded the discussion.

III

I turn now to a different aspect of Ryle's treatment of the question, "What is Thinking?" In the earlier papers Ryle sometimes interprets this as a question, not about what thinking is, but about whether thinking requires an "apparatus" or "vehicle," *i.e.*, words, images, or "symbols," a question which, with certain exceptions, he either answers negatively or rejects. It could of course be true that any "programme of *identifying* thinking with some procession or other is radically misguided" (*TR* 210, my italics), yet still true that some such processions were nevertheless required in thinking. I shall briefly consider Ryle's arguments against such necessary "vehicles" of thought.

At least three doctrines are suggested by things Ryle says. The first is unexceptionable: the man tying knots and the conversationalist are both thinking, but they do not require images of knots or silent soliloquies in addition to their overt performances. Hence not all thinking requires processions of private items. But this leaves open whether the thinking of the outwardly inactive *Penseur* requires silent soliloquy, imagery, etc. The second doctrine, which concerns this question, may be only the relatively weak claim that silent thinking requires no one particular species of items, *e.g.*, unspoken words, or visual images, but only some members of a perhaps lengthy disjunction. This weak claim is suggested by the remark that thinking requires no proprietary things in the way that singing requires noises (PE 137). But this would not establish the third and much more extreme doctrine, that silent thinking can occur without *any* private processions at all. Only this extreme view denies the position of those who have held that thinking cannot occur without images, words, "symbols," or, in Price's phrase, "quasi-sensible particulars" *of some sort*, and perhaps Ryle never intended to hold it; but when, in the earlier articles, he denies the need of any "vehicle," "medium," or "apparatus" for thought, it often sounds as if he does, and he has certainly been understood thus.

Unfortunately, the vagueness and variety of his locutions make it impossible to say what exactly his view is, while providing some easily demolished straw men. "No necessary apparatus" suggests that with which an act is performed, *e.g.*, spades for digging. "No necessary stuff, materials" suggests that out of which thoughts are constructed, as pots are out of clay. "No necessary medium" suggests that in which something is done, as swimming is in water; and "vehicles" suggests that which carries thought, as transportation requires a carrier. But unless these are merely metaphors, they are easily rejected. We do not need, literally, tools for thinking, materials to make thoughts out of, a medium to think in, etc., nor presumably has any reputable recent philosopher thought so. So while Ryle may rightly "deny that it even makes sense" (PE 134) to ask *these* questions, one wishes to know whether, under these locutions, he was also rejecting the *not* obviously absurd view, held by many, that when silent thinking occurs, there must occur some sequences of imagined words, pictures, diagrams, gestures, or other quasi-sensible particulars in which the thoughts are, at least in minimal degree, "embodied," "expressed," or "clothed"; the opposite view being, in Price's words, that there is such a thing as "pure or naked thinking."

I shall not presume to pronounce on whether Ryle intended this latter extreme position; certainly his own later "adverbial" views seem to run counter to it. The *Penseur's* X-ings precisely are such things as manipulating words, tunes, images, or diagrams in the mind's eye or ear; so either Ryle was not espousing the extreme view, or else that view is in *prima facie* conflict with his later views. However, since the topic of interest is, and historically has been, the conflict between the two extreme views, that silent thinking *can*, and that it *cannot*, occur without sequences of imagined or inner particulars, I shall make some comments about it and the bearing of Ryle's other arguments on it.

I shall simplify this traditional dispute by distinguishing, within cases of thinking, an "activity" and an "object." The "activities" (or, on an adverbial or dispositional account, the *supposed* activities) include pondering, considering, trying to solve, accept, reject, call up, etc. The "object" is what we ponder, consider, try to solve, etc., and varies from case to case. It may be a question or problem, theoretical or practical, verbal or musical; it may be an answer, a possible solution, or a list of kings. It is, like Ryle's X-ings, whatever might be expressed overtly in words or diagrams, or spoken *sotto voce*, visualized, etc. It might be a half-written or half-imagined after-dinner speech which one considers, seeks to change, or decides to accept. It might be the question, uttered aloud or silently, "Whether a mallet is more suitable than a hammer," or the proffered solution, "that there is no prime number between 405 and 409." The difference between "act" and "object" might be stressed by pointing out that these questions or solutions might occur to someone and be understood by him without his thinking about or considering whether to accept them at all. Understanding what might be thought about, or what might be thought about it, is not thinking about it.

I shall take it that there must be some such question, solution, list, or speech as the grammatical object of one's pondering, and that the traditional dispute is over whether it must have, or need not have, an expression or embodiment. One party asserts that, without an actual or *sotto voce* verbal list, or an actually drawn or inwardly imaged genealogical table, etc., however fragmentary, we have not called up, cannot think about, accept or reject the list of Kings; that we cannot consider whether a mallet is preferable to a hammer without actually or inwardly saying or hearing these words, or having similar bits of verbal or other imagery. Thinking requires both an object, O, and that O be embodied or expressed, however partially. This is how I interpret the doctrine that Ryle may, at least at moments, be attacking. (I must ignore the question whether *thinking* also (the "activity") must, or need not, have some expression in "heard" words or "seen" pictures, and whether this question is even intelligible.)

Oddly, the dispute is often traditionally discussed as if, at least by implication, it were an empirical one, resolvable by introspection or memory. Ryle himself says that "when I recollect, however clearly, a stretch, however recent, of my musing or pondering, I do not seem to be . . . automatically primed with the answers to questions about the concrete ingredients of the thoughts the having of which I have no difficulty in recounting . . ." and goes on that, if asked, "my answer might be, 'No; I don't recall saying anything to myself at all . . .'" or "'No; I am sure that I did not visualize anything'" (*PE* 131–32). But such denials will not refute the opponent who concedes that, contingently, we often cannot recall in what guise our thoughts occurred, but insists that they must have had some embodiment. The dispute cannot, by Ryle or others, be intended as empirical; and for a conceptual question, to establish or reject a necessity, arguments appropriate to a conceptual question are needed. So it remains to see what other arguments Ryle gives, and what others might perhaps be given.

If, at least at times, Ryle is arguing for the extreme position that, in general, thinking requires no embodiment, he also seems to admit one kind of exception: some thinking necessarily involves words rehearsed either subvocally or aloud. He says, "I do in fact think that an unworded argument belongs where an unworded quatrain belongs—nowhere" (TR 218). But it is not obvious that these are mere isolated exceptions to the extreme thesis. For if, until you have in some degree formulated the quatrain or argument *in words*, you cannot have thought it out, it would seem by parity of reasoning that, until you have formulated in words, pictures or some appropriate way that you must use a mallet, or that Henry I follows William II, you have not thought these out either. Alternatively, anyone who totally denied the necessity of thoughts being somehow expressed might deny that Ryle's quatrain provided a relevant exception at all. For, he might say, Ryle's remarks merely reflect the necessary truth that composing quatrains is dealing with words, not diagrams or pictures, just as calculating is dealing with numbers, not sounds or faces, and thinking about kings is dealing with names, not machine-diagrams or mallets. While it is true that thoughts about numbers, he might say, *if expressed*, aloud or subvocally, will be expressed in written, spoken, or pictured numerals, and thoughts about speeches, *if expressed*, will be in words, spoken, written, or imagined, the present issue is whether they can be thought about without any expression. The question, what certain thoughts are about, and hence what forms they must take *if* expressed (outwardly or inwardly), is being confused with the question whether one can think about anything, speeches included, without such expressions or formulations.

The question remains, what arguments, if any, could settle the issue; for, assuming Ryle to have been at times discussing it, we have come to the end of any arguments of his that might seem relevant. I shall mention briefly some considerations that those who have thought the issue settled with necessity one way or the other may have implicitly relied on.

One argument has been indicated already. Thinking consists necessarily in running over, trying out, or pondering *something*, an "object." When thinking is overt, the something is embodied in written or spoken words, sketch-plans, piles of bricks, etc.; these are rearranged, rejected, erased, allowed to stand, and so on. So non-overt reflecting, which involves these same activities, must, if anything is to be going on and if the *Penseur's* mind is not a blank, have its objects too, *imagined* speeches, diagrams, or building bricks. But, like the quatrain-maker argument, this is inconclusive. The thinker is, on any account, manipulating *thoughts*. The question is precisely whether, to think of a road or a word, one must picture a road or a word, and so on.

There are other genuinely conceptual considerations which may explain why proponents of the opposing views are always to be found. Apparently favouring the view that thoughts can occur unexpressed are the often stressed facts that we frequently have to search for words to express what we mean or think. We must be able to accept one formulation as appropriate, and reject others as inadequate. Even when, as in ordinary conversation, the words come effortlessly, the thinker will be vetting his words, either letting them stand, or, occasionally, withdrawing what he has said. This creates the pull towards regarding thinking as necessarily prior to its expression.

The opposite pull is that, until a man can express his thought in some appropriate way, we do not allow that he has really thought it out. If someone claims to have just composed a couplet silently and we ask him to recite it, we would not allow him to pause till he had *also* found the words, even if he claimed to have done his thinking wordlessly. Inability to express one's thoughts, at least when one has just done the thinking and the thoughts are not lengthy or complex, is something we disallow. Of

course we need not always insist on words; the village
carpenter satisfies us if, without faltering, he can demon-
strate with pieces of wood or a sketch. In general, whether
thinking silently or aloud, the struggle to find some form
of expression for what we think *is* regarded by us as thinking something out; if we hesitate, retract and try again,
we are not allowed to have thought the matter out adequately. And this seems to contradict the other claim, that
knowing what one thinks logically precedes the possibility
of expressing it. These necessary, yet apparently contradictory features of thinking provide temptations to take
one side or the other of the traditional dispute. But the
contradiction is no more than apparent if thinking is, or
in part consists in, acquiring the ability to express, to oneself or others, one's solution, reasons, etc., and *vice versa*.

Nor, after all, does it bear on the "imagery-vehicle"
dispute. For instance, the protagonist of "naked" or unexpressed thoughts could agree that having thought
something out entails having acquired the ability to express one's thoughts in some appropriate way; yet he
might, for all the arguments mentioned so far, deny that,
while thinking silently, one must already have *exercised*
this ability at all in addition to acquiring it. Expressing, in
spoken or "heard" words, etc., is more than the ability
or readiness to do so. If at t_2, after thinking out a problem, a man is able, when tested, to produce a ready
account of his solution and the steps to it, and if he insists that between t_1 and t_2 he was thinking about it and
is not merely thinking it out now while talking, there is
nothing in any of the arguments considered in this paper
to refute, as necessarily false, a claim on his part to have
engaged in no subvocal talk, imagery, etc., while thinking. To insist that, without any processions of imagined
items, he could not have been thinking is only to assert
one of the opposing views dogmatically. Of course we do
know what it is for solutions to problems to occur to us
after our minds have been blank or elsewhere engaged;
solutions sometimes come to us after sleep or during some-

thing irrelevant. But the man who claims to have been thinking without quasi-sensible vehicles is presumably denying that his mind was blank or wandering in these ways.

Two additional points. We certainly disallow, with a lengthy and complex problem, that a man can have thought it out if he performs in a disproportionately brief time. And the time we allow is roughly proportionate to the time it would take, for instance, to recite the steps, even if fragmentarily, to oneself. Barring calculating prodigies, who baffle us partly for this reason, we say of the man who provides an instant correct answer that he must have known the answer already. Secondly, as Ryle admits, most of us can usually recall some subvocal calculatings, etc., after we have been thinking; and we might generally be unwilling to allow that our minds could have been, in this respect, blank. But if these facts tempt many of us to the "no naked thinking" view, they seem to me too weak to establish it. In the required sense, "no thinking without vehicles" has not been established, or refuted, by any considerations mentioned in this paper or, I think, in any of Ryle's papers either.

RYLE ON PERCEPTION

ANTHONY QUINTON

1. INTRODUCTORY

The very special vigour and attraction of Ryle's philosophical work are due to the highly personal way in
which it is written as well as to the force of the ideas and
reasonings it contains. A notable source of its vitality is
the resolution with which he avoids the ordinary devices
of scholarly exposition. Other philosophers are seldom
mentioned by name and even less often quoted. The
positions criticised are not precisely and historically
identified. As a result his books and articles are delight-
fully unencumbered by footnotes. He will, furthermore,
go to some trouble to exclude from his work the usual
technical vocabulary of philosophical debate. Sense-data,
universals, pure egos, and so forth are mentioned from
time to time but only with an explicit cautionary apparatus of initial capitals and inverted commas that has
the effect of assimilating them to the Great Boyg, the
Will-o'-the-Wisp, and Uncle Tom Cobleigh.

As well as the stylistic pleasures it provides, Ryle's manner of writing must also have helped many of his readers to free themselves from the constricting influence of
a habitual, and distorted, way of viewing a philosophical
problem. But there is, in some cases, a price to be paid.
His approach can have the effect of allowing the central
issues in a given field of discussion to escape effective
consideration. I believe that this has happened, to some
extent anyway, in his treatment of perception, whose
main constituent is Chapter 7 of *The Concept of Mind*
but which is continued and elaborated in the article
"Sensations" in *Contemporary British Philosophy, Third
Series* and in Chapters 5, 6, and 7 of *Dilemmas*.

Ryle maintains that there is no such thing as *the* philosophical problem of perception, but he does not back up this claim by any direct examination of the position of those philosophers like Price and Ayer who believe that there is. As a result the arguments designed to show that material objects are not directly perceived are never really confronted: these are the arguments that pose what is usually taken to be the central problem of perception, that of how, if at all, our beliefs about material objects can be justified by what we do perceive directly. The soil is loosened here and there but Ryle is hesitant about taking a critical axe to the main obscuring growth. Thus the traditional view has been that since no perceptual belief about material objects is absolutely certain, it cannot be physical realities that we really perceive, but only their appearances. But in Ryle's discussion the concepts of absolute certainty and of appearances get only marginal attention.

The somewhat more nebulous issue which he does mainly discuss is that of why philosophers should have thought it necessary to discuss sensations when considering perception. He accepts, with evident reluctance, the usual assumption that sensations are essentially involved in perception and concludes that even if the perception of common objects always involves the having of sensations this having of sensations is not itself a kind of perception or observation, supplying premises about our inner experience from which conclusions about the external world can be more or less cogently derived. (A further conclusion is that sensations are not the causes of perceptions, a thesis advanced on the ground that perceptions are not the sort of things about which causal questions are appropriate or even significant.)

But his discussion is obstructed by his unwillingness to make use of the well-thumbed vocabulary in which the topic is usually explored. He gives good reasons for saying that "sensation" is not a happily chosen word with which to refer to the subjective, experiential element in perception. Perhaps an implicit recognition of the fact that to use it for this purpose is to deviate from its established employment underlies the almost universal practice among philosophers of perception of using other words instead: idea, representation, appearance, sensum, sense-impression, sense-datum, and many others. Mill is perhaps the only major philosopher of perception to make predominant use of the word "sensation." But Ryle sticks firmly to it, with only the most occasional recourse to terms like "sense-datum" and "sense-impression."

Ryle's preference for talking about observation rather than perception is a further obstacle of the same kind, a preference motivated, as far as I can see, by nothing more than a desire for elegant variation. "Perception" is perhaps a slightly more artificial word than "observation" to apply to our fundamental way of discovering empirical facts about the external world, but this is a direct outcome of its convenient generality. Ordinarily when we have occasion to talk about the discovery of such facts by the use of our senses we can specify the particular sense involved and so can speak of what we have seen or heard rather than of what we have perceived. It might be argued, on Ryle's behalf, that "perceive" is ambiguous, in that there is a non-sensory use of the word: "I perceive a consistent pattern in the Ruritanian government's treatment of religious minorities," "I perceive a hardening of the attitude of the Football Association to foul play." But, as Ryle himself points out, there is also an ambiguity in the word "observe" which is of a more potentially troublesome kind. To be engaged in the observation of something can be either to be trying to find things out about it or to be succeeding in this enterprise. ("Observe" can also, of course, mean the same as "say," "announce," or "declare.") But the interest of the principle that observation necessarily involves sensation attaches entirely to observation in the second sense, as perceptual discovery, which is effectively singled out by the word "perception." Watching earnestly in total darkness for some

chink of light that might indicate the whereabouts of the
door, I may not have any sensations, or at any rate any
relevant sensations, at all. The ambiguity of "perceive"
is very venial in comparison; it parallels a perfectly familiar ambiguity in the specific verbs of perception, "see,"
"hear," etc., which it so conveniently embraces.

In general Ryle's mode of approach to and manner of
exposition of the topic of perception has a slightly puzzling eccentricity. An underlying reason for this, no
doubt, at least as far as the discussion in *The Concept of
Mind* is concerned, is the general strategy of that book.
Its overall aim is to show that in describing the workings
of the mind it is not necessary to admit the existence of
private, mental objects, states, and events to which their
owner has privileged, introspective access. Perception is
one of the most important ways in which the mind works.
It is alleged to entail the having of sensations, in a special, theorist's, sense of the word and these seem to bear
all the marks of Cartesian mentality. In the face of this
problem Ryle could either take the heroic step of denying
that there are any sensations in the sense intended, and
he does at times come near to doing this, or he could
give an account of our reports of sensation which does
not have the Cartesian implications he finds unappetis-
ing, which seems to be his preferred tactic. But beyond
saying that sensations are not things or episodes, that
sensing is not a cognitive relation to a sensible object and
that we have no "neat" sensation vocabulary but must
describe our sensations in terms of common objects, he
does not get very far with his overall, strategic project in
this field.

But despite his view that there is no central problem of
perception he does provide an answer to the problem
about perception that has usually been taken to be central. In effect he denies the first, problem-posing step of
the argument, that our ordinary perceptual beliefs about
common objects require logically prior beliefs about our
immediate sense-experience for their justification. Sensa-

tions cannot be observed, he holds, so there are no purely
sensory premises from which inferences to conclusions
about material objects can be drawn. To see a thimble,
is to have visual sensations in a thimble-seeing frame of
mind: it is not to reason from the perceived visual sensations to some assertion about a thimble.

2. THE WORD "SENSATION"

Ryle's thesis that the word "sensation," as ordinarily
understood, has two senses, in neither of which is it
identical with the subjective, experiential element in perception, is well-founded but of limited significance for the
philosophical discussion of perception. Other words than
"sensation" are available for the technical task to which
he reluctantly subjects it and are much more commonly
used for that task than it is. So it would seem unlikely, on
statistical grounds, that any confusions there may be in
received philosophical doctrines about perception can be
traced to this more or less unhappy choice of technical
terminology.

He says that in ordinary speech to have a sensation,
or, in one of its senses, to feel something, is either to perceive something tactually or kinaesthetically, as when one
has a sensation of, or feels, the pressure of the table's
edge against one's leg, the rough texture of the curtain,
the warmth of the water, or is to experience some pain or
discomfort, a twinge, itch, stabbing, tingle, or what have
you. A sensation of the tactual-kinaesthetic kind is simply
a specific sort of perception, it is the exercise of a learnt,
and more or less skilled capacity, comparable to seeing
or hearing. It is obvious that perception, or observation,
does not generally entail sensation in this sense. Some
perceptions just are sensations of this kind. But it is
perfectly possible to perceive something by sight or hearing without perceiving anything at all tactually or kinaesthetically, either as an essential part or as an accompaniment of doing so.

Nor need sensation of the second ordinary kind help to constitute or accompany perception. We can, happily, see things without there being any noticeable discomfort in our eyes. Ryle remarks that to the extent that sensations of this uncomfortable kind, located in my sense-organs, do accompany my perceptions, as they sometimes do, as when being interrogated under a bright light or when one is trying to hear what someone is saying to one at a party, they obstruct rather than assist one's perception.

The natural thing to do, in view of all this, would be to follow common practice and use some word other than "sensation" for the subjective, experiential element in perception. But for the most part Ryle continues, under some protest, to use the word "sensation" in a technical and unusual way. Now one of his main theses about perception is that what I shall call "sense-impressions" are not observed or perceived. But if sense-impressions are, as he convincingly argues, quite distinct from sensations as ordinarily understood, no conclusion about sensations so understood can be confidently applied to sense-impressions. It is important for Ryle to show that sensations are not observed. One reason he gives for thinking they are not is that we do not observe the pinches given by a tight shoe, do not have them under observation, do not witness our qualms, do not bring observational aids to bear on our sensations. But from the premise that discomforts are not observed it does not follow that sense-impressions are not observed.

Ryle's adherence to the word "sensation" causes him unnecessary difficulties as well as encouraging him to draw conclusions to which he is not entitled. He maintains, for example, that I must be conscious of any sensations, in the ordinary sense of the word, that I have. But if this is so it does not follow, as the sense-datum theorist supposes, that in every perceptual situation I am incorrigibly aware of the sense-impression that I am having, that it is present to my mind and thus cognitively available, so to speak, for the theorist's purported inferences to conclusions about material objects. It would need to be established independently that sense-impressions are necessarily self-intimating in the way he takes sensations in the ordinary sense to be.

It may, indeed, be questioned whether sensation as tactual or kinaesthetic perception is necessarily self-intimating. Can I not touch or feel something inside or outside my body without being conscious of the fact? Fishing from a small boat in a rough sea I brace myself against the side of the boat, adjusting my stance appropriately to its movements. I can surely be said to perceive the relative movements of the boat and my body although my attention is fully concentrated on what is going on at the end of my line and I should have to make an effort of attention to answer any questions about these movements. It can even be questioned whether one is always aware of pains and discomforts. The man whose attention is distracted for a minute or two from his toothache by a fascinating piece of gossip and who then becomes aware of it again once the news has been digested, having continued to rub the painful area all the while, might be said to have been in pain throughout the period but not to have been continuously aware of the fact.

3. SENSATION AND OBSERVATION

One of the points Ryle is most anxious to establish is that even if sensation, in the technical sense of having sense-impressions, is an essential ingredient in observation, sensations, or sense-impressions, are not themselves observed. He deploys a variety of arguments for this purpose but even if they were valid it is not clear that anything very substantial would have been achieved. The discussion is complicated by the fact that he has two ends in view: first, the refutation of a Cartesian account of the having of a sense-impression as a matter of standing in a cognitive relation to a private, sensible object or event,

and, secondly, the refutation of the sense-datum theory
with its claim that perceptual belief about common objects is justified only to the extent that it is supported by
an antecedent awareness of sense-impressions. These two
distinct birds are assailed with a variety of stones of as-
sorted shapes and sizes.

The two objects of Ryle's criticism are not wholly unrelated to one another. It is often argued that the sense-
datum theory requires an illegitimate reification of appearances, a practice, that is misleading if it is more than
merely idiomatic, of identifying the fact that there appears to be something green with there being a green
appearance. If this reification is improper then a sense-
datum is not a private, Cartesian *object*. But even so the
event of having a sense-impression, of something's appearing to be green, could still be held to be a private
event, to which its possessor has a privileged access. It
might also be argued that if perception does not require
antecedent awareness of private objects or events for its
justification a Cartesian view of self-knowledge is under-
mined. But in fact it is at most weakened. For even if
private sense-data are not needed to explain and under-
write perception there remain many other objects of
knowledge which invite Cartesian treatment: images,
pains, emotions and thoughts. Cartesianism could, therefore survive either of these styles of objection to the
sense-datum theory. On the other hand, it seems that
the sense-datum theory, although not entailed by Cartesianism, does entail or presuppose it, unless it is presented in a curious and unusual form. How could the
awareness of sense-data be incorrigible in the way the
theory requires if they were not private? However in his
doctrine of avowals Ryle combines the view that our reports of our sensations are incorrigible with the denial
of their Cartesian privacy so for him at any rate the pre-
supposition does not hold: the epistemologically crucial
requirement that our knowledge of our immediate experiences is incorrigible does not have Cartesian implications.

Let us turn to the arguments with which Ryle seeks to show that sense-impressions are not, and cannot be, observed. The first is that observation and sensation, in other words perceiving and the having of sense-impressions, are entirely different kinds of activity: to perceive is to bring off a more or less skilful and arduous achievement, whereas sense-impressions just happen. Sensation, he says, is not any kind of apprehension, it is not the exercise of any qualities of intellect or character. Everything hangs here on whether sense-impressions are self-intimating, whether there is an intelligible distinction between having a sense-impression and recognising it as the precise kind of sense-impression that it is. Ryle's view is that they are self-intimating and that there is no such distinction. As mentioned earlier, he appears to derive this from the fact, if it is a fact, that sensations, in the two ordinary senses of the word that he countenances, are self-intimating. But even if sensations, so understood, are self-intimating, it does not follow that sense-impressions are.

But let us suppose that they are. In that case having a sense-impression surely is an apprehension or is at any rate the exercise of a quality of intellect, of a learnt skill, in particular the skill of recognising them as the kind of sense-impressions that they are. What could be more indubitably cognitive than recognition? It may well be that "observation" is not the right word to use for either the pursuit or the achievement of this kind of recognition but it is clearly some kind of awareness, the acquisition of knowledge or belief. Only if a sense-impression can be had without being recognised can the distinction of kind that Ryle insists on be admitted between perception and sensation. Furthermore the assumption that sense-impressions *can* be had without being recognised does not entail the exclusion of the opposite possibility, it does not entail that they are never recognised. So the line Ryle wants to draw between what merely happens and what is more or less skilfully achieved separates the occurrence of unrecognised sense-impressions on the one hand from the recognition of impressions and the perceiving of objects on the other. Only a kind of sense-impression he does not admit falls on the passive side of the distinction he draws.

Ryle presents his conclusion to this, and some more elusive arguments to the effect that we do not witness sensations in the ordinary sense of discomforts, in terms of a characteristic analogy. Sense-impressions cannot be observed in the same way that letters cannot be spelled. But the analogy is vague and very tenuous: correct spelling is using letters the right way, veridical perception is using sense impressions the right way. But it does not really go any further than that. To spell a word correctly is to write down the letters that the conventional rules of spelling assign to it in the correct sequence. But to perceive an object is not to have, let alone bring about, the correct sense-impressions in the correct order, even for a phenomenalist.

In the course of developing this analogy Ryle makes an important admission. No question arises about the spelling of an individual letter: it is only groups or sequences of letters that can be spelled or misspelled. But, he says, there is a comparable question about letters, that of whether they are *written* correctly. "The fact," he goes on, "that we may not talk of the observation of sensations by no means precludes us from talking of the notice or heed that people can pay to their sensations, or of the avowals and reports that they can make of the sensations of which they have taken notice" (*Concept of Mind*, p. 206). To admit this is to admit all that the sense-datum theorist requires. He has no commitment to the view that sense-impressions are strictly *observable*. It is enough for him that they can be noticed and reported. Their being unobservable is at most a formal disability which deprives them of nothing they need for the role in which the sense-datum theorist casts them, that of being the logically prior items of empirical knowledge from which perceptual beliefs about the external world are derived. Furthermore this admission undermines the whole distinction between active observation and passive sensation since noticing and reporting are as "active" as observing.

He goes on to argue that to have a sense-impression is not to stand in a cognitive relation to a sensible object. Sense-impressions, he says, do not have shape, position, temperature, volume, or smell. No one would maintain that the event of having a sense-impression is endowed with perceptible characteristics of this order. But that does not prove that sense-impressions cannot significantly be described in this sort of way. A construction, considered as a process of *constructing*, cannot be dark brown, six feet high, and made of wood, but a construction, considered as something *constructed*, can be. There are, I believe, objections to the unrestricted application of a reifying idiom to reports of sense-impression. But Ryle does not develop them, although he provides some of the material for such a development elsewhere in what he says about the tentative character of statements about what appears to be the case. At most, then, he has shown that the ascription of ordinary perceptual characteristics to sense-impressions is problematic, not that it is clearly mistaken.

To enforce his conclusion that sense-impressions are not things or episodes he argues that the purported objects of the cognitive relation of "sensing" (glimpses, views, looks, appearances, sounds, flavours, whiffs, tingles, and twinges) are the cognate accusatives of the verbs that figure in reports of them such as *have, get,* and *feel*. To get a glimpse of something is not to stand in a relation of getting to a thing called a glimpse and likewise for the parallel cases. One can no more talk of seeing the looks of things than one can talk of eating nibbles of biscuits. In fact one can surely talk about both: "I saw the look on her face," "I had time to eat only a nibble of the sandwich." But in doing so one is not talking about anything peculiar or special: the look on her face is the publicly visible character of her face at the time, or an aspect of it, the nibble of the sandwich is probably a small corner of it. In general these colloquial terms that Ryle prefers to technicalities like "sense-datum" for the supposedly immediate and private objects of perception are not well chosen for the purpose since most of them have an accepted application to what is public. Views, looks, appearances, flavours, and sounds are all, like nibbles, parts of the common public world. The view of Edinburgh from Arthur's Seat, for example, consists of those literal parts of the public, material entity Edinburgh that can be seen from that position and exists when no one is viewing it. Glimpses, admittedly, do have the required subjectivity and although they may be had, got or caught they cannot properly be said to be seen. But even if a glimpse is not some kind of visible object, but rather an event of seeing or seeming to see, it still has to be shown that in catching a glimpse of something there is not something else, such as an array of coloured patches in my visual field, that I see.

The argument most stressed by Ryle is, of course, his attempted proof that to regard sensation as a kind of observation gives rise to an infinite regress of sensations. I observe a tree. In doing so I must have a sensation somehow related to the tree. If this event of sensation is itself an observation it must be of something other than the tree since it can occur when there is no tree there. But this implied observation of the tree-surrogate must, observation being what it is, involve a further sensation, which will itself be an observation of a tree-surrogate of the second order, involving its proprietary sensation and so on ad infinitum.

Marc-Wogau has suggested a simple way of bringing this regress to a virtuous halt. The sensation involved in the observation of the tree can be treated as itself an observation of a sensible object without implying a further sensation, distinct from itself. Ryle anticipates this objection, saying "such a defence in effect explains the having of sensations as the *not* having any sensations. It avoids the imputed regress by the heroic device of suggesting that sensing is a cognitive process which does not require its owner to be susceptible of stimuli or to be describable as either highly or slightly sensitive" (*Concept of Mind*, p. 215). But, as Ayer remarks, since observing a sense-datum *is* being sensitively affected, Ryle's counter-attack fails. It can, perhaps, best be seen as a rhetorical way of reformulating the principle that observation entails sensation as the assertion that observation entails having a sensation that is a proper part of itself.

Ryle is taking observation to be a way of becoming aware of the existence of something independent of oneself through the action of that independent something upon one. If this is correct, and it does seem to be a reasonable account of the established use of the word, it follows that sense-impressions or sense-data cannot be observed. Many sense-datum theorists have treated the immediate objects of perception as such observable things but only by inadvertence: Berkeley appears to do so at times, Moore and Broad do so when they concede that the apparent and actual properties of sense-data can differ. But this is a lapse and destructive of their position, for it exposes sense-data to all the doubts about immediate perceptibility that are brought against material objects. The vital point is that nothing is lost by the sense-datum theorist who admits that sense-data cannot, logically, be *observed*. All he requires is something that Ryle readily admits, that it should be possible to notice and report them. They can be objects of empirical knowledge, even if not, strictly, of observation.

4. APPEARANCES AND CERTAINTY

Having, he believes, blocked the only possible line of escape from his demonstration that the sense-datum theory involves an infinite regress, Ryle turns to consider the more or less empirical protest that since in double vision, when squinting at a candle say, we surely see two bright somethings in circumstances where only one bright physical thing is present, it must be the case that in a perceptual situation we do non-inferentially discern a sensible object. It is at this point that he comes closest to a direct confrontation with the argument from illusion.

His first response is, as before, to resist the reification of looks. When a plate looks elliptical to me it does not follow that I see the elliptical look of a round plate. To say that what I see looks elliptical is not to say that I see something that actually is elliptical but rather that I might be seeing something that is elliptical. When I say how something looks, he goes on, I am not giving a direct and uncomplicated description of something immediately present to my mind but I am making a statement of a rather sophisticated logical sort, a "mongrel-categorical" which is the application of an "open hypothetical recipe." To say that the tilted plate has an elliptical look or looks as if it were elliptical is to say that it looks as an elliptical but untilted plate would look in ordinary circumstances. It is like describing someone as behaving judiciously or talking like a pedagogue.

Ryle is explicit that the statement about how the plate looks is a compound and the same conception of its logically conjunctive character is implied by the comparison with the statement that someone is talking like a pedagogue. This illustrative assertion is approximately equivalent to the statements (a) that he is talking in a certain discernible way and (b) that most pedagogues talk in that way (as it might be, in a measured and sarcastic fashion, although this is not specified by the original remark). Thus the looks-statement must be interpreted as a conjunction of something like "this plate presents a certain discernible appearance" and "elliptical plates generally present this appearance in ordinary circumstances, i.e. when viewed straight on."

The sense-datum theorist will at once fasten on the

first, pedigree-categorical, component of the Rylean mongrel about which Ryle has very little to say. There must, on his account, be such a component in the whole statement, an item of given knowledge for the hypothetical recipe to apply to. Both Ryle's theoretical account of looks statements as mongrel-categoricals and his illustrative comparison of them with descriptions of people talking like pedagogues imply that looks-statements are inferences from independently established premises, one of which, the categorical one, is a report of immediate experience of the kind that the sense-datum theorist regards as basic to all empirical knowledge. The more or less public look of things which Ryle is seeking to explain turns out to be an inference from premises one of which is just the sort of statement about private looks which hs is anxious to discredit as a theorist's fabrication.

It could be objected that this argument rests on the unfounded assumption that all statements which are formally conjunctive, to the extent that they can be analysed into a conjunction of other statements, can be asserted with justification only as the result of an inference. Whatever else it may be an inference from, "that is a child" is not an inference from the premises that that is a human being and that it is younger than most human beings, even if it means the same as that conjunction.

But although this objection is correct it does not, I think, suffice to protect Ryle from the charge of having surreptitiously reintroduced sense-datum statements in an account of statements about how things look which is intended to dispense with them altogether. The reason why "that is a child" is, in the relevant sense, noninferential is that we learn to recognise children before we explicitly apprehend or formulate any principle about the typical age-relation between children and human beings in general. But in the crucial pedagogue case we cannot understand what it is to talk like a pedagogue until we have accumulated some information about how pedagogues generally do talk and to do this we must be able to recognise a pedagogue when we come across one. It is the element of comparison, embodied in the word "like," that has this consequence and the same word occurs in the fully articulate form of the looks-statement Ryle is concerned with: this plate looks *like* an elliptical plate viewed head on.

What Ryle needs to show is that statements about how things look, in his more or less public interpretation of them, are uninferred or basic and that the explanatory things he has to say about the application of recipes to something he does not clearly specify is, so to speak, not logic but psychology, not an account of the reasoning that must lie behind the assertion if it is to be well-founded but an account of the psychological processes which terminate in the assertion and of which the assertor may be quite unaware. Ryle is prevented from doing anything like this by his total dismissal of the "Euclidean model" which regards beliefs as either intuited or inferred. There are certainly objections to the standard version of this "model," in particular to the usual assumption that a belief does not require to be justified by inference only if it is intuited in a strong sense, if it is some kind of incorrigible certainty. But the alternative inferred-or-uninferred cannot be so easily brushed aside. It has the force of the law of excluded middle behind it. So even if it is too much to say that Ryle has definitely committed himself to the existence of sense-datum statements, as indispensable to the justification of statements about how things look as he interprets them, he has not succeeded in showing that his account of looks-statements does not have this disconcerting implication.

Statements about how things look are only one of the many familiar forms of everyday language with the help of which philosophers have introduced the concept of a sense-datum. At least as common a recourse for the sense-datum theorist is our ordinary way of talking about the appearances of things or, again, about the way they seem.

Ryle discusses this briefly in his article "Sensations" (*Contemporary British Philosophy*, Third Series, pp. 434–35). He makes the important point that words like "appear" and "seem" are used to make guarded, tentative, and non-committal assertions. But the aspect of this fact that he stresses is not that in saying "this appears to be green" we are talking guardedly about the possibly green thing rather than about something else, viz., an appearance, that certainly is green. His main theme is that we talk guardedly about subject-matter of all kinds in most of which there is no question of sense-impressions being what we are really talking about. "Statements of the form 'it looks as if'—'there seems to be'—'Apparently . . .' are not," he says, "*ex officio* dedicated to the wanted reports of the experiences alleged to be the basic ingredients in sense-perception."

But this proves very little. Even if not all of what we say about appearances has something to do with the reporting of perceptions it is clear that a good deal of it has. One might as well argue that seeing has nothing to do with the eyes because the expression "I see that . . ." is not *ex officio* dedicated to the reporting of discoveries made by the use of the eyes, since we can see that there is no largest prime number when we have heard someone set out the proof.

Nevertheless it is worth insisting against the more extravagant identifications of sense-data with how things appear that not all uses of the verb "appear" are perceptual and that those that are perceptual are ordinarily in guarded assertions about material things and not in unguarded assertions about non-material things. It still remains possible, and is, I believe, true, that we can use the verb "appear" in a purely phenomenological way. But this is an unusual and sophisticated activity that has to be more or less arduously learnt by those who are already fully qualified perceivers of material objects and can be undertaken only by a special redirection of attention. This makes it utterly unplausible to suppose that incorrigible phenomenological information of this sort is always available to the ordinary perceiver in every perceptual situation as the jumping-off point for his alleged inferences to material objects.

Perhaps the most deep-seated epistemological source of the sense-datum theory is the conviction that any belief less than incorrigibly certain must be an inference from a belief that does have this kind of certainty. The point is made clearly in Ayer's definition of the sense-datum theorist's technical expression "direct awareness." "If someone is directly aware of an object x," he says, "it follows that x exists and that it really has whatever properties it is appearing to have" (*Foundations of Empirical Knowledge*, p. 61). The object of direct awareness, in other words, is that which necessarily has the properties it is believed to have. But those who define direct awareness in this way have not fully emancipated themselves from the ordinary sense of the word "direct." An object of belief which does not satisfy the stringent requirements of the definition is said to be indirectly known, that is, to be known, or reasonably believed in, only on the basis of an inference. But this is a wholly unwarranted step. It does not follow from the fact that something is not known directly in the technical sense, is not, that is to say, known incorrigibly, that it is not known directly in the everyday sense, is known only by way of an inference.

Ryle, in the course of his discussion of phenomenalism in *The Concept of Mind*, enters a justified protest against the assumption, common both to phenomenalists and their traditional representationist opponents, that genuine perception must be incorrigible. "We do not say that no one ever reasons, just because no one ever has a certificate guaranteeing that he has not committed a fallacy, so why should it be supposed that there is a kind of mistake-proof operation to which the verb 'to observe' alone is consecrated" (*Concept of Mind*, p. 237). The business of ascertaining does not, he goes on, base a superstructure of guesses on a foundation of certainties; it is a process of making sure. Certainties are ascertained, not given.

He offers two explanations for this mistaken assumption. First, since it would be absurd to say that any matters of empirical fact could not be found out by observation and "since any ordinary observation actually made might be mistaken there must be a special mistake-proof observation, in order that 'empirical' may be defined in terms of it" (*Concept of Mind*, p. 237). Secondly, verbs of perception are achievement verbs. One can perceive only what is really there or that something is so which really is so. But "the fact that doctors cannot cure unsuccessfully does not mean that they are infallible doctors" (*Concept of Mind*, p. 238). And "a person who claims to have solved an anagram and is then persuaded that that is not the solution, withdraws his claim to have solved it. He does not say that in a 'strict' or 'refined' sense of the verb he solved a 'solution-object,' which happened not to coincide with the word camouflaged in the anagram" (*Concept of Mind*, p. 239).

Although these factors may have contributed to the widespread acceptance of the principle that the ultimate foundations of knowledge must be incorrigibly certain I do not think they are the crucial ones. For they do not bring out the essential connection this principle asserts between being corrigible and being inferred. What is needed is an explanation of the idea that any method of forming beliefs which is less than infallible must derive this weakness from the processes of inference that it embodies.

In this general connection Ryle observes that although perceptual recognition is an intellectual activity that does not mean that it is a kind of thinking. Furthermore, even if it were a kind of thinking that would not mean that it is a kind of inferring or, as he typically puts it, pondering. Perceiving, he says, is not a matter of having sensations and thereupon initiating "lightning cognitive episodes." It is, rather, having sensations in a vigilant and expectant way. Perception should not be treated as a kind of detective work; to use one's senses is not necessarily to use one's sensations as clues from which to draw inferences.

These remarks are very apt, although the identity Ryle assumes between inferring and the altogether more exploratory business of pondering might be questioned. So also might his resistance to describing perception as a form of thinking. The main point is that perception can be intellectual without being inferential. What Ryle fails to do is to draw the conclusion that the perception of common objects is a non-inferential way of discovering matters of empirical fact of the kind that there must be if inference is ever to yield any empirical knowledge. What he does say really amounts to this but he hesitates on the brink because of his hostility to the "Euclidean model," with its apparent implication that non-inferential discovery must be some kind of infallible intuition. But it does not follow from the fact that there must be uninferred empirical beliefs if there are to be inferred ones that those uninferred beliefs are incorrigible. Once the "Euclidean model" is divested of the requirement that non-inferential knowledge is incorrigible it ceases to be a controversial speculation and becomes a truism.

5. PERCEPTION AND CAUSATION

One of the most recurrent and emphatic themes in Ryle's treatment of perception is that it is an achievement. The prime importance of this as regards traditional accounts of perception is, in his view, that it implies that causal questions about perception are improper. In his article "Sensations" he says that one of the principal sources of the erroneous doctrine that ordinary perceptual beliefs necessarily involve sense-impressions is the assumption that the latter are needed as the mental link in the causal chain that reaches from the external object perceived to the perception of it. But, he argues, this embodies a radical error about the nature of perception.

Questions about how we perceive are not causal but technical; they concern the bringing off of an achievement. The same theme is taken up in Chapter 7 of *Dilemmas*. To ask "how do we perceive" is not to ask "of what is perceiving the effect?" We do not, he goes on, postpone giving an answer to the question whether we have perceived something until someone has "probed our insides." Perceiving is not a phenomenon, not an act I can catch myself performing. Equally it is not a state or a process. The alleged fact that verbs of perception have no continuous present is adduced to show that perceiving is not a process.

I shall make three main criticisms of this body of ideas. I shall argue, first, that the doctrine of sense-impressions is introduced to explain not just perception as an achievement but also perception as a failure, botched or unsuccessful perception, in other words the forming of false perceptual beliefs as well as true ones. Secondly, I shall attempt to show that achievements in general are proper subjects of causal investigation, even if the description of their causally necessary conditions will not itself contain or constitute an elucidation of what the achievement itself consists in. Finally, and most important, I shall argue that perception is itself a causal notion, in that for someone to have perceived something it is necessary that the impact of his environment on his senses is a causally necessary condition of his forming the belief about his environment that he does.

(1) *What do sense-impressions explain?* What sense-impressions are invoked to explain is not perception proper, the achievement of forming a true belief about the external world, but only a part of it, namely the formation of a perceptual belief, true or false. For it is a central feature of the ordinary doctrine of sense-impressions that two sense-impressions indiscriminable from one another can accompany the formation of very different beliefs, a true belief about what is actually there and a false belief that registers an illusion or hallucination. The

causal question, then, to which the occurrence of sense-impressions is offered as an answer is not "how do we perceive?" but "what causes us to form perceptual beliefs?" Further and different considerations are needed to account for the truth or falsity of these beliefs. In rough outline these are that we are taught to come out with a given perceptual sentence when our senses are stimulated in a particular way in more or less ideal conditions. Gradually we learn how to use it when differently stimulated in non-ideal conditions. In any given case of sensory stimulation the part of this complex skill we shall exercise will depend on what we take to be the prevailing conditions of observation. If they are not what we suppose, and the difference may be one for which our training has not equipped us, we shall, unless very lucky, come out with a false statement.

It might be argued, at this point, that the formation of a perceptual belief, true or false, is also an achievement in its way. It is, at any rate, not as much of an achievement as perception proper. But it is something we have to learn how to do and that we can try to do and fail in. The usual form such failure takes is that of finding oneself with no perceptual belief at all. Someone asks "what is that?" and I candidly reply, "I haven't the faintest idea" or "what's what? I don't see (hear, etc.) anything." (The latter is the stronger example since in the former case of not having the faintest idea what one has no belief about is what the thing in question is ordinarily called. One will usually have formed some perceptual belief in the circumstances, for instance, to the effect that it is a small, complicated, metallic object.) To think that one has formed a perceptual belief when one has done nothing of the kind would seem to be less usual. But the thesis that the concept of perception is essentially causal, which I shall develop in the third part of this section, shows one way in which it could happen, namely when I form a belief about the external world in a dream or as the result of a complete hallucination, unaware of the fact that my belief does not have amongst its causes the operation of the external world on my senses.

But if the formation of a perceptual belief is an achievement it is a very modest achievement like falling over or smiling. It is something that one sometimes does deliberately and intentionally but which for the most part just happens, not necessarily against one's will but independently of it. The continuous flow of fairly uninteresting information (and misinformation) about my physical environment that pours in on me is not something I have to sustain like a dietary regime or a firm resolve to speak French all day or a stiff upper lip.

One of Ryle's favourite examples of an achievement is solving a crossword puzzle. In order to bring this off I have to fill in the blank squares with the appropriate letters. There is a more modest activity of simply filling in the squares, not all of them with the correct letters. But even filling them in with letters that make words in whatever direction the lines of letters are read is a kind of achievement as, for that matter, is filling each square with one and only one letter or again filling them with letters rather than little diagrams or faces. We do not have names for these humbler approximations to solving a crossword puzzle but all of them must have been accomplished for the crossword puzzle to have been solved. Are all of these immune from causal investigation? Behind Ryle's position on this subject there seems to lurk an extreme libertarianism which rules out causal inquiry into any activity that can embody an exercise of the human will.

(2) *The causation of achievements.* The achievement that sense-impressions are invoked to explain, then, is not the one Ryle takes it to be, but only a logical part of it, and it is an achievement only in a small way. But even if it were a full-blooded achievement like winning a race, another of his favourite examples, would it be improper to ask causal questions about it? If I have won a race this is, logically not causally, because I got to the finish before

any of my competitors and this, in the absence of handi-
capping, logically presupposes that I ran, on the average,
faster than they did. It is surely perfectly proper to inquire
into at least the causally necessary conditions of any of
these three, logically nested achievements. I ran faster
(and finished first and won) because I am stronger than
they are or have longer legs or trained for longer or under
a more experienced instructor and so on.

In the case of perception we commonly look for explanations of failure, at any rate. Why did Jones not see what
Smith saw when they were standing side by side? Because
there was the branch of a tree in Jones's line of vision.
Thus a causally necessary condition of Smith's seeing the
thing in question was the absence of an opaque object
between his eyes and it. There is no question that Jones's
failure to see the thing was caused by the intervening
obstacle: it causally interfered with the light reflected
from the thing under discussion towards his eyes. If its
presence in the circumstances caused failure, why should
not its absence in the closely comparable circumstances
of Smith be part of the cause of his success? If the mere
absence of an obstacle seems too negative to be a cause,
the passage of light from the thing to Smith's eyes is
surely positive enough.

It may well be true that in the ordinary course of events
we do not ask causal questions about success. We are
more concerned with causes of failure, not because we
hope to prevent its recurrence by suppressing them, since
we could just as well secure success by initiating its causes,
but because in everyday activities like perception, success
is the usual thing. This does not make causal questions
about success, or the normal, improper. If it were, New-
ton's legendary attention to the desperately stereotyped
behaviour of the apple would have been misguided. It is
no doubt true, as Ryle says, that in connection with a
more or less deliberate and skilled activity like attempting
to win a race or perceive the external world we ask how it
is done rather than why it happened, our pursuit of ex-

planation takes a technical rather than explicitly causal form. We ask "what do I have to do to achieve that result?" not "what causal conditions have to be satisfied for that result to ensue?" But these two questions are not unrelated. The technical question, indeed, is causal but it restricts itself to those causal conditions which are known or believed to be fairly clearly under the agent's control. "How do I make a white sauce?" "Put some flour into some hot fat and stir, adding milk." This is an adequate technical answer just to the extent that the correlated causal statement, that the addition of flour and milk to hot fat causes a white sauce to come into existence, is true. The practical interests that confine our questions about why things happen to cases of failure and about how they happen to causes we can control in no way rule out causal explanations of success or explanations in terms of causes not readily answerable to our wills. There is, then, nothing objectionable about the causal explanation of successful achievement.

(3) *Perception as a causal concept.* To argue, against Ryle, that the concept of perception essentially involves causal dependence on the impact of the external world on our senses I shall have to go into a little more detail about this causal relationship. A perception occurs: I see a passing car, for example. How is this brought about? (a) The car passes, causing light of a particular kind to be reflected towards my eyes. My eyes are stimulated in a certain way by the light that strikes them and a characteristic pattern of brain activity is set up. I form, without inference, the belief that there is a car passing by. Now there are several other ways in which I might come to believe this. (b) A high wind blows a large sheet of tin rapidly down the road, but the rest of the story is much the same. In that case my belief that a car is passing is false. But it is still a perceptual belief. But it might be (c) that I am fast asleep and dreaming that a car is going by or (d), more mysteriously, I may just find myself firmly believing that a car is passing in circumstances where my

senses are, as it were, quiescent, subject to no new stimulation at all. In (c) and (d) the immediate cause of my belief is not external to me. Of these four cases (a) is a genuine perception, (b) is the forming of a perceptual belief, but a false one, (c) and (d) are not perceptual beliefs at all, although their natural verbal expression, and thus, one might say, their content, is the same as that of (a) and (b). A perceptual belief proper is one caused by some stimulation of the senses by the external world and a genuine perception is a true perceptual belief, or, more accurately, a belief that some fact obtains in my physical environment which was caused by the effect on my senses of that fact. (The longer formula is more accurate since I may truly believe that Mrs. Jones is in the group over there, when she is, although what actually caused me to believe it is the impact on my optical apparatus of light reflected from the surface of her twin sister Mrs. Smith, who is also there. In such a case my belief that Mrs. Jones is there is true and perceptual, since caused by the external stimulation of my senses, but I have not actually seen Mrs. Jones.)

The concept of perception is, then, intrinsically causal. Without the causal implication there would be no distinction between perception and lucky guessing about the contents of one's physical environment. Ryle reluctantly accepts the principle that observation entails sensation but he never really considers why it should have been generally accepted, even if he offers a number of explanations for particular constructions that have been put upon it. If sensations are taken to be stimulations of the senses by the external world their necessary involvement with perception is simply the factor that is needed to distinguish perceptual beliefs from beliefs about the environment with the same sort of content that occur in dreams, hunches, or guesswork. In terms of this causal implication we can go on to distinguish genuine perceptions from perceptual beliefs that merely happen, more or less fortuitously, to be true.

Now it could be objected that all this is an elaborate way of missing the point about the principle that perception entails sensation. Because, as it is ordinarily understood, the sensations that the principle mentions are not physical or physiological happenings in the sense-organs or brain of the perceiver but mental events. Perception may indeed involve physical stimulation of the sensory apparatus but it does not follow that it involves sense-impressions.

I should agree that sense-impressions, as ordinarily understood, do not occur as links in the causal chain between the stimulation of the senses and the formation of the perceptual belief. When I see the car go by, it is said, it appears to me that a car is going by. This is true but does not amount to much. In particular it does not draw attention to some state of affairs prior to, distinct from and thus potentially a cause of my seeing the car go by. For it is no more than a minimal expression of the belief which is a constitutive part of my perception of the car. "There appears to be a car going by" is simply a cautious way of stating the belief, integral to my perception, that a car is passing.

However when I see a car going by I can ordinarily say with confidence, not merely that it is doing so, but that I perceive that it is doing so. And for me to be in a position to do this, if my account of the causal implications of perception and perceptual belief is correct, I must be aware, at least in general terms, that this belief is caused by something happening to my senses. I am often able to distinguish beliefs about the current state of my environment that are perceptual from those that are not. I may be taken in by dreams and total hallucinations but I can tell a perception from an intuitive hunch.

I suggest that what I am aware of in making this distinction is not how things appear to me in the ordinary sense, which is the content of my belief whether perceptual or not, but that my senses are being stimulated. I am aware of this not perceptually, by looking at them or feeling sensations in them in Ryle's everyday tactual-kinaesthetic sense of the word, but introspectively. But this introspective awareness is not usually very detailed. I can, however, direct my attention to the character of my experience and, with practice, give a more or less precise and definite description of it, either in terms of colour patches or, confusingly to philosophers of perception, in terms of how things appear to me now. But in the normal case I am aware of no more than that something is going on in my sense-field which I could acquire a detailed knowledge of if I put my mind to it. Unless I have some such generalised introspective awareness my capacity for distinguishing perceptual beliefs from nonperceptual beliefs with the same content cannot be accounted for. Nor can my capacity for distinguishing perception in one sensory mode from perception in another, since it is not from the content of the belief involved, which is the same in both cases, that I am able to distinguish seeing a car go by from hearing it do so.

External events causally influence my senses, stimulate them and my brain physically in certain ways. Correlated with these physical states of the brain and nervous system, and perhaps identical with some part of them, are sense-impressions or appearances in the phenomenological sense. I am usually introspectively aware *that* such impressions are occurring and that they are of a particular sensory type; visual, tactual, auditory etc. These phenomenological events cause me to form beliefs, which are sense-impressions in the epistemic sense. These are perceptual to the extent that they are so caused and I know them to be perceptual to the extent that I know them to be so-caused. But my knowledge of the perceptual character of my beliefs is far from infallible. In a dream or total hallucination I take a belief to be perceptual which is not. In such cases the phenomenological impressions occur without their usual external cause. (If they are in fact identical with some state of the brain it must be the terminal brain state and not the stimulated condition of the sense-organs which is its immediate cause since my rods and cones are presumably not in a stimulated condition in such circumstances.) But I can form a belief about my environment when I am aware that there is no relevant phenomenological occurrence and, on the basis of this awareness, I realise that the belief in question is not perceptual. I can, of course, go wrong about this. When I "just know" that there is someone lurking in a completely dark room I have entered, I may believe this belief to be non-perceptual when in fact it is caused by minute digestive noises emanating from the lurker.

Perception, then, involves not only sensations, conceived as physical states of the brain and nervous system, but also sense-data, in the phenomenological sense of that expression. To the extent that I am aware that my beliefs are perceptual, and with which specific sense they are connected, I am aware of these phenomenological data. Nevertheless I do not ordinarily infer my belief from these data, for what I normally know of them is far too vague and generalised to account for the detail and complexity of my perceptual beliefs. I can acquire detailed knowledge of their character if I put my mind to it, but in general this detail only causes my beliefs, it does not figure in ascertained premises from which they are inferred.

As far as the particular doctrine of Ryle's that is under consideration is concerned: far from its being improper to ask causal questions about perception, it is necessary to have answered a causal question about the belief it embodies to establish that what we take to be a perception really is one. "X perceives that S is P" is like "A was killed by B." Each asserts something about its subject (that X truly believes that S is P and that A is dead) and something about the causation of that fact (that X's belief was caused by the effect on his senses of the fact that S is P and that A's death was caused by some action of B's). Although both concepts are logically causal it is perfectly proper to ask specific causal questions about cases to which they apply. We can still ask how A was

killed by B even if we are already committed to the view
that some action of B's caused A's death. Similarly we can
ask how the fact that S is P caused X's belief even if in
saying, for example, that X sees that S is P we are already
committed to the view that X's belief was somehow
caused by the effect of S's being P on X's optical equipment. Just as there are many ways in which B can cause
A's death so there are many ways in which the fact that
S is P can cause X to believe it by stimulating his senses.
In each case we know that some causal account must logically be forthcoming; but that does not preclude us from
setting to work to find out precisely what it is.

6. CONCLUSION

In this discussion of Ryle's writings about perception
I have concentrated on the ungracious task of criticising
various elements of comparative detail in his presentation. It would be incongruously disproportionate to leave
the subject without taking a larger view of Ryle's contribution to the philosophy of perception. The chapter
on perception in *The Concept of Mind* was the first large-
scale attempt to undermine the whole structure of ideas
and assumptions about the subject initiated in the revival
of the British empiricist tradition by Russell and Moore
in the first decades of the century and brought to a high
pitch of subtlety and sophistication by Price and Ayer. At
a time when Austin, in the lectures eventually published
as *Sense and Sensibilia,* was carrying out his brilliant but
unsystematic guerrilla intrusions into the territory of the
sense-datum theory, Ryle was engaged on the larger and
more serious task of mounting an invasion in full force.
All subsequent critics of the sense-datum theory are indebted to him for his penetrating objections to a host of
received ideas. Of particular value, I believe, have been his
contentions that sense-impressions are not things of
which we have a constant perceptual awareness; that
statements about how things appear are commonly

guarded assertions about how they are and not categorical assertions about the appearances they present; and that certainty is something ordinarily ascertained, not something given. If those who have followed his lead have thought it possible to improve on the way in which he has defended these claims and developed their detailed implications it is only because he provided them with a set of fundamental ideas of true philosophical originality and importance to add their small improvements to.

IMAGINATION

In his chapter on Imagination,[1] Professor Ryle seeks to
show that "seeing things in the mind's eye does not involve the existence of things seen or the occurrence of
acts of seeing them," and that "The question 'Where do
the things and happenings exist which people imagine
existing?' is a spurious one." His argument appears to run
as follows. When we say someone "sees" something we
mean something quite different by the word " 'see' " from
what we mean when we say he sees something. The
quotation marks are important. "Whereas they (people)
see trees and hear music, they only 'see' and 'hear' the
objects of recollection and imagination." Again "A person
who says that he 'sees' the home of his childhood is often
prepared to describe his vision as 'vivid,' 'faithful,'
'lifelike,' adjectives which he would never apply to his
sight of what is in front of his nose." This shows how entirely different "seeing" is from seeing. What then is the
difference between the two? To "see" something is to
imagine that one sees something. "Having a mental picture of Helvellyn is imagining that we see Helvellyn in
front of our noses, and having a tune running in one's
head is imagining that one has the tune being played in
one's hearing." The point of such phrases is that they are
factual disclaimers. They deny that we saw Helvellyn
and do not assert that we saw something else, namely a
sort of copy of Helvellyn, or a mental image. Mental images therefore do not exist. We do not see them, and it is
a spurious question to ask about their locations.

Mind, Vol. LXI, 1952, pp. 528–42. Reprinted with permission
of the author and the Editor of *Mind*.
  [1] *Concept of Mind*, Ch. viii.

Now it may be admitted that "seeing" something is not to be described as seeing a special sort of copy of something. Though it is not very far out in some cases of "seeing." For example, we may say " 'See' an oasis" or "See a mirage." Apart from this, however, most of what Ryle says is not correct.

In the first place he seems a little arbitrary in deciding what are and what are not spurious questions. "Do mental images exist?" is a genuine question to which the answer is that they do not. On the other hand "Where do they exist?" is spurious. This way of talking suggests a parallel between "Do unicorns exist?" and "Where are they to be found?" The latter may be regarded as spurious because there are not any unicorns. But "spurious" is surely the wrong word here. In a philosophical context "spurious question" implies "meaningless question." But in this case the question makes perfect sense, but, the world being what it is, it just does not arise. Anyone who asks it is misinformed about the empirical facts. In the case of images this is not the case. What Ryle really seems to have in mind is that both questions make no sense. Both arise from thinking that any question that may be asked about such things as tables, chairs, or unicorns, can also be asked about mental images. However, this point need not be pressed. It is not uncommon to express the fact that it is nonsense to talk of something existing by saying that it does not exist. It is a more or less recognised alternative to saying that the question about its existence is a spurious one. But it is dangerously misleading to combine both ways of talking.

There are, however, other errors. Ryle fails to make any distinction between the various senses of the word "see" when it is used in quotation marks. It is this failure which makes his account of visualising seem plausible. Indeed he does not just blur or ignore such distinctions, but positively denies their existence. Visualising, or having Helvellyn before the mind's eye, is "a special case of imagining."[2] A man suffering from delirium tremens may imagine that he sees snakes. A perfectly healthy person, casting his mind back to his holiday in the Lakes, may imagine that he sees Helvellyn. Presumably the only reason that we do not use the word "visualise" in the first case is that the man is in a peculiar state. This is clearly incorrect. If a man imagines that he sees snakes, he is mistaken, he thinks he sees snakes but does not. If he visualises snakes, he may do this quite deliberately and does not think there are really any snakes about. The concept of imagining is to be illuminated by distinguishing visualising or picturing from the sort of imagining that a drunkard does, not by identifying the two. One can see that it is wrong to identify the two from the fact that, as Ryle points out, we can use with the verb "to picture" adverbs like "faithfully." But can the drunkard's "vision" be described as faithful any more than our "sight" of something in front of us?

It is illuminating to make explicit the reason why we can use words like "vivid," "faithful" and "lifelike" in connexion with picturing or visualising. The reason is that the logic of words like "picture," "visualise," and "see in the mind's eye" is to some extent parallel to that of "depict," and "draw a picture of." We can depict something vividly, faithfully or in a lifelike manner, or we can picture something in these ways. Thus when it is said that "seeing in the mind's eye is one thing and seeing is another," there are two points to be added. First "see in the mind's eye" is a misleading expression in a way that "picture" is not. The analogue of "seeing" and picturing is not seeing, but depicting. Second, seeing in the mind's eye or picturing, what might best be called " 'depicting,' " is not the same thing as depicting. It is depicting only in a metaphorical sense and is not even metaphorical seeing.

This analogy (partial logical parallelism) between depicting and visualising throws light on a number of

2 *Op. cit.*, p. 256.

points. It shows what is wrong with saying that visualising Helvellyn is the same thing as seeing an image of that mountain. It is wrong for the same reason that it is wrong to say that drawing a picture of Helvellyn is drawing a picture of a picture of Helvellyn. When I depict Helvellyn it is Helvellyn itself I depict, not the picture I make while depicting Helvellyn. The things I can visualise are just the things I can depict, real physical objects like lions, or else imaginary ones like unicorns, not pictures in the one case or visual images in the other. Again Ryle says that visualising is not a matter of "pure sentience." But this is not because visualising belongs to that aspect of perceiving that might be described "in a strained sense" as thinking. It is because visualising does not correspond to perceiving at all. Visualising is not mock-seeing. Visualising is *doing* something in a way that seeing is not doing something, and more in a way that depicting *is* doing something. One can be ordered to depict or to visualise something, one cannot be ordered to see it.

We have now shown that visualising something is not seeing a mental image of something. We have not shown that we do not see mental images. This, however, would have to be something different from visualising, just as seeing a picture is different from depicting something. We have stated that the logic of "visualising" is parallel to that of "depicting." We do see pictures. So, if the parallel was complete, we would see mental pictures also. That is to say the expression "see a mental picture" would have a use. But it has not got a use. It is not normally used. Moreover, when it is introduced by philosophers it is supposed to be synonymous with "visualise something," and to elucidate what we mean by this phrase. In this case it is not parallel to "see a (real) picture," which is not synonymous with "depict something." The parallel is just not complete, and this is a fact about the English language. It is not, however, *just* a fact about language. For it is a fact about the non-linguistic world that it is not of such a nature that it would be convenient to give a use to the expression "see a mental image." One might express this, not improperly, by saying that the parallel between depicting and visualising extends only a certain way. The same applies to other questions such as "Do mental images exist?", "Are they in a space of their own?" and so on. We have no use for such expressions as "Such and such a mental image is no longer in existence." Such expressions have no use because we do not do anything that it is natural to describe in these terms. Let us make this point clearer by indicating what it would be like to "visualise" in a way that might tempt us to give a use to these expressions. To do this it is necessary to use familiar words in an extended sense, as is usually the case when we are describing phenomena different from any we have met before. This procedure is justified, though it must be used with care, and is in accordance with ordinary practice. We are not debarred from extending the use of a word where convenient, and others usually contrive to understand what we are getting at provided that they are co-operative. Suppose that when we visualised anything the image stayed put until we visualised it being rubbed out. If we had visualised a house and then wanted to visualise a triangle, we should have to visualise a house and a triangle side by side unless we first "rubbed out" the house. Perhaps we might visualise a triangle superimposed on a house, but that would be confusing. Again suppose there is a limit to the number of things we can visualise, if we go on visualising new things without "rubbing out" the images of the old ones. That is to say we just cannot produce another image to the right of our right hand image, and so on. Moreover, if we visualise things very small we can get more on to our "mental screen." Now, if things were like this, it might be convenient to ask questions that it is in fact not proper to ask. One might ask "Is that mental picture you produced yesterday still in existence, or have you rubbed it out?" Or, "Where is it?"; to which the reply might be "At the bottom left hand corner of my mental screen." If this were so, it would be as correct to say "mental images exist" as it is to say "physical objects exist." Both these statements would be logical statements to the effect that statements like "that chair no longer exists" or "the image of the chair I had yesterday no longer exists," have a use in English. That mental images do not exist is therefore best described as both a logical and an empirical fact. Alternatively one might say that it can be taken in two ways. (1) Such expressions as "That image no longer exists" have no use. (2) The world is such that it is not convenient to give a use to such expressions. The former expresses a linguistic, the latter a non-linguistic fact.

We may now examine more closely the various senses of " 'see.' " It was by confusing these different senses that Ryle was led to equate seeing in the mind's eye with imagining that one sees. We say someone "sees" something in a variety of different situations. At the cinema we may "see" a car driving along the road. Now in this sense the theory of "seeing" that Ryle attacks comes into its own. We do really see a picture of a car. Only this sort of "seeing" has nothing to do with imagination. A case which has something to do with imagining, and is fairly like this is that of "seeing" an oasis. We can say either " 'see' an oasis" or "see a mirage," but not " 'see' a mirage." Similarly at the cinema it is wrong to say " 'see' a picture of a car." A mirage, however, is not a picture of anything. What is the difference between the expressions " 'see' an oasis" and "imagine that you see an oasis?" It is that the latter tends to be reserved for cases where one is taken in or is in some danger of being taken in. An old hand at desert travelling might be said to have "seen" several oases in the course of a journey, but he would indignantly deny having imagined that he saw any. "He imagined he saw" is closer to "He thought he saw"; though perhaps the former implies that he definitely did not see, whereas the latter suggests only that he may not have done. The former is in fact a factual disclaimer, whereas the latter expresses doubt about the facts. These two same expressions cover a wide range of phenomena. The man who has an hallucination thinks he sees and imagines he sees. In a normal state of mind I might quite gratuitously think I see something when there is nothing there. Now to describe all these cases we may use the word " 'see' " (*i.e.* "see" in a special tone of voice). But none of them are at all like seeing in the mind's eye. If I have an hallucination, I do not see anything in my mind's eye. I do not visualise anything. I make a mistake about whether I see or whether I do not see something. I think I see something, but I do not. But when I visualise Helvellyn, I do not make any sort of mistake at all. Nor am I even tempted to do so, as in the case with the sufferer from delirium tremens who knows what is wrong with him but still cannot help being frightened by the snakes he "sees." I cannot deliberately "see" snakes, but I can quite deliberately visualise Helvellyn, and to do this is not to indulge in a bit of self-deception. One can imagine that one sees Helvellyn, and one can visualise Helvellyn. They are two quite different things. One exception to this may be worth noticing. If I say to someone "Imagine that you see Helvellyn," this means the same as "Visualise Helvellyn." The usage in the imperative does not correspond to that in the indicative. It is easy to see why this is so. One cannot order someone to be mistaken, so one clearly cannot use "imagine" in the imperative in a sense that implies error. This is presumably why "imagine that" in the imperative comes to mean the same as "visualise."

Another description given by Ryle of visualising is that it is sham-seeing.[3] We have seen that this is wrong in that if visualising is sham-anything it is sham-depicting. Is it then sham-depicting? In a way it is, and this has been one of our main points so far. But it is not sham-depicting in the way that sparring is sham-fighting. Sham-depicting in this sense would be drawing something in the air with your finger, going through the motions of depicting with-

[3] *Op. cit.*, 264 ff.

out actually producing a picture. Just as in sparring one goes through the motions of fighting without actually punching hard. Sham-seeing would presumably consist in pretending to see something when one did not. Visualising is not sham-anything. It does not involve any sort of pretence, or the going through of any motions. It may, however, be involved in pretence and make believe, and often in fact is. If I trace a triangle with my finger on a sheet of paper, I usually visualise a triangle on the paper at the same time. I visualise the lines I do not actually draw. If I pretend to see a boat I probably visualise one. Moreover, if I really enter into the spirit of the thing, I may almost take myself in. An actor may find it hard to return from the world of fancy to that of reality. Visualising is an ingredient in make-believe, and make-believe may shade off into delusion. Perhaps there is no hard and fast line between cold-blooded visualising and one sort of imagining that I see. Nevertheless there is some visualising that has no element of pretence or deception about it. Suppose that someone sets me a fairly simple problem in geometry. He says, "There is a rectangle with its longest side horizontal. The bottom left hand angle is bisected. What side of the rectangle will be cut if the bisecting line is produced?" Now if I am very familiar with this sort of thing, I may be able to produce the answer pat without any thought. If I am very unfamiliar with geometry, I may have to draw a diagram. It may, however, be enough to mock-draw the diagram with my finger. Or, better than this, I may just visualise the rectangle instead and get the answer that way. This brings out how wrong it is to describe visualising as a sort of abstaining.[4] Rather visualising is a substitute for doing something else. Similarly it is wrong to describe reading to oneself as merely abstaining from reading out loud. One way of doing this is not to read at all. But reading to oneself is a way of spending the afternoon. One cannot spend the

[4] *Op. cit.*, p. 270.

afternoon in abstaining from going for a walk. Of course visualising may involve refraining from drawing. I may want very much to draw a diagram. In complicated cases it is so much easier than solving the problem in one's head. I may refrain in order to exercise my powers of visualising. Usually, however, I do not have any such urge to draw, and so cannot be said to refrain. One cannot refrain from doing what one does not want to do. One just does not do it. Often one combines visualising and drawing. One draws so much, and this enables one to visualise the rest.

So far we have dealt mainly with visual imagery. Auditory imagery cannot be dealt with in quite the same way. There is nothing in the realm of sound that corresponds to depicting. One can reproduce a sound, but one cannot make a model of it. Without going into all the differences between "seeing" and "hearing," which are mainly the result of the differences in the logics of the words "hear" and "see," many of the conclusions we have reached about visualising apply here also. "Hearing" a tune in one's head is not the same as imagining that one hears a tune. It is not pretending to hear, it is not mock-hearing. It is no sort of abstaining.

We have seen that the verb "imagine" is often used when there is no question of anyone doing any visualising, "hearing," "smelling" or "tasting." In other constructions, however, it is used to refer to just this sort of thing, as for example in sentences like "He imagined himself doing so and so." Sentences like this imply that the subject was engaged in various sorts of imagery. If I imagine myself playing tennis, I "see" what I would see, "feel" what I would feel, "hear" what I would hear, if I were really playing tennis. If I imagine someone else playing tennis, I "see" and "hear" what I would see and hear if I were watching him play tennis. It is partly for this reason that imagining myself looking at something is not the same as visualising that thing. Similarly "hearing" a tune is not the same as imagining oneself humming it or imagining oneself listening to it. At least if I myself was asked to imagine myself humming a tune, part of what I should do would be to visualise myself from the "outside," so to speak, in a humming attitude. However perhaps different people would do different things when asked to imagine themselves doing something. Perhaps, if one was asked to imagine oneself playing tennis, one might visualise what a spectator of oneself would see. This is an empirical matter to be decided only by asking people what they do.

I now want to consider another question about visualising to which no very satisfactory answer has yet been given. Why cannot a man blind from birth visualise anything? Is the impossibility logical or empirical? Ryle makes it a purely logical matter. It is like the impossibility of pretending to be a bear if one does not know what a bear is. To take a parallel example from depicting, one cannot depict the Taj Mahal if one has no idea of what it is like. Now this is correct as far as it goes. But the fact remains that a man who has never seen a bear may (logically) do just what someone might do who was in fact giving a skilful imitation of a bear. A blind man might take a pencil in his hand and produce on a sheet of paper a good likeness of Mr. Churchill. Now to say that it is logically impossible for a blind man to portray Churchill is misleading in that it suggests that he cannot (logically) produce the likeness. Similarly it may be misleading to say that a blind man cannot visualise anything. May it not be logically possible for him to do something we might describe as "visualising without knowing it?" What would we say if a man came to see for the first time late in life and stated that he had always been able to visualise in a way, though he had not known that that was what he used to do? To state baldly that the impossibility of a blind man's visualising is logical is to commit oneself in advance to answering the above question. We would have to say that whatever he did it was not any sort of visualising. It is to say that no imaginable occurrence would lead us to say that a man who had never seen anything could visualise. This is not to find a logical impossibility but to extend language in such a way as to manufacture one. One would make a similar mistake if one said the impossibility was empirical. For to say this is to say that there are certain imaginable situations that would lead one to say a blind man could visualise, but that in fact they never arose. What then are we to say? It is tempting to say that the sentence "This blind man can visualise" is meaningless because we do not know what would count as a blind man visualising. But this will not do either, because it is certainly meaningful and true to say that no blind man can visualise. If it is meaningful to say that a blind man cannot visualise, it cannot be meaningless to say that he can. However, the position is not really very puzzling. I can safely say something is not green even if I do not quite know what "green" means, provided I know that the object in question is not green. Similarly I can say that a blind man cannot visualise, because I know that nothing he does would count as visualising, even though I am not clear what would count, and even though it is not clear whether anything would count. All I know is that some things would come nearer to counting than others, and that no decision has been made as to the correct terms in which to describe them because they have not occurred and no decision has been needed.

Let us now consider the use of such phrases as "being imaginative," "having a vivid imagination" and so on. In general Ryle seems to be right. There is no nuclear operation that consists in exercising the imagination. But I do not think that a man's excellence at visualising counts at all in favour of saying that he is imaginative. Nor does constant indulgence in make-believe make a child imaginative. The notion of imagination is close to that of originality. If the child's make-believe is dull, or if he always makes believe about the same thing in the same sort of way then he shows that he lacks imagination. If I can visualise complicated diagrams, solve problems in my head, or have a good visual memory, this does not mean I am imaginative. There is no specific connexion between visualising and make-believe on the one hand and imaginativeness on the other. I can, of course, show my imaginativeness in my make-believe just as I can in story telling, or producing a play, but I can also show my lack of imagination in these ways. The phrase "he has no imagination" tends to be used particularly, though not exclusively, of our ability to put ourselves in someone else's place, and to understand how others feel about things. Many other expressions too tend to have their own special uses, but we need not go into that here.

Part of the answer to the very vague question "What is imagination?" has now been given. Visualising must be distinguished from other sorts of "seeing," and not confounded with them. Roughly to visualise is to *do* something, whereas to "see" snakes is not to do something. Again we are not talking of any sort of "seeing" when we say that someone is imaginative. Of course, there are further distinctions that can be made. For example, we have not considered a number of expressions in which the word "imagine" occurs. We have talked as if "see in the mind's eye" is synonymous with "visualise." This is not quite true. Apart from this, however, it may still be felt that certain questions have been left unanswered which are not touched by the procedure we have so far followed. What, positively, is visualising? Granted that visualising is doing, what exactly is it that we do when we visualise? Now, if these questions are taken in one way, they are unanswerable. But the desire to ask them may be allayed by seeing why they cannot be answered. It may be that what is wanted is a description of visualising that would enable someone who could not visualise to know what visualising is.

But ultimately the only answer to the question about "what visualising is" is something like, "It is what you do when you solve a geometrical problem in your head, re-

member someone's face and so on." Similarly if a man has
never had a pain, you cannot make him understand just
what it is like to have a pain. You can perhaps give him
some idea by saying it is a very unpleasant bodily sensation. You can give a man who cannot visualise some idea
of what it is like, by saying things like, "It is the visual
analogue of having a tune running in your head." If this
is not the sort of thing that is wanted, then there is nothing that is wanted. However, there do remain certain
other questions about imagery to which some sort of answer can be given. These may be expressed in a vague
form as follows: "Are there mental images?" "Are mental
images things?" "What sorts of things are they?"

The best way of approaching such questions is to ask
whether mental images can be said to be vague, and by
comparing together describing, visualising, and depicting. The relevance of this will become clearer as we proceed.

Some philosophers have held and some have denied
that such images can be vague, indeterminate, non-
specific and general. Consider for example the view expressed by Sartre in *The Psychology of Imagination*:[5]

> "To be vaguely conscious of an image is to be con-
> scious of a vague image. We are far from Berkeley and
> Hume who denied the possibility of general images *or*
> non-specific images—Berkeley's error lay in ascribing to
> the image conditions that apply only to perception. A
> hare vaguely perceived is nevertheless a specific hare.
> But a hare which is the object of a vague image is a
> vague hare."

Now such a view as this may appear paradoxical or even
nonsensical. So at least it would have seemed to Berkeley. One can bring out the nature of the paradox by
putting the matter in a way that seems to involve a denial
of the law of excluded middle. Suppose that I have an

[5] Ch. 1 §5.

image of a head that is non-specific about baldness, is this not rather queer? For presumably this head must be neither bald nor not bald nor even a half-way house with just a few hairs. Again it will not do to say that what is visualised is a head without a top (*e.g.* a scalped head) so that the question of its baldness cannot arise. For to visualise such a head is quite different from visualising a head without considering the question of baldness at all.

Yet at the same time there does seem to be a point in saying that images are in some way non-specific. For if one tells someone to visualise something, and then asks about some detail of what he visualised, he is often unable to give an answer. I may say "visualise a rabbit," and then ask "What colour did you visualise it as having?" Sometimes the reply will be something like this, "It did not have any particular colour, the question of colour did not enter my head." Or again he may say he visualised something as red, but not be able to say whether it was scarlet or crimson. Can one here avoid talking of an image that is red but no particular shade of red by saying that the image was perhaps scarlet but that the visualiser did not notice this? This would be an attempt to preserve the analogy between images and things, for one can notice that the wallpaper is red without noticing what particular shade of red it is. But this will not do. Not only have we got no established use for expressions like "notice a feature of my mental image," but if we did decide to apply it in the situation we are now considering, we would still be unable to give criteria establishing what the overlooked feature was like, what the colour really was. But we do have such criteria in the case of the wallpaper, and this is just what gives the word "notice" its point. In fact we do not preserve the analogy with seeing an object just by using the word "notice" in this context, for the word is left without point.

There seems then to be something of a dilemma. It is both natural and paradoxical to describe mental images as vague or non-specific. Now there are a number of dif-

ferent things that incline one to say that images are
vague, a number of senses in which they may be said to
be vague. One of these senses may be clarified and isolated by comparing visualising with describing. The ways
we use these words run parallel to a considerable extent.
Visual images are always images *of* something, and so are
descriptions. We may visualise men as bald and we may
describe them as bald. We may visualise or describe something correctly or incorrectly, and if we want to check on
our accuracy, we must do the same thing in either case, go
and have a look at the object in question. Visualising and
describing can be done in greater or less detail.

Let us consider what it is for a description to be vague,
and see if there is anything at all analogous in the case
of visual images. There is clearly nothing at all odd in
speaking of a vague or non-specific description. If a description is non-specific about colour, this means only that
the colour of the object was not mentioned, or that it
was described only in vague or general terms, as being
light or dark. A man may not be described as being
neither fair-haired nor not fair-haired, but in an incomplete description he may well be neither described as fair
nor described as not fair. His hair may not be mentioned.
There is no paradox in this. Let us then try to manufacture one that is like the one that arose about imagery.
To do this one must say not, "The man was described
neither as bald nor as not bald," but instead "The description was neither bald nor not bald." The absurdity of
this way of talking is of course obvious. Descriptions are
not material objects and cannot sensibly be said to have
or not to have the characteristics that belong to such objects. Now we may note that to construct the paradox
about visualising we had in that case too to talk in an artificial way. We do not normally speak of red mental images, any more than we speak of red descriptions. We visualise red things and we visualise things as red. It does not
sound odd to say, "The man was visualised neither as fair
nor as dark" instead of "The image was neither fair nor

dark," or "The image was of a man who was neither fair nor not fair." Shall we then say that to talk in this way about imagery is as absurd as to speak in a parallel way about descriptions? Is it impossible to ascribe to mental images the properties of material objects or at least analogous properties? Is the vagueness of visualising just like that of describing, and do all puzzles vanish once this is pointed out? We may say that part of the desire to say that images are vague springs from this likeness between visualising and describing. Descriptions and images have to be *of* something and this is why they can both be described as vague, indeterminate and so on. The things they are "of" cannot sensibly be said to have this sort of vagueness.

Nevertheless we must not assume that our original difficulty about saying that images are vague has now been dispelled. No trouble arises about descriptions because they clearly cannot be said to have the properties that material objects do. But to ascribe such properties to images is not so obviously absurd. To put the matter in another way, we are tempted to think of images as things, though of a special sort. Like pictures, it seems that they can be regarded in two ways, as objects in their own right as well as representations of other things.

How far then are they like pictures? What is the need or justification for introducing a word like "visual image" at all?

We can approach this question by asking why it is we need a word like "picture" to which nothing corresponds in the case of describing, and then seeing if there is any similar need in the case of visualising. In some respects we can liken depicting to describing. The police can circulate both pictures and descriptions of criminals for roughly the same purpose. Reading a description of a murderer and looking at his picture both enable one to say "So that's what he's like." One may talk of descriptions metaphorically by using words that apply literally to pictures. One may call a description a caricature, a pen portrait or a verbal picture. Portraits and descriptions can be accurate or inaccurate representations, detailed or not detailed, lifelike or not lifelike. Portraits and descriptions have to be *of* something. More detailed parallels can be worked out. A bald description is rather like a conceptual or schematic drawing. An impressionistic picture in which much is suggested is like a vivid but oblique description. However, there is one big difference about the ways we can talk about the two. For pictures are things, just as much as the things they are pictures of. For this reason one can ascribe to pictures the properties that one can ascribe to other material objects. A statue can have no hand, and this does not mean that it is a statue of a man without a hand. In saying that a statue has no hand we are not thinking of it in its representational aspect, but, so to speak, as a thing in its own right. We cannot do this in the case of a description. The case of a picture is rather more complicated. We can speak of a picture as a thing, as when we say that it is brightly coloured, and do not mean it is a picture of something brightly coloured. Also we have phrases like "the man in the picture" where the object is thought of as a man (a picture-man). We may say "this (picture-) hand is delicately drawn" or "this (picture-) hand has blurred edges" and we do not mean that it is a picture of a hand with blurred edges. A statue may be regarded as a stone man as well as a statue of a man in stone. For all these reasons we need a word like "picture" or "statue" to which ordinary material object adjectives may be applied. Now quite clearly a mental image is not an object, but it may be in some way analogous to one in that it is useful to have a way of talking about visualising that does not refer to the representative aspect of visualising. It seems to me that in fact there *is* this much excuse for the introduction of the word "image." It is a fairly well known fact that it is often difficult to visualise the faces of people we know very well. We can get so far, we can perhaps put in the outline of the head, but the features elude us. Now when people describe this they tend to say things like this. "I tried to visualise the face but all I got was a blur," or "His face was a blur" or "It was a blur." Now we may ask "What was a blur?" What does "his face" refer to? It does not refer to the face we are trying to visualise, nor do we mean that we visualise his face as blurred. What we are referring to is something analogous to the "face in the picture," the picture-face. The blur does not represent anything in the face visualised. It is, so to speak, a feature of the image in its own right. Similarly there is such a thing as visualising a scene in black and white, as opposed to visualising a black and white scene. If we do this and are asked what colour we visualised the sky as being, we may say "I didn't visualise it as any particular colour, the whole thing was various shades of grey." "The whole thing" is not the scene but what is best called the image of it, or the mental picture of it. The word "picture" is a good one here because of the analogy between painting in black and white and visualising in black and white. Of course, there is danger here. One may press the analogy too far, and talk of seeing mental images as though having produced them one could afterwards do something analogous to examining them. This is one of the ways in which mental images are not like pictures.

The answer to the question "Are there mental images?" is contained in the above discussion. There is no straight answer because the purport of the question is not clear. If it is taken as meaning "Do people visualise things?" then the answer is that they do. On the other hand a desire to deny that there are images may spring from a number of sources. We do not need a word like "image" in the normal course of events, and it may be felt that its introduction is not justified. More particularly the denial that there are images may be at bottom a rejection of a philosophical account of imagination that is felt to be misleading, and to lead to the asking of absurd and therefore unanswerable questions. This appears to be part of the motive for Ryle's denial that there are images. The concept of visualising is not illuminated but obscured by saying that it consists in seeing a private picture located in the mind. In so far as it is some such theory as this that is denied, we may agree with Ryle. But it will not do to express this by saying there are not images. It is very natural to talk of visual images, and we can make ourselves understood when we do so. I have argued that it is sometimes more convenient to talk about images than to use more normal forms of expression. For these reasons the denial that there are images seems quite paradoxical to the educated non-philosopher. It is far better to say that there are mental pictures, and at the same time issue a warning against asking questions about them that can sensibly be asked only of real pictures. There remains the question "What sorts of things are images?" The answer to this may be put briefly thus: "They are the same sorts of things as pictures and descriptions. They are a sort of half-way house between pictures and descriptions." This answer as it stands is of course very misleading, and its meaning is not obvious. It is intended merely as a short-hand reminder of our earlier comparison of the concepts of describing, visualising, and portraying. Moreover, this answer is not the whole story. Rather it illustrates a method of answering questions like "Are there mental images?" This method is to try to talk about visualising in the same sort of language as we talk about depicting and about pictures, and to see how far such a way of talking is possible and useful. We draw certain distinctions in our talk about pictures, how far can parallel distinctions be made in talking about mental pictures? In this article this method has been applied to one very important part of the field. We can talk about pictures without talking about what they are pictures of. How far is it convenient and possible to talk in a similar way about mental pictures?

MENTAL COPIES

G. B. MATTHEWS

"The language of originals and copies," writes Gilbert Ryle in *The Concept of Mind*, "does not apply to smells."[1] Nor, according to Professor Ryle, does it apply to tastes and feelings. "It makes no sense," he says, "to apply words like 'copy,' 'likeness' and 'dummy' to smells, tastes and feelings" (p. 253). Ryle thinks this is important for the following reason. When a philosopher says that to imagine[2] a face or a sound is to perceive an internal picture of the face, or an internal echo of the sound, what he says makes sense only because we already know what pictures of faces and echoes of sounds are. But since the language of copies and originals does not apply to smells, tastes, and feelings, none of us, not even the philosopher among us, is tempted to try a similar explanation of imagining smells, tastes, and feelings.

Ryle's talk of the "language of copies and originals" and how it applies to one kind of thing and not to another gives, I think, an oversimplified picture of the situation. It encourages one to suppose that there is a reasonably well-defined vocabulary having to do with copies and originals and that one can make a quite general judgment about whether this vocabulary fits a certain range of entities.

It is clear from Ryle's discussion that he would include "snapshot," "effigy," "picture," "echo," "recording," "copy," "likeness," "dummy," "facsimile," and "original"

Reprinted with permission from the *Philosophical Review*, Vol. LXXVIII, No. 1, January 1969.

[1] (London, 1949), p. 252.

[2] Ryle wants to say something similar about an imagist's account of memory. In this paper, however, I shall concentrate on the imagist's account of the imagination.

in the vocabulary of this language. It may not be equally clear to his readers exactly what other words belong.

More important, it seems quite misleading to suggest that a list of words like this is, as a whole, either appropriate or inappropriate for talking about visible objects and sounds. We may indeed speak of an effigy of a person—for example, Guy Fawkes—but we should be unlikely to speak of an effigy of the Empire State Building, let alone an effigy of the sound of motorcycles. I may refer to the echo of a falling tree, but I should need poetic license to refer to the echo of a smiling face, or even to the echo of middle C. We talk of facsimile coins and facsimile signatures, but not usually of facsimile people or of facsimile noises.

To be sure, the words "replica," "copy," "echo," "facsimile," and so forth have points of overlapping application. But I suspect that no two of them would be appropriately applied to just the same range of things. So to say that words like these apply to visible objects, but not to (for example) tastes seems a misleading way of putting things.

Still, at least part of Ryle s claim can be rephrased so as to avoid the quarrel I have raised thus far. We certainly know what it is for something (for example, a daguerreotype of Abraham Lincoln) to bear to a visible object or person (in this case to Lincoln himself) the relation of likeness to original. Similarly, we know what it is for something (for example, the sound a phonograph makes in playing a recording of one of Churchill's speeches) to bear to a sound (in this case, one made by Churchill in a BBC studio) the relation of likeness to original. But we do not really know what it would be for something to bear to a smell, a taste, or a feeling the relation of likeness to original. Hence it is not tempting—perhaps it is not even intelligible—to speak of imagining smells, tastes, and feelings as though it were a matter of perceiving (internal) likenesses.

This line of argument is immediately suspect on account of the falsity of its conclusion. When Ryle refers to the temptation to speak of internal likenesses or copies he seems to have in mind as one prime target Hume and his copy theory of ideas. Yet Hume certainly thought we have ideas of smells, tastes, and feelings. Hume was happy to talk about the ideas of sweet and bitter (for example) in the same context in which he discusses the ideas of scarlet and orange.[3] On Hume's account, smells, tastes, and feelings are exactly like colors and sounds in so far as they first come to us as impressions and turn up later in memory and imagination as ideas—copies of the original impressions. Not only was Hume subject to the "temptation" which Ryle denies we can have; Hume succumbed to it.

In fact, Ryle's own statement shows that we do have the verbal means for talking about smell replicas, smell facsimiles, and smell echoes. Such a way of talking may be odd, misleading, or confused; but it is a way of talking and therefore there is such a way of talking. Perhaps Ryle means only to point out that this is no *ordinary* way of talking.[4] But the significance of that fact, if it is a fact, remains to be determined.

Let us ignore the question about what ways of talking there are, ordinary or otherwise, and see if we can still salvage something of Ryle's point. If it is a mistake, perhaps a mistake certain philosophers have made, to apply the language of originals and copies to smells, tastes, and feelings, then it is also a mistake to conceive of imagining smells, tastes, and feelings as the perception of inner or mental copies. Now the question is, is this application a mistake? What might lead us to think that it is? Ryle's answer seems to be that "it makes no sense to apply words like 'copy,' 'likeness' and 'dummy' to smells, tastes and feelings." But then we need to know why it makes no

[3] *A Treatise of Human Nature*, ed. by L. A. Selby-Bigge (Oxford, 1928), p. 5.
[4] As he does when he says this: "How should we describe this 'smelling in the mind's nose'? Ordinary language provides us with no means of saying that I am smelling a 'likeness' of a singed hoof" (p. 252).

sense, if indeed it does make no sense. The reason cannot be simply that, as a matter of fact, there are no smell copies, taste likenesses, feeling dummies, and so forth. For it might still make sense to apply these words to smells, tastes, and feelings even though, as a matter of fact, there happened to be nothing in the world to fit the resulting descriptions. The reason why these combinations make no sense, if indeed they do make no sense, must be that there is something about (for example) "smell" and "copy" such that it is nonsensical to suppose there could be a smell copy.

Ryle's reasoning may go like this. For anything to be a smell copy it would have to be a non-smell that is nevertheless very like a smell. But that is impossible, since no non-smell would be very like a smell. Therefore there could be no smell copies. By a similar line of reasoning there could be no taste or feeling copies.

Unfortunately, this way of arguing will do Ryle's cause no good, for it applies not only to smells but also to sounds (and to colors) as well. That is, in just the same way as it might be thought nonsensical to talk about a smell copy it is also nonsensical to talk about a sound copy, for just as no non-smell could be very like a smell, so no non-sound could be very like a sound. Yet Ryle says there are sound copies—namely, recordings and echoes.

Surely Ryle is wrong. Surely there could be smell copies and taste copies, perhaps even feeling copies, in just the same way in which there are sound copies. Consider what counts as the reproduction of a sound made on some particular occasion. Sound S_2 counts as the reproduction of sound S_1 when S_2 resembles S_1 in pitch, loudness, density, and volume and when some procedure has been carried out to record S_1 as a result of which S_2 could be produced.[5]

---

[5] These conditions are, I think, sufficient, though perhaps not necessary. The sound a bird mimic makes might count as the reproduction of a bird's song, even though the mimic employs no procedure to achieve the reproduction. (I owe this point to the editors of the *Philosophical Review*.)

Compare the smell case. According to psychologists, the quality of a given smell may be located uniquely in a so-called "smell prism" whose corners stand for the qualities flowery, foul, fruity, burnt, resinous, and spicy. A smell Sm_2 could count as the reproduction of a smell Sm_1 (for example, the smell of my basement after the rain one spring afternoon) provided Sm_2 resembled Sm_1 in quality and provided that Sm_1 had been recorded by some procedure which made the production of Sm_2 possible. Perhaps we have not in fact developed the technology of smell reproduction so as to be able to record or produce smells easily according to quality specification. Nor is it easy to conceive of situations in which the interest in smell reproduction would make the technology worth developing. Still, movie producers once thought of adding realism to their offerings by using smell-producers. And documentary films, so produced, would certainly aim at reproducing the smell of a certain locale at a certain time much as they aim at reproducing sounds made on particular occasions.

Taste reproduction is similarly conceivable. No doubt feeling reproduction would be the most difficult undertaking of all, if for no other reason than because there is no simple ordering of feeling qualities to correspond to those of sound, smell, and taste. It is, however, conceivable that we might one day be able to record, for example, the feeling a given astronaut had when he entered the gravitational field of Venus.

Someone might object that smells, tastes, and feelings cannot be recorded—that all we could conceivably record are certain chemical characteristics of air which have been correlated with the smells people report, or certain chemical characteristics of food correlated with tastes eaters report, or certain physiological states correlated with feelings people report. But the answer to this objection is simple. In just the same way it is not a sound of a certain loudness, pitch, density, and volume which is recorded, but rather the frequency and intensity of air vibrations, which are correlated with the sounds people report hearing.

II

A sympathetic reader of *The Concept of Mind* might be moved to state the following thesis about the imagination:

(*i*) To imagine *x* is not to perceive something like *x* —that is, a dummy or copy *x*—but in some cases to imagine *x* is to do something like seeing *x* (or something like hearing *x*, or something like smelling *x*, and so forth).

Ryle himself puts things in a somewhat different way. For example, he says this:

a person picturing his nursery is, in a certain way, like that person seeing his nursery, but the similarity does not consist in his really looking at a real likeness of a nursery, but in his really seeming to see his nursery itself, when he is not really seeing it [p. 248].

Still, (*i*) is, I think, sufficiently close to what Ryle says to count as one way of trying to make his point. In any case, I propose to discuss the merits of (*i*) with an eye to Ryle's own discussion.

(*i*) has two parts, an affirmation and a denial. Let us consider the affirmation first—namely, the claim that in some cases to imagine *x* is to do something like seeing *x* (or something like hearing *x*, and so forth). One might question whether this is really so.

A rather striking bit of evidence is due to C. W. Perky.[6] Perky conducted a series of psychological experiments in which he placed his subjects before a ground-glass wall,

6 "An Experimental Study of Imagination," *American Journal of Psychology*, 21 (1910), 422–52.

asked them to fix their attention at a point on the wall and to visualize various objects there (for example, a tomato, a book, a leaf). Each time he asked a subject to visualize something, he had an appropriate image projected faintly on the ground-glass wall. He did not tell his subjects about the image projections and (except when the projector was jogged inadvertently) they did not realize they were there. But when the subjects were questioned about what they had visualized, they described objects corresponding to the faintly projected images. For example, if a subject had been asked to visualize a book and the image of a book with a blue cover had been projected, the subject, upon being questioned, would report that the book he had visualized was blue. Thus the subjects apparently saw the faint projections, but took them for their own visualizations.

Of course, to say that in some cases imagining *x* may be like seeing *x* or hearing *x* (and so forth) is not to say very much. Anything is like almost anything else in some respect or other. Perky's results suggest one way of trying to specify a respect in which, for example, imagining a tomato at a certain point in space might be like seeing one there. Perky's results suggest that imagining a tomato at a certain point in space may be phenomenologically similar to seeing a faint image of a tomato there; for one may confuse the latter with the former.

A great deal more remains to be said on this subject; but I shall not try to say any of it here. For I want to concentrate on the second, and more controversial, half of thesis (*i*)—namely, the part about how imagining *x* is not, in any case, an instance of really perceiving a dummy *x*. This is certainly what Ryle is most concerned to defend. I find myself sympathetic with it; but I consider unsatisfactory the reasoning Ryle offers in support of it. One line of reasoning we have already considered. It is that, since the language of copies and originals does not apply to tastes, smells, and feelings, imagining a taste, smell, or feeling could not be a case of perceiving a copy taste, copy smell, or copy feeling. I have argued that there is nothing conceptually outlandish about talk of taste, smell, and feeling copies.

Perhaps the main line of reasoning that Ryle thinks supports his contention is this.[7] One can describe imagining something by the use of an ordinary perceptual verb. To picture the White House trimmed in gold is to "see" the White House decked out in this fashion. To imagine all the church bells in Paris tolling at once would be to "hear" them all tolling together. But when one uses "see," "hear," "taste," "smell," or "feel" in this fashion, one uses them metaphorically. To "see" the White House trimmed in gold is not to *see* anything at all—the White House or anything else. One could "see" the White House after it had been burned down or after one had gone blind. Nor is to "hear" all the church bells of Paris tolling at once really to hear anything at all.

At work in this line of reasoning are the simple truisms that in "seeing" we do not really see, in "hearing" we do not really hear, in "tasting" we do not really taste, and so forth. Ryle seems to think that the imagist philosopher supposes that a man who "sees" the White House trimmed in gold must really see something, only not the White House; what he really sees is a White House image, or a White House copy. And, in general, Ryle thinks the imagist philosopher supposes that a man who, as it were, sees (or hears, tastes, smells, or feels) so-and-so by imagining it, must really see (or hear, or taste, and so forth) an as-it-were so-and-so.

In fact, the imagist philosopher need suppose nothing of the sort. He may agree that to "see" the White House trimmed in gold is not really to *see* anything at all; it is, he may agree, to do something like seeing the White House. But what, he asks, could be like seeing the White House except perceiving, in some way or other, an object that somehow resembles the White House?

[7] *The Concept of Mind*, p. 246.

A partially developed analogy misleads Ryle on this issue. There are not, Ryle assures us,

> two species of murderers, those who murder people, and those who act the parts of murderers on the stage; for these last are not murderers at all. They do not commit murders which have the elusive attribute of being shams; they pretend to commit ordinary murders, and pretending to murder entails, not murdering, but seeming to murder. As mock-murders are not murders, so imagined sights and sounds are not sights or sounds. They are not, therefore, dim sights, or faint sounds [pp. 250–51].

Suppose a mock murder takes place—say, the murder of McKinley enacted on the stage. We need not charge the actor with homicide, for the murder of McKinley in a play is, fortunately, not usually a real murder of a stand-in McKinley, but only something like the real murder of McKinley. Similarly, according to Ryle, a mock look at the White House is not a real look at a mock White House, but merely something like a look at the White House.

Unfortunately for Ryle's argument there could, in fact, be a number of different kinds of mock murder. A mock murder of McKinley might be a case of:

(1) doing something to McKinley like murdering him; or
(2) murdering someone like McKinley; or
(3) doing something to someone like McKinley which resembles murdering him.

The last-named possibility is actually the most usual. It is what we expect in a play. And, contrary to Ryle, its analogue in the interpretation of " 'seeing' the White House trimmed in gold" is *doing something like seeing*, where the object of one's quasi-seeing is *something like the White House.*

So the image theorist and Ryle may agree that (in a given case) to "see" the White House in one's imagination is to do something like really seeing the White House. But the image theorist goes on to say that what is like really seeing the White House (in such a case) is perceiving (by a means other than ordinary seeing) something that looks like the White House—namely, a mental picture or copy. It is on this last point that Ryle demurs. As we have seen, the justification he gives for demurring is unsatisfactory. We can perhaps suggest a justification on his behalf, however, that is at least somewhat more satisfactory.

Suppose we concentrate for a moment on the imagined gold trim of the White House. I can imagine—that is, I can "see"—gold trim on the White House. Either the mental picture of the White House I am supposed to perceive when I "see" gold trim is colored (presumably gold and white, or at least yellow and white) or it is not colored at all. If it is not colored at all, how can it portray the qualities I am imagining the White House to have? How can anything but a color portray a color? If, on the other hand, the mental picture is itself colored, then how can it be perceived except by vision?

Or suppose I can "hear" the "Star-Spangled Banner" every morning when I wake up. The image theorist says I perceive a sound copy. But is this copy also a sound, or a group of sounds, like those my phonograph produces? If so, how is it that I do not need some auditory organ to hear it? Or is it only something like a sound? But what could be really like a given sound except some other sound?

Similar worries arise with respect to tastes, smells, and feelings.

The image theorist asks: what could be like seeing a building except perceiving a copy building? What could be like hearing a song but perceiving a likeness of the song? What could be like tasting a beefsteak but perceiving a facsimile beefsteak taste? And so forth.

The point of his rhetoric is to suggest that the analysis of imagination into perception and object of perception makes imagination more easily understood. But I think this is not so. Instead, it introduces a dilemma we do not know how to resolve. Either the objects of "inner" perception are colored objects (such as pictures), sounds, tastes, smells, and feelings—or they are not. If they are, and we perceive them, then surely it must be that we really see, hear, taste, smell, and feel them. If they are not, then how can they be copies? That is, how can it be that they truly resemble what we see, hear, taste, smell, and feel?

I thus remain sympathetic to thesis (*i*). I think we should content ourselves with saying (for whatever it is worth) that to imagine a sensible thing may be to do something like seeing, hearing, smelling, tasting, or feeling that thing. We should not add, thinking to clarify matters, that what is like seeing, hearing, and so forth is the real perception of mental copies. The addition does not clarify.

III

I should like now to move toward a somewhat more incisive verdict on image theories of the imagination. It will be helpful first, however, to say something about the logic of contexts governed by the word "like." In what follows I shall call contexts governed by "like" "ikonic contexts." I might title this section of the paper (rather grandly, if not grandiosely) "The Logic of Ikonic Contexts."[8]

I shall be chiefly interested in four statement schemata. Using parentheses to mark off the ikonic context, I can indicate *roughly* what the four schemata are as follows:

[8] I owe the idea for this section and several of the detailed points to discussions with S. Marc Cohen.

(*a*) Olaf does something like (cutting) wood.
(*b*) Olaf does something like (cutting wood).
(*c*) Olaf does something like (cutting something like [wood]).
(*d*) Olaf does something like (cutting) something like (wood).

In (*a*) the object of Olaf's action is wood. The force of (*a*) is brought out by this:

(*a'*) Olaf does to wood something like cutting it.

(*d*) is subject to a similar paraphrase, thus:

(*d'*) Olaf does to something like wood something like cutting it.

Clearly (*a*) cannot be true unless there is some wood to which Olaf does something. Nor can (*d*) be true unless there is something like wood to which Olaf does something. By contrast, (*b*) may be true even though Olaf is stranded on a woodless island. If he mimes wood-cutting, (*b*) will be true. Similarly, (*c*) may be true without there even being ersatz wood available to Olaf. To do something like (cutting something like [wood]) is to do something like fibrous-material-cutting. One way to do that would be to mime fibrous-material-cutting.

The device of marking ikonic contexts by parentheses is imprecise in a way I should now like to remedy. I shall do this by introducing a bit of symbolism. The symbolism is not meant to conform to anyone's idea of canonical notation. I have, however, allowed myself only such departures from symbolic orthodoxy as seem to make more perspicuous the relationships in which I am interested.

In what follows "*o*" will be an individual constant standing for "Olaf." "*D*" will be a two-place predicate such that "*oDy*" will stand for "Olaf does (or performs) *y*." "*D'*" will be a three-place predicate such that "*oD'yz*" will stand for "Olaf does *y* to *z*" (or "Olaf performs *y* on *z*"). "*w*" will be an individual constant standing for "wood" so that "$oD'yw$" will stand for "Olaf does y to wood." "xLy" will stand for "x is like y" and "$x:xLw$" will stand for "an x such that x is like wood" or, more simply, "something like wood." Finally, "k" will stand for "cutting," "k^w" for "cutting wood" and "$k^{w:wLw}$" for "cutting something like wood."

Now the four sample sentences in which I am interested can be symbolized this way (in each case the whole sentence is to be understood as bound by the existential quantifier, "there is a y such that"):

(α) $oDy \cdot oD'yw \cdot yL(k^w)$
(β) $oDy \cdot yL(k^w)$
(γ) $oDy \cdot yL(k^{w:wLw})$
(δ) $oDy \cdot oD'y(x:xLw) \cdot yL(k^w)$

These sentences are meant to bring out one interpretation each of (a), (b), (c), and (d). Other interpretations are possible. (And, incidentally, the fact that other interpretations are possible shows that our rudimentary symbolism is capable of marking more distinctions than we could mark with the device of parentheses alone.) (a), for example, might also be interpreted as saying: there is a y such that

(α') $oDy \cdot oD'yw \cdot yLk$

On this interpretation (a) would be true if Olaf took a piece of wood and pretended to cut it with scissors. (He would be doing to wood something like cutting, but not, in this case, something like wood-cutting.)

Now let us say something about the entailment relations among (α), (β), (γ), and (δ). By simplification (that is, by appeal to the fact that $\ulcorner \phi \cdot \psi \cdot \chi \urcorner$ entails $\ulcorner \phi \cdot \chi \urcorner$) we may infer (β) from either (α) or (δ). But what about the relation between, say, (δ) and (α)? What would justify an inference from (α) to (δ)? Clearly one thing that would is what I shall call the Rule of Self-Ikonicity. It enables us to replace "w" in any sentence with "$x:xLw$" *salva veritate*. The idea is that a given thing is itself among the things that can be said to be like it.[9] (For example, wood is itself among the things like wood.)

By appeal to the Rule of Self-Ikonicity we may get (δ) from (α), and (γ) from (β), though not the other way around. And by appeal to Self-Ikonicity plus simplification we may get (γ) from (α).

I suspect many people would reject Self-Ikonicity on the grounds that if I say, "Olaf is cutting something like wood," I imply either that what Olaf is cutting is not wood or else that I am not sure whether what he is cutting is wood. I am myself inclined to reject this reasoning. It seems to me on a par with arguing that $\ulcorner \phi \urcorner$ does not entail $\ulcorner \phi$ or $\psi \urcorner$ because if I say, "Either it is a baseball bat or it is a softball bat," I imply that the bat is a borderline case or at least that I do not know for sure whether it is a baseball bat or a softball bat.

Often enough it is misleading to make a weaker claim when one is in position to make a stronger claim—so long as the stronger claim would clearly be of interest. But that, I think, does not show that the weaker claim is not entailed by the stronger.[10]

But is a thing really like itself? I suspect we have conflicting inclinations here. In some contexts it seems natural to say "Yes." If, for example, there are two styles of chair in a room and I say, pointing to a ladder-back chair, "Please put all chairs like that in the storeroom," I would surely be taken to want the specimen chair I pointed to stored with chairs like it.

And suppose I have given my son the warning, "If you do anything like that again I'll spank you." Provided a future offense is serious enough, I will not be prepared to

[9] The Rule of Self-Ikonicity makes "There is nothing like it" either trivially false or else elliptical for "There is nothing else like it."

[10] Cf. H. P. Grice, "The Causal Theory of Perception," in *Perceiving, Sensing, and Knowing*, ed. by Robert J. Swartz (New York, 1965), esp. pp. 449–51 and 458–59.

accept the plea, "But, Papa, I did the very same thing again, not something like it."[11]

In any case, the application of the Rule of Self-Ikonicity has to be restricted. For one thing, we will not want to allow the substitution of ⌜something like θ⌝ for ⌜θ⌝ in the antecedent of a conditional or in either side of a bi-conditional. "If it is poison ivy, it will have three leaves" does not entail "if it is something like poison ivy it will have three leaves."

Then there are contexts governed by verbs expressing propositional attitudes. "Amy wants maple syrup" does not entail "Amy wants something like maple syrup." The main trouble here, we might say, concerns the placement of the quantifier. If we put it outside we get this: there is something like maple syrup (presumably maple syrup itself) that Amy wants. But that is too strong for the reason that the original statement ("Amy wants maple syrup") might be true even though maple syrup and its likes were only a figment of Amy's imagination. But if we put the quantifier inside we get this: Amy wants it to be the case that there is something like maple syrup that she has. In prudence we dare not infer from Amy's desire for maple syrup that she has any desire at all for the likes of maple syrup.[12]

Anyway, what I want to establish in this section does not depend upon the acceptability of the Rule of Self-Ikonicity. Quite to the contrary, one main reason for including this brief discussion of ikonic logic is to show

[11] I owe this example to Peter Geach, who took it, he said, from real life.

[12] Reasoning in support of this last claim might go this way. S wants it to be the case that S has x if, and only if, its coming to be the case that S has x would satisfy a desire S has. Then, (1) Amy wants it to be the case that she has maple syrup if, and only if, (2) its coming to be the case that Amy has maple syrup would satisfy a desire Amy has. And (3) Amy wants it to be the case that she has something like maple syrup if, and only if, (4) its coming to be the case that Amy has something like maple syrup would satisfy a desire that Amy has. But (4) does not follow from (2). So (3) does not follow from (1).

that an entailment that might be thought to depend
upon Self-Ikonicity in fact does not.

The second rule I want to consider I shall call the
Rule of Ikonic Transfer. This rule, like the Rule of Self-
Ikonicity, permits the substitution of *"x:xLw"* for *"w."*
But it permits this substitution *only within an ikonic context.* The idea is that if, for example, what I am doing is
like smoking a cigar, what I am doing is also like smoking
something like a cigar (it is like, for example, smoking
a dummy cigar). Again, if what I am doing is like counting money, it is also like counting something like money
(it is like, for example, counting counterfeit money).

The Rule of Ikonic Transfer enables us to infer (γ)
from (β). Furthermore, by using this rule and also sim-
plifying, we may infer (γ) from (α).

I know of no reason to reject the Rule of Ikonic Transfer. Whatever worries we may have about Self-Ikonicity,
there seems to be no good reason to reject Ikonic
Transfer.

Let us see now what relevance this brief consideration
of the logic of ikonic contexts has for an imagist account
of the imagination. Thesis (i) from the last section
would allow us to suppose that when Olaf imagines the
White House trimmed in gold he does something like
seeing the White House trimmed in gold. That is, there
is a y such that

$$(\epsilon) \quad oDy \cdot yL(s^{wh})$$

(where, of course, "s^{wh}" stands for "seeing the White
House trimmed in gold"). To this the image theorist replies that when Olaf imagines the White House trimmed
in gold he does something like seeing something like the
White House trimmed in gold. How are we to interpret
the image theorist's claim? If we interpret it this way—
there is a y such that

$$(\zeta) \quad oDy \cdot yL(s^{x:xLwh})$$

—then, by the Rule of Ikonic Transfer, it will be entailed
by (ϵ). And just as it does not follow from (ϵ) that there

exists any such thing as the White House, so it does not follow from (ζ) that there exists anything *like* the White House. The object slot in the gerundive phrase "seeing the White House"—as in the gerundive phrase "seeing something like the White House"—must be taken to be, in Quine's phrase, referentially opaque. The reason for this is clear. If the notion of doing something like seeing x is to be at all helpful in giving an account of what it is to imagine x, it must be possible to do something like seeing objects that fail to exist. The force of "$yL(s^z)$" would therefore be this: y is like what it is or *would be* to see z.[13]

We thus find ourselves in an odd position. The "*wh*" in "$yL(s^{wh})$" is inaccessible to external quantification. Writing the "*wh*" as a superscript is meant to mark this fact. Yet, although the position of the "*wh*" is referentially opaque, a certain kind of substitution is nevertheless vouchsafed by the fact that "s^{wh}" falls within an ikonic context. The substitution vouchsafed is the replacement of "*wh*" by "*x:xLwh*." But of course the quantifier implicit in that substitution cannot be exported. That is, in so far as "A is doing something like seeing something like the White House" follows, by the Rule of Ikonic Transfer, from "A does something like seeing the White House," the former does not entail that there is something like the White House—a dummy or copy White House.[14]

---

[13] Ruth Marcus has made me more aware of the importance of the subjunctive "would be" here. To imagine a unicorn cannot be to do something like seeing one—there being none to see. But to imagine a unicorn on a given occasion is, perhaps, to do something like what it *would be* to see one.

[14] The expression "ikonic transfer" is meant to suggest that the *respect* in which one thing is said to be like another is also carried over to the second occurrence of "like." Thus suppose, for example, that I think I hear a voice late one night and then decide I was just imagining it. My imagining a voice might be understood as my doing something which is like hearing a voice in at least this respect: it could be easily mistaken for hearing a voice. The Rule of Ikonic Transfer authorizes us to go on and say that my imagining a voice late that night is also like hearing something like a voice. And since the respect is also to be passed on, "something like a voice" is to

In order for the image theorist's claim to amount to anything beyond what a supporter of thesis (i) from the last section would be quite happy to grant, the image theorist must therefore give the notion of "something like the White House" a role outside the ikonic context in a referentially transparent context. Thus he might claim that there is a y such that

$$(\eta) \quad oDy \cdot oD'y(x{:}xLwh) \cdot yL(s^{wh})$$

or that there is a y such that

$$(\eta') \quad oDy \cdot oD'y(x{:}xLwh) \cdot yL(s^{w{:}xLwh})$$

Is there any way for the image theorist to make good on the contention that a case of imagining fits (η) or (η'), and not just (ζ)? That is, is there any way for the image theorist to make good on the contention that in imagining x one is not just doing something which is like seeing (or hearing, and so forth) the likes of x, one is also doing *to something like x* something like seeing it?

For the image theorist to make good on his contention, it would be necessary for him to find some role for the notion of a mental copy in addition to the role it is given in reporting that one imagines something. In the next section I shall discuss the only attempt along these lines with which I am familiar.

IV

The image theorist wants to say that in doing something like seeing the White House one is as-it-were-seeing an as-it-were-White-House. Taken in one way his sugges-

---

be taken as meaning "something which is like a voice in that it could easily be mistaken for a voice." Making the respect explicit for both occurrences of "like" we get this: my imagining a voice that night was a case of doing something like (in respect of being easily mistaken for it) hearing something like (in respect of being easily mistaken for it) a voice.

I have omitted a full development of this matter for fear of obscuring with technical detail the main point of this section.

tion is trivial. By the Rule of Ikonic Transfer anyone who does something that is like seeing the White House thereby does something like seeing something like the White House. And just as one can do something like seeing the White House though there is, in fact, no White House to see, so (for all we yet know) one could do something like seeing something like the White House without there being a quasi-White-House to quasi-see. This is the point of our discussion in the last section.

The only way to rescue image theory from this sort of trivialization is to find some role for the concept "mental copy of x" beside that of picking out the objects of quasi-seeing, quasi-hearing, quasi-smelling, and quasi-feeling. To find such a role may seem impossible, for surely the concept "mental copy of x" is applicable, if at all, only on those occasions when one can be said to be doing something like seeing x (or hearing x, and so forth).

Yet image theorists have traditionally sought to do something which, if successful, would actually provide the needed independence for the concept of a mental copy. They have used the concept of a mental copy in a theory about how it is we can imagine some things and not others. The theory goes this way.

We get our basic stock of mental images through our senses; and we are able to form additional images only by taking the ones given in sense experience and "operating" on them. Possible operations include enlarging them in whole or in part, cutting them up and putting together whole images or image parts. But each of us is limited in the formation of mental images to the image materials we have on hand and to the possible operations of mental "carpentry." Our image material in stock can be enriched only by new and different sense experience. Since to imagine x is to perceive an image or copy of x, we are limited in our ability to imagine things by the stock of our image materials (and so, ultimately, to the range of our sense experience). In particular, since we cannot our-

selves form an image "simple" (for example, a color or
taste or smell image) but only image composites, we cannot imagine an unfamiliar color or taste or smell and we
can imagine composite things only when we have the
simples on hand needed to construct an appropriate
image composite.

I think it is clear that this theory of "image mechanics,"
if successful as an account of how it is we can imagine
some things and not others, would provide a reason for
saying flatly that to imagine x is to do *to* a mental copy of
x something like seeing (or hearing, and so forth) it. But
is the theory successful? In particular, does the story
about inner copies do any real explanatory work? Or does
it simply exploit an attractive metaphor to state a generalization about the limits of what we can imagine?

I think it might be instructive to attempt a full answer
to that last battery of questions. There is, however, a
prior question to be considered—namely, this: Is the theory at least right about what we can and cannot imagine?
That is, are we in fact able to imagine what, according to
the theory, we should be able to imagine and unable to
imagine what, according to the theory, we should be unable to imagine?

Let us consider the following cases:

(1) You can't possibly imagine who's coming to supper tonight! Your Aunt Matilda!
(2) I can't imagine Queen Victoria in a bikini.
(3) An Eskimo can't imagine what pineapples
taste like. (Or: An Eskimo can't imagine the taste
of pineapple.)

It may be initially tempting to think (1) equivalent
to this: "You can't possibly imagine the person who is
coming to supper tonight." But that is really not so. The
point in (1) is not that the party addressed cannot imagine Aunt Matilda, who is, after all, the person coming to
supper. It is rather that he cannot imagine what the an-

swer is to the question "Who is coming to supper to-night?"[15]

If being unable to imagine who is coming to supper tonight were a matter of being unable to imagine Aunt Matilda, image mechanics might at least seem relevant to this case, even though it would have one able to do what, *ex hypothesi*, one is unable to do. Or if being unable to imagine who is coming to supper tonight were a matter of being unable to form in imagination the name "Aunt Matilda," image mechanics would again be relevant (though, again, it would have one able to do what, *ex hypothesi*, one is unable to do). But in fact image mechanics is simply irrelevant to this case.

Consider now the second case:

(2) I can't imagine Queen Victoria in a bikini.

It is certainly outlandish to suggest that Queen Victoria might have clad herself in something so un-Victorian as a bikini. But the problem is not, as image mechanics suggests, that we lack the parts out of which to construct an image of Victoria in a bikini. In fact, if the image-mechanics account were correct, anyone who had seen, or seen pictures of (1) a woman in a bikini and (2) the face of Victoria should be able to imagine Victoria in a bikini. But, of course, to say that one cannot imagine Victoria in a bikini is to say something about what would be completely out of character for her. An inventory of general image parts "on hand" in one's mind is quite irrelevant to what would be in character and what out of character for Queen Victoria to wear.

Consider now this last case:

(3) An Eskimo can't imagine what pineapples taste like. (Or: An Eskimo can't imagine the taste of pineapple.)

[15] Compare John Austin's discussion of the relative "what" and the interrogative "what" in "Other Minds," *Collected Papers* (Oxford, 1961), p. 64.

According to the traditional account of image formation, one is unable to form an image of *any* unfamiliar taste or color or sound or smell or feeling. The reason is that an image is a sort of picture or representation. And, although we get new colors by mixing pigments and new tastes by mixing foodstuffs and spices, we do not get new colors by putting together color patches or new tastes by putting together taste representations or images. All this, we might suppose, explains (3). But will such an explanation do?

Suppose, for example, that the project is to imagine what nectarines taste like. Anyone who is familiar with the taste of peaches and the taste of plums should be able to manage this, with proper instructions, at least, since nectarines taste like a cross between peaches and plums. Or suppose that the project is to imagine what my morning cup of coffee would taste like with one more teaspoon of sugar in it than I have ever put in before. I do not have to be very imaginative to be able to manage this.

In a famous passage in the *Enquiry* Hume himself points out this difficulty in image mechanics. Here are his words:

Suppose . . . a person . . . to have become perfectly acquainted with colours of all kinds except one particular shade of blue, for instance, which it never has been his fortune to meet with. Let all the different shades of that colour, except that single one, be placed before him, descending gradually from the deepest to the lightest; it is plain that he will perceive a blank, where that shade is wanting, and will be sensible that there is a greater distance in that place between the contiguous colors than in any other. Now I ask, whether it be possible for him, from his own imagination, to supply this deficiency, and raise up to himself the idea of that particular shade, though it had never been conveyed to him by his senses? I believe there are few but will be of opinion that he can: and this may serve as a proof that the simple ideas are not always, in every instance, derived from the correspondent impressions.[16]

What Hume proposes for blue could also be proposed for other colors and for tastes, smells, sounds, and feelings. And anyway, one clear exception is as damaging to the theory as a hundred.

So the image-mechanics account of how it is we can imagine some things and not others fails. It is irrelevant to some cases, and in other cases it would have us able to imagine what we cannot imagine and unable to imagine what we can.[17]

[16] *Enquiries Concerning the Human Understanding and Concerning the Principles of Morals*, ed. by L. A. Selby-Bigge (Oxford, 1902), p. 21.

[17] One might think to improve the image theorist's position by withdrawing the story of "image mechanics" as a *general* account of what we can and cannot imagine and by offering it instead as an account of what we can and cannot imagine in some *limited sense* of the word "imagine." Taking the verb "to visualize" as our model we might coin the words "to audialize," "to olfactorize," "to gustatize," and "to senticize." Then we could say that to imagine *x* in the appropriately limited sense of "imagine" (call it "imagine*") is either to visualize *x* or to audialize *x* or to olfactorize *x* or to gustatize *x* or to senticize *x*.

I think there is, as a matter of fact, no such sense of the verb "to imagine." But let us suppose, for purposes of argument, that there were such a sense. A moment's reflection will reveal that the story of image mechanics will not provide a satisfactory account of what one could and could not imagine*. A single example will suffice, I think, to show that this is so. To imagine* a certain selection of new furniture arranged in a bare apartment would be to (e.g.) visualize it there. But I may be unable to do that even though I have had not only a good look at the colors, shapes, etc., that might be thought to make up a picture of the furnished apartment, but also a good look at the furniture itself and the apartment as well (though not, of course, a good look at the furniture *in* the apartment). People often have trouble visualizing a familiar room with but one new piece of furniture added to it, perhaps even the piece they are standing in front of as they try to decide whether or not to buy it.

It seems that image mechanics is thus no more satisfactory as an account of what one can and cannot imagine* than it is as an account of what one can and cannot imagine.

An imagist account of the imagination, I have been arguing, is threatened by trivialization. If a given case of imagining x is a case of doing something like seeing or hearing or smelling or tasting or feeling x, then, trivially (by the Rule of Ikonic Transfer), it is also a case of doing something like seeing (or hearing; and so forth) *something like x*. To avoid this trivialization the image theorist must suggest some non-trivial role for the concept of a mental copy.

Traditionally image theorists have tried to use the concept of a mental copy in explaining how it is we can imagine some things and not others. Their account, if satisfactory, might supply a non-trivial role for the concept of a mental copy and might thereby provide some warrant for the claim that in imagining x one is doing *to* something like x something like perceiving it. But our discussion suggests that the account does not fit the facts.

My over-all conclusion thus remains as before. We may as well content ourselves with saying simply that in some cases to imagine x is to do something like seeing, hearing, tasting, smelling, or feeling x. We should not add, thinking to clarify matters, that what is like seeing x (or hearing x, and so forth) is the inner perception of a copy x. Either the addition is not an addition at all, or else what it adds is only the basis for a faulty account of how it is we can imagine some things and not others.[18]

[18] The original version of this paper was prepared for delivery at the University of Illinois at Chicago Circle, whose Philosophy Colloquium is supported by a grant from the Carnegie Foundation. The present version owes a great deal to discussions of earlier versions at Chicago Circle, Brown, Dartmouth, McGill, and the University of Illinois at Urbana.

CATEGORIES

P. F. STRAWSON

Ryle's introduction of the topic. The matter is introduced by Ryle in his 1938 article in a sufficiently striking way. It is, he says, a matter of some importance, "for not only is it the case that category-propositions (namely, assertions that terms belong to certain categories or types) are always philosopher's propositions, but, I believe, the converse is also true. So we are in the dark about the nature of philosophical problems and methods if we are in the dark about types or categories."[1] In *Philosophical Argument* (1946) he seems, though less explicitly, committed to the same view. It appears again, robustly enough, in the Introduction to *The Concept of Mind* (1949): "Philosophy is the replacement of category-habits by category-disciplines."[2] It is echoed in his declaration, made in the first chapter of that work, that the "official theory" he is bent on destroying is "one big mistake . . . namely a category-mistake;"[3] or, perhaps, a "family" or "batch" of category-mistakes.[4]

A few years later the note has changed. The idiom of sameness and difference of category "can be helpful as a familiar mnemonic with some beneficial associations." There is no "exact professional way of using it"; but there is "an inexact, amateurish way of using it" in which, though "it gives the answers to none of our questions," it can nevertheless be made to arouse people to the questions in a properly brusque way.[5]

It looks as though Ryle came later to abandon, if he

[1] "Categories," *P.A.S.* 1937–38, p. 189.
[2] *Concept of Mind,* p. 8.
[3] *Ibid.,* p. 16.
[4] *Ibid.,* pp. 18, 23.
[5] *Dilemmas,* p. 9.

ever held, the view that there could be such a thing as a
theory of categories—a clear and general explanation of
the notions of sameness and difference of category and
hence of the notions of category-confusion and category-
mistake. Did he ever hold it? It is clear that there is one
view he never held: the view, namely, that there is some
definite short list of nameable categories, comparable
with a traditional grammarian's list of word-classes or
parts of speech. The following sentence from *Dilemmas*,
with the substitution of "category" for *"métier,"* could be
introduced without incongruity in any of his earlier treatments of the subject: "The truth is that there are not
just two or just ten different logical *métiers* open to the
terms or concepts we employ in ordinary and technical
discourse, there are indefinitely many such *métiers* and
indefinitely many dimensions of these differences."[6]

Still, to hold that there are indefinitely many differences of a certain sort is not the same thing as to hold
that the general nature of that sort of difference must
be indefinitely resistant to explanation. A hard-liner
might indeed say that no one who holds the second view
has a right to the first. Whatever the reply to this may
be, if there is one, and whatever the state of Ryle's views
on the question when he came to write *Dilemmas*, it
seems reasonable to suppose that at the time of composi-
tion of the earlier works cited he did think that some
general theoretical account could be given of the notions
of category, of category-difference and category-mistake.
It was not for the sake of elegant verbal variation that he
declared philosophical problems to be category-problems
and philosophical error to rest on category-confusion. He
held, at least, that the notions of the category group
could be connected, in an explanatory way, with certain
other notions already available in the professional vocabulary.

The most striking of these connexions were those be-

6 *Ibid.*, p. 10.

tween the logical types or categories of proposition-factors and the logical forms and powers (or "liaisons") of propositions; where the "logical powers" of a proposition were explained as the set of facts about what other propositions it followed from, was incompatible with, and implied. The connexions were declared to be very close indeed; to amount, in fact, to identities. In *Categories* we find the following passages:

> To know all about the logical form of a proposition and to know all about the logical types of its factors are to know one and the same thing. (p. 196)
> Now, any respect in which two propositions differ in form will be reflected in differences in their liaisons. So two propositions which are formally similar in all respects save that one factor in one is different in type from a partially corresponding factor in the other, will have liaisons which are correspondingly dissimilar. Indeed the liaisons do not merely *reflect* the formal properties of the proposition and, what this involves, those of all its factors. In a certain sense, they are the same thing. To know all about its liaisons is to know all about the formal structure of the proposition, and *vice versa*. . . .
> The operation of extracting the type of a factor cannot exclude the operation of revealing the liaisons of propositions embodying it. In essence they are one operation. (p. 205)

and in *Philosophical Arguments* the following:

> In fact the distinction between the logical types of ideas is identical with the discrimination between the logical forms of the propositions from which the ideas are abstractions. If one proposition has factors of different types from those of another proposition, those propositions are of different logical forms and have different sorts of logical powers. The rules governing the conjunctions of propositions in valid arguments re-

flect the logical constitutions of their various abstracti-
ble factors and features. There are as many types of
terms as there are forms of propositions, just as there
are as many uphill as downhill slopes.[7]

It seems clear that Ryle cannot, in these passages, be
using the expression "logical form" as a formal logician
uses it. Any two propositions exemplifying the schemata
"*p* or *q*" and "*p* and *q*" are classically different in form; as
are any two propositions exemplifying the schemata "All
F are *G*" and "Some *F* are *G*." But if we exclude the connectives and the quantifying adjectives themselves, there
need be no difference between the types of the proposition-factors in one proposition of such a pair and the
types of the proposition-factors in the other proposition
of that pair; for they may be the very same factors. If we
make no such exclusion, we have, certainly, the difference
between "or" and "and" in the one case and "all" and
"some" in the other. It may be questioned whether the
notion of type or category has any application to such
factors as these. But assuming an application for it—such
as both texts seem to favour—then one might surely have
expected that if any pair of non-synonymous expressions
exhibit non-difference of type or category, "or" and "and"
would be one such pair and "all" and "some" another.

There is a complementary reason, equally potent, for
holding that "logical form" must in these passages receive an interpretation enlarged beyond the formal logician's. Just as it appears to be false that differences of
form of proposition (in the logician's sense of "form")
carry with them differences of type of proposition-factor,
so it appears to be false that differences of type of
proposition-factor carry with them differences of form of
proposition (in this sense of "form"). The mathematical
proposition "There exists just one number which is both
even and prime" is of the same form as the theological
proposition "There exists just one person who is both

[7] *Logical Positivism*, ed. Ayer, p. 333.

human and divine"; but surely some of their factors exhibit category-difference if any factors do.

Ryle cannot mean by "logical form" what a logician means by this phrase; for a logician, in exhibiting form, is concerned to abstract from *all* differences in subject-matter and hence all differences in type or category of subject-matter.

If we now seek help by invoking the remaining identity —the identity of the logical form of a proposition with the totality of its logical powers—we are in no better case. We are still obliged to say that "or" and "and" belong to different categories, if the notion applies to them; and we are now also obliged to say that "29" and "31" are expressions of different types, as are also "red" and "green," "tall" and "short," "father" and "mother," "round" and "square" and so on. For it is easy to construct pairs of propositions of which the factors are identical save that one member of one of these pairs of expressions replaces the other and which are also such that each member of a proposition-pair has different powers or liaisons from the other. But then, if their liaisons are different, their forms (in our new sense of "form") are also different; and if their forms are different, there is a difference in the types of their proposition-factors; and this difference must be located in the only place where there is any difference at all.

It may be said that this is to press unsympathetically hard on the interpretation of the identities which appear to be announced in the quoted passages. It is not a matter of *all* differences in the liaisons of a pair of propositions implying a difference in their form and hence a difference in the types of their factors. Only certain *sorts* of differences in proposition-powers imply these further differences.

Certainly this is a more sympathetic interpretation, and we must adopt it. But in adopting it, we forfeit the expected benefit of the connexions. We hoped for light on the relatively ill-understood notions of type or category of proposition-factor, to be cast by the relatively well-understood notions of the logical forms and powers of propositions. But if the explanatory application of these notions is to be understood as subject to certain enlargements and restrictions, our understanding of the problematic notion is no firmer than our grasp of these enlargements and restrictions. Just *what* sorts of differences in propositions' powers, we must ask, imply differences in their logical forms (in the relevant sense) and hence differences in the types of their factors?

Unfortunately no direct answer is offered to this question. And what indirect hints there are seem unconvincing, seem to point, even, in the wrong direction. In *Philosophical Arguments* it is repeatedly suggested that, since to mistake the logical type of a proposition-factor will be implicitly to credit propositions containing it with logical powers they do not possess, the working out of the consequences of the mistaken interpretation will eventually issue in contradiction; for (e.g.) the mistakenly attributed powers will be found to be irreconcilable with the genuinely possessed powers. Hence the instrument *par excellence* of the exposure of type-confusion is the *reductio ad absurdum* argument. But this thesis is not stated in such a way as to be easily assessed. It is not convincingly illustrated. And it leaves one with a strong sense of misdirection; for contradiction, in its clearest cases, seems to be a relation of terms, or of propositions in respect of terms, between which we are the least disposed to find differences of type or category. Finally, even if the thesis could be made out, it would leave us with the same question as before on our hands. For it is not maintained that all *reductio ad absurdum* arguments reveal type-confusions in their premises, that all contradictions emerge from category-mistakes. So we should still have to ask which are the ones that do, and why these and not the others.

However, there are different kinds of absurdity, and, hence, different kinds of reduction to absurdity. When Ryle speaks of the absurdities which result from violating category-restrictions, it is clear that he does not always have in mind that rather stiff and formal kind of absurdity which we find at, or just before, the terminus of a *reductio ad absurdum* argument. When he offers, in the most frequently quoted of all the sentences he has written on the topic, his criterion for difference of type or category of proposition-factors, it is again clear that it is not this kind of absurdity he has in mind. If it were, the criterion would yield immediately unacceptable results.[8] There must be a *distinctive* sort of absurdity which a sentence suffers from, when "at least one ingredient expression in it is not of the right type to be coupled or to be coupled in that way with the other ingredient expression or expressions in it."[9] In putting us on the track of this distinctive kind of absurdity—which he does by means of a host of vivid examples scattered throughout his writings—Ryle does more to point the way towards a general theory of the topic than he does by the over-general references to logical forms and powers. He points the way, but does not follow it. Instead, he ends his classical article on the subject with a question: "What are the tests of absurdity?"

Something of the unresolved character of Ryle's treatment can, I think, be understood. Listening attentively to what he has said on the topic, one can detect, not just one theme, but two or even three. First there is a concern with philosophy in general; a sense that philosophical problems typically arise from limitations or imperfections—which may be recognized as such, or not recog-

---

[8] The sentence, from "Categories," runs: "Two proposition-factors are of different categories or types, if there are sentence-frames such that when the expressions for those factors are imported as alternative complements to the same gap-signs, the resultant sentences are significant in the one case and absurd in the other" (*op. cit.*, p. 203). One should try importing first "27" and then "37" as complements to the gap-sign in "She is over . . . and under 33 years old"; or first "mother" and then "father" into "It's not your . . . but your father"; or first "Green" and then "Red" into ". . . is a more restful colour than red."

[9] *Op. cit.*, p. 200.

nized—in our reflective understanding of our own equipment of ideas or forms of thought; or, what is the same thing, from limitations or imperfections in our reflective understanding of the force, and modes of functioning, and mutual relations, of the items which make up our own equipment of linguistic expressions and constructions. In particular we may be prone to overlook differences, to assume or imagine non-existent parities. So it may be useful to multiply classifications, in the process of forestalling, or correcting, mistaken assimilations. And so we may come to speak of different *types* of expression in a sense of this phrase generous enough to harbour *any* classification which a philosopher finds it useful to employ or worthwhile to invent. When Ryle says, as in the sentence I began by quoting, that type-concerns are the philosopher's whole concern, it must be at least such a capacious sense of the phrase as this that he has in mind; as also when he shows himself prepared to speak of the logical type of connectives or quantifiers or token-reflexive words. Even this generous conception of a type, however, seems not wholly adequate to cover the field of a philosopher's activity. The classical procedure of analysis, for instance—as applied to a concept like "cause" or "intention"—seems incompletely characterized by reference to such a conception. Here, then, is a motive for extending the notion of a type yet further, so that our knowledge of the type of a problematic concept embraces knowledge of the unobvious liaisons of propositions in which it figures. And this extension Ryle effects, as we have seen, through the mediating notion of form. But by now—indeed before now—the notion of a category or type has become over-extended.

The second theme, included in the first, yet emerges with a certain distinctness in *Dilemmas*, where Ryle is concerned with the apparent conflicts which may arise between different specialist accounts of the same thing or between a specialist and a non-specialist account. Propositions emerging from backgrounds thus diverse, yet concerned with what is in some sense the same subject-matter, may appear to have incompatible consequences regarding the nature of that subject-matter. But when they do, this is often because we have, in our thinking, allowed one or both of the apparently conflicting propositions, and the terms they contain, to become detached from the background of theoretical or practical concern from which they derive their life and their force. Concepts which do not clash during their working hours may generate imaginary conflicts as they idle through the speculative mind; and the discipline re-imposed by the critical philosopher—who, indeed, may have to be prepared for certain reforming adjustments—is a species of category-discipline. Evidently this application of the notion of a category has some affinities with Wittgenstein's conception of a "language-game" or of a "form of life." (I do not at all mean to suggest, what would clearly be false, that in *Dilemmas* Ryle is thus intentionally re-interpreting the notion of a category; only that we have here an aspect of his use of the term which comes most prominently to the fore in that work.)

There remains the third theme. It is not something quite separate from the other two, but, rather, something which can be extracted from them and which offers, as they, being so general and indeterminate, do not offer, at least the hope of systematic elucidation. We hear this theme whenever we are confronted with an example of a sentence which is absurd in the sense already alluded to, which resists literal, and sometimes invites figurative, interpretation, and which lends itself to a certain familiar style of elaborated disjunctive negation: as

> People are born and die and sometimes wear boots; *meanings* are not born and do not die and they *never wear boots—or go barefoot either.*[10]
> *Letters are not easy to spell nor insuperably hard to spell.*[11]

[10] "Theory of Meaning," in *British Philosophy in the Mid-century*, p. 245.
[11] *The Concept of Mind*, p. 206.

Here, and in all such examples, we have, stimulated in "a properly brusque way," that sense of conceptual disparateness which is the sense of our topic, if we have a topic. But have we? Is the sense of a distinctive kind of absurdity to be trusted?

Doubts and difficulties; clues and encouragements. The doubts go more, or less, deep. The deepest-going of all are the doubts—or, rather, the negative certainties—of those who find no irreducible difference properly described as the difference between propositions acceptable or rejectable "in virtue of meaning alone" and propositions acceptable or rejectable in virtue of the constitution of things.[12] Why bother to distinguish categorial absurdity from, or as a special case of, analytic falsity, if the more general distinction which both notions presuppose is itself an illusion? Why distinguish vaporous illusions within a vaporous illusion?

These doubts I shall disregard. To put it with maximum concessiveness: we miss too much if we refuse to try to draw distinctions at one level of philosophical analysis because of a persuasion that viewed from another, sufficiently lofty, level, those differences will appear simply as differences of degree or will be in some other way, as it used to be said, "transcended."

To disregard these doubts is to allow ourselves the distinction between what is rejectable or acceptable "in virtue of meaning alone"—or, as I shall say, what is a priori acceptable or rejectable—and what is not. Then the domestic difficulties begin; and they are difficulties of a familiar kind. The notions we seek to explain form an interconnected group: the notion of category-inappropriateness or category-absurdity, the notion of sameness or difference of type or category, and the notion of a categorial predicate. The difficulty is to explain any one of these without the explanation's resting on one of the

[12] Here and in what follows, "acceptable" = "true"; and whether or not "rejectable" = "false," "false" implies "rejectable."

others in the way in which Ryle's explanation of type-difference rests on the notion of category-absurdity. Consider, by way of illustration, the problem of distinguishing sentences which are a priori rejectable because they involve contradiction but no type-absurdity from those which are a priori rejectable because they involve a category absurdity. Thus we wish to say that the sentence "She is younger than her own daughter" cannot, taken literally, express a truth because it is, taken literally, self-contradictory; whereas the sentence "The number 5 is more than twice as tall as the number 2" cannot, taken literally, express a truth, because numbers are not of the right type to have spatial dimensions predicated of them, because such predication is categorially absurd. Pressed for a further account of the difference which does not rest on a free invocation of the problematic notions, we may say that a contradiction is distinguishable from a category absurdity by the fact that from it we can derive, by linguistically certifiable steps, a *formal* contradiction. But cannot we do the same in the case of the category absurdity? Cannot we derive from it the consequence that there is something which (as being a number) does not have, and (as being taller than something else) does have, spatial dimensions? To this the reply might be that we can derive the formal contradiction in this case only by making use of a predicate ("having spatial dimensions") which, as being a *categorial* predicate, is not to be permitted in such test-derivations. What, then, is a categorial predicate? A traditional answer here is that it is a predicate which is a priori acceptable of some subjects and which is either a priori rejectable or a priori acceptable of any subject. But now we need some restrictive interpretation of this last phrase. For if I say "What John is thinking of has spatial dimensions" or "The first item mentioned on p. 22 of John's book has spatial dimensions," I do not say something a priori acceptable or a priori rejectable. And the question arises: can we impose the necessary restriction without once more invoking a notion of the problematic group?

If there are doubts and difficulties, there are also clues and encouragements. The grammarians, and linguistic theorists, are willing enough to distinguish classes of linguistically deviant sentences in terms of a technical apparatus worked out (not indeed fully, but at least partially) with quite other purposes in view than the protection of philosophical investments. The distinctions the philosopher wishes to draw between the grammatically irregular, the category-absurd and the merely contradictory are in a fair way to finding their counterparts in distinctions between kinds of rule-violation involved in the generation of sentences so classified.[13] Thus reinforced, the category-minded philosopher may feel in a position to serve the deep-going doubters from their own table. The latter accept a distinction between the true and the false, between sentences which stand up to the pressures of experience and those which do not. They question only whether any clear distinction can be drawn between those which collapse without, as it were, being touched and the other non-survivors (the "empirically falsified"); and, *a fortiori*, question whether any clear distinctions can be drawn *within* the former class. Yet, if the undifferentiated notion of *falsity* is to be tolerable at all, it would seem that they must accept one further distinction; viz., that between a (declarative) sentence and a non-sentence, between strings of words which qualify for assessment as true or false and those which fail to fulfil some minimal grammatical requirement for such assessment. But then surely mere intuitions of minimum grammaticalness should be regarded with no less suspi-

[13] Cf. in Chomsky, *Aspects of the Theory of Syntax*, the distinction between "strict subcategorization rules" and "selectional rules" (p. 95) and its suggested application in distinguishing types of grammatical "deviance" (p. 153); also the contrast with "purely semantic incongruity" (pp. 76–77), of which the examples given are all in fact contradictions.

cion than those other linguistic intuitions which provide the basis for differentiation within the favoured, undifferentiated concept of falsity. It may be said: linguists can construct sets of rules which yield results conformable with intuitions of minimum grammaticalness. But the rejoinder to this we have already before us. It would be rash indeed to maintain that linguists cannot construct sets of rules which yield results conformable with the other intuitions in question.

Discouragement from (some) logicians, then, may be offset by encouragement from (some) linguists. And against the domestic difficulties we may set the strength, and the *form*, of the relevant intuitions. The form, especially; for this gives us a clue we badly need to the direction in which we should look. When category-points are made with that "proper brusqueness" which Ryle commends, it is the inappropriateness of some range of *predicates* to some class of *subjects* that is normally stressed in the style of the making. "Xs are not the sort of thing that can be Φ"; "*xs* neither Φ nor fail to Φ"; "'Φing' (or 'being Φ') cannot be significantly predicated of *xs*." This is the brusque style of making category-points; and there is no such point that cannot be made in this style, even though category-mismatch may manifest itself in other *grammatical* relations, e.g., as between verb and adverb or noun and modifying adjective. If we can give a non-circular account of category-inappropriateness in predication, of category-mismatch as between subject and predicate, we may assume that the explanation of the other notions of the problematic group will present comparatively little difficulty.

A satisfactory philosophical account will have two aspects. First, it will fit our intuitions. It will distinguish the cases we want to distinguish from other cases. That is the technical problem. Second, it will have some explanatory force. It will give us some understanding of the distinctive character which category-points seem to have and of their place in philosophy. I do not think I can produce anything like complete solutions either to the technical or to the explanatory problem. I can at most sketch some lines of approach which may possibly lead in the right direction. This, at any rate, is what I shall try to do.

Category-mismatch and categorial predicates. We attend, then, to singular subject-predicate propositions in which some single item is somehow specified by the subject-expression (a definite singular term) and somehow characterized by the predicate-expression. One favored way of characterizing category-mismatch for these propositions is as follows. We have such a mismatch when the individual item specified by the subject-expression is of such a sort that both the affirmation and the denial of the predicate in question of that individual are a priori rejectable. Such a characterization raises questions. We must be careful that the expression "of such a sort" does not conceal a reference to another notion of the group of notions to be explicated and hence import the kind of circularity we are to avoid. We must be prepared to take account of scepticism regarding the implied distinction between two styles of a priori rejection of an affirmative predication, viz., that in which the rejection is consistent with rejecting the denial as well as the affirmation of the predicate and that in which it amounts to just the same thing as the denial of the predicate.

Perhaps we can ultimately guard ourselves on both these points by attending to a prior question. To predicate having a certain colour of a number or having a certain temperature of an after-image would, one is inclined to say, be a clear case of category-mismatch if anything was. Yet if I say "The item I have in mind is blue," what I say is not a priori rejectable in any style, even if the item I have in mind is a number; and if I say "The green thing currently engaging my attention is at a temperature of 10°C," what I say is not a priori rejectable even though it is in fact a green after-image which is currently engaging my attention.[14] Clearly, then, the proposed characterization of category-mismatch is to be understood as relative to some restricted style of specification of individuals. Let us consider the suggestion that an individual is specified in the required style when it is specified by an "adequately identifying" designation. I have now to explain this phrase.

A sufficient condition of a designation's being adequately identifying is that it *completely specifies* the individual it designates. Only those individuals of which the identity is completely determined by their *essential* properties (or character) can be "completely specified," in the sense in which I am using this phrase; and any designation of such an individual completely specifies it when the *essential* properties (or character) of that individual are determinable a priori from the meaning of the designation. The following expressions satisfy this condition for being adequately identifying: "the proposition that snow is white"; "the number 5"; "justice"; "the colour blue"; "the number which, when multiplied by 12, yields 36."

There would be objections, both remote and immediate, to making it a necessary condition of a designation's being adequately identifying that it should be completely specifying. An immediate objection is that there can be no completely specifying designations of (empirical, or spatio-temporal) particulars. However, there are many general terms or descriptions under which particulars fall, and many others under which non-particular individuals fall, which embody in their meaning principles for distinguishing or picking out individuals which fall under them from other things, for counting or enumerating such individuals (though perhaps only under favourable circumstances) and for identifying such an individual en-

---

[14] It may be that a satisfactory characterization of the notion of logical subject would rule out such "subject-expressions." But I do not wish to discuss this here.

countered in one connexion or referred to under one description as the same item as one encountered in another connexion or referred to under another description. Thus for particulars we have such general terms as animal, person, island, storm, shipwreck, river, day and a host of others, more or less specific. For non-particular individuals we have such general terms as sentence, natural number, flag, sonnet, sonata, disease, game, word, and many others, more or less specific. (It is to be noted that some of these general terms under which non-particular individuals can be individuated are also terms under which particular individuals can be individuated.) Any specification of an individual item, whether a particular or a non-particular, which embodies or implies any such general characterization of that individual I shall say is adequately identifying. Thus the expression "The natural number I have in mind" is an adequately identifying expression in the stipulated sense, and so is "That number which is in fact the number of planetary satellites in the Milky Way," even though no one knows what that number is and the expression is not likely to have much use for the ordinary purposes of identifying reference. Of definite singular terms which include no general terms we may count ordinary proper names—e.g., "Socrates," "France"—as adequately identifying on the ground that they cannot be commonly understood by different users unless they are taken as implying a term of the kind just described; or, as some would say, their sense in use includes the sense of such a term.

The requirement that an adequately identifying designation, if not completely specifying, should embody or imply a general term of the kind I have just described is still too stringent. Let us call terms which clearly satisfy that description "clearly individuating terms." There are other terms which, in one way or another fall short of being clearly individuating, yet are such that if a designation of an individual brings that individual under one of these terms, that designation is to count as adequately identifying. One relatively uninteresting case in which a term may fall short of being clearly individuating is the case in which the criteria of identity to be associated with the term are in dispute. Thus philosophers dispute about the criteria of identity for propositions and hence, perhaps, for facts. This does not mean that there are no such criteria; only that the criteria are, so to speak, adjustable, depending on the purposes for which we wish to use the notion or the place we wish to give it in our theories. What we have here is the case where the meaning of the term is unsettled or disputed, but where any settlement of it would yield a clearly individuating term.

More interesting and more extensive is the class of cases in which (a) the meaning of the term is not in dispute, (b) the term does not of itself supply quite definite criteria of distinctness and identity for items falling under it but (c) the term is such as to supply principles for determining such criteria. The last provision is perhaps not very clearly stated, and I must illustrate it. Another way of putting it would be this: the term allows for a certain measure of play in the criteria of distinctness and identity for items falling under it, but determines the dimensions of play. Examples of such terms would be: for non-particular individuals, the terms "colour" and "sound" or "noise"; for particular individuals, the terms "sound" or "noise" again and, say, the term "extent of ground." Take the term "colour." It will not do to say that there are no criteria of distinctness and identity for colours; only that they are more or less elastic and not wholly determined in advance by the term "colour" itself. Or take the term "sound" as used to refer to particulars. Here again, and more determinately, there is a variety of possible principles for counting and identifying particular items to which the term applies. When two instruments play together, we may speak of the single sound they jointly make or of the two separate sounds they severally make. Or where one speaker refers to a succession of temporally separated sounds, each lasting for a few seconds, another may speak of a single discontinuous sound, lasting for, say, a minute-and-a-half. The concept of a sound in general is indeterminate in relation to this variety of possible principles; but it determines the range of the possible variation of principle. We know a priori what is permissibly but not obligatorily used to count for difference (e.g., difference of source, discriminable timbre, variation of pitch, discontinuity). Consider, finally, the somewhat different case of the concept of *an extent of ground*. This leaves open to us any way we please of tracing out the boundaries of such extents, and thereby determining particular individuals which fall under the term; but it also *requires* that we adopt some boundary-indicating procedure if we are to specify *any* individual under the term. And in contrast with this tolerance of boundary-indicating procedures for initially distinguishing such individuals, the concept is very strict as regards their subsequent identity-conditions. We are free to distinguish individuals of this kind by tracing boundaries as we please; but once created, then, unlike the boundaries of fields, counties or countries, they can never change. (Of course the phrase itself is ambiguous. In "The extent of ground now occupied by College X was formerly parcelled out in small lots" we have the sense of the phrase we are concerned with; in "The extent of ground occupied by College X has grown over the years" we have not.)

I am aware that I have only indicated, rather than clearly defined, the character of the class of terms which I have been illustrating. Nevertheless I hope that my indications are clear enough to justify my naming the class. I shall call it the class of variably individuating terms, and I shall define individuating terms in general as the logical sum of clearly individuating and variably individuating terms. A sufficient and necessary condition for the designation of an individual item to be an adequately identifying designation is that it either completely specifies that item or that it embodies or implies an individuating term under which the item is presented as falling.

Next, some remarks about the relevance or appropriateness of this notion. It is, I think, now generally recognized that any adequate theory of categories must provide for a distinction which may be described as the distinction between relative and absolute categories.[15] Two items belong to some one relative category if there is a predicate or set of predicates such that that predicate or every member of that set of predicates can be predicated without category-mismatch of both items. Two items belong to the same absolute category if every predicate which can be predicated without category-mismatch of one can also be predicated without category-mismatch of the other. Evidently two items belong to the same absolute category only if they have all their relative categories in common; and any single item can belong to a number of different relative categories but only to one absolute category.

The items thus assignable to categories are not necessarily expressions or concepts, though they will include both expressions and concepts. They are individuals in the sense in which I have throughout been using this expression. An individual is anything whatever; i.e., anything which can in principle, in any way whatever, be distinguished, as the single thing it is, from all other items and identified as the same item under different presentations or descriptions or in different manifestations. Belonging or not belonging to some relative or absolute category is not a characteristic which an individual can, as it were, put on or shrug off; it is a characteristic which belongs essentially to the individual and covers its whole temporal span, if it has one. Further, it

[15] See, for example, Sommers, "Predicability," in *Philosophy in America*, ed. Black, p. 280; and the same author's definitions of α-types and β-types in "Types and Ontology" (*Philosophical Review*, 1963).

is a feature which adheres essentially to the individual not in virtue of its being the particular individual that it is, but in virtue of its being the *sort* of individual that it is. The word "sort" is not by itself very helpful; for any sort of sorting constitutes a sort. But one sort of sorting imposes itself here; viz., the sort of sorting to which individuals in general, we may say, owe their very existence (i.e., their discriminability and identifiability) as individuals. And this is just the sort of sorting provided for by individuating terms: terms which embody or imply principles for distinguishing, counting and identifying individuals, as clearly individuating terms do, or terms which supply principles for determining such principles, as variably individuating terms do. It seems prima facie reasonable to suppose that the a priori assignment of individuals to categories depends on some knowledge of what sort of individual, in *this* sense of "sort," we have to deal with.

However, a qualification is necessary here. For it is not quite true that all individuals owe their existence, i.e., their discriminability as individuals, to the sort of sorting provided for by individuating terms. Thus we have the idea of moral qualities or qualities of mind or character. And we can certainly discriminate individual qualities (such as justice, honesty, perseverance, or benevolence) which fall under one or another of the general heads, moral quality, quality of mind or quality of character. But it would not be very plausible to represent the general heads, in these cases, as supplying either clear or variable principles for distinguishing and identifying individuals (e.g., justice or benevolence) which fall under them. For it would be too difficult to state what the principles, or the principles of variation of principle, were. However, it is always possible completely to specify the individual, by naming it or giving a defining description of it, in such a case. And we can be a priori certain that such a complete specification of the individual will imply a priori all the information about its sort, in a now looser sense of "sort," which is relevant to its a priori assignment to a category. This, then, is why I defined "adequately identifying designation of an individual" disjunctively: such a designation *either* brings its individual under an individuating term *or* completely specifies it.

Now from the point we have reached, there is more than one path we might follow. We might try to define the category-inappropriateness of a predicate to an individual directly as follows: an individual i and a predicate P are category-mismatched if, and only if, P and the denial of P are alike a priori rejectable for every adequate indentifying designation of i. Apart from other possible objections, such a definition would leave us unprotected from scepticism of a kind I have already alluded to, viz., scepticism regarding the distinction, within the general class of a priori rejections of an affirmative predication, between those which involve simply the denial of the predicate and those which do not, but are consistent with rejecting that denial. A sceptic on this point will challenge us to show a basis for this distinction of two styles of a priori falsity, to explain why the a priori rejection of the denial of a predicate is not to be taken as equivalent to the affirmation of that predicate.

Clearly it would be desirable, if possible, to circumvent this demand by freeing the definition of category-mismatch from dependence on such a distinction. (In doing so, one will incidentally go some way to meeting the demand and explaining the distinction.) Prima facie it should be possible to do this. For when one makes a category point in the brusque, informal way by saying of an individual that it is not the sort of thing which can be or fail to be Φ, then there is surely one predication here that one is rejecting in a quite unproblematic style, viz., the predication (of that individual) of the predicate "is the sort of thing which can be or fail to be Φ." It should surely be possible to find a less questionable characterization of that *sort of thing* which would yet yield the same consequences as regards category-mismatch. For example, instead of saying that the predicate "is in the drawing-room" is mismatched to some individual because both that predicate and its negation, viz., "is not in the drawing-room," are alike a priori rejectable for all adequately identifying designations of that individual, we should seem to miss no essential point if we said that the predicate in question is mismatched to that individual because it *implies* a predicate *of a special kind,* viz., "has some spatial location," and this *implied* predicate is a priori rejectable for all adequately identifying designations of that individual. The a priori rejectability of the implied predicate is not a special style of a priori rejectability consistent also with the rejectability of its denial. We do not wish to say that the individual in question neither has nor does not have spatial location. We wish to say, *sans phrase,* that it has no spatial location, and that is why any predicate ascribing a spatial location (such as "is in the drawing-room") is category-mismatched to it.

As our example illustrates, it is easy enough in some cases to find a predicate of the desired kind—a categorial predicate. Even when we cannot find a very natural-sounding predicate of the desired kind, it should be possible to devise one. For if we really have a topic at all, then—to repeat the point—the predicates the non-mismatching applicability of which define a relative category must form a unified range and there must be ways of stating the principle of its unity other than the jejune form of observation that any individual which lies outside its range is neither Φ nor not Φ (for some value or values of Φ). We should not be unduly dismayed if, in framing predicates which incorporate such principles, we find that some of them have a pretty artificial look; nor even if we find that we are *guided* in their selection and construction by that jejune but, after all, intuitively apt form which I have just referred to. Neither fact would mean that we could not *explain,* in a more long-winded

way, the principle we were seeking to compress into a
predicate.

Of course, this reflection, though it indicates a possible
direction of escape from our difficulty, does not actually
get us out of it. We need a *general* characterization of
the kind of predicate in question and one which does not
rest on the distinction held to be questionable. However, if the general line I have hitherto followed is correct, it seems reasonably clear what form that general
characterization should take. Let us define a categorial
predicate as follows. A categorial predicate is a predicate
which satisfies the following two conditions: (1) it is a
priori acceptable for at least some individuals under all
adequately identifying designations of those individuals;
(2) it is either a priori acceptable or a priori rejectable
for any individual whatever under all adequately identifying designations of that individual. The definition of
category-mismatch follows at once. A predicate is
category-mismatched to an individual if and only if it implies a categorial predicate which is a priori rejectable for
all adequately identifying designations of that individual.[16] Since every predicate implies itself, this means that
we shall have to say that the predication of a categorial
predicate itself may involve category-mismatch, even
though (as already suggested) such a predication does
not involve the distinctive style of absurdity we associate
with category-mismatch. E.g., we shall have to say that
"The number 5 has spatial location" involves category-
mismatch no less than "The number 5 is in the next
room," even though the first does not have, and the sec-

[16] On the basis of a definition of category-mismatch of predicates
to individuals, we can of course easily frame a definition of category-
mismatch as between predicates—and hence, derivatively, as between
predicates and subject-expressions. Two predicates are mismatched if
and only if for every individual to which one is *not* mismatched the
other *is* mismatched; i.e., there is no individual such that neither is
mismatched to that individual. It is easy to see how category-
mismatch between expressions combined in other grammatical relations can be derivatively characterized.

ond does have, that characteristic feature. But this is surely a consequence of no importance, one not worth making special provision to avoid. It is easy enough to explain why the distinctive air of absurdity should attach to one case and not to the other; and I shall not dwell on the point.

Would a theory on the above lines give us what we want? Would it enable us to locate category-mismatch in all the cases in which our intuitions find category-mismatch and in none in which they do not? Well, it is clear that what such a theory *would* give us depends on the notion of an identifying designation, or the class of all identifying designations, of an individual. And this notion in its turn rests on that of principles of identity for individuals. Neither notion, it might be said with some justice, has been adequately clarified, let alone adequately explored. And I shall not explore them now. Instead I shall make some general comments on the acceptability of a theory of categories.

The merit of the sort of theory suggested is that it offers us a way of escape from the circle of problematic notions in which discussions of this topic seem otherwise destined to wander. It is peculiarly important for any theory of categories to find such a way of escape. For if none is found, the very idea of this topic is exposed, not just to that general style of scepticism to which, say, the notion of analyticity and related notions are exposed, but to a specific and argued scepticism. Let me try to sketch the nature of this specific scepticism.

The notion of a question being applicable or not applicable is not one that requires any philosophical justification. Thus if it is said of someone that he is a flute-player, the question with what degree of accuracy of intonation he plays is an applicable question. So, also, if he is said to play any other wind or string instrument. But if someone is known not to play any musical instrument at all, then *eo ipso* that question is not applicable in respect of that person. Similarly if something is acquired by purchase, the question of how high a price was paid is applicable in respect of the transaction; if it is given, the question is not applicable. All propositions purporting to specify the kind of information sought by such a question suffer, if that question is not applicable, from a peculiar kind of inappropriateness defined by this very description of them. Now, given any general classification or description, we can in general correlate with it sets of questions which are at least prima facie applicable and sets of questions which are at least prima facie inapplicable to anything to which that general classification or description applies. And correspondingly we can correlate with that general description sets of sets of predications which will prima facie suffer, or prima facie be free, from the special kind of inappropriateness just referred to.

These notions of applicability and inapplicability of questions and the associated notions of appropriateness or inappropriateness of predications or propositions require, as I have said, no special philosophical justification. Neither does the notion of such correlations as I have mentioned. (Some may indeed say of the correlations that they depend only on the meanings of the expressions involved on either side, while others may be unwilling to say this. But both parties to *this* dispute may admit the existence of such correlations.) Now the sceptic notes that *some* of these correlations between general classification or description on the one hand and applicability or inapplicability, appropriateness or inappropriateness, of question or predication on the other excite a particular interest in some philosophers; and this interest they mark by willingness to employ the terminology of categories, and of category match or mismatch. But this kind of interest is excited only in some cases, not in others. We can take the points that an individual who is dead neither cares about, nor is indifferent to, some issue; that someone blind neither spots nor overlooks the fly in the ointment; that a gift costs its recipient neither a large nor a small sum; that not being a player of any instrument is not being the sort of thing which has perfect or poor intonation. But philosophers show no disposition to treat these as category points. In yet other cases a philosopher might feel, or be induced to feel, hesitation. Thus, as an earlier quotation suggests, Ryle might be disposed to treat "having a spelling" as defining a category; but if we say of a word that, being written, if at all, only in ideograms, it is neither hard nor easy to spell, then will it seem clear that we are making a category-point —or rather one of those points which one is not disposed to treat as category points?

The sceptic suggests, then, that the particular interest excited by some cases of these correlations and not by others reflects nothing but a sense of *depth* or *striking-ness* or, sometimes, of philosophical *importance*, as attaching to some cases and not to others; and that this is why theories of categories tend to move in circles. For this is the result that inevitably ensues when an attempt is made to present as resting on a clear and general distinction a habit of classification which in fact rests on nothing but differences in degree of impressiveness.

If we are to resist such scepticism, a way of escape from the circle must be found; and if one can be found on the lines indicated, then perhaps we should be willing, if necessary, to pay a certain price for it: the price, namely, of readiness to correct *some* intuitions in the light of theory.

In the foregoing I have said nothing about the equivocal or non-equivocal use of terms. It seems to be unnecessary to do so. For where a term is unequivocally predicable, without category mismatch, of items which do not have all their relative categories in common, we should be able to *give an account* of its common sense; whereas when a term is only equivocally so predicable, we cannot do this, but can only give accounts of its disparate senses, supplemented, perhaps, by an explanation of its having these disparate uses.

Categories, grammar, and philosophical criticism. Under this head I have not even the sketch of a theory to offer. But I wish to bring together two kinds of consideration in the hope that they may suggest a way of approach to a part of the explanatory problem.

Theorists of categories have normally differentiated category-absurd sentences from ungrammatical sentences. They have even, surely with some exaggeration, suggested that only grammatically correct sentences are capable of suffering from category-absurdity. Some modern theorists of grammar, on the other hand, have claimed that such sentences owe their oddity to a violation of syntactical rules, i.e., they are a species of ungrammatical sentences. Suitably interpreted, these claims need not conflict. For the grammarians distinguish different kinds of syntactical rule, and hence different kinds of violation of syntactical rule. And in such differences the traditional theorist of categories may find, redescribed, the distinction (between the "ungrammatical" and the "absurd") which he was concerned to draw.

Let us for the moment consider a restricted or traditional notion of grammar according to which category-absurdity is *not* a species of grammatical fault. Then among the strings of words which, according to this notion, would count as ungrammatical sentences if they counted as sentences at all, we can draw certain non-sharp distinctions. Roughly speaking, we can distinguish between those which, while being certainly ungrammatical, are obviously corrigible and those which are not obviously corrigible. Corrigibly ungrammatical sentences abound in the exercises of schoolchildren translating sentences of their native language into sentences of other languages. They result from ignorance, or failure to bear in mind, for example, the fact that French grammar requires the agreement of adjectives in gender and number with their nouns, while English grammar does not; that English grammar lays down a principle for selecting "whom" instead of "which" or conversely in certain relative pronoun positions in which French or Spanish permit

an undifferentiated "que"; that German grammar embodies requirements about the position of verbs in clauses
which are equally alien to English, French, or Spanish
grammar.

When theorists of categories said that category-absurdity presupposes grammaticalness, they did not mean
freedom from obviously corrigible ungrammaticalness.
They did not mean that it was impossible to preserve a
category-mistake in translation while making a grammatical slip. They meant that category-absurd sentences had
to satisfy a certain condition of minimum grammaticalness. They meant that the grammatical classes of sen-
tence-parts or elements supplied—noun-phrases, nouns,
verbs, verb-phrases, adjectives, pronouns, prepositions
etc.—had to be such, and so disposed, that we could read
off the main grammatical relations which were supposed
to hold among the parts or elements of the sentence. For
only under this condition could we even raise the question whether these parts or elements were semantically
such that they could, without category-mismatch, stand
in those relations.

I have remarked that modern grammarians are inclined, or half-inclined, to claim for the domain of syntax
those restrictive rules the violation of which issues in
category-absurdity. Suppose the claim granted. (The
question is admitted to be one of convenience in organisation of the theory of a language.) Then we must point
out that this part of syntax at least must be admitted to
have a semantic basis. That the verb "hit," for example, at
least in its basic, literal employments, is restricted to taking expressions for corporeal things as its grammatical
objects can scarcely be regarded as a truth independent
of the sense of the word.

For this part of syntax the relation is obvious. May not
some such relation also hold for that part which bears on
the satisfaction of conditions of minimum grammaticalness? The notions of the grammatical classes and those
of the grammatical relations are definitionally intercon-

nected. It may be thought improbable that there are no
lines of connexion which join this network to broad
semantic classifications of language-elements. To determine just how and where these lines of connexion run is
no doubt a matter of the greatest difficulty. But if they
run at all—if for example there are certain semantic types
of language-element which are *basically* nominal or verbal
or adjectival—then their discovery may help us to understand better the place of the notion of category absurdity
in philosophy.

To suggest a reason why this may be so, I now introduce the second of the two kinds of consideration I
mentioned. It is often remarked that category-absurd sentences, though they resist literal interpretation, frequently lend themselves to figurative interpretation. Ryle
remarked that many jokes were type-pranks. In the same
spirit one might say that many tropes are type-trespasses.
Some analogy, some imaginative stretch or more or less
remote connexion can often be found, or made, to bring
the categorically absurd in from the cold of the blankly
nonsensical to the wide and welcoming domain of figurative speech. Now philosophers do not often, if ever,
produce, in all seriousness, sentences which flatly offend
against category-propriety. If they use what are plainly
metaphors, as they often do, it is usually as metaphors
that they use them; and hence they are not obliged to
take them any further than they wish. What is consciously
taken up as a figure can, as a figure, be consciously
dropped at any point beyond which it would be unwelcome to pursue it. But it is a commonplace that philosophers are prone to be influenced in their theorising by
models or pictures or figures of which they are not fully,
or at all, conscious as such; to think they are advancing
a literally correct account of some phenomenon when
they are actually engaged in elaborating, or being puzzled
by, features of the figurative mode in terms of which they
are thinking about that phenomenon. It is when the
theorist is thus engaged, when he is unconsciously com-

mitted to this sort of thinking, that the brusque style of making category points is most appropriate and effective. It has the damaging effect of bringing the concealed figure out into the open. And the effect is damaging because you cannot say "Thus far and no farther will I go with my figure" when you did not think it was a figure at all, but thought it was the literal truth about the phenomenon in question.

And now to try to bring these two kinds of consideration together.

"Sincerity" is a noun; "smile" is sometimes a noun; "the death of Caesar" is a noun-phrase. But the noun "sincerity," we say, is formed from the adjective "sincere"; the use of "smile" as a noun is secondary to its use as a verb; the noun-phrase "the death of Caesar" is derived from a clause in which the noun "death" does not figure, though the verb "die" does. Such thoughts as these are given a more systematic shape in the work of modern grammarians, who distinguish between "deep" and "surface" grammatical structure and study their relations under the name of transformations. The operation of revealing deep structure points to certain sentences as having a relatively basic or underived character. These are sentences corresponding to the most deeply embedded sentence-forms in the deep structure of given sentences. If we want to find, as it were, the basic models for (at least some) grammatical relations and classes, it is presumably to such basic sentences that we should look, seeking for general connexions between types of element-meaning and potentialities of grammatical role in such fundamental sentence-structures. Here we should find our primitive nominals, adjectivals, adverbials, transitive and intransitive verbals; and our primitive cases of grammatical combinations and relations. Next, we should seek to understand the analogies, partly logical and partly other than logical, which underlie the vast extension in the scope and coverage of those grammatical classes and relations, an extension which involves bringing in new meaning-elements such as have no place in basic sentences as well as allowing for transformed or derived forms of elements which already have a place. Thus we might get a grasp of our grammar and, to that extent, of the structure of our thinking.

But we might also get something more, and more relevant to our immediate concerns. We might get some insight into the source of those unconscious models or figures which haunt the philosophical imagination and which it is the function of brusquely made category points to expose. Grammatical relations and classifications which we find in surface grammar are modelled in part on those we find in deeply embedded sentence-forms of deep structure. It is to be supposed that genuine analogies, in part logical, in part semantical, underlie this modelling. But may not the modelling be escorted, even helped on its way, by imaginary analogies as well? May not a deceptive ghost of the semantics of the original nominals, verbals, and adjectivals cling to the emergent nominals, verbals, and adjectivals? The theorists of categories, I repeat, have normally contrasted the grammatical acceptability with the semantic unacceptability of their category-absurd sentences. A proper use of such sentences, I repeat, has been to expose the unconscious figures which plague philosophical thinking. May we not find a clue to the appeal of those figures by asking just how, and why, it is that what makes (critically useful) category-nonsense, makes (at one level) grammatical sense? In looking for the ancestry of the grammatical sense that it makes, we may also turn up the features of the figure which fathers the nonsense it makes.

KNOWING HOW AND KNOWING THAT, WHAT

D. G. BROWN

The distinction between *knowing how* and *knowing that* has an odd status. It is one of Professor Ryle's best known ideas, and there seems widespread agreement, in which I share, that it is a substantial contribution. But where has it been put to work, in a more than corroborative or decorative capacity, by anyone else? Who has troubled to explain the distinction carefully and accurately, when it is obvious, as I will show, that Ryle himself did not? At one time there was a suggestion in the air that the distinction opened a third way through an objectivist-subjectivist dilemma in ethics.[1] The possibility, however important, has been neither explored nor discredited. In other fields, a constant drizzle of allusions to the distinction sinks into the ground without substantial effect on the arguments in hand. Even in a sensible attempt, like Scheffler's,[2] to apply the distinction in the theory of education, the attentive reader, interested in the nature of learning and teaching, must find himself baffled by scraps of linguistic fact. We can know how but not believe how, believe in but not know in—where does that leave us?

[1] Such remarks were common enough in conversation. The only one I can find in print is by R. C. Cross, in "Ethical disagreement," *Philosophy* XXV, 1959, pp. 301–15. On p. 314: "I do not think that what is primarily involved in morals is knowing that something is the case, any more than having certain feelings. I think that what is involved rather is knowing how to act, how to cope with situations, and that our ethical utterances are neither true nor false, at least in the sense usually given to true and false in this connection, nor merely emotive. . . . A commentary in terms of rules or prescriptions for action is likely to be more illuminating. . . ." And towards the end he speaks of "the importance of 'knowing how' in moral conduct, and rules or prescriptions in moral language."

[2] Israel Scheffler, *Conditions of Knowledge* (Chicago: Scott, Foresman and Company, 1965). See Chapters One and Five.

This history testifies both to the undeniable interest and power of what Ryle was doing and to the unmanageable state in which he left his account, and thereby I think it raises questions of method. If we have been trying, these twenty-four years, to bring the facts about natural languages to bear on the solution of philosophical problems, it seems that our approach to such work may leave something to be desired.

Our difficulties seem due in some measure to the fact that two kinds of theory simultaneously offer to organize the linguistic data and focus them on the philosophical tangles needing illumination. The two kinds of theory are roughly (a) old-fashioned analysis or description of concepts, and (b) empirical linguistics. The one kind of theory attempts to systematize a body of necessary truths about knowledge, or propositional attitudes, or mental states, or the mind, or whatever. The concepts it deals in are sometimes as profitably invented as they are discovered in the natural language; the old game (which Ryle plays in this case) of oscillating between old and new concepts, by oscillating between ordinary and technical uses of expressions, creates half the excitement and light as well as half the frustration and darkness. The other kind of theory, in linguistics, is comparatively obvious in its aims and methods; the syntactic part of this theory seems at last to be on the sure path of a science. Interest in developing either theory has typically gone with neglect of the other. But I think that the philosophical study of particular concepts must submit to the constraints of both kinds of theory at once.

In this paper I will try to show first that Ryle's distinction is indeterminate, and that what he says about it is unsatisfactory even for the immediate purposes he had in mind. Then I will offer an alternative description of the field of distinctions in which he was working. This positive account will try to benefit from the intermingling of considerations drawn from generative grammar with philosophically structured piecemeal semantics of the kind Ryle practised.[3] Finally I will consider some implications of the account for questions in philosophy of mind and ethics.

1. DIFFICULTIES IN RYLE'S ACCOUNT

The difficulties concern, first, the drawing of the distinction, and second, that which is known in knowing how.

The phrases "knowing how" and "knowing that" are merely tags. What are they, or should they be, attached to?

There are two places in which Ryle appears to do no more or less than say what the two things are which he is about to contrast. Presumably the tags, being his property, are attached to these two things and only these.

Philosophers have not done justice to the distinction which is quite familiar to all of us between knowing that something is the case and knowing how to do things.[4]

When a person is described by one or other of the intelligence-epithets such as "shrewd" or "silly," "prudent" or "imprudent," the description imputes to him not the knowledge, or ignorance, of this or that truth, but the ability, or inability, to do certain sorts of things. Theorists have been so pre-occupied with the task of investigating the nature, the source, and the credentials of the theories that we adopt that they have for the most part ignored the question what it is for someone to know how to perform certain tasks.[5]

[3] I am grateful to Jonathan Bennett for criticisms which substantially altered the account, and also to F. Bowers, J. D. Dybikowski, and Gary Wedeking.
[4] "Knowing How and Knowing That," *Proceedings of the Aristotelian Society* XLVI, 1945–46, p. 4.
[5] *The Concept of Mind* (London: Hutchinson, 1949), p. 27.

The first passage firmly attaches "knowing how" to knowing how to do things. But then, in the second one, are knowing how to perform certain tasks, the ability to do certain sorts of things, prudence, shrewdness, and intelligence implied to be the same as knowing how to do things, or to be part of it on all occasions, or is the phrase "knowing how" rather to be extended to cover them all? Much of the context of each passage is concerned with the application of intelligence-predicates or the exercise of intelligence in practice. If knowing what to do and where to begin, and even knowing that some way to do a thing is the right way, involve the exercise of intelligence in practice, are they therefore also to be called "knowing how?" The answers are far from obvious. Yet these three sentences comprise all that Ryle says by way of drawing his distinction.

He gives many clear examples on both sides. The difficulty is rather, for each kind of knowing, to find out what is not an example. What is obscure is the boundary of each class, and as a result, the principle of division itself.

Evidently "knowing how" means something like knowing how *to do* things; for knowing how a projectile will fall is "knowing that." But does it then not cover knowing *when to* stop and *where to* draw the line? On the other side, it may seem that there can be no slip if "knowing that" is attached to knowing that something, anything, is so; but is it quite clear whether or not it covers knowing *that* one way to slow down is to change down a gear? On both sides of the contrast then, there are, along with cases that clearly do belong there, cases which at first one does not know how to classify, or how one ought to classify.

Of course he also expresses views about the things he has distinguished, as when he says[6] that knowing how is a disposition whose exercises are observances of rules or canons or the applications of criteria. Here he is talking

[6] *Ibid.*, p. 46.

about something, namely about knowing how, and is not defining "knowing how." But what he says about knowing how and knowing that in such passages as this might betray his use of the words "knowing how" and "knowing that." Actually, as should later become clear, what he thinks true of the things suggests that he sometimes, but not always, used the words "knowing how" for much more than knowing how to do things, and the words "knowing that" for much less than knowing that something is the case. Such evidence, however, is too indirect and complex to be worth sifting here.

As our final resort, we have Ryle's mention of a set of related distinctions:

> There are certain parallelisms between knowing *how* and knowing *that*, as well as certain divergences. We speak of learning how to play an instrument as well as of learning that something is the case; of finding out how to prune trees as well as of finding out that the Romans had a camp in a certain place; of forgetting how to tie a reef-knot as well as of forgetting that the German for "knife" is "*Messer*." We can wonder *how* as well as wonder *whether*.
>
> On the other hand we never speak of a person believing or opining *how*, and though it is proper to ask for the grounds or reasons for someone's acceptance of a proposition, this question cannot be asked of someone's skill at cards or prudence in investments.[7]

Here, the words "learning how," "finding out how," "forgetting how," and "wondering how" are left in the same position as "knowing how." "Wondering whether" is either a quite unexplained tag, or else clearly inappropriate; for wondering whether to do something has nothing to do with knowing that. The remarks about believing and about reasons seem correct, but do not help.

[7] *Ibid.*, p. 28.

Since there is not, to my knowledge, a better account of the distinction, no one has drawn it precisely. And although the phrases "knowing how" and "knowing that" have been commonly used, I do not think they have acquired a determinate use at all.

Aside from the fact that the distinction is not fully determinate, Ryle's account even of clear cases of knowing how to do something provokes a problem which seems hard to resolve within the terms of his analysis.

It seems that knowing how to ride a bicycle involves being able to. But why only *involves?* Knowing how to just is being able to, unless there is something to it over and above being able to. Is it that one must have learned to do it? Not that alone, because there are things one must learn to do, like drawing a circle freehand, which one is merely able to do. It would be natural to suggest that besides being able to there is involved knowing something. What then is known? How to ride a bicycle. But we started from here, in search of some reason to speak at all of knowing. Very well then, something must be known, namely ordinary facts, and it is the necessary presence of this knowing which makes it appropriate to speak of knowing how to. But since, according to Ryle, such knowledge may leave one still unable to do the thing, some account is needed of how it contributes to the ability. If this account relies on knowing how to exploit the information, the same problem recurs; on any other account, it is obscure why the part played by this knowledge should justify calling the resultant whole itself knowledge.

For to state such facts, even if they must be known, would seem to give at best a partial formulation of what is known. How could the rest of it be put into words? It seems fair to ask, not only to be told which bit of knowledge someone has, but also to be *told that which* he knows. Perhaps what is known is a rule, and a rule can be formulated in words. The suggestion is unclear, but on any relevant conception of a rule it makes doubtful sense to say "He knows . . . ," filling in the formulation of a rule. In any case, if knowing a rule is said to be exhibited in performance, one has the analogous problem of why it is called knowing, rather than being able to act in accordance with, the rule.

This maze has further turnings, but none that brings one to what it seems legitimate to seek, a statement of the content of the knowledge in cases of knowing how to do things. But is it legitimate? Surely one of the points of Ryle's distinction is that some knowledge can be put into "that" clauses, while some can only be exhibited in practice; one cannot ask for knowledge that is both at once. We shall see whether one cannot.

2. TWO KINDS OF KNOWING HOW

The most direct way forward is to attempt a positive account of some distinctions in fact to be found in the territory Ryle was mapping. The distinction immediately needed, without which Ryle could not go straight, is that between two kinds of meaning for sentences of the form

1) John knows how to V

where "V" takes verbs as instances. It will turn out that when such a sentence has both kinds of meaning it has a different grammatical structure under the two interpretations. But I can begin by distinguishing the two meanings in straightforwardly semantic terms, in terms namely of the implications of the statements made.

The explanation of the distinction may be easier to follow with examples in mind. The one sense for "know how to V" is exemplified in

2) John knows how to run a projector.
and 3) John knows how to build frame houses.

The other sense is exemplified in

    4) John knows how to move about in a canoe.

and 5) The accused does not know how to address the magistrate.

To provide working labels, I will call the use of "know how to V" in examples (2) and (3) *the English use* (in the sense of English-language use), and I will call the use of it in examples (4) and (5) *the standard use*. In justification of these labels, I remark that the English use of the words (which has given us "American know-how") has no counterpart in French, German, or Dutch, and that within English grammar it proves to be syntactically non-standard.[8] In other words, the distinction now to be drawn will prove to mark off a use of "know how" which is both characteristic of English and anomalous within English from a use which is found in many languages and is in the relevant respects straightforward.

The English use of "know how" I define as that in which if John does not know how to V then John is unable to V (where the same substitution is made on "V"). The standard use of "know how" I define as that use in which the above condition does not hold.

To show that sentences (2) and (3), and sentences (4) and (5), exemplify the English use and the standard use respectively, we can point out that John's succeeding in running a projector or building a frame house, not by luck but in a way which exhibits that he is able to do these things, establishes that he knows how to do them. By contrast, when John moves about in a canoe, or the

[8] I have not found much commentary on the English use. But see R. B. Lees, *The Grammar of English Nominalizations*, Fourth printing (Bloomington: Indiana University Press, 1966), pp. 61 and 108 (note 40); G. O. Curme, *Syntax* (Vol. III of *A Grammar of the English Language*) (Boston: D. C. Heath and Co., 1931), p. 249, Sec. 24 III d; and E. Kruisinga and P. A. Erades, *An English Grammar*, 7th ed., Vol. I (Groningen: P. Noordhoff N. V., 1950), p. 291, Sec. 230.

accused does address the magistrate, and clearly is able to do so, nothing is established by that fact alone about whether John knows how to move about in a canoe, or whether the accused knows how to address the magistrate. The actual performance may equally well provide evidence of the performer's knowing or of his not knowing; it is the manner of the performance which is relevant. John's not knowing how is best seen when he does move about, and capsizes the canoe; the accused's not knowing how is best seen when he does address the magistrate, and addresses him as "man."

3. HOW, WHERE, WHEN, WHAT, WHICH

Of the two uses of "know how," I have called the one *standard* because it runs closely parallel to uses of "know where," "know when," "know what," "know which," and so on, and seems adequately accounted for by an analysis which covers all these expressions and which draws on grammatical rules of wide application. I suggest that the standard use of "know how" exemplifies a construction which is also found in the following cases:

6) The plumber will know where to use half-inch pipe.
7) The stenographer knows where to send the notices.
8) As a politician he knows when to keep quiet.
9) He doesn't know what to say.
10) Our guests know which road to take.

It seems obvious in all the examples (4) to (10), in which "how," "where," "when," and the rest follow "know," that this construction goes with other constructions in which these words follow "ask," "tell," and "learn"; and that at the heart of all such sentences there lie question forms. (I will argue in Section 7 that the same holds for the English use of "know how.") When we can say John knows how to V, we can also say that he asked how, was told (or shown) how, and learned how. When we can say John knows where to V, we can also say that he asked where, was told (or shown) where, and learned where. It is the question of how to V, or the question of where to V, to which he knows the answer, or to which he asked, was told, or learned the answer.

The similarity among these uses of "how," "where," "when" and the rest extends to a contrast with the English use of "know how." For the question-words other than "how" nearly always follow the pattern of the standard use of "how."[9] If John does not know where to V, he may quite well be able to V, and may show by the places of his actual V-ing that he does not know. The plumbers may well use half-inch pipe, and by that very fact show that they do not know where to use half-inch pipe. As in the standard use of "know how," where it is the manner of actual V-ing which exhibits both knowing how and not knowing how, so in general for "know where" and the others, it is, e.g., the place, time, object, or instrument of actual V-ing, which exhibits both knowing and not knowing where, when, what, and with what to V.

These standard uses invite us to add some specification of the form "in order to . . . ," "in doing . . . ," or "by the standards of. . . ." John knows how to move about in a canoe without capsizing it, or in order not to capsize it, or safely. The accused does not know how to address the magistrate by the standards of formality and etiquette customary in courts of law. Our guests know which road to take in order to get to our house. The politician knows when to keep quiet as a politician, that is to say, in the pursuit of his political interest. In general, I see no

---

[9] The condition which defines the English use, namely that if John does not know how to V, then he is unable to V, can sometimes be paralleled by conditions marking off analogous uses of "know where" and the rest, but such uses seem infrequent and confined to limited classes of verbs. For example, "I do not know where to find him" implies that I am unable to find him. See the end of section 7.

ground for regarding the examples as elliptical, where such specifications are not given and have to be supplied from the context or from background information. But we can say that in many such cases knowing something is a part or an aspect of some larger accomplishment or competence. Commonly this larger accomplishment or competence can be attributed to its possessor by means of the English use of "know how." So knowing how, where, when, or what to V is often a part or aspect of knowing how to handle a canoe, knowing how to build a house, knowing how to succeed in politics, or knowing how to get there.

Where a person does know how to V, in the English use of "know how," it may be a matter for discussion whether this knowing on his part is itself to be identified as one of his accomplishments or competences, or whether it is more properly the *ability* to V which is so identified, the *knowing* being one of a number of necessary conditions of the ability. In such a case as knowing how to build a house, it would appear that both knowing how and being able to build a house should be counted as accomplishments, the former being one necessary condition of the latter; the remaining necessary conditions would include some degree of persistence and organization of mind, and either manual skills or the ability to work with men. At any rate, it is intelligible that Ryle should have come very near to identifying knowing how to V with being able to V, provided we observe one thing about Ryle's discussion. A review of his examples would show that he has the English use of "know how" almost exclusively in mind.

It follows that in proceeding to analyses of the standard use of "know how," and the similar uses of "know where" and the rest, we are entering territory neglected in Ryle's account. Nor will any conclusions apply without further argument to the English use.

4. QUESTIONS AND ANSWERS

At this point we need some account of the syntactic structure of sentences (4) to (10). I think it will often prove to be the case that considerations of syntax are insufficient to settle a semantic problem of a philosophically interesting kind, and yet are able at the same time to throw a strong light on it. They may leave open the philosophically decisive options, and yet contribute to philosophical understanding; and that in three ways. They may provide a precise statement of the semantic issues; they may set substantial and helpful limits for an acceptable solution; and they may suggest particular philosophical theories. In the present case I think some philosophical benefit of these kinds flows from recent work in the syntactic analysis of embedded questions, of imperative sentences, and of modal auxiliaries. Unfortunately these are topics on which work in linguistics remains maddeningly fragmentary. But I think it would be a mistake to postpone our enquiries until the syntax is well understood. I venture to suggest, as a layman, that syntax in turn might find philosophical theories suggestive.

I wish to emphasize that the grammatical suggestions I make are offered as conjectures. I have no great confidence in them, and I will be content if their refutation proves useful. But I am sure that such theory is needed, and I hope that students of syntax will at least be moved to provide something better.

Let us first consider embedded questions with factual answers. It is not that anyone ever took knowing how, in Ryle's sense, to include knowing how things in fact happen, and are done, and are. It is just that the embedding of questions is a general process in the language, most of whose instances probably are factual, and it seems reasonable to suppose that embedded questions with imperative or modal answers should be treated as special cases of the general process.

Several points about questions are relatively uncontroversial, and can be stated independently of the technical problems of giving an explicit grammatical analysis. One is that the meaning of a question determines and is determined by a range of possible answers to it, in the sense of a range of answers which would be intelligible as answers, whether or not they would be true or would have any analogous kind of acceptability. In particular, it is convenient to divide questions into those to which "yes" and "no" are possible answers and those to which they are not. Questions which are not yes-no questions very typically contain a word like "which," "what," "who," "when," or "where," and may for a first approximation be called *wh-* questions. Both kinds of question appear in indirect speech, and the most straightforward kind of embedding of questions would seem to be with the verb "ask." Thus we can say that John *asked* me *whether*[10] I had seen his friend, or that John *asked* me *when* I had seen his friend. It also seems clear that, whatever further complexities may be introduced, we have essentially parallel constructions in which "ask" is replaced by "tell," "say," "wonder," "consider," "hear," "discover," "learn," "know," and "remember." Thus I can tell John when I saw his friend, and then John will *know* *when* I saw his friend. Here evidently "know when" means roughly "know the answer to the question of when."

Analysis of the structure of embedded questions on the lines of a theory like that of Chomsky in *Aspects of the*

10 Or we can say that John asked me *if* this was the case. The use of the expression *"wh-* question" for a kind of question which excludes the question of *whether* something is so may not be happy. But any *wh-* element in the deep structure of a yes-no question is not realized in this obvious way in the surface structure unless the sentence is embedded.

Theory of Syntax,[11] while it accommodates the foregoing points easily enough, must of course commit itself to particular syntactic rules, and must face the technical problems of doing so. Katz and Postal suggest[12] that phrase structure rules provide for questions by a question marker (Q) in the deep structure of any sentence, i.e., in the general rule for expansion of S, together with a second marker (*wh-*) which, in any sentence marked with Q, must be attached to at least one element of the sentence and may be attached to noun phrases or to a sentence adverbial. Where *wh-* is attached to a sentence adverbial, we can generate a yes-no question, and this will be in factual cases a question of *whether or not* something is so. Where *wh-* is attached to a noun phrase, that element is said to be questioned, and we can generate various kinds of *wh-* questions. In simpler cases we get questions in "what," "which," and "who." For the rest, adverbs are analyzed as involving a preposition and a noun phrase, and questions in "where," "when," and "how," are generated by questioning the noun phrase in adverbial phrases of the form "in some place," "at some time," and "in some way."

I think such an analysis can be straightforwardly extended to deal with embedded questions. Presumably, where an embedded sentence has a Q marker, selectional restrictions will govern what can appear in the matrix sentence. Thus, for example, a question can be embedded as the direct object of "ask," "tell," and "know," but not of "deny" or "believe." To illustrate how such an account works out for embedded *wh-* questions of a factual kind, the sentence

11) John asked Bill when the Board would meet.

can be assigned a deep structure roughly like this:

[11] Noam Chomsky, *Aspects of the Theory of Syntax* (Cambridge, Mass.: M.I.T. Press, 1965).

[12] J. J. Katz and P. M. Postal, *An Integrated Theory of Linguistic Descriptions* (Cambridge, Mass.: M.I.T. Press, 1964), Section 4.2.4.

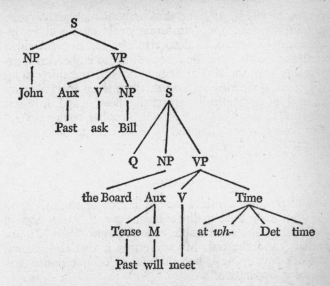

One odd feature of this deep structure will prove to be relevant to later problems. It appears that the tense of the embedded sentence has to be Past, even though the direct question being reported is "When will the Board meet?". An alternative view, which might be adequate to deal with cases such as this one, would be that the embedded tense is Present, following the direct question, and that Present comes to be replaced by Past in the surface structure, by the operation of transformational rules with the effect of traditional rules for "sequence of tenses." Perhaps there are such transformational rules, but I think it is clear that they will not provide a general solution to the problems of constructing embedded sentences for indirect speech. The question "Will it meet the day after tomorrow?" has to be reported as the question of whether it would meet two days later, or the day after the day after the time of asking. Such adjustments depend on the meanings of particular words or particular classes of words, and the direct question, together with phrase structure and transformational rules, will be insufficient to determine deep structure for the embedded sentence. In the transition from direct to embedded question, as also for similar reasons in the transition from direct to embedded statement, there is an inevitable intrusion of semantically governed choices, and it seems obscure to me what sort of rule, or what component of the theory of the language, will be able to account for them.

6. PRACTICAL QUESTIONS

We can now consider the application of an analysis on the foregoing lines to the standard use of "know how to V" and to the comparable uses of "know when," "know where," and the rest. My suggestion is that the analysis applies equally well, but the embedded questioned sentence is imperative.

Let us begin with some relatively uncontroversial occasions, philosophically, for the use of the construction in question. These are occasions on which we are among other things ascribing to a person knowledge of his orders, instructions, prescribed duties, and the like. For example:

12) The artillery commander knows when to open fire.
13) The janitor knows how to arrange the tables.

In typical contexts for (12) and (13), it would be implied that someone knew when or how he *was to do* something, or *was supposed to* do it, in that he was in possession of his orders or instructions. He might, in a case like (12), have asked when to do something, and been told when; or he might have read written orders from which he learned when to do it. The familiar pattern of "ask," "tell," "learn," and "know," with *wh-* forms strongly suggests embedded questions. It is less obvious what questions these can be.

In these selected cases, it seems that the person in ques-

tion, when he asks something, is asking for orders; and
when he is told what to do, he is being given orders. It
is therefore natural to suppose that what is said to him
will be in the imperative. By analogy with cases in which
he is told something in the indicative, it might further
seem natural to arrive at the relevant questions from the
deep structure of the answer sentences by adding question markers and replacing determiner elements with
question markers. For even though a given answer sentence can serve in answer to a variety of questions, we can
expect to arrive easily at some at least of these questions
by "questioning" elements in the deep structure of the
answer. However, in the case of imperatives there are special problems. The surface structure of most imperatives
lacks both a subject and most of the auxiliary; and it is obvious that a speaker inviting an imperative and a speaker
uttering one must use different pronouns if they are to
refer to the agent of the verb. In addition, it seems a serious possibility that there might exist no question at all to
which an imperative was an answer, but only a range of
requests, statements, or provocations which would make
the uttering of the imperative in various ways appropriate.

But there is one kind of question which has seemed to
some writers, on semantic grounds, to be the most
straightforward kind to which an imperative could supply
an answer. Such questions are, in R. M. Hare's phrase,[13]
of the form "What shall I do?". For (12), the direct
question would be "When shall I open fire?". An answer
like "At 5 o'clock" will be short for the order "Open fire
at 5 o'clock." Now it happens that on one generally received and relatively conservative analysis of imperatives,[14]

[13] R. M. Hare, *The Language of Morals* (Oxford: Clarendon
Press, 1952), e.g., p. 29. Hare's idea suggested much of my account
of deliberation, in D. G. Brown, *Action* (Toronto: Toronto U.P.,
1968), Ch. 1.

[14] See Katz and Postal, *op. cit.*, Section 4.2.3, and E. S. Klima,
"Negation in English," in J. A. Fodor and J. J. Katz, eds., *The Structure of Language* (Englewood Cliffs, N.J.: Prentice-Hall, 1964), e.g.,
pp. 258–60. More recent analyses are mentioned in notes 16 and 17.

they have in their deep structure, along with an imperative
marker, *Imp*, a modal verb which is usually deleted, and
is always deleted when the subject is; the modal is taken
to be "will." The appropriateness of imperatives in answer to the question "What shall I do?" suggests that if
there is such a deleted modal it may be "shall" rather
than "will."[15] For the time being, let us adopt the received analysis with this modification. On such a view, the
deep structure of the imperative "Open fire at 5 o'clock"
has "Imp + you + shall + open fire at 5 o'clock."
This allows us to treat our embedded questions with imperative answers in a standard way, that is to say as questioned imperative sentences, and thus to arrive at the
analysis we seek.

There is just one difficult problem to be faced before
setting out the combination of my conjectures in a proposed deep structure for (12), and that is the problem
of the subject of the embedded questioned imperative. It
is evident that once again we must exercise our options
according to the sense. For in an ordinary, unimbedded
imperative it is plausible, at the least, to suppose the
subject is "you." But in this embedded imperative the
asker of the question would have to say "I," and we must
use neither "you" nor "I." As a first approximation to our

[15] The main arguments for "will" seem to depend on taking "you
will do it" as actually a form of "do it" or "you do it," and on assuming that the tag question in "Close the door, will you?" must
reveal the modal in the main sentence. As to the first, there are many
non-imperative forms that can fill some of the roles of imperatives,
like "you are going to do it," "you must do it," "you might do it,"
and "you are expected to do it." As to the second, it is not obvious
why tag-questions should not be quite distinct sentences, when they
have the force of coupling a speech act to another of a different
category. (If they join question to statement, why not request to
command?) In favour of "shall," I find in my dialect a use of "shall"
I suspect to be very old, in which it serves in all persons to express
the entitled will of the speaker as to the action of the subject of the
sentence.

analysis, let us consider making the subject of the embedded question identical with the subject of the main sentence.[16] For (12) this would yield the following deep structure:[17]

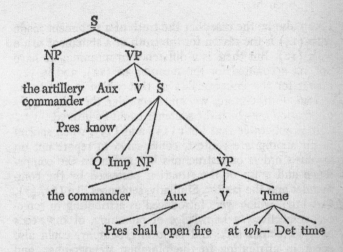

[16] Of course to do this we must allow Noun Phrases of many kinds, and not just "you," as subject of an imperative sentence. But this has already been seen to be required on syntactic grounds not related to the embedding of imperatives. See J. P. Thorne, "English imperative sentences," *Journal of Linguistics*, 2, 1966, pp. 69–78. Thorne derives "you," when it does occur in an imperative, from a Vocative marker which is required by the presence of the Imp marker. Thorne's analysis will provide for the structures I need if the Vocative marker is required only when Imp occurs in the main sentence, and this seems reasonable anyway.

[17] On one alternative analysis of imperatives, proposed by R. B. Lees ("On passives and imperatives in English," *Gengo Kenkyu* No. 46, 1964), the imperative marker Imp does not merely require a particular modal, Tense and Modal elements normally being deleted later, it replaces those elements of Aux as one possible expansion of Aux in the phrase structure rules. On this analysis, the diagram would be amended by deleting "Pres" and "shall" and moving the "Imp" into their place under "Aux."

This analysis, however, can be seen on reflection not to be adequate. Perhaps it is adequate for a different sentence, namely

14) The artillery commander knows when *he is to* open fire.

It can also be the case that the truth of a statement made with (14) is the reason for the truth of a statement made with (12). But there is a difference in meaning; we have not yet accounted for the meaning of (12), and in particular for the impersonality of that which is said to be known. Furthermore, we must consider the other types of occasion on which the sentence could be uttered.

It is noticeable that both (12) and (13), when spoken in an appropriate context, could serve to report not on anyone's orders or instructions but rather on the competence and grasp of the situation possessed by the commander and the janitor. Similarly, sentences like (6), (7), and (10), which were introduced as attributing to someone respectively a knowledge of plumbing, of the needs of a secretarial task, and of local geography, could also occur in attributing to the plumber, stenographer, and guests a knowledge of the instructions or advice that had been given to them. What we need to correct the analysis of (12), and what we need to accommodate the cases of attributing competence, are I think one and the same adjustment. For both purposes a simple conjecture seems to me the most probable. This is to suppose that the subject of the embedded imperative question is not the same as the subject of the matrix sentence but is unspecified. In the diagram of the deep structure we can show a dummy element Δ, which would be marked as carrying a syntactic feature "Personal." Such unspecified personal noun phrases, when they survive into the surface structure, may be realized as "one" or "someone" or "anyone." Here they would be subject to obligatory deletion. Accordingly, we reach the following deep structure for:

12) The artillery commander knows when to open fire.

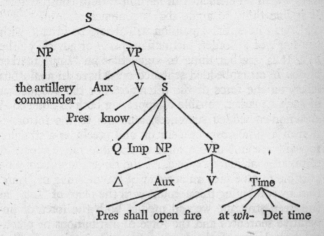

This analysis goes for all occurrences of (12), and this avoids a claim of ambiguity. Knowing when to do something may in some cases be founded on orders and one's reasons for obeying them, and in other cases be founded on circumstances which in the light of one's own competence are seen to make some time the time which is right or best or necessary. But these differences do not, on this view, affect the analysis of what is known.

The analysis may of course arouse objections analogous to those which greet R. M. Hare's idea of an enriched imperative mood.[18] For we now seem to be postulating imperatives directed to any hearer by any speaker at and concerning no particular time, and it seems obvious that the attempt to combine such features with those which actually belong to imperative sentences in English leads to absurdity. But such an issue cannot be resolved without distinguishing the meaning of whole utterances from the meaning of elements in a deep structure, and distin-

[18] R. M. Hare, *op. cit.*, Section 12.4.

guishing, within the latter kind of meaning, among the
roles which an element can have in various constructions.
It is one thing to argue that a sentence with an "Imp"
marker in its initial expansion will always be uttered with
the force of an order, instruction, piece of advice, or the
like. It is another thing to argue that an "Imp" marker
buried in an embedded sentence must have an analogous
effect on the force of the utterance. For the postulation
of such a marker, capable of appearing both in embedded
and non-embedded sentences, amounts to the introduction of a more abstract element, and precludes a straightforward account of the force of the imperative mood in
terms of that marker alone. At the same time, it may be
possible to give such an account of the meaning of "Imp"
that by combining this account with the place of "Imp" in
the deep structure we can predict both the force of imperative sentences and the force of attributions of practical knowledge of the kind under examination. In that
case, the syntactical analysis will have helped to vindicate
Hare's idea as an insight into a concept deeper and more
abstract than imperativeness. As to how this might be
done, I think some useful intuitive hints can be offered.

I have suggested elsewhere[19] that the agent's question
of what to do is not essentially verbal, and can be settled
by action, but that its formulation in language depends
upon question and answer forms whose primary role is
found in speech situations of command, instruction, advice, and the like. Given the agent as both asker and
answerer of practical questions, and given a notion of the
point of view of the agent which is defined for any action,
we begin to see how syntactic structures which are most
at home in specific social situations become adapted to
formulating the consideration of reasons for and against
action by any agent at any time. The necessary leeway in
the syntactical rules is provided by the necessity, noticed
above, of relying on semantic considerations for the con-

[19] D. G. Brown, *op. cit.*, p. 78. (Cf. sec. 1.4.)

struction of embedded sentences. Not only is it grammatical and semantically correct to embed sentences which never occurred unembedded: it is grammatical and becomes semantically correct to embed sentences which never could occur unembedded. For it is easy to regard the agent, when he tries in exercise of his skill and judgement to decide what to do, as considering what any agent in such a situation would be well advised to tell himself to do, or simply would be well advised to do. That piece of advice which any rational man would be looking for could come from any rational man, including himself. Call it a command of reason.

There is another class of questions and answers which might naturally be supposed to be highly relevant to practical knowledge, but which cannot actually be taken to provide analyses for (4) to (10), (12), and (13). It is instructive to consider both why they are relevant and why they cannot enter the analysis. These are questions and answers which concern how, when, or where one *should* do something, or *must* or *ought to* or *had better*. There is evidently a close connection between knowing when one should do something and knowing when to do it, and between knowing when one must do something and knowing when to do it, and so on. In reply to the question "When shall I do it?" when the question asks for advice, the statements "You should do it at 5 o'clock" or "You must do it at 5 o'clock" are appropriate and relevant, even though instead of strictly answering the question they go on to contribute something which helps the agent to settle his question of when to do the thing. From the stark advice "Do it at 5 o'clock" there radiate many kinds of advice, of which these two are typical, which have in common that in some way they assess or comment on the reasons for and against the course of action in question.[20] Correspondingly, from the stark question of what

[20] This idea is developed somewhat in my book: D. G. Brown, *op. cit.*, sections 1.4, 1.7, 1.9, 3.3, and 3.9.

to do, there radiate many kinds of question, which have in common that they concern the reasons which bear on this original question. One ground for supposing that these further questions might actually be parts or versions of the original question is that the availability of some answer to one of them, which in the context of advice implies the availability of some judgement on the reasons for or against a course of action, is a necessary condition for speaking of the agent as *knowing* what to do. If the question facing the agent is simply what to do, or whether to do something, or when to do it, that which is called for on his part is simply decision and action, not knowledge. Even having a policy or rule, or having his mind made up on what to do, does not amount to his *knowing* what to do. Something must enter, on the side of some course of action, capable of rendering it the thing *to be done*. This source of objectivity can involve authority, as in the case of orders or instructions. It can also be the independent existence of reasons, as it is when knowing exhibits competence. But the agent must know either what he *must* do, or what he *ought* to do, or something of the kind, if he is to *know what to do*. So it seems that the real content of his knowledge is given in the modal assertion. But I think this conclusion is not merely unwarranted but also open to a strong objection. The need for some judgement to be available does not entail that the judgement is the content of knowing what to do. And if we supposed that it was, we would be faced with a wide variety of judgements on different occasions. This would have to be reflected in a variety of embedded questions in the deep structure, all represented in the surface structure as the question of what to do. Even if it is possible to regard any one modal as deleted in reaching this surface structure (as some theories take "will" or "shall" to be deleted in reaching an imperative) it will not do to say that sometimes one modal is deleted and sometimes another. This variety could not be reconciled with the principle of recoverability of deleted elements[21] without the unplausible consequence that "know when to V" has dozens of senses. We must clearly stay with the commonsense view that knowing what to do is distinguishable from knowing what one *must* do and so on for the rest.

Do we thereby deprive ourselves of a content for knowledge of when, where, and how to do things in the standard uses for which I have suggested a deep structure? This is the problem of whether we can give an indicative sentence or a "that" clause which will formulate what the knower knows, granting that we are not to use "should," "must," and the like. A natural solution is provided by sentences of the form "The time (place, way) to do it is _____." Thus what the competent commander knows, when he has practical knowledge, is that the time to open fire is 5 o'clock. To find the deep structure of such a sentence, we can observe that the subject of "is _____" is a definite description picking out a time, place, or way of doing something as the time, place or way to do it. The only problem is to specify this relative clause, by giving the sentence in the deep structure which is dominated by the relative marker. I will not try to develop the details here, but evidently this sentence must be the analogue, with use of *"wh-"* as a marker for relativization, to the question embedded with "know," in which *"wh-"* occurs as an interrogative marker; the sentence will be imperative, and its subject unspecified. Roughly, if he *knows when* to do it, he knows the time *at which* to do it, and this is to know *that the time at which to do it is* such-and-such. The same rules for obligatory deletion of the subject and Aux which yield a bare infinitive in "know when *to*" yield a bare infinitive in "the time (at which) *to*."

Such uses of the infinitive in relative clauses, attached to the time, place, and way of doing something, or attached to a thing that can be done, in indicative sentences with "is," provide what is syntactically the most

[21] See N. Chomsky, *op. cit.,* pp. 138, 144 f.

stripped-down form of "evaluative" term. Instead of saying that something should or must be done, we say merely that it is the thing *to be done*. This might be called a degenerate case of "prescriptive language in the indicative mood," where the uses of "should" and "must" are full-blooded cases. But it is also a central case, and it allows us to speak of *knowledge* of what to do.

7. THE ENGLISH USE

I turn now to the English use of "know how to V," which clearly has affinities with the standard uses just considered, but requires a different account and raises further problems.

The defining characteristic of the English use is that, in this use, if a person does not know how to V then he is unable to V. We need to see how the meaning of the English use differs from that of the standard use, and how this difference accounts for the presence or absence of the implication which defines the distinction.

First let us notice that although "how" is a pretty abstract word, there seems no need to regard it as ambiguous. The breadth of its application corresponds to that of "way," and it can on occasion be paraphrased by "in what way" or "the way in which," or simply "the way" (cp. "how it looks" or "how it is"). The way in which something is done can be more specifically classified as the manner in which it is done or as the means, method, procedure, or route by which it is done. Some grammarians speak of *manner* adverbials, but it would be too specific to give "in what manner" as underlying "how"; for such purposes as the phrase structure rules, we ought to provide the more abstract "in what way," relying on restrictions of a different kind to specify manner as opposed to means, procedure, respect, and the rest. (Of course, the use of "manner" may here be stretching for technical purposes, in the direction of the dialect spoken by sergeants and civil servants.) In any case the extreme versatility of "how" does not justify us in looking to some convenient ambiguity of the word for the difference between English and standard uses.

At the same time, the contrast between manner, on the one hand, and on the other hand, the list of things like means, method, procedure, and route, does seem relevant to our distinction. For a manner is necessarily a way of doing something which is being *done* and not merely attempted or begun. That is to say, a description of a person's manner of V-ing presupposes that he V-ed; and when a person is advised on the manner in which to V, his having followed or not followed the advice can be reported only when he has V-ed. By contrast, means, methods, procedures (usually), and routes provide ways of doing something such that these ways can be undertaken successfully or unsuccessfully. A description of a person's means or the like of V-ing may be part of a description either of his V-ing or of his failing to V. In such cases, a way of V-ing consists in doing something the doing of which is distinguishable from V-ing, and hence, even though the doing of it may on occasion be part of V-ing as well as the way of V-ing, it is possible for this ancillary action to occur in the course of failing to V. Evidently knowing how to V in the standard use is typically knowing the manner in which to V; and knowing how to V in the English use is typically knowing means, methods, procedures, or routes the knowledge of which will in favourable conditions enable one to V. Nevertheless, if the words "how" and "way" are not ambiguous, the contrast just drawn is not due to any equivalence between senses of "way" and the respective meanings of "manner," "means" and the rest. The contrast is only an indirect consequence of the distinction we want to draw, and we have yet to locate the distinction itself.

The peculiar force of the English use lies not in the sense of "way" in which the utterance concerns ways of doing things, but in the structure of its reference to them.

I have said that knowing how in the standard use is knowing that some particular way of V-ing is *the* way in which *to* V, and that in fact this way of V-ing will typically be a manner of V-ing. We cannot similarly construe knowing how in the English use as knowing that some particular way of V-ing is the way in which to V, where this way of V-ing happens to be instead (say) a *means* of V-ing, because there need be no particular way of V-ing which is required or favoured; and where there is a variety of ways it is sufficient for knowing how that one know any single way. Further, granting that one knows at least one way, what is it to know this one way? It is to know of some course of action only that it is *a* way of V-ing, that is to say a way in which one *can* V, or in which it is possible to V. It is to know of it only that *by* doing that thing one *can* V.

It seems evident, then, that we can analyze the English use in terms of an underlying modal which is deleted to yield an infinitive in the surface structure. In fact, since we need to provide for the ambiguity of "know how to V," we can do it by postulating for one of the two senses the very structure which we had to reject earlier for the standard uses of *wh-* forms, on the ground that it would generate unwanted ambiguities. Accordingly, I suggest that in the English use "know how to V" is derived from "know how one *can* V." Once again, there is an embedded question, this time a fairly straightforward one: "How can one V?," in the sense of "In what way is it possible (for one) to V?."

That this should be the question simultaneously accounts for the fact that knowing how to V, in the English use, is knowing *a* way rather than *the* way. For this question, in its direct form as well, is unusual among questions with many correct answers, and unusual in a relevant respect. With most such questions, like "Who is on the committee?" or "Where did they go in Mexico?," which can be correctly answered by a number of names or places, knowing who and knowing where mean knowing the whole list of correct answers. But with the question "How can one V?," knowing how means merely knowing one from the list of correct answers.

In section 3 (cp. note 9), I alluded to uses of "know where to V," and other such expressions, which satisfied a condition analogous to that defining the English use of "know how to V." For example,

14) I know where to find him.

in most contexts would imply that if I did not know where to find him, I would be unable to find him, and my success or failure in finding him would be the test of whether I did know where to find him. The present analysis adapts well to dealing with such uses since (14) can be paraphrased as "I know where one can find him" or "I know where he can be found," and these in turn as "I know with respect to some place that it is a place at which . . .".

Now that I have stated the meaning of each use of "know how to V," I can test the account against certain turns of phrase which might seem to cast doubt on the claim to find an ambiguity. Sentence (3) can be used to convey the sober piece of information that John has a certain competence in the building trade. Perhaps he was a contractor at one time, or has been to a training college. In that case my analysis diagnoses the utterance as the English use. But building houses allows every degree of knowledge from shocking incompetence to mastery and flair. For exceptional performance, we hear praise of the form "John sure knows how to build a frame house," and the force of this remark is not to imply ability to build a house, which is taken for granted, but something more, such as ability to do it very well. I think my analysis must call this a standard use, and take it as saying that John knows *the* way *to* build houses (roughly the best way or the right way). We also hear comments, on houses undoubtedly and repeatably built, of the form "John just does not know how to build a frame house." Once again I must say that this is a standard use, denying of John what the praise asserted of him. Further, it is simultaneously true of him that, in the English use, he does know how to build a frame house. Is it plausible to suggest that the same form of words flips from one sense to another and back again over this range of degrees of competence? Not only do I find this plausible, it is the only explanation I have found for the impression of punning irony given by such remarks. A solemn hearer or reader, or one deprived of context, could in fact be misled as to John's ability or inability to get some kind of house built.

8. WHAT IS LEFT OF RYLE'S DISTINCTION

If my account is right, all knowing how is knowing that. We are allowed to return to the common assumption, which Ryle wanted to upset, that knowing in general (other than knowing in the sense of being acquainted with) is knowing that. In other words, knowing how to do things, in either of the two senses of the expression, just as much as knowing how things are, is formulable in "that" clauses. The contrast between *wh-* forms and "that" forms is a very general grammatical phenomenon, associated everywhere with a relation between questions and answers. Further, the exemplifications of this contrast can be either theoretical or practical, and either plain indicative, modal, or infinitival. Finally, the contrast is irrelevant to any of the contrasts which are of interest in classifying kinds of knowledge. I conclude that we have good grounds for abandoning the use of the tags "knowing how" and "knowing that."

At the same time it is evident that Ryle has brought to light important differences between kinds of knowledge, and roughly speaking between two main kinds of knowledge. In addition, the form of his account can be substantially maintained, and needs to be corrected and elaborated rather than given up. For we can regard such an account as having two stages. The first is to draw distinctions which enable us to identify kinds of knowledge in straightforward terms, and in particular to achieve this straightforwardness by relying heavily on grammatical terms. The second stage is to show that the kinds of knowledge so identified differ in philosophically interesting ways. It turns out that a revised identification of a kind of knowledge which we could call practical does enable us to contrast this kind of knowledge with other knowledge in a way closely following Ryle's original intent. In short, a revised account preserves much of Ryle's insight. In the rest of this section I sketch a revised distinction. In the final section I will try to foresee philosophical implications.

A revised distinction can deal in either questions or answers; it can distinguish either among *wh-* forms or among types of "that" clause. It is more helpful in enforcing the criticisms already made to present the revised Ryle as distinguishing kinds of "that" clause, or simply kinds of indicative sentence. Thus knowing is knowing that, and has a content, but two main kinds of knowledge can be distinguished by differences in content. In order to begin on such a distinction it should not be too difficult (though I cannot do it here) to give a precise definition of a particular kind of indicative sentence. This would be the kind of sentence (to describe it roughly for now) in which we speak of something which an agent can do, often using an infinitive construction to introduce the concept of that thing, and in which we either say of that thing that it is the thing to do, or say of some time that it is the time at which to do it, or say of some place that it is the place at which to do it, or say of some way of doing it that it is the way in which to do it—and so on for other constructions. The extreme abstractness of the concept of a thing to do, which allows us for example to count V-ing at two different times as two different things to do, allows us to sum up this projected definition as a definition of the class of sentences in which something is said to be the thing to do. By adding to this class

of sentences one corresponding to the English use of
"know how" together with the analogous uses of other
wh- forms, we would arrive at a corresponding kind of
knowledge which we could plausibly offer as the kind
Ryle wanted to pick out.

However, before settling on such a definition for our
new distinction, and proceeding to the second stage of
revision, it would be wise to consider the familiar kind of
"that" clause discussed in Section 6 above, in which something is said to be the thing which must be done, ought
to be done, had better be done, or the like. The way in
which Ryle stated his distinction automatically precluded
this and any other type of "that" clause from candidacy
for classification as "knowing how." But we are free to
ask whether or not knowing the time at which something
must be done should be classified with knowing the time
at which *to do it*. The relation between them is very
close. As we have seen, there are similarities in their grammatical structures. I suggest, further, that the statement
that something must be done entails that (other things
being equal) that thing is the thing to do. In my view,
if we are to define an interesting kind of knowledge which
we might want to call *practical knowledge,* and might
want to install as heir to Ryle's "knowing how," we ought
to include such knowledge as this. So let us add to the
previously defined kind of knowledge, roughly knowledge
that something is the thing to do, knowledge which has
two properties, namely a) that the sentences in which
it is formulated have certain structural similarities with
the sentences already included, and b) that the thing
known entails a statement to the effect that some thing
is (other things being equal) the thing to do.

The resulting category of practical knowledge would
bear a suspicious resemblance to that of knowledge stat-
able in what Hare once called "evaluative" terms. We
might invite Hare to consider whether the entailment relations (in the usual sense) used in my projected definition would not embody one aspect of the property with

which he sought to define "value-judgements." Hare's formulation was that value-judgements entail imperatives in his extended uses of the terms "entail" and "imperative."[22] The full unpacking of his formulation connects "value-judgements" with actual action. Mine so far connects knowledge in "evaluative" matters with knowing what to do. But in the second stage of my revised account we will find a connection between knowing what to do and doing it, and thus will provide in some form for the remaining aspect of Hare's property.

9. IMPLICATIONS FOR FAMILIAR PROBLEMS

To proceed to this second stage, we can ask whether practical knowledge, as delimited by some definition on the lines just sketched, has properties which are of interest for various philosophical issues. Of the many problems that could be raised, I think it will follow the drift of Ryle's account most closely to select the problem of the criteria for ascribing knowledge to a person. In his introduction to the chapter on "knowing how" in *The Concept of Mind*, Ryle says (p. 26):

> The main object of this chapter is to show that there are many activities which directly display qualities of mind, yet are neither themselves intellectual operations nor yet effects of intellectual operations. Intelligent practice is not a step-child of theory.

Accurate exegesis of the chapter would have to take account of constant intersubstitution of such terms as "competences," "abilities to do things," "intelligence in practice," and "knowing how to do things." But it is obviously a substantial part, at least, of the strategy of the chapter to argue that "knowing how" is a disposition whose exercises are "observances of rules or canons or the applications of criteria," but are not "tandem opera-

22 R. M. Hare, *op. cit.*, sections 2.4, 11.2.

tions of theoretically avowing maxima and then putting them into practice" (p. 46). In order to defend such a view, Ryle argues that ability to perform is primary in "knowing how" and that ability to formulate is secondary. He comes close to saying that certain kinds of performance are necessary and sufficient for "knowing how," and that ability to state anything is not relevant. Of the boy who is learning chess he says (p. 41):

> It should be noticed that the boy is not said to know how to play, if all he can do is to recite the rules accurately. He must be able to make the required moves. But he is said to know how to play, if, although he cannot cite the rules, he normally does make the permitted moves, avoid the forbidden moves and protest if his opponent makes forbidden moves. His knowledge how is exercised primarily in the moves that he makes, or concedes, and in the moves that he avoids or vetoes. So long as he can observe the rules, we do not care if he cannot also formulate them.

The implied contrast with "knowing that" is evident. In ascribing to a person the knowledge, say, of a matter of particular empirical fact, the person's ability to state the fact and to acknowledge formulations of it is in some way central to the criteria of ascription. As to behavioural or performance criteria, on the other hand, no type of performance not involving formulations of the fact is uniquely relevant. There is only an indefinitely wide variety of actions, corresponding to the variety of intentions, motives, desires and the like in the light of which the fact in question would make those actions appropriate. Thus to act as if one knew that it was raining would be a quite different thing according to whether one was afraid to get wet, enjoyed walking in the rain, or wanted to catch a train.

Such a contrast survives under the revised definition of practical knowledge. For in the formulation of the content of such knowledge a particular kind of action is singled out. The primary criteria for ascription of such knowledge concern action of the specified kind, whether these criteria lay down success in action of that kind or lay down some time, place, manner, or the like for action of that kind. These performance criteria can be read off from the statement of that which is known. Moreover, when such criteria are relevant, the person's ability or inability to state or acknowledge formulations of what he knows recedes to the status of weak evidence either way.

Ryle, being preoccupied with the English use of "know how to V," gave a simple version of this primacy of behavioural criteria. For the test of knowing a way to V is whether or not one succeeds in V-ing. But there is no problem about including the standard uses. For it is just as crisp a matter to specify the test of knowing that some way or time of V-ing is the way in which to V or the time at which to V: it is whether or not one V-s in that way or at that time. Similarly, the test of knowing that one must or ought to V is whether or not one does V. So when we have finished revising Ryle's account, we have arrived at the opening sentence of Hare's *The Language of Morals*: "If we were to ask of a person 'What are his moral principles?' the way in which we could be most sure of a true answer would be by studying what he did."

It would be foolish to suggest that the criteria for ascription of knowledge, or of belief, were anything but extremely complex. It is easy to oversimplify the relation between knowledge and action, and the relation between knowledge and acknowledgement, on both sides of our contrast. But it seems obvious that there is an important reversal, on the side of practical knowledge, of the relative importance of verbal formulation and of action. The significant aspect of Ryle's achievement seems to me the realization that there is such a type of knowledge, and that the very definition of it can supply the material for stating this contrast in criteria of ascription. That there is a kind of propositional content for knowledge, such that the knower need not be able to say what he knows but exhibits his knowledge in performance, is no less striking a claim than Ryle's original claim that there is a kind of knowledge which has no propositional content.

On the other hand, it may be apparent by now why the revolution in ethics was never heard from. One problem in ethics is to analyse the meaning of utterances to the effect that someone ought to do something. On my account, knowing what one ought to do involves knowing what to do. We could equally well say that it involves knowing how to act. Consequently, as long as these points are the substance of what is meant, there is no objection to the thesis that for the agent at least, moral knowledge is "knowing how." Indeed it might be argued that the cases for which this holds will be central in any adequate analysis of moral utterances. What my account of practical knowledge shows, however, is that the relevant "knowing how" is still propositional and still formulable in a "that" clause. Analysis of the judgement *that such-and-such is the thing to do* raises the same old problems as analysis of the judgement *that such-and-such ought to be done*. No immunity from objectivist-subjectivist dilemmas is conferred by such streamlining of the content of the moral judgements. So the concept of "knowing how" is unable in principle to contribute anything new in ethics. Or perhaps it would be fairer to say that it makes its contribution to ethics under other names, in the work of Hume and Kant, and in that of Reginald Jackson and Hare.

POLYMORPHOUS CONCEPTS

J. O. URMSON

Few philosophers can have been more fertile than Gilbert Ryle in detecting groups of concepts with some noteworthy set of characteristics and christening them. In his contribution to a symposium on *Thinking and Language*, read at the Joint Session of The Aristotelian Society and the Mind Association in 1951, he diagnosed and christened polymorphous concepts. To remind the reader of Ryle's account of these polymorphous concepts, it would be well to quote three paragraphs from that contribution:

If asked "What does working consist of?" we should quickly object that there was no general answer. Some sorts of work are done with some sorts of tools, others with other sorts. But sometimes the same work might be done with alternative tools. Some work does not require tools at all. The dancer uses her limbs, but her limbs are not implements. A headmaster might do his work though deprived of the use of his arms, or his legs or his eyes. Some sorts of work are done with special materials, like string or Carrara marble. But the work might be done with different materials, and some work does not require materials at all. An artist's model need not even be attending to her work. She might be paid for sleeping or playing patience in the studio. There need be no action, inner or overt, performed by the policeman on his beat, which he may not also perform when strolling round the same streets when his work is over. Not all work is for pay; not all work is unpleasant; not all work is tiring. Nothing· need be done, thought, or felt by the professional footballer at work, that might not be done, thought, or felt by the amateur at play. *Work* is a polymorphous concept. There is nothing which must be going on in one piece of work which need be going on in another. Nothing answers to the general description "what work consists of." None the less, each specific job is describable. The workman can be told what he is to do. The concepts of *fighting, trading, playing, housekeeping,* and *farming* are also polymorphous concepts, where the concepts of *boxing* and *apple-picking* are nearly enough non-polymorphous.

The concept of *thinking* is polymorphous. There is no general answer to the question "What does thinking consist of?" There are hosts of widely different sorts of toilings and idlings, engaging in any one of which is thinking. Yet there need be nothing going on in one of them, such that something else of the same species or genus must be going on in another of them. Where certain specific sorts of incidents must be going on for someone to be counting, any of a wide variety of heterogeneous incidents can be going on when he is thinking. Just as there are hundreds of widely different operations, including apple-picking, to be occupied in any one of which is to be doing farm-work; so there are lots of widely differing operations, including multiplying, all of which are proper specimens of thinking.

Consider the dictum that in thinking the soul is talking to itself. It is clearly both too wide and too narrow. An actor's part may be running through his head while he eats and walks, even though he wishes it would stop. If he is not deliberately rehearsing his part or even considering the merits and demerits of his words, he can deny that he is thinking, while allowing that he is saying significant things to himself. Conversely, a poet, essayist, or philosopher may be trying hard to find the word, phrase, or argument that he needs, but the time when he is thinking what to say is the time when he still has nothing to say. In some thinking, the soul is only stammering to itself.

I propose to examine, rather than to attack or defend, this technical concept with which Ryle has presented us. Whatever may be etiquette with regard to live-stock, it is right and proper to look a philosophical gift-horse closely in the teeth. It is particularly desirable to do so in the present case, since, naturally enough, in the paper quoted Ryle does not develop the notion further than is necessary for its application to the problems raised by his fellow symposiasts.

If we do scrutinize carefully what Ryle has to say it is by no means clear how he wishes to characterize polymorphous concepts. It sometimes appears that a concept, such as the concept of X-ing, is polymorphous if there is no general answer to the question "What does X-ing consist of?" Let us, for syntactical convenience, coin the expression "action-content" as equivalent to "that of which the action consists." It might seem, then, that the concept of X-ing is polymorphous if there is no action-content which is a both necessary and sufficient condition of X-ing. But if what the action consists of contrasts, as presumably it does, with such things as the context, merits, and intention of the performance, the status of the agent, relevant social and legal customs, and the like, there is no action-content which is a necessary and sufficient condition of the vast majority of our concepts of action. Consider the action-concepts expressed in English by words beginning "ab . . .": *abandon, abbreviate, abdicate, abduct, abet, abjure, abolish, abridge, abrogate, abscond, absolve,* and *abuse*; it is surely clear without argument that the action-content is in none of these cases a necessary and sufficient condition of their application. It cannot be so prevalent a feature as this that Ryle wishes to isolate.

Let us start again. After saying that *work* is a polymorphous concept, Ryle adds: "There is nothing which must be going on in one piece of work which need be going on in another. Nothing answers to the general description 'what work consists of.'" If this is to count as a sufficient characterization of a polymorphous concept, it would seem that Ryle is here treating a concept as polymorphous, not because no action-content is both a necessary and sufficient condition of the application of the concept, but because no action-content is even a necessary condition of its application. Clearly the criterion that no action-content is a necessary condition of the application of a concept picks out a smaller class of concepts than does the criterion that no action-content is both a necessary and sufficient condition; thus hurrying satisfies the latter criterion but not the former, since moving fast is a necessary but not a sufficient condition of hurrying. So the concept of *hurrying* is not polymorphous by the criterion we are now considering, but, like most other concepts, would have been according to the criterion we first considered.

Perhaps this interpretation of what Ryle has in mind best suits the name "polymorphous"; the polymorphous will be that which may take different forms, no form being necessary to it. But it is in fact difficult to believe that it is what Ryle intends. Not only does this interpretation still pick out a very wide and heterogeneous class of concepts; more importantly, it will make many of his examples he gives in elucidation simply irrelevant. Thus Ryle says: "There need be no action, inner or overt, performed by the policeman on his beat, which he may not also perform when strolling round the same streets when his work is over"; and again: "Nothing need be done, thought, or felt by the professional footballer at work, that might not be done, thought, or felt by the amateur at play." But these points are irrelevant to showing that the action-content is not a necessary condition of working; they are clearly designed to show that the action-contents mentioned are not sufficient conditions of working. Similarly Ryle criticises the dictum that in thinking the soul is talking to itself on the ground that "it is clearly both too wide and too narrow." That the soul be talking to itself is not a sufficient condition (too wide) nor a necessary condition (too narrow) of thinking.

It seems to me, therefore, that the most plausible interpretation of Ryle's notion of the polymorphous concept is as follows. A concept, such as the concept of X-ing, is said to be polymorphous if there is no general answer to the question "What does X-ing consist of?". But there may be two quite different reasons why such a general answer may be impossible. One reason is that X-ing may consist of totally disparate activities; working, for example, may consist of using tools or of sitting in a studio. The other reason is that some quite specific performance may count as X-ing against one background but not against another; the professional footballer is working, for example, the amateur is not. We have, then, two distinct possibilities; the concept of X-ing may be such that either

> (1) No action-content is a sufficient condition of X-ing,
> or (2) No action-content is a necessary condition of X-ing.

I take it that Ryle regards a concept as polymorphous only if it satisfies both these conditions, not if it merely satisfies one of them. My grounds for this interpretation are: first, and most importantly, that Ryle insists that both these conditions are satisfied by his two paradigm examples of working and thinking; secondly that it selects at least a narrower class of concepts than either of the other interpretations that we have considered, both of which were manifestly too wide. It is clear that our present interpretation is much more restrictive than our first suggestion that a concept was polymorphous if no action-content was both a necessary and sufficient condition of X-ing. For it could be the case that making a movement A was a necessary condition of X-ing and making movements B+A was a sufficient condition of X-ing, but that neither A nor A+B was a necessary and sufficient condition of X-ing, since making the movements A + C was also a sufficient condition of X-ing. In this case the concept of X-ing would be polymorphous on our first suggestion, but not according to our present interpretation.

This interpretation of the notion of a polymorphous concept could be correct, even if it emerged that according to it neither *working* nor *thinking* turned out to be polymorphous. But one obvious difficulty must be faced at once. "Not all work is for pay," Ryle says in the passage quoted above, and this is no doubt true. But surely *writing a philosophical article for pay* is a sufficient condition of working. So, if Ryle wants to claim that *doing it for pay* may be part of an account of what X-ing consists of, it is plain that he must allow that we have provided one clear case of an action-content which is a sufficient condition of X-ing and *working* will therefore not be a polymorphous concept according to our present interpretation. Being paid is not, indeed, on its own a sufficient condition of working; if I am paid a lump sum as a condition of abstaining from publishing a piece of information I shall not therefore count my abstention as work. Nor, obviously, is being paid a necessary condition of working. But writing or playing football for pay is inevitably working, even if it be a labour of love. My solution to this problem is to suggest that Ryle is making a slip when he brings in "doing it for pay," which it is surely wrong to regard as being part of what the action consists of, as part of what is going on. "He was paid for doing it" no more tells us what he did than does "He was despised for doing it."

Let us then take it that the concept of X-ing is polymorphous if no action-content is a sufficient condition of X-ing and no action-content is a necessary condition of X-ing. As we shall see, there certainly are concepts which satisfy these two conditions, whether or not *thinking* and *working* are included among them. Even more certainly there are many concepts which satisfy one or other of these conditions. It may throw some light on polymor-

phous concepts which satisfy both if we first examine
some of the ways in which it may come about that a concept satisfies one or the other.

We shall first consider the case of concepts of action
such that some action content will be a necessary but not
a sufficient condition of the application of the concept.
But clearly one or more sets of conditions must be jointly
sufficient for the application of any concept, if we are to
be able to know that we have correctly applied it; if no
set of conditions were sufficient for the application of
the concept of X-ing we should never be able to say of
anyone with certainty that he was X-ing, or know exactly
what we were asserting of him in asserting that he was
X-ing. So if an action-content is a necessary but not a
sufficient condition of X-ing, one way in which a sufficient condition of X-ing could be achieved would be by
finding another necessary condition, other than action-
content, which, together with the action-content, would
constitute a sufficient condition of X-ing.

The further necessary condition may be a certain intention. Thus it is a necessary condition of *pruning* that
the action should consist of the cutting of twigs and
branches from a bush or tree; but it is not a sufficient
condition, since I may do this when gathering roses or
collecting wood for a fire, neither of which counts as
pruning, though I may chance to do it in a way indistinguishable from the performance of a skilled pruner. I
must perform an action with this content with the intention of improving the future growth of the plant pruned,
if it is to count as a case of pruning. I think it is also
clear that *weeding* must consist of removing plants from
the earth, but that a further necessary condition of weeding is that it should be done with the intention of freeing the ground of undesirable plants (so that the making
of some value judgment will be a subsidiary necessary
condition of weeding). Again, to *hurry* one must move
quickly, but must do it to save time and not from mere
love of high velocities or for exercise. It is unnecessary

to multiply examples further; but we may note that very many names of crimes involve an action-content with a certain intention—theft, for example, involves taking goods with the intention of permanently depriving the owner of them.

We have noticed, incidentally, that a necessary condition of the application of an action-concept may be that the agent to whom it is applied has made some value judgment; to weed I must judge the plants removed to be undesirable for otherwise I may be merely thinning out or lifting plants to give to a neighbour. But also a necessary condition of the application of a concept may be that the person applying it should make some value judgment. If I listen to a conversation to which I am not a party, you will say that I am *eaves-dropping* only if you judge that I ought not to be listening; if I make my way through a crowd, you will judge me to be *jostling* only if you think that I ought to be less self-assertive. A favourable judgment of what is done is implied by speaking of giving back as *restitution* or of conceding as *acknowledging*. The evaluation may also be of the skill of the performance rather than, as in the cases so far considered, of the merit of engaging in it at all; thus to say that I have *misdescribed* involves the judgment that I have described badly, and to say that I was *gabbling* involves the judgment that I was speaking badly. Further examples are legion.

Further necessary conditions, other than action-content, arise from status and similar matters of background and convention. Thus anyone who can speak can perform the act which consists of telling somebody that he may do something; but he will be performing the act of *authorising* only if he has a certain status. It is unnecessary for us to elaborate this point, since Austin has provided us with so many examples in his discussion of illocutionary forces. *Marrying* was his paradigm case.

There is clearly no theoretical upper limit to the number of types of extra necessary conditions beyond

A Collection of Critical Essays 257

action-content that may be part of the sufficient condition of the application of a concept. Thus we have concepts which can be applied only to actions which have a certain content and are also performed at a certain time; presumably *noctambulate* and *breakfast* are examples (though I have seen in Detroit a notice proclaiming "Breakfast served all day and all night"). But there is no point now in any attempt at being exhaustive. It is much more to the point to notice that we have now to hand a recipe for creating, and perhaps a clue for finding, concepts which will formally satisfy Ryle's criteria for being polymorphous. A concept will clearly be polymorphous, formally, if some one or more of the necessary conditions other than action-content which we have so easily found are treated as being a necessary and sufficient condition of its application. If some feature other than action-content is a necessary and sufficient condition of the application of a concept, action-content will clearly be neither.

We could clearly invent such concepts; we could have a concept of *seven-o'clocking*, the necessary and sufficient condition of the application of which should be that what was done should be done at seven o'clock. But we do not need to invent them, for there are already many such concepts. Thus it is a necessary and sufficient condition of *misbehaving* that the action-content, whatever it may be, should be something that ought not to be done. It is a necessary and sufficient condition of *copying* that one should act with the intention of producing a copy, and any action content may either be a case of copying or of mere incidental resemblance. The concept of *ruling* covers all, but only, actions performed in virtue of a certain status. *Wronging, taking revenge, competing, responding, helping, tantalizing,* and *complying* are just a few further examples of concepts for the application of which no action-content is either a necessary or a sufficient condition.

There is something very disturbing about the situation

at which we have arrived. When Ryle says that the concept of *working* is polymorphous and that the concept of *thinking* is importantly like it he seems to be saying something both true and exciting. But it would be ridiculous to imagine that *thinking* could be helpfully compared to *wronging* or to *taking revenge*; nor can *wronging* and *taking revenge* be helpfully compared to each other. It is clear that, if it is true that no action content is a necessary or sufficient condition of either thinking or working, this only places these concepts in a class the membership of which is large and heterogeneous in the extreme. Either, therefore, we have still misunderstood Ryle's explanation of the polymorphous concept or his explanation was insufficient to pick out the special features of such concepts as those of working and thinking that he had in mind. There is clearly a difficulty here that needs our attention.

We understood that for a concept to be polymorphous it must satisfy two criteria:

1) No action-content must be a sufficient condition of its application;
2) No action-content must be a necessary condition of its application.

We have seen that the first of these two criteria will be satisfied if there is some other necessary condition such that it and the action-content are jointly sufficient for the application of the concept (as the cutting of branches and a certain intention are separately necessary and jointly sufficient for the application of the concept of pruning). We have also seen that the first criterion will be satisfied if there is some condition other than action-content which is both a necessary and a sufficient condition of the application of the concept (as the impropriety of behaviour is a necessary and sufficient condition of the application of the concept of misbehaving). The second criterion of the polymorphous is that no content shall be a necessary condition of the application of the concept. It is obvious that this criterion will be automatically satisfied whenever there is some condition other than action-content which is a both necessary and sufficient condition of the application of a concept. Hence the awkward situation in which we find ourselves; the second criterion has been trivialized and we find ourselves faced with a useless miscellany of polymorphous concepts.

But it may be that there is no action-content which is necessary for reasons other than the existence of a sufficient condition of some other type. Aristotle has brought to our attention two ways in which this may happen, though he gives no examples of action-concepts to which they apply. Things not in the same genus may be given the same name without punning if they contribute to a single end or stem from a single case; Aristotle's favourite example is that of the healthy man (the central case) and the healthy food, healthy way of life, healthy place, and the like, which are called healthy because they contribute to the health of the healthy man; we may modernize another of his examples by instancing the academic enterprise, garment, person, and institution. Thus what is a sufficient condition for applying the concept *healthy* to a food will not be a necessary condition for the application of that concept to a man. The other way suggested by Aristotle is what he calls *analogia*. Intellectual argument and information is the sustenance, food, or pabulum of the mind because it stands to the mind as organic matter stands to the body; a note, a number, a mountain are all high if they stand in the same relation to their backgrounds. But a high note and a high mountain do not share a generic feature. Wittgenstein brought out another way in which there need be no generic sameness of content to justify the application of the same content when he drew our attention to the phenomenon of family resemblance; there is no single necessary condition for something to be a game, though many different contents will severally be sufficient conditions of it being a game.

Thus there is nothing very exotic about the absence of a necessary condition for the application of a concept. Admittedly the examples considered in the last paragraph were not of action-concepts; but we can perhaps find family resemblance cases among action-concepts. Perhaps *picking* will serve as one. There seems to be no action-content necessary to picking, if we assemble such diverse cases as picking a flower, a winner, a team, and a seat; if you ask me to pick a certain rose for you, you are not asking me to do any selecting; if I pick a winner and a seat, I am in both cases selecting, but I select one seat from many seats while I try to pick out the winner from the losers. Yet *picking* is surely not a polymorphous concept, since it would be easy to find action-contents which were a sufficient condition of its application.

So we have now found two ways in which a concept may satisfy the two criteria under consideration. In the first case no action-content will be either a necessary or a sufficient condition for the application of the concept because there is some other type of necessary and sufficient condition, as in the case of *misbehaving*. This case is without interest; it embraces many quite heterogeneous concepts, as we have already clearly seen. But there is another possibility. It may be that no action-content is sufficient because there is another necessary condition other than content for the application of the concept, and that no action-content is necessary because there is a set of different action-contents, related by family resemblance or in some similar way, each of which will be sufficient, jointly with the other necessary condition, for the application of the concept.

Can this possibility, or some variation on it (of which there are many), be used to illuminate the special features of working and thinking which Ryle seeks to illuminate with his notion of the polymorphous concept? Before we tackle this question directly, there is an interesting feature of these two concepts that I should like to bring out.

Working has no strict opposite or contrary; but it is

most typically contrasted with recreation and leisure pursuits. One of Ryle's leisure pursuits and recreations is gardening; I should never be surprised to hear that he has spent the afternoon working in his garden. But perhaps I ought to be surprised when I hear this, for if gardening is his recreation how can he be working when he is gardening? Yet in fact it does not ring at all oddly if somebody says that his favourite recreation is working in his garden. However, we should be surprised if a professional philosopher, filling in one of those tiresome statisticians' questionnaires, were to include his hours of gardening in his answer to a question about the number of hours he worked each week; we should be shocked if he were to refuse a legitimate professional call on his time on the ground that he had other pressing work to do, if it emerged that this other pressing work was lawn-mowing; if he can find much time for gardening over a certain period, then for that period he cannot have been very busy. It is clear that only for certain limited purposes can a professional philosopher's gardening be called work, and that for many important purposes it must be contrasted with his work. It is also worthy of attention that not all recreation, however strenuously pursued, can be called work. It is all very well in the case of gardening, knitting, carpentry, and rug-making; these are most naturally categorized as working; it is perfectly reasonable to speak of somebody as working on his stamp-collection · or on a painting. But we should require some special explanation if we were told that somebody was working on a game of ludo or a detective story, or that he was working at a country walk or a game of cricket. No doubt, if I am writing a detective story, even for fun, I may be said to be working at or on it, but not when I am sprawled in an armchair reading it.

Let us call occupations which would be counted as work in all standard contexts, primary cases of work, and those which would be called work only for some purposes, but not for many important ones, secondary cases of work.

Something similar can be detected in the case of thinking. Ryle rightly reminds us (*op. cit.*):

The title "thinking" is not reserved for the labours of trying to decide things. I am thinking if I am going over, in my head, the fortunes of the heroine of a novel that I have been reading; or if I am re-savouring a well turned argument, though I have long since accepted its conclusion. Or if I am drifting in idle reverie from one topic to another. Only some thinking is excogitation; only some thinking is work; only some thinking has a topic or problem.

All this is very true, but are these primary or secondary cases of thinking?

If I were to start to speak to Ryle and he said "Hang on a bit, I am thinking," it would be a bit upsetting if it later emerged that he had been drifting in idle reverie from one topic to another, or going over (not, for example, trying to reconstruct) the fortunes of the heroine of a novel. Or what should we think of the intelligence of a man who rejected the view that thinking is as tiring as manual labour on the ground that reverie was minimally fatiguing? Do I comply with the injunction "Think before you act!" if I daydream a little about my future actions before performing them? Should Benn's *Thinkers' Library* have included detective stories to be ruminated over by the evening fire? It seems to me that these cases of idly running over the real or imaginary are quite parallel to what we called secondary cases of working.

It is also worth noting that not everything that, purposefully done, would count as the action-content of thinking could be counted as even a secondary case of thinking if done idly. No doubt Ryle's architect is thinking out his design for a war-memorial as he arranges and re-arranges toy bricks on the carpet; but if he idly groups toy bricks together it will be at best an irrelevant accompaniment to his thinking, not in any way a part of it.

In the light of all the considerations that we have before us I shall now try to sketch the general character of the concept of *working*. The central among the primary cases of working are those in which one does something, whatever it consists of, because it is necessary or useful in a practical way. Since people typically have the duty to do such things and are frequently paid for doing them, we also extend the primary cases of working to include doing anything, whatever it consists of, if it is done as a matter of duty for pay. In this way the game-playing of the professional comes to be counted as a primary case of work. Perhaps this is also how the activity of the professional philosopher comes to be counted as work; Aristotle could still think of philosophy as a leisure-activity (*schole*) to which business or work (*ascholia*) was but a necessary means. We, of course, still have the distinction between workingmen and such as are called to the "gentlemanly" vocations and professions.

In the case of primary work we thus have a slide, excluding action-content, from whatever is practically necessary or useful, to the same done as a matter of duty for pay, to anything which is done as a matter of duty for pay. Secondary cases of work are those which resemble reasonably closely in action-content typical and common forms of work. One of these, for example, is the cultivation of the soil, and thus the construction of an ornamental rockery for the pleasure of its construction comes to be counted as (secondary) work. Also, since central cases of work typically require effort and concentration, we are even prepared to say of an enthusiastic amateur game-player that he is working hard, though we are unlikely to say that he is working *simpliciter*. It would seem that we will not say that the solver of crossword puzzles is working because he is not doing anything sufficiently similar to what people commonly do in the way of primary work, though we can say that the amateur carpenter is working at his bench without any qualms.

But even so, the motive and background of an activity must not be too grossly dissimilar to that of the same activity performed as primary work if it is to count as secondary work. You may say that I am working in the garden if I am cutting down a tree just because I enjoy cutting down trees and think that the one I am cutting down will not be missed. But if it is your favourite tree and I am angry with you and am cutting down the tree purely as an act of spite against you it would surely be distinctly off-colour to call my activity "working in the garden." I am inclined to agree with the view which I have attributed to Ryle that no action-content is indefeasibly a sufficient condition of working. There is a story of Oxford undergraduates disguising themselves as workmen and digging up Carfax under the noses of the police; they appeared to be working, but surely they were not.

It seems to me that the story is essentially the same in the case of thinking as in the case of working. Primary thinking is any activity devoted to the answering of a question or the solving of a problem, theoretical or practical. It is surely clear that the manipulation of toy bricks or of chessmen and similar forms that thinking may take, as Ryle shows in his article, would count as part of thinking only when undertaken with some such end in view. Again, Ryle's insistence that we want histories and not chronicles of thinking is no doubt correct; but how could we give a history, as opposed to a chronicle, of "drifting in idle reverie from one topic to another"? The history is surely possible only when we have primary thinking which has a form—a beginning and a middle and an end—distinct from mere temporal succession. Such secondary thinking as idle reverie seems to be called thought only from the similarity of its content to typical cases of primary thinking. Idly going over the fortunes of the heroine in one's head is very like an attempt to reconstruct from memory the plot of the novel, so far as what the activity consists of is concerned, and so we call it thinking. But thinking is not typically done by manipulating toy bricks, so that idle play with such bricks is not counted as thinking, even in a secondary way. But as I should not be pre-

pared to call the cutting down of a tree as an act of revenge a case of working in the garden, so, with Ryle, I
should not want to count having a tune or a poem on the
brain as a case of thinking.

So, in summary, I wish to suggest that the reason why
the cases of working and thinking satisfy the two criteria
which I have taken to be the criteria for being polymorphous is that:

(1) For primary cases of thinking and working we can
find necessary and sufficient conditions for the application of the concept other than action-content. This adequately explains why action-content is neither a necessary nor a sufficient condition.

(2) Cases where we are willing to apply the concept,
though the necessary and sufficient conditions for primary
employment are not satisfied, are to be explained by similarity in content to typical cases of the primary application of the concept. But these are cases of secondary
thinking or working, in that the activity will be counted
as thinking or working only for certain limited purposes
and in certain contexts.

It seems to me that Ryle was following a sound instinct
in concentrating on these two examples. For the concepts
of *fighting, trading, housekeeping,* and *farming* do not
seem to me to have the same sort of complication, though
they formally satisfy the criteria for being polymorphous,
as Ryle claims. It seems that Ryle's formal account of the
polymorphous concept, if I have interpreted it aright, is
too wide for his purposes. There are too many significantly different ways in which a concept may satisfy the
criteria for it to be very helpful to characterize *thinking*
as a polymorphous concept. I have tried to offer a more
specific account of the concept of *thinking,* and incidentally for that of *working,* though one based on Ryle's
work, rather than in opposition to it. Not that what is
said in this paper is in fact close-grained enough to deal
with all nuances; according to the account of the matter

which I have offered washing one's face should be an
example of working, but we should not usually account it
as such. Such details have been beyond my scope.

My thesis, then, has been that Ryle's account of polymorphous concepts is capable of more than one interpretation. I have suggested that with regard to *working*
and *thinking* the most acceptable interpretation is that in
their primary employment these concepts are such that
no action-content is a sufficient condition and no action-
content a necessary condition of their application. I have
further suggested that this is because in each case there is
a necessary and sufficient condition of application other
than action-content. But these concepts have the peculiarity that they can be applied secondarily when the necessary and sufficient condition is not satisfied, provided
that the action-content is very similar to that of typical
and common cases of primary employment. The secondary cases, I have suggested, can be recognized as such by
the fact that we are willing to apply the concepts to them
only for some purposes and in some contexts, but not in
all.

WORDS AND SENTENCES

G. J. WARNOCK

Gilbert Ryle has written often, wittily, and well about meaning. From what he has written on that subject I want to pick out for further scrutiny one particular topic —namely, that of the relations, or some of them, between the notions of *words, sentences, use,* and *meaning.* On this topic, on which Ryle has written more than once,[1] he seems to me, though battling on the side of the angels, to have gone wrong in some respects; and I believe he has gone wrong through seeking, as one might put it, to cut a longish story too short. If that is right, then there is more to be said, and not only in the sense in which there always is.

The issues I shall consider are these. First, Ryle remarks that, while we talk perfectly smoothly and intelligibly of "using" words, expressions, phrases, there is by contrast something jarring about, perhaps even wrong with, talking, as nevertheless some philosophers do, of "using" sentences. Second, and consequentially, he maintains that, whereas knowing what a word means can usefully be said to be a matter of knowing "how to use" that word, knowing what a sentence means cannot be said to be a matter of knowing how to use that sentence. And third, he seeks to explain this alleged linguistic asymmetry by reference to what words and sentences respectively are. I shall look at these matters in the reverse order. I shall try to show that Ryle goes wrong about what words

[1] I shall refer to "Ordinary Language," in *Philosophy and Ordinary Language,* ed. C. E. Caton (1963)—hereafter "O.L."; and also to "Use, Usage, and Meaning." Aristotelian Society Supplementary Volume XXXV (1961)—hereafter "U.U.M." "Ordinary Language" appeared originally in the *Philosophical Review* in 1953, but I shall refer to pages of the Caton volume.

and sentences are, and in consequence does not properly explain, and even does not quite correctly present, the linguistic data to which he calls attention.

Ryle's account of the difference between words and sentences presents it as a very radical difference indeed. He says, for example: "Words, constructions, etc., are the atoms of a language; sentences are the units of Speech. Words, constructions, etc., are what we have to learn in mastering a language; sentences are what we produce when we say things" (U.U.M., p. 224). Now this looks well enough at first. Ryle seems to be making merely the correct points (1) that to know a language is to have acquired (at any rate a good deal of) its vocabulary and grammar, and so (some) ability to construct and construe sentences in which that vocabulary is employed, whereas (2) to say something in a language, it is normally necessary actually to produce, not just some words, but a sentence.[2] But it emerges that Ryle wants to hold that "sentences are the units of Speech" in a much stronger sense than this; for a sentence, he goes on to say, is not merely what I have to produce in saying something; it actually *is* my saying it, or (sometimes) it *is* "what I say." (See, e.g., U.U.M., p. 229, and O.L., p. 120.) This puts things badly wrong, as soon appears.

"In daily life," Ryle continues (U.U.M., p. 225), "we do not often mention as such the sentences that people produce. We speak instead of their allegations, complaints, promises, verdicts, requests, witticisms, confessions, and commands." No doubt this is true. Sentences are something of a special interest—of, Ryle says, "people like grammarians, compositors, translators, amanuenses, and editors." But what these people do, he says, is to "refer to the things that people say as 'sentences'"— "what they are interested in are instances of someone,

---

[2] We can of course sometimes say something in a single word. You ask me "Are you going to London today or tomorrow?", and I say "Tomorrow." We need not dwell on this.

actual or imagined, alleging, complaining, warning, joking, etc., though their special concern is with the punctuation of them and not with their humorousness; with their length and not with their truth; with their moods and tenses and not with their relevance or rudeness." But this last bit is surely wrong, and wrong in more than one way. For one thing, "people like" grammarians, etc., are actually interested in very different things—grammarians in syntax, compositors in spaced strings of letters, translators in style and meaning, amanuenses and editors in lots of other matters. But more importantly, reference to sentences is only very misleadingly indeed to be described as reference "to what people say as 'sentences.'" Consider the sentence "That dog won't eat bananas." In what sense, if any, is this "something that people say?" Perhaps no one has ever said of any dog that it won't eat bananas; further, if anyone ever had said of some dog that it wouldn't eat bananas, someone else might have said something else, viz., that some other dog wouldn't eat bananas, by uttering the very same sentence. The sentence, then, is "something that people say" only in the very unnatural sense that it is a grammatical and meaningful sequence of words of English, which accordingly a competent speaker of English *might* utter. But, "What sentence did he utter?" is not usually what is meant by "What did he say?" The sentence itself is not, in the usual sense, "what someone says," only referred to in a rather specialized way; it is a certain grammatically structured sequence of words, in the utterance of which something, perhaps many different things, *could* be said, whether they ever *are* said or not.

Nor is a sentence an "instance" of "someone, actual or imagined, alleging, complaining," etc. You allege that Smith's dog won't eat bananas, I complain that my dog won't eat bananas; what we do, and say, is different, but the sentence that we utter may be the same; and if one wishes to talk simply about the sentence, there is no need to bring in anybody's allegations or complaints, whether actual or imagined—though indeed one might have occasion to mention that, of course, one who uttered that sentence *could* therein be alleging, complaining, etc. Again, a sentence is a grammatical item that can have moods and tenses; but *it* cannot have relevance or rudeness (except perhaps in the interesting special case of its containing a "rude word")—though, in uttering that sentence, something relevant or rude might be said from time to time. Conversely, a joke does not have punctuation, though the sentences may have in which a joke is told.

Things stay very similarly awry in Ryle's next paragraph. Mentioning the well-known dictum attributed to Julius Caesar, he observes, rightly, that there is something queer about the question "Is 'vici' a word or a sentence?"; but then he seems to mis-identify what is queer about it. There is, he says, firstly, the word "vici," a word in the Latin language; then there was Caesar's boast, "Vici," in giving his self-consciously laconic account of his dealings with Britain; and there perhaps was, on some other occasion, the nervous gladiator's query "Vici?", as his concussion wore off. That is, there is the word, and there are various speech-episodes, cases of boasting, inquiring, etc., in which that word is used. But there is nothing that could be one of these *or* the other, any more than there is anything which could be a cricket-bat *or* a cover-drive, a gibbet *or* an execution. These simply are not permissible disjunctions. But here one must object that there are not enough pieces on the board. By distinguishing *only* the word from episodes of its utterance, Ryle gives, and gets, the impression that sentences *are* speech-episodes. "The boast 'vici,'" he writes, "was a different sentence from the question 'vici?' . . ."; well, two sentences perhaps, but not, as he implies, because the episode of Caesar's boasting was a different episode from that of the gladiator's enquiring. For a sentence could not *be* a boast, though it might be uttered in boasting; and a sentence could not *be* a question, though it might be interrogative, i.e., such that its utterance would standardly be the asking of a question. If "vici" and "vici?" are different sentences, this is not because boasting is different from enquiring, still less because Caesar's boasting was a different episode from someone else's enquiring. Boasting, after all, is different from not boasting, but if I say boastfully, and you say modestly, "Vici," we have certainly each uttered the very same sentence. "Vici" and "Vici?" perhaps are different sentences, but if they are, the reason must be that they are syntactically distinguishable, as "Vici," said boastfully, and "Vici," said modestly, are not. Thus, what is queer about "Is 'vici' a word or a sentence?" is nothing so extreme as what is wrong with "Is that a bat or a cover-drive?". The trouble is that it is not answerable in the simple manner that the form of the question invites, since "vici," in Latin, *may* occur simply as an element, a word, in some larger linguistic structure, but may *also* occur by itself as a one-word sentence. To say which it is, we need a syntactic setting. The cause of the trouble, then, is the syntactic versatility of "vici," not the relatively harmless disjunction "word or sentence." After all we can say readily and properly enough that "Dogs bark" is a sentence, not a word, and that "sky" is a word, not a sentence; also that "Bark dogs but" is not a sentence, though it is a series of words, whereas "Dogs sometimes bark" is not simply a series of words, it is a sentence. And listening bemusedly to a highly polysyllabic language like German, I might quite naturally ask, after listening for quite a long time, "Was that a sentence?", and be given the dispiriting but intelligible answer "No, that was just the first word."

Finally (on this point) Ryle says (U.U.M., p. 229): "My last sentence but three, say, is not something with which I once learned how to say things. It *is* my saying something." But surely not; the sentence is neither his saying something, nor for that matter, in the most natural sense, what he says. It is what he uttered—in this case, wrote—*in* saying something, to the effect (if I've

counted right) that philosophers wrongly assimilate
words and sentences through neglecting the distinction
between Language and Speech. Someone else's saying of
this would be a different saying, not the same "episode,"
even if he happened to come out with the very same sentence; and also, of course, he (or Ryle) might have come
out with a different sentence, and yet said the same thing.
It is true that the sentence in question is not something
with which Ryle once learned how to say things; it is
something that he was able to compose, and write down
in saying what he wished to say, because of something
else that he once learned, namely, English. Nevertheless,
the sentence that he wrote down, and which was subsequently printed, is not to be identified (in the most natural sense) with what he said in doing so, or (in any sense)
with his saying it. His saying it, which took place in 1961,
was, as I happen to think, ill-judged; but the sentence
itself could not be said to be ill-judged, nor to have taken
place at that date or any other.

Can anything be said about how Ryle was led to mis-
characterize sentences in this way, or in these ways? Two
things, I think. First, having remarked to start with that
some of the things we say smoothly and intelligibly
enough about words "do not go," as he puts it (O.L.,
p. 119), when we seek to say the same things about sentences, he looks, rightly no doubt, for the relevant difference between words and sentences; but I suspect that he
had a preconceived idea of what this relevant difference
would be like. At least it would not be surprising if he
had anticipated that it would be a *difference of category*,
so that the dicta that "do not go" would be specimens
of that philosophically interesting species, *category-
mistakes*. I take no stand here on what sort of difference
a difference of category is; but at least one feels that it
ought to be a good, big difference, really clear and
radical, like that between an implement and what one
does with it, a bat and a cover-drive, a coin and a pur-

chase, a gibbet and an execution. So, if words, phrases, expressions are things used, and if sentences are to go into another *category*, what sort of things must sentences be? Surely they must be, not items used, but *usings*, i.e., speech-acts, episodes of saying. This is one of the answers Ryle gives—partly at least, I believe, just because it was the answer which his very Rylean proforma of a solution temptingly left room for.

Second, in his later discussion (U.U.M.) of much the same issue, I think that his philosophical movements were hampered by his initial introduction of Sir Alan Gardiner's distinction between Language and Speech.[3] Not that there is anything essentially wrong with this distinction; there clearly is a distinction to be made between languages, Latin, French, English, and so on, and "the activity or rather the clan of activities of saying things, saying them in French, it may be, or English or some other language" (U.U.M., p. 223). But in fact, when one comes to talk about sentences in particular, pre-occupation with this distinction is inevitably liable to confuse the issue. What happens, I suspect, in Ryle's case is that, finding that sentences cannot happily be located on one side of this distinction, he concludes that they must belong on the other side. Since learning French is a matter of acquiring the words, the syntax and semantics of French, and not of learning all, or most, or even any French sentences, sentences do not go on the "Language" side; so they must go on the "Speech" side, that is, must *be* the sayings of things in (e.g.) French. But this is a case of false alternatives; the Language-Speech distinction, as so far set out, has not put all the requisite pieces on the board, and in particular not enough for the proper location of sentences. If one does try to fit sentences, without distortion, into this distinction, one finds them, in a sense, recalcitrantly hovering on both sides of it. They hover on the Language side, since, while it is indeed true that learning

3 Alan H. Gardiner, *The Theory of Speech and Language* (1932).

a language does not consist in learning a list, or stock, or repertoire of sentences, it does consist precisely in acquiring, by way of mastering a vocabulary and a "grammar," the (some) *ability* to construct and construe sentences of that language; but then sentences seem to hover also on the Speech side, for the reason that (roughly, by and large) the activity of saying things essentially involves the utterance of sentences, and conversely the utterance of a sentence is (typically, usually) an instance of saying something. A sentence perhaps is not "part of" a language;[4] but nor is it an act of saying something in a language. It is, more complicatedly than this distinction allows for, something which (a) one who has fully acquired the relevant language has (therein) acquired the ability to construct and construe, and which (b) one who says something (whatever it may be) *in* that language must, or at least may, utter in doing so. We need, to repeat, more pieces on the board—words, sentences, what sentences mean, acts of uttering sentences, "what is said" when such acts are done, "what is done" when such acts are done, doubtless other things too. Words and "speech-episodes" are not enough to get on with.

So now we must look again at our use of the verb "use." For if there is something amiss with talk about "using" sentences, that cannot be so for the large, knock-down reason that Ryle has suggested; it is not that sentences are *usings*, sc. of words, and thus categorially cannot themselves be used. So should we look for some other reason? I think we should not, since I submit that, as a matter of fact, talk—some talk—of using sentences is in no way objectionable. For example, I might, in rendering one of Kant's arguments into English, use five

[4] Though some linguists in fact define a language as a "set of sentences," not of course that set which one learns in learning the language, but the ideal set, perhaps infinite, "generated" from its vocabulary by its grammar. This seems a bit artificial perhaps, but unobjectionable.

sentences where Kant used only two: Hemingway was fond of using very short sentences, without connectives, to create an effect, one may suppose, of non-literary toughness: interrogative sentences are often, perhaps usually, used in asking questions. And so on. There should surely be nothing surprising about this. For, omitting complications, a sentence is a certain kind of verbal structure, a syntactically ordered sequence of words of some language; and we do not in general concoct such sequences idly, just for fun. Usually, we want to do something with them, we produce them for a purpose, indeed, often, for several purposes at once; and what is this but to say that we do not just compose them, we *use* them? One of Ryle's own examples might here be turned against him. He compares (O.L., p. 119) the composer of a sentence with a cook; somewhat as a cook uses ingredients, and also uses kitchen utensils, in making a pie, so I may use certain words in composing a sentence. But then, a cook is unlikely to make a pie for no reason, purely for the sake of making it; having made it, her idea is probably to use it for something, perhaps as an item in the evening meal, or conceivably as a missile in a music-hall routine. Rather similarly, I am unlikely to compose my sentence just for fun; the likelihood is that I shall make some use of it, will use it in saying—and doing—something or other. Ryle's text in fact betrays some uneasiness here; for, after observing that the cook uses her ingredients and utensils, he says cautiously that she does not *in this way* use the pie—that the speaker who uses certain words in composing a sentence does not *in this way* use the sentence. That may be so; but it may be, too, that the cook does use the pie she has made, and the speaker the sentence he composes.[5] No doubt it is true that, as Ryle insists, cooks keep the ingredients they need to use "in stock," and not what they make from time to time out

---

[5] Not, usually, *after* he has composed it; we usually compose and utter, as it were, in one breath.

of those ingredients; similarly words are, so to speak, the "stock" of a language, in a way in which sentences are not —there are no dictionaries of sentences. But then it will obviously not do to suggest that only items "in stock," there, beforehand, ready for use, are ever used; I may construct something out of such items, and proceed to use *that*. Bat-makers use pieces of wood in making bats; and the bats they make are used by cricketers. Machines are often used in making other machines.

It is probably true that we do not often *have occasion* to speak of people as "using sentences." In fact the examples I gave of that locution suggest this, since each suggested a rather special interest in language, an interest of a sort that we perhaps do not often take in what people say. That Kant used only two sentences in stating some argument is something that, perhaps, only a translator would have occasion to remark upon. That Hemingway used a lot of short, bald sentences is of interest from the rather special angle of stylistic criticism. Normally, that someone in some way asked a question will be of more interest than that he did, or perhaps did not, use an interrogative sentence in doing so.

But if so, it is not of course at all surprising that philosophers should speak of using sentences more frequently than people usually do; for philosophers in their own way, as translators and critics and grammarians in theirs, have a special interest, not only—sometimes even not at all—in what people say, but in the manner and means and *minutiae* of saying it. One might add that, even given such special interests, occasions for speaking of using sentences may still be relatively few; for an interest in language will often be an interest in the *words*, and not particularly, perhaps not at all, in the sentential structures in which those words are syntactically embedded. Perhaps, then, talk of people using sentences is somewhat unusual, something we don't often have occasion for; but it seems to me wholly natural, indeed unavoidable, when we do have occasion for it. There is here, then, no genuine linguistic jarring to be accounted for.

But the case is somewhat different with Ryle's other, and perhaps his major, concern. "We talk about the meanings of sentences, seemingly just as we talk of the meanings of the words in it; so, if knowing the meaning of a word is knowing how to use it, we might have expected that knowing the meaning of a sentence was knowing how to use the sentence. Yet this glaringly does not go" (O.L., p. 119). Now this indeed does *not* go, at least not smoothly; so we have to ask why.

Well, first, does this way of speaking really go all that smoothly, even in the instance to which Ryle, here, does not object? "*If* knowing the meaning of a word is knowing how to use it . . ."—but *is* it? It seems to me that, in many cases, this should be recognized as at the very least a very strange thing to say. For it seems to me that, philosophical habits apart, "knowing the meaning of" and "knowing how to use" would more naturally be *contrasted*—or if that is too strong, at any rate not thus identified. It seems to me that the sort of word we "know how to use" (or don't) is typically the sort of word that plays a specific part in what might be called the tactics of discourse, and which in *that* sense has a special function. The Greek particles would be an excellent example of what I have in mind. What one knows about that famous pair "μέν" and "δέ," for instance, is exactly how to use them, partly where to put them in the sentence, but also what they *do* in the sentence, what their special point is; but I can think of no straight answer to the question, what they mean.[6] Rather similarly: what does "but" mean? Or "however," or "nevertheless"? What one knows about "but" is again, I think, how to use it—that is, as a conjunctive device, the special point, or effect, of which

[6] I note, for what it is worth, that Liddell and Scott conclude that they "must often be left untranslated."

is to imply (to put it very inaccurately, no doubt) that the conjunction, though it holds, might not have been expected. ("We were in Oxford during August, but it didn't rain.") "However," similarly, seems to have a role in discourse, rather than "a meaning"; I know how to use it, but I should not find it easy to say what it means. But now, with lots of other words, it seems the other way around. I know what the words "trombone," say, and "emigrate" mean; but I should be puzzled by the question whether I know how to use them. After all, unlike "but" and "however" and "δήπου," they just are *not* used in any special way; we have here a quite ordinary sort of noun and an intransitive verb, used just as other such nouns and verbs are, that is, in all sorts of ways, whenever what they mean makes such use appropriate.

Ryle says that understanding a word is "knowing how to use it, i.e., make it perform its role in a wide range of sentences." Now "but," it seems to me, clearly does have "its role" in sentences, as does "δήπου"; and "understanding" those words is, in that pretty clear sense, knowing how to use them. But does "trombone" have "its role" in sentences? At least it is not at all clear what this would mean. Surely it does not function in the same way in every sentence—in "The trombone is a brass instrument," "Promise not to play your trombone!", "Is that a trombone?". Or does it? Is there perhaps always *something* that is the same? Perhaps there is; but then that would be its *meaning*; and if so, in this very common sort of case "knowing how to use the word" would not elucidate, but would itself need to be elucidated by, the notion of knowing what it means. "Do you know how to use the word 'trombone'?"—"Well, I know what it means, *if that's the question you're asking.*"

Of course it is not, I suppose, untrue to say that I do know how to use the word "trombone." I know that it is a pretty ordinary sort of noun, and I know what it means, so that, whenever it happens to be the word that I want, I have no difficulty in bringing it out. I sometimes use the word, and all goes smoothly when I do, so presumably it's true that I know how to use it. But that I know how to use it is nevertheless, it seems to me, a strange thing to say, and particularly so when there is the further suggestion that my knowing what it means *is a matter of* my knowing how to use it. For the fact seems to be that "trombone," like a lot of other words, just isn't the sort of word of which we would naturally speak in this way. Since there isn't any particular "way of using" such a word, except of course to mean whatever it is that it does mean, to speak of knowing what it means seems natural, and of knowing how to use it, by contrast, strange; and the other way around, it seems to me, for "but," "δή," "donc," and words (I say vaguely enough) of that sort. But let me make quite clear what I am, and am not, maintaining here. I am *not* maintaining that to equate "knowing the meaning of" with "knowing how to use" is *wrong;* I am *not* denying that to do this might be a legitimate and valuable, though in itself cryptic, introduction to an illuminating account of meaning and understanding. Nothing so ambitious as that. What I *am* maintaining is that to propound this equation is, on the face of it at least and until something further is said, to say something *strange;* and this is pertinent to our present topic, since, if we are to consider an alleged oddity in the locution "knowing how to use the sentence . . . ," we ought not to contrast this suspect locution with "knowing how to use the word . . ." on the supposition that in the latter there is no whiff of oddity at all. To do this is to allow our philosophical habits to dull the sharpness of our ears for ordinary English, and thus to present our linguistic data in too black-and-white a guise.

So what about "Knowing how to use the sentence . . ."? Having suggested that "Knowing how to use the word . . ." is, at least in some cases, a less smooth, unsurprising idiom than Ryle implies, should we go on to suggest that the substitution of "sentence" for "word" is correspondingly less offensive? Well, yes, I think so; but only up to a point. The notion of knowing how to use a sentence does not seem to me so *glaringly* outrageous as Ryle says it is—in particular it seems to me not categorially wrong, not a case of speaking of using what categorially cannot be used. Even so, there is perhaps not much to be said for it, and something fairly serious to be said against.

I would suggest first that, very much as in the case of words, there is a sense in which it is presumably, but uninterestingly, true that people do know how to use sentences. If, in response to your asking me what time it is, I, wishing to inform you that it's nearly half past six, come out with the sentence "It's nearly half past six," then I have not just uttered that sentence idly but used that sentence, viz., used it in answering your question. Whether or not my answer is right, the sentence is perfectly intelligible to you as an answer, and conveys furthermore just the answer that I intended to give. So all has gone smoothly in my use of that sentence; and presumably it is thereby shown to be true, or at least not untrue, that I know how to use it. Nevertheless, that I know how to use the sentence does not seem a very *pointful* thing to say—it certainly does not even begin to make clear what exactly it is that one knows, in knowing what the sentence means, or what this knowing consists in. It is also, certainly, a pretty *strange* thing to say; very much as in the case of (some) words, if I were asked whether I know how to use the sentence "It's nearly half past six," I should find the question a puzzling one, and, in trying to construe it, would take it perhaps to be just a queer way of asking whether I know what it means.

But in this case surely there is more to be said, and in saying it we must go along with Ryle, even if not quite so far. One might say that, in talk of knowing how to use words, and of knowing what they mean as a matter of knowing how to use them, there is, even if such talk is in itself a little strange, at least a valuable *suggestio veri;*

there are important truths (I shan't here say what they are) about what it is to understand discourse, and to discourse meaningfully, which can quite naturally be introduced in this way, even if (as is obvious) the truths are really a good deal too complex to be adequately summed up in those dicta without further explanation. By contrast, even if we do know how to use sentences, and even if talk of knowing how to use them could be construed as a queer way of talking about knowing what they mean, there is in *this* way of talking an undoubted *suggestio falsi*—the suggestion, namely, that to understand a language is to be able to operate with some finite stock or set of sentences, the uses of which one has individually learned. Linguists, very properly, are never tired of insisting that a conspicuous feature of mastery of a language, the feature most crucially to be accounted for by any theory, is the ability of speakers to construct and construe sentences which they have never encountered before, and which may very well never have been uttered before. My vocabulary, like everyone else's vocabulary, is limited; and if I have never come across some word before, I cannot know, though perhaps I may guess, what that word means.[7] By crucial contrast, the number of sentences I could construct and construe is (theoretically, doubtless not actually) unlimited; and my ability to understand sentences is wholly independent of the question whether I have ever heard, read, written, or spoken those sentences before. In so far as talk of knowing how to use sentences, as a way of saying, or even beginning to say, what it is to know what sentences mean, does tend, as it very well might, to draw off our

[7] This is really too brisk and sweeping. I can get to the sense of "eating" or "eatable" from that of "eat"; if I know what "communist" and "anti-semitic" mean, I shall not be puzzled by "anti-communist"; and if I knew a bit about Italian, I might work my way from "trumpet" to "trombone." It is obvious, however, that there is not *in general* any principle or set of principles by which the sense of one word is derivable from that of another.

attention from this crucial contrast, then certainly such
talk is very greatly to be deprecated. If it is not quite so
radically wrong as Ryle suggested, nor wrong for at any
rate all the reasons he offers, he was surely quite right
here in scenting danger as he did. The way of speaking
he objected to could indeed be dangerously, disastrously
misleading; and that makes a good enough case for not
speaking in that way.

RYLE IN RELATION TO
MODERN SCIENCE

J. J. C. SMART

I.

Modern science presents a view of the universe which is very different from that which was available to previous generations. Man is now thought of much more as simply part of nature, rather than as set over nature. Even statistically there has been a great change in emphasis. Thirty years ago it seemed quite likely that the origin of the solar system was due to a highly improbable celestial accident and that it was not unreasonable to suppose that our own planet was the only place of intelligent life in the universe. There are at present still a number of competing theories of the origin of the solar system, none of them completely satisfactory, but opinion seems to have moved towards thinking it much more plausible that planetary systems and intelligent life should be a feature of innumerable stars even in our galaxy alone. We get an even greater sense of the relative unimportance of the human race in the universe as a whole when we consider the huge number of galaxies in the observable part of the universe. It is even quite a salutary corrective for human arrogance to look at a photograph of (say) the great nebula in Andromeda and reflect on the huge number of stars which appear as a misty cloud. When we go from the very large to the very small we also find that science has changed our views about man's place in the scheme of things. Biology has become increasingly biochemical, and it is hard to recapture the mood in which even so modernistic a prelate as E. W. Barnes, the Bishop of Birmingham, could write (in a book published in

1933[1]): "The mystery of life is unsolved, probably insoluble." Recent developments, such as the discovery of the structure of DNA and the synthesis of certain macromolecules, are spectacular cases of the general background to an increasingly mechanistic view of man. In particular, it looks as though the main difficulty in understanding the functions of the human brain lies in the difficulty of discovering its organisation, and does not lie in the adequacy for this purpose of the known laws of physics and chemistry. The chief evidence in the other direction would seem to come from the comparative lack of success of endeavours to produce artificial intelligence, which have given rise to Chomsky's judgment[2] that we should not be surprised if we find that known physical laws are inadequate to explain the functioning of the brain. But on the whole the indications do not seem to me to support the view that there is anything mysterious about life or mind.

I would suggest, therefore, that it is science, not metaphysics, which has been mainly efficacious in conditioning our present austere and unromantic view of man and his place in the universe, though in some respects the work of philosophers, such as Gilbert Ryle in *The Concept of Mind*, does useful mopping-up work. However, even in Ryle there can perhaps be found a residue of traditional ideas about the place of man in the world. If we read Ryle we feel that we are in a cosy sort of world of rowing, golf and cricket, card games and cooking, drill movements, tables, chairs and gardens. As Stuart Hampshire remarks in the last paragraph of his critical notice[3] of *The Concept of Mind*, there is a suggestion of "a sharply . . . definite view of the world: a world of solid and manageable objects, without hidden recesses, each

[1] E. W. Barnes, *Scientific Theory and Religion* (London: Cambridge University Press, 1933). See p. 420.

[2] Noam Chomsky, *Language and Mind* (New York: Harcourt, Brace & World, 1968), p. 12.

[3] MIND, 59 (1950), pp. 237-55 [reprinted in this volume].

visibly functioning in its own appropriate pattern." When we read Ryle neither vast astronomical spaces nor the strange world of the atomic nucleus is likely to be near the forefront of our consciousness. Now Ryle might justifiably say, "Well, why should it be?" and indeed for most of the time he is not concerned with issues in which his cosy examples do not do the job. But sometimes he does seem to me unjustifiably to play down the way in which the world view suggested by modern science does conflict with our cosy common sense view of the world, and in *Dilemmas* he even suggests that any conflicts between science and traditional religion are merely the products of conceptual confusion.[4]

Now I can see Ryle wincing a bit here, because he is (often rightly) suspicious of terms like "world view," and "Science" (with a capital "S"). In fact in *Dilemmas*[5] he does a bit of deflation of what he calls "two over-inflated ideas," the idea of *Science* and the idea of *world*. Let me attempt to carry out a bit of re-inflation.

Ryle says that "There is no such animal as Science." There are scores of sciences, he says, and most of them are "such that acquaintanceship with them or, what is even more captivating, hearsay knowledge about them has not the slightest tendency to make us contrast their world with the everyday world."[6] It is indeed true that there are scores of sciences, but we must not overlook the extent to which this is due to arbitrary departmentalism. Thus the study of DNA in plants or bacteria is much like the study of DNA in animals, and more like it than is the study of animal ecology. This example shows the philosophical unimportance of the division "microbiology—botany—zoology." No doubt with advancing knowledge new sciences develop, but it is

[4] See *Dilemmas* (London: Cambridge University Press, 1954, and henceforth referred to as "D"), p. 81.
[5] pp. 71–74.
[6] D, p. 71.

also true that old ones coalesce. There is a move towards unity and simplicity just as much as there is a move towards diversity and proliferation of detail.[7] I would therefore suggest that there is quite a lot of truth in saying that there *is* such an animal as "Science." Incidentally I would not think it illuminating to employ the cluster concept "science" quite as widely as Ryle does, when after saying that there are scores of sciences he proceeds to illustrate his point with the example of philology. For philosophical purposes I think that it is far more illuminating to classify philology as a *history*. I would also concede to Ryle that there is a non-arbitrary and philosophically important diversity between sciences, in as much as some of them, namely physics and chemistry, are concerned with the discovery of laws of nature, whereas others, like most of the biological ones, are mainly concerned with the application of known laws of nature (physical and chemical ones) to the explanation of generalisations of natural history. (Roughly, in the way in which electronics is physics plus wiring diagrams, biology is physics and chemistry plus natural history.)

Now for "world." Ryle's deflation of this idea begins by drawing attention to the use of the word "world" according to which there might be a periodical entitled "The Poultry World."[8] He points out that here the word "world" could be paraphrased by "field" or "sphere of interest" or "province." In this sense to speak of the world of physics would just be to speak of the physicist's sphere of interest. Here "world" does not mean "*the* world" or "the cosmos," any more than it does in "the poultry world" or "the entertainment world." Ryle says: "In the articles and books that [physicists] write for their colleagues the word 'world' seldom occurs, and the grand word 'cosmos,' I hope, never occurs." Actually

[7] On this point see the very instructive remarks by P. B. Medawar in his *The Art of the Soluble* (London: Methuen, 1967), pp. 114 ff.
[8] D, p. 73.

the most common synonym is "universe" and this word occurs very commonly (as might be expected) in cosmology. At its most fundamental physics seems to merge with cosmology, and in cosmological contexts "world" or "universe" tends to be used quite unsolemnly. There is, it is true, a tendency (perhaps for unnecessary positivist preconceptions) for cosmologists to mean by "universe" the observable part of the universe: that is, they may not include as part of "the universe" galaxies whose velocity of recession is greater than that of light or of events which (on the assumption of a "big bang" theory of cosmic evolution) occurred before the big bang. However, it is dangerous to set *a priori* limits to knowledge, and hypotheses about the world before the big bang (for example, hypotheses about an oscillating universe) and hypotheses about the nature of space extending beyond the observable part of the universe are indirectly testable, or at least may be to some extent supportable by considerations of simplicity or plausibility.[9] In any case, whether a cosmologist uses "universe" in the wider or narrower sense, he is talking about all or part of "the world" in the sense in which the metaphysician uses this shudder quoted word.

II.

Let me consider a particular way in which science in the past has been thought to suggest consequences for our general metaphysical view of the world, and Ryle's method of dealing with the ideas in question.

In the nineteenth century the philosophical view which seemed most natural to many sciences was a materialistic one. Scientists tended to think of mechanics as the basic science to which all other sciences should ultimately be

[9] See R. G. Swinburne, *Space and Time* (London: Macmillan, 1968), Chapter 12.

reduced. They thought of mechanics (and therefore of the universe) as rigidly deterministic: the idea was that if an infinite intelligence were to know the whole state of the universe at a certain moment it would be able to calculate the state of the universe at any time before or after that moment. E. Du Bois-Reymond put it with what now seems quaint nineteenth-century imagery: "As the astronomer predicts the day on which, after many years, a comet again appears on the vault of heaven from the depths of space, so this 'mind' would read in its equations the day when the Greek Cross will glitter from the mosque of Sophia or when England will burn its last lump of coal."[10] This is the form in which what Ryle has called "The Bogy of Mechanism"[11] reared its ugly head, and I think that it is here convenient to discuss mechanism in these nineteenth-century terms. It is true that mechanics is no longer thought of as the fundamental science to which all others, such as the theory of electricity and magnetism, will ultimately be reduced. Moreover, modern physics is indeterministic, so that even an infinite intelligence could not make the sort of predictions envisaged by Du Bois-Reymond (or by Laplace[12]). However, Ryle rightly rejects any attempt to provide a loophole for free will by means of quantum-mechanical indeterminism. As he says: "The modern interpretation of natural laws as statements not of necessities but of very, very long odds is sometimes acclaimed as providing a desiderated element of non-rigorousness in Nature. . . . This silly view assumes that an action could not merit

[10] Quoted in F. A. Lange, *The History of Materialism*, 3rd edition, translated by E. C. Thomas (London: Kegan Paul, 1925). See Bk. ii, p. 308.
[11] *The Concept of Mind* (henceforth referred to as "CM"), pp. 76 ff.
[12] See P. S. de Laplace, A *Philosophical Essay on Probabilities*, translated from the 6th French edition by F. W. Truscott and F. L. Emory (New York: Dover, 1951), p. 4.

favourable or unfavourable criticism, unless it were an exception to scientific generalisations."[13]

Let us therefore discuss the bogy of mechanism in nineteenth-century terms. Most of what we have to say will easily be adaptable to modern indeterministic physics, by making the appropriate qualifications. This will enable me to make my discussion more simple, and will avoid irrelevant difficulties.

In what way is mechanism a bogy? I think that there are two reasonably respectable reasons for thinking that the truth of a mechanistic world view would imply emotionally unpalatable consequences. Most importantly, I think that a mechanistic metaphysics implies a threat to those who set their hearts on a life after death. Belief in a life after death is *perhaps* consistent with a mechanistic outlook, provided that one allows certain very unplausible factual assumptions (resurrection of the body, and so on), though there are of course well-known difficulties over personal identity here. But it is surely more plausible to believe in life after death if we regard the soul more on the model of a Cartesian spiritual substance than on the model of some sort of complex of digital or analogue computers. The other possible source of worry about the bogy of mechanism is the thought that if our brains are mere mechanisms, devoid of souls or vital principles, then relatively intelligent people like ourselves will perhaps be superseded by electronic devices, just as the unskilled laborer has been superseded by earthmoving machinery, and the process worker has been done out of a job by automation in factories. (But surely this is also good, if it makes us relatively clever chaps more sympathetic with the Luddite fears of the workers.) There may even lurk in the background of our minds fantasies of electronic Newtons and Beethovens, with a consequent threat to human dignity. (I strongly suspect that

[13] CM, p. 80.

much resentment at the threat which a materialistic philosophy makes to traditional religion comes from the fact that materialism is felt as a threat to human vanity.) Already we are beginning to pass from the relatively respectable reasons for seeing mechanism as a bogy, namely the threat to hopes of immortality and the threat posed by extensions of automation, to dark fears perhaps best probed by a psychiatrist. In other ways, however, a mechanistic world view is very far from being a bogy. It appeals to those who treasure theoretical simplicity, classicism rather than romanticism.

How does Ryle deal with the bogy of mechanism? In particular, how would his considerations appear to someone like Du Bois-Reymond? Ryle points out that not all questions are physical questions, and that the laws of nature "do not ordain everything that happens."[14] He then remarks "Indeed they do not ordain anything that happens. Laws of nature are not fiats." Well, I don't know much about Du Bois-Reymond, but I would expect him to have wanted to say not that laws of nature are fiats, but simply that everything that happens would seem to be determined by (a) a set of initial conditions and (b) a set of laws of nature. As an answer to most mechanistic philosophers surely the remark that laws of nature are not fiats is an *ignoratio elenchi*. (Du Bois-Reymond's own way out from his worries seems to have been a quite different one from Ryle's. He argued that physics could never explain *consciousness*, and thence to a Kantian type of metaphysics. This solution would presumably appeal to Ryle as little as it does to me.) However, Ryle might have meant something else by the remark that laws of nature do not ordain what happens. This is that even in a completely deterministic universe it is not possible to deduce what happens from the laws of nature alone. Also needed is a specification of initial

[14] CM, p. 76.

or "boundary" conditions. (Thus given "Everything is such that if it is F then it is G" we can deduce "Something is G" only if we have the additional existential premiss "Something is F.") I am not sure whether this is Ryle's point, because if it is then his immediate remark that laws of nature are not fiats seems irrelevant. However if it is Ryle's point here, then it is of course a good and sound one, but it does nothing to exorcise the bogy of mechanism. Du Bois-Reymond would of course have agreed with it. The point never was that the laws of nature might determine everything that happens: his point was that *together with suitable initial conditions* they might determine everything that happens.

The difficulty of deciding just what Ryle's point is supposed to be here is increased when we look at an illustration which he gives of it.[15] He points out that in a game of chess the rules govern every move but they do not determine the moves. However, what ice would this illustration cut as far as someone like Du Bois-Reymond is concerned? He would agree that the laws of nature do not determine even the motions of the planets. What determines the motions of the planets is laws plus boundary conditions. Moreover these boundary conditions have to relate either to the whole universe or at least to a sufficiently large part of the universe which can be regarded as a closed system for the period of the prediction in question. The chess analogy is weak because there is not even the possibility of determinism. The configuration of the pieces on the board together with the rules do *not* determine (even probabilistically) the actual moves. In fact, were this not so there would be no real game. Du Bois-Reymond might have been worried that the moves in the game might be determined by the configuration of pieces on the board, together with a great number of other facts, such as the molecular structures of the

15 CM, p. 77.

players' brains (perhaps contingently identifiable with their intelligence, knowledge, intentions, etc.[16]).

A similar objection could be made to Ryle's other analogies. Thus consider his comparison of laws of nature with the rules of grammar, which did not confine Gibbon to "a fatal groove."[17] Just because there are no philological initial conditions which together with the rules of grammar determine what Gibbon will write, the analogy becomes a totally misleading one. Similarly Ryle makes use of the analogy of billiards and remarks that "a scientific forecaster, who was ignorant of the rules and tactics of the game and of the skill and plans of the players, could predict, perhaps, from the beginning of a single stroke, the positions in which the balls will come to rest. . . ."[18] This is not helpful precisely because the balls and the billiard table constitute an open system, not a closed one, and because surely the particles about which a Du Bois-Reymond is most concerned are not those which constitute the balls and the table but those which exist in the spaces between the players' ears.

We can connect this with Ryle's discussion in *Dilemmas* about alleged incompatibilities between the world of science and the world of everyday life.[19] Physics, he tells us, is *ex officio* about such things as fundamental particles, and has no place in it for either a description or a misdescription of such things as chairs and tables. He compares the situation with that in a college, where every transaction is reflected in the college accounts. If books are bought then a suitable entry is made in the accounts. But though, in a sense, the accounts cover everything that goes on in the college, they neither describe nor misdescribe such things as the literary or scholarly qual-

---

[16] I do not wish here to argue for such a contingent identification, but see for example D. M. Armstrong, *A Materialist Theory of the Mind* (London: Routledge and Kegan Paul, 1968).

[17] CM, p. 79.

[18] CM, p. 80.

[19] D, Chapter 5.

ities of the books. Once more, the analogy fails to do its job. There are things left indeterminate by the accounts (for example, the exact shape of a bought book), whereas according to a Laplacean determinist everything that happens *does* follow from the laws of nature plus a suitable set of initial conditions. (I hope that we have already agreed that as far as the discussion of the bogy of mechanism is concerned, the issue of quantum-mechanical indeterminism is a bit of a red herring.) Of course the concept of a chair or table is tied to the purposes for which it is used: thus a chair is something normally used for sitting on. This consideration, however, does not cut any metaphysical ice either, since the mechanist is presumably willing to identify intentions or purposes (contingently) with brain states, or at any rate to propose some general account of them which would be consonant with mechanism. Once again, of course, Ryle's point here might be that the laws of nature do not determine what happens. This would not be contested by even a Laplacean determinist, whose thesis would be that the laws of nature *together with suitable boundary conditions* determine everything that happens. I am more inclined to think, however, that Ryle's point is the slightly different one that a concept like that of "chair" or that of "table" is one which connects with the concepts of intention and purpose, as do concepts like "carpenter."

Even if this is so, it seems to me that Ryle is being rather misleading. He says: "A bit of the theory of ultimate particles has no place in it for a description or misdescription of chairs and tables, and a description of chairs and tables has no place in it for a description of ultimate particles. A statement that is true or false of the one is *neither* true *nor* false of the other. It cannot therefore be a rival of the other."[20] First, a pedantic quibble. It is unclear to me what "true of the one" and "true of the other" mean here, since it is predicates that are "true of" or "false of," whereas statements are true or false *simpliciter*. However, we may plausibly interpret Ryle as saying here that a description of a table or chair cannot mention ultimate particles. I think that he has over-reached the mark here, even though we can concede that concepts like "chair" and "table" are partly anthropological ones. Consider the explanation of why an X-ray photograph of a chair is darkened rather slightly but is heavily darkened at the images of the nails in it. This would have to include the statements that the wood of the chair consists of certain sorts of atoms and that the nails in it consist of other sorts of atoms. Or again, consider an explanation of why the chair becomes electrically charged when it is rubbed with a rough cloth.

Here, when I say that the chair *consists of* atoms, I am following Feyerabend in denying that a useful distinction can be made between "observation language" and "theoretical language." As Feyerabend has put it: a theory can be its own observation language.[21] However, Ryle, in sharply distinguishing between talk about chairs and theoretical talk about ultimate particles, might have at the back of his mind a quite different philosophy of scientific theories, of the sort which is often called "instrumentalism." According to this sort of view there are sharply different classes of expressions, *observation* words and *theoretical* words. Ryle would probably object to talking of "observation language" and "theoretical language" in that a scientist uses one language (say, English . or Russian), but if one is permitted to use the word "language" in the slightly technical sense in which it occurs in logic (e.g., "metalanguage") we may put the instrumentalist theory as follows: a theory is not in itself a meaningful description of the world, but it is a useful

[21] See P. K. Feyerabend, "Comments on Sellars' 'The Language of Theories,'" in H. Feigl and G. Maxwell (eds.), *Current Issues in the Philosophy of Science* (New York: Holt, Rinehart and Winston, 1961), pp. 82–83.

device whereby on the basis of certain statements of the observation language we can deduce certain other statements of the observation language. In fact instrumentalism is what is very naturally suggested by Ryle's account of laws of nature as "inference licences." Let us now look at this side of Ryle's work.

III.

Ryle says:[22] "At least part of the point of trying to establish laws is to find out how to infer from particular matters of fact to other particular matters of fact, how to explain particular matters of fact by reference to other matters of fact, and how to prevent or bring about particular states of affairs." The "at least part of" disarms criticism, but it is not at all clear what *else* Ryle thinks is the point of trying to establish laws.

Now it is true that according to any philosophical account of laws of nature they can function as inference licences. Suppose that we have two premisses A and B from which we can deduce a conclusion C in accordance with the rules of formal logic. Then the production of B licences a person who already is in possession of A to assert C. This will be the case whether or not B is a universally quantified statement (perhaps a law statement) or whether it is a statement of particular fact. It follows that in *this* sense *any* statement can function as an inference licence. It must therefore be in some stronger sense than this that Ryle wishes to characterise law statements as inference licences. This is presumably that laws are supposed to licence inferences in the way in which rules of inference do, and not in the way in which extra premisses do. But once again we run into difficulties, because *any* premiss, whether a law or not, could be replaced by a corresponding rule of inference. Even a par-

[22] CM, p. 121.

ticular or existential premiss could be construed as a rule of inference. Thus H. Gavin Alexander remarks[23] that instead of the statement "Flossie is a cow" as a suppressed premiss in the inference "All cows are ruminants; therefore Flossie is a ruminant" we could introduce the material rule: "From a premiss of the form '(x)(x is a cow ⊃ *F* x)' deduce '*F* (Flossie).'"

The above example shows that statements of the form "*F* (Flossie)" cannot *always* function as inference licences, because even if "Flossie is a cow" is elucidated as an inference licence, it is here used to infer to "Flossie is a ruminant." That is, not only the licence but the conclusion of the licenced inference is of the form "*F* (Flossie)." It is true that we also deduce laws from laws, so that perhaps it could be argued that this shows that law statements cannot always be construed as rules. However it would be more plausible to say that this is a case of deducing rules from rules, whereas if we always construed *all* statements, even particular ones, as rules, it would be hard to see what the point of the whole business would be.

"Flossie is a cow" and "Flossie is a ruminant" could both be observation statements. Someone who is trained to tell cows from other animals can be caused by an objective situation which contained Flossie to respond immediately and without conscious thought with "Flossie is a cow." If he can see Flossie's teeth and is well trained in the difference between ruminant and non-ruminant teeth he can equally respond with "Flossie is a ruminant." Hence despite the fact that "Flossie is a ruminant" has, according to Ryle, a law-like or dispositional character, it can be an observation statement, in the sense of Carnap's

[23] H. Gavin Alexander, "General Statements as Rules of Inference," in H. Feigl, M. Scriven, and G. Maxwell (eds.), *Minnesota Studies in the Philosophy of Science* (Minneapolis: University of Minnesota Press, 1958), pp. 309–29, especially pp. 310–11.

pragmatic criterion for observation statements.[24] An observation statement is a report on some particular chunk of the world which causes the relevant utterance of the statement, and hence it must contain names or descriptions or be preceded by existential quantifiers. Thus "Fa," "$(\exists x)Fx$," "$(\exists x)\ (\exists y)\cdot Fx\cdot Fy\cdot x\neq y$" are some possible forms of observation statements. Thus "Flossie is a cow," "The cow is a ruminant," "Two people have been hurt" could all be observation statements. Something of the form "$(x)(Fx \supset Gx)$" could not be an observation statement, because of the universal quantifier at its left-hand side. (It is true that some universally quantified statements could perhaps be observation statements if they contained predicates, such as "is a lion in this room now," which contain references to small chunks of space-time. However this does not matter in the present context, since statements containing such predicates would not be laws of nature.) Thus if it is the purpose of inference licences to get us from observation statements to other observation statements, then it is easy to come to think of law statements as being somehow *essentially* inference licences, because (not being observation statements) they cannot function as start or terminus of such a licenced inference.

Ryle follows Ramsey in calling laws "variable hypotheticals."[25] Ramsey held that these are not judgments but "are rules for judging 'If I meet a Φ, I shall regard it as a Ψ.'"[26] According to him this "general enuncia-

---

[24] See Rudolf Carnap, "Testability and Meaning," *Philosophy of Science* 3 (1936), 419–71, and 4 (1937), 1–40. See also P. K. Feyerabend "Explanation, Reduction and Empiricism," in H. Feigl, M. Scriven, and G. Maxwell (eds.), *Minnesota Studies in the Philosophy of Science*, Vol. 2, pp. 28–97, especially pp. 36–37.

[25] CM, p. 120.

[26] F. P. Ramsey, *The Foundations of Mathematics* (London: Kegan Paul, Trench Trubner and Co., 1931), p. 241. (Something seems in fact to have gone wrong with Ramsey's syntax here. Perhaps a colon should have been inserted after "judging.")

tion" expresses a "habit of singular belief."[27] Ramsey seems to have thought, for reasons which he sets out in some detail but which nevertheless are still not very clear to me, that the only alternative to this view would be to regard laws as conjunctions, and such conjunctions would have to be infinite and so could not be written out. Laws therefore cannot be conjunctions, for, as Ramsey said, "what we can't say we can't say, and we can't whistle it either."[28]

There would seem here to be a reliance on the rather dubious notion of meaning as *expressing* a belief (analogous to the dubious notion of emotive meaning in ethics), but if we eschew this notion what is the advantage of construing a variable hypothetical as of the form "If I meet a Φ I shall [ought to?] regard it as a Ψ"? This is of the form "(x) $(\Phi x \cdot$ I meet $x \cdot \supset$ I shall regard x as a $\Psi)$," and so we have presumably replaced an infinite conjunction of statements by an infinite conjunction of imperatives. Possibly this is why later in his paper Ramsey expresses the variable hypothetical not as a universally quantified statement but as an open sentence, "If Φx then Ψx." Perhaps Ramsey was under the influence of Wittgenstein's *Tractatus*, where sentences are regarded as pictures of facts. One trouble about this is that observation statements might well have the form "$(\exists x)Fx$," and these could not be pictures or truth functions of pictures any more than universally quantified statements could be. We can thus envisage a language for science (a Quinean canonical language) of which *no* sentences were proper statement-making sentences according to Ramsey's criteria. It should also be noted that undecidability- and unsolvability-results of modern logic, which have accrued since Ramsey's time, point up an additional infelicity in regarding laws of nature as rules of inference. Surely we should demand that there should be an *effective* way of

[27] *Ibid.*, p. 240.
[28] *Ibid.*, p. 238.

telling whether or not a sentence was a rule of our system. Yet with any reasonably strong scientific theory there is no *effective* way of deciding whether or not a theorem follows from the axioms. Hence if laws of nature be taken as rules of inference there is no effective way of telling whether something is a rule of inference.

I have been construing Ryle's talk of laws as "inference licences" as following Ramsey's account of laws largely because of Ryle's use of Ramsey's term "variable hypothetical."[29] It is worth noting that as *ordinarily* construed these law statements are neither variable nor hypothetical. Thus "$(x) Fx \supset Gx$" is not of the form "$A \supset B$," since the scope of the quantifier extends beyond the "$\supset$." What is variable or "open" and hypothetical is not "$(x) Fx \supset Gx$" but "$Fx \supset Gx$." Should we therefore, in spite of Ryle's remark about "any" and "every," be dealing with "$Fx \supset Gx$?" What is the rule of inference here? Perhaps it could be rephrased: "If you find anything of which 'Fx' is true expect 'Gx' to be true of it." But what on earth is the point of ascending to the metalanguage here? (Especially as we still need a universal quantifier in the formulation of the rule.)

Perhaps, then, the term "inference licence" is a mere metaphor which should not be taken very seriously. After all, Ryle does say that law statements are true or false,[30] though he qualifies this by saying that "they do not assert truths or falsehoods of the same type as those asserted by the statements of fact to which they apply or are supposed to apply. They have different jobs." Well, perhaps they do have different jobs, but this does not imply that they are inference licences in any sense other than that in which any statement (perhaps a statement of a particular fact) might (as a suppressed premiss) licence an enthymeme. Earlier on the same page Ryle says: "We have to learn to use statements of particular matters

29 CM, p. 120.
30 CM, p. 121.

of fact, before we can learn to use the law-statements which do or might apply to them." He concludes that law statements belong to "a different and more sophisticated level of discourse" from the statements of fact which satisfy them. But equally we have to learn how to make non-disjunctive statements before we learn to make disjunctive ones, and yet there does not seem to be much temptation to say that disjunctive statements belong to a different level of discourse from non-disjunctive ones. An even more doubtful remark of Ryle's is that "knowing or even understanding the law does involve knowing that there could be particular matters of fact satisfying the protasis and therefore also satisfying the apodosis of the law."[31] Those philosophers who argue that science can be done entirely in an extensional language will presumably hold that a person might understand law statements, say of the form "$(x)(Fx \supset Gx)$," without having to understand the modal word "could."

I am inclined to think, therefore, that Ryle has not succeeded in giving any reason for thinking of laws of nature as inference licences, except perhaps in the innocuous sense in which a suppressed premiss of an enthymeme may licence a deduction.

In his "Predicting and Inferring"[32] Ryle talks of laws and theories as "recipes" for generating inferences from observation statements to observation statements. Clearly "recipe" is a variant on the term "inference licence." Ryle here uses it to make a point about the problem of induction. The success of inferences which are in accordance with the laws *shows* the goodness of the laws in the same way in which the successful making of soufflés in accordance with a recipe *shows* the goodness of the recipe. Therefore there does not have to be "a special

[31] *Ibid.*
[32] In S. Körner (ed.), *Observation and Interpretation in the Philosophy of Physics* (New York: Dover, 1962), pp. 165–70.

sort of argument, to be called an 'inductive argument,' *from* the successes and failures of the inferences *to* the truth of the theory."[33]

I do not think that Ryle has here succeeded in dissolving the philosophical problem of induction. Indeed, I do not think that he has even done much to help the down-to-earth worry of a scientist who knows that a theory has been successful within a restricted range of circumstances, but wonders whether observations in new circumstances may show the theory to be false after all. Newtonian mechanics provides (within the limits of observational error) as good predictions and retrodictions as does special relativity, provided that we are dealing with bodies at small velocities; high velocities show the theory to be false. Indeed, after accepting special relativity, we can see that the theory is even false about small velocities, though the errors in the theory are too small to show up experimentally. It is true that the last sentence makes no sense to an out-and-out instrumentalist philosopher of science, and if Ryle were to hold that within the domain of small velocities Newtonian theory is as good as special relativity, because it works as well in providing correct experimental inferences, then this would suggest (what I suspect) an instrumentalist tenor to his philosophy of science.

Still less does Ryle's manoeuvre deal with the not so down-to-earth worry about the philosophical problem of induction. For this applies to recipes as much as to laws: how do we know that a recipe which works in certain circumstances today will work in even exactly similar circumstances tomorrow? The successes of the recipe (or of a law) certainly show that it works today, but how

[33] *Ibid.*, p. 170. Criticisms of Ryle were made by Peter Achinstein, "From Success to Truth," *Analysis* 21 (1960–61), pp. 6–9 (with a reply by Ryle *ibid.*, pp. 9–11), and by H. V. Stopes-Roe, *ibid.*, pp. 115–20.

do we know that even the best tested recipe or law will work tomorrow?

Ryle's attempted dissolution of the problem of induction here partly rests on an interesting suggestion of his, that there is no such thing as inductive inference. (In one of his Gavin David Young lectures at the University of Adelaide in 1956 he argued interestingly that "deductive inference" and "inductive thinking" make sense, but not "deductive thinking" or "inductive inference.") But even if (as could plausibly be maintained) scientists never (or hardly ever) explicitly argue "This theory has survived a great number of varied tests, *and so* it is probably true," nevertheless they do suppose that it is rational to believe well-tested theories. The question of the rationality of this belief is still the philosophical problem of induction, even though it has been formulated with reference to the rationality of a belief and not with reference to the validity of an inference. It has long been agreed that inductive procedures cannot be deductively justified (validated) but it is perhaps still an open question whether they might be pragmatically justified (vindicated) in some way. It is interesting that though Ryle follows Ramsey in his account of laws as "variable hypotheticals," he does not follow up Ramsey's attempt at a pragmatic justification of induction.[34] Perhaps such an attempt is (despite the contemporary efforts of people like Wesley Salmon) doomed to failure, but a too quick dissolution of the problem can prevent us from at least investigating this possibility.

IV.

I have suggested that Ryle's attitude to science, as something metaphysically neutral, and his treatment of laws of nature, perhaps presuppose an instrumentalist

[34] Ramsey, *op. cit.*, p. 197.

point of view, even though he never makes this explicit.
I shall now suggest that a similar conclusion can be got
from a consideration of his views on the science of psychology. In CM, Chapter 10, Ryle argues that psychology
is not concerned with explanations of our mental competences or of usual behaviour, but it is typically concerned with explanations of our incompetences and our
more peculiar actions. "The question why the farmer will
not sell his pigs at certain prices is not a psychological
but an economic question; but the question why he will
not sell his pigs at any price to a customer with a certain
look in his eyes might be a psychological question. . . .
We cannot, from our own knowledge, tell why a straight
line cutting through certain crosshatchings looks bent.
. . . Yet we feel that the wrong sort of promise is being
made when we are offered corresponding psychological
explanations of our correct estimations of shape, size, illumination and speed."[35] We may agree that we would
seldom desire an explanation of a particular exercise of a
competence, but nevertheless this could be given *via* psychological explanation of the general fact that humans
possess such competences. Such an explanation would be
a causal one *via* hypotheses about the central nervous
system. These may be put in functional[36] rather than
neurological terms. But then an explanation of the working of a radio may be fairly abstract, perhaps because of
lack of detailed knowledge: it may talk of, say, "a frequency changer," rather than about the specific circuitry
of the item in question. Just as in electronics we find
explanations of the correct functioning of pieces of apparatus, and not merely of their misfunctioning, so in
psychology there are explanations of human and animal
competences and normalities. As against Ryle's claim to

[35] CM, p. 326.
[36] On this point cf. J. A. Fodor, "Explanation in Psychology," in
Max Black (ed.), *Philosophy in America* (Ithaca, N.Y.: Cornell
University Press, 1965), pp. 161–79.

the contrary, this can be checked by looking at psychological journals.[37]

Ryle's idea that (as far as normal behaviour is concerned) psychology does not go deeper than our ordinary commonsense explanations is evidently connected with the view that if it did give causal explanations these would be para-mechanical ones, based on the Cartesian "two worlds" myth.[38] It looks as though he cannot see a third possibility beyond either behaviourism or Cartesian dualism. He seems strangely reluctant to allow the identification of "mental" causes with structures or processes in the central nervous system, whether these are described neurophysiologically or functionally.[39] Neglect of this possibility indeed clouds his whole concept of a mental disposition. Thus vanity can naturally be taken as the structure which explains typically vain behaviour. No adequate translation into hypotheticals about behaviour can be produced. Similarly for physical dispositions. We cannot *translate* "This glass is brittle" by "If a stone hits it then it breaks," because conditions can exist in which the stone hits the glass without breaking it. We can, however, identify brittleness with an inner structure which *explains* typically brittle behaviour of the glass. This strategy of identifying dispositions with physical structures is as efficacious as Ryle's in disposing of "ghosts" and it avoids obvious difficulties in Ryle's account.[40]

Suppose that something mysterious happened to our

[37] See my paper "Ryle on Mechanism and Psychology," *Philosophical Quarterly* 9 (1959), pp. 349–55, and Maurice Mandelbaum, "Professor Ryle and Psychology," *Philosophical Review* 67 (1958), pp. 522–30.

[38] CM, pp. 324–25.

[39] See B. H. Medlin, "Ryle and the Mechanical Hypotheses," in C. F. Presley (ed.), *The Identity Theory of Mind*, pp. 94–150.

[40] See Hilary Putnam, "Psychological Concepts, Explication, and Ordinary Language," *Journal of Philosophy*, 54 (1957), pp. 94–100, and Isaac Levi and Sidney Morgenbesser, "Belief and Disposition," *American Philosophical Quarterly* 1 (1964), pp. 221–32.

window pane, so that we couldn't see through it. Well, then, that would be something for which we should want an explanation, whereas most of the time we do not demand an explanation of why we can see through a (normal) window pane. (We usually can, and so we have the answer "Because it is transparent.") However, if we always were satisfied with such simple explanations there would be no real science. It is often the most familiar phenomena (for example the transparency of glass) that require the deepest explanations. A lot of children's "Why?" questions can be answered only on the basis of something difficult like solid-state physics. Similarly, in psychology, some familiar things, such as normal vision, require quite deep hypotheses about neural circuitry. Yet in his discussion of psychology Ryle seems as though he is satisfied to stop at the rather trite level of commonsense explanation of *normal* behaviour, much as though "Because it is transparent" were an adequate explanation of the light-transmitting properties of glass.

This attitude once more suggests an instrumentalist philosophy of science. If the commonsense explanations provide as good predictions as the deeper scientific ones, then what need is there of the latter? Of course, even on an instrumentalist philosophy of science the deeper explanations can be defended because of the way in which they do lead to new predictions in unusual cases, and because of the simplicity and unity which they bring to theory. So even an instrumentalist will want to go deeper than the phenomenological generalisations of commonsense. Nevertheless he has not *as much* motivation as the scientific realist whose ideal is not just ability to predict or retrodict, but *understanding*.

v.

In this essay I have been trying to extract from the many hints which Ryle drops in various places some sort of coherent attitude to science, which boils down to two inter-related tendencies: (a) an inclination to believe that science is metaphysically neutral, and that it is no threat to ordinary commonsense ways of thinking about the world, (b) an instrumentalist attitude to laws and theories. These are at best tendencies only, and perhaps I have been unfair in foisting ideas on to Ryle which he might wish to repudiate. With typical modesty he has disclaimed competence to arbitrate in boundary disputes between sciences, and he says, "I have long since learned to doubt the native sagacity of philosophers when discussing technicalities which they have not learned to handle on the job, as in earlier days I learned to doubt the judgment of those towing-path critics who had never done any rowing."[41] I fear that he may well discern a fair amount of hot air in the present essay. Nevertheless, even if only by way of hints and metaphors, Ryle has been widely influential in matters of interest in the philosophy of science, and it seemed worth while to try to bring some of Ryle's implicit views into the open. By fastening on to these matters my area of disagreement with Ryle appears greater than it in fact is. At one time Ryle's ideas were the dominating ones in my own thinking. However my attempt to extract from his writings an explicit and coherent attitude to science may have been doomed to failure, simply because what I seek to find was perhaps never there in the first place, but at least it has seemed a useful exercise to have a go at it.

[41] D, p. 12.

PHILOSOPHY AND COMPUTER SIMULATION

KEITH GUNDERSON

INTRODUCTION

The sticky issues involved in characterizing the mental, form a philosopher's tar-baby to which many fists are fastened. The point of minding about machines lies simply in the hope that Br'er Robot might prove more formidable an opponent than Br'er Rabbit.

Not all philosophers have shared or now share this vision, of course. And not all who have shared the reluctance to share it have shared each other's alternative outlook. Rudeness to robots has been practiced from Descartes through Ryle, who, in *The Concept of Mind*, cautions us that "Man need not be degraded to a machine by being denied to be a ghost in a machine" (p. 328). In the face of eclectic antagonism the perennial popularity of mechanistic analogues of the mind seems all the more fascinating. What explains the philosophical relevance of this *idée fixe*, how should we assess it, and what attractions and limitations attend the current art of robotology?

As a path to philosophical enlightenment there may be no *a priori* reason to prefer analyzing analogues between minds and machines to analyzing analogies between minds and mud. *A posteriori*, however, there is much to recommend the former. Mud is as it always was, and as it was and is holds no particular promise as a medium for modeling the mind. Machines, on the other hand, have, since the seventeenth century, dealt us diachronic delights. Through a process of unnatural selection the Cro-Magnon robot has at last evolved equipped with enough self-adaptive, problem-solving prowess to compel the collective concern of philosophers, psychologists, and miscellaneous camp followers.

Computer science in the twentieth century has forced philosophers to re-draw the line between men and machines in a variety of respects and has thereby given at least a suburban status to what seemed to be the time-hollowed credos of a mechanistic materialism. Cybernetics has thus had much the same force which the technical innovations of the Swiss clockmakers had in the seventeenth and eighteenth centuries when their compelling mechanisms inspired a new surveying of the boundaries between the living and the mechanical. From the vantage point of this century it is all too easy to belittle the philosophical surprise that Vaucanson's mechanical duck and flute-playing boy held for his contemporaries who were inclined to associate the movements involved in ambulation only with living organisms. But that these inventions gave impetus to La Mettrie's mechanistic speculations, which in turn became a guidebook for later French materialists such as the philosophes, Cabanis, *et al.* is now a matter of historical record.

Indeed the most important, though casual and almost inadvertent, implications which computer science has had for philosophy, are the new insights it has given us into some of our old concepts. Some examples: that a purely mechanistic system can display some degree of self-adaptiveness; that certain highly complicated problem-solving activities can be carried out by indisputably non-living machines; that certain kinds of creative abilities are not at odds with rule-governed behaviors; etc.

However, this general account of the interplay between mechanistic models and philosophical insight can be contrasted with the attitude of another recent surveyor of the same terrain, Kenneth Sayre, who in his *Recognition: A Study in the Philosophy of Artificial Intelligence* writes concerning machine analogues of human recognition:

We simply do not understand what recognition is. And if we do not understand the behavior we are trying to simulate, we cannot reasonably hold high hopes of being successful in our attempts to simulate it. (p. xii)

Contra Sayre, I find it unsatisfactory to maintain this. (Here for the sake of exposition let us assume [as Sayre does] that the goals of pattern-recognition research have been to *simulate* human pattern-recognition behavior.)

Now certainly the main motivation for this has been to further our understanding of the behavior and/or psychological process to be simulated. To require detailed understanding of the phenomenon to be simulated prior to devising the simulation is to guarantee that the simulation be theoretically irrelevant. Its utility in psychological explanation will reduce to that of a sort of visual aid—a method for displaying what is already known.

The point is that the theoretical efficacy of computer simulation depends on our having some knowledge of the phenomenon to be simulated, *but not too much*. Preliminary clarification of the nature of the phenomenon to be simulated is no doubt required. But this more as a way of charting the course, than as making the journey. Sayre seems to assume that only after we have clarified the concept of recognition will we understand how to programme a machine with recognition capacities, whereas I want to suggest that by trying to programme a machine with recognition capacities we will perhaps improve our understanding of the concept of recognition—and, of course, of recognition itself.

A book such as Ryle's *Concept of Mind* seems to me best appreciated as an attempt to arrive at a preliminary clarification of mental phenomena. And it may be that the enormous difficulties in doing even this well, has led some philosophers to assimilate philosophical activity *per se* to the kinds of analytical tactics employed in that work.

Sayre's (early) work cited above presents a somewhat curious mixture of attitudes in this regard. On the one hand there are remarks such as the last-quoted. Yet on the other hand he openly uses Rylean-type distinctions

(between achievements, attainments, and processes) as a
preface to and not a substitute for working on simulation programmes. One drift of his argument against
pattern-recognition studies is that if such researchers had
read their Ryle, they would not have used interchangeably an "attainment" verb such as "to recognize" with
verbs such as "to classify" or "to identify." The latter are
said to range over behavior admitting of greater or lesser
degrees of success, whereas recognition is said to be
"evaluation neutral"—something not done more or less
well. Clearly, unless one is able initially to specify the
phenomena he wishes to simulate, it is highly unlikely
that the desired simulation will be brought off. And
obviously conceptual analysis (what else?) can be an aid
in carrying out the initial specification.

It would, of course, underrate the philosophical importance of computer science to suppose the conceptual
insights alluded to earlier would have been gained without the technological illustrations. They might have
been, but what's important is that they weren't. Yet it
would overrate the philosophical implications of those
same types of illustrations to suppose they provide a kind
of panacea to most previously intractable problems in
philosophical psychology.

In a series of informal discussions of such questions as
"Can machines think?" and "Could a robot have feelings?" philosophers have sought to clarify our hazy intuitive notions regarding the mental life. Simulation psychologists, by contrast, have focused on the flow charts
and routine constructions involved in actual programming and hoped thereby to grasp in detail the ways in
which it is or isn't possible to model mentality with current computers.

The two tactics are surely quite compatible, if not in-
separable, and a formal marriage between philosophical
analysis and computer simulation seems desirable.

I certainly agree with Sayre to this extent: unless some
initial clarification of the nature of the phenomenon to

be simulated is attempted, the simulation is likely to lack direction and its evaluation will seem arbitrary. As Walter R. Reitman has said (*Cognition & Thought*):

> . . . although we are interested in natural phenomena, we can only work with what we have ways of thinking about. The trouble arises when we try to discover just what our constructs simulate. (p. 6)

Furthermore, many informal philosophical problems pertaining to minds and machines reflect themselves in the methodological disorders of computer simulation (CS) and artificial intelligence (AI). But as I've said elsewhere, I think it is no longer important to decide whether these matters are empirical issues with conceptual overtones, or conceptual issues with empirical undertones.[1]

Another way of characterizing the implications which computer science has for philosophy is to say that for certain problems it provides new and sharper ways of rephrasing them—namely in terms of programming problems. To rephrase is not, of course, to solve. But it is sometimes a useful first step to a solution. We come to see more clearly the edges of our ignorance.

In what follows I shall try to illustrate how certain programming problems may be viewed as rephrasals of certain philosophical problems. I shall then make some critical comments on the craft of computer simulation as well as on the statements of certain (philosophical) commentators who have for different reasons been critical of it. Finally I will try to show that an understanding of the limitations of current simulation techniques helps us to detail some interesting differences between what has traditionally been called the sapient and sentient aspects of the mind.

But first some orienting remarks on pattern-recognition, computer simulation, and artificial intelligence. (Note:

[1] See my "Minds and Machines—A Survey," *Contemporary Philosophy—A Survey*, ed. by Raymond Klibansky (Firenze, 1968).

most problems which computer simulation programmes deal with such as theorem-proving, chess-playing, etc. are problems in pattern-recognition of one sort or another. Sometimes in the literature, however, pattern-recognition is equated with letter- or character-recognition [in cursive script, say]. It should be clear from the context exactly what sort of pattern-recognition problem is under discussion.)

II
PATTERN-RECOGNITION, COMPUTER SIMULATION, AND ARTIFICIAL INTELLIGENCE

A discussion of PATTERN-ReCogNition is, of course, a discussion of Pattern-Recognition which is, of course, a discussion of pattern-recognition, and hence we have exhibited the phenomenon many would like to explain.

Roughly, the aim of pattern-recognition research is to devise mechanical means whereby non-uniform instances of an auditory or visual pattern, the letter "M," say, would be distinguished as M's. As Newell and Simon have pointed out, however, ("Computers in Psychology," in Luce, Bush, and Galanter) it is possible to view a pattern-recognizer as virtually any system which makes different responses to different stimuli. But it will prove satisfactory for our purposes to confine our examples to those where a machine has been programmed to recognize a given character or characters of the alphabet.

To follow Newell and Simon, the possible stimuli might be combinations of ones and zeros in a large two-dimensional grid of ones and zeros:

Figure 1

```
1001011000
1010110100
1011101011
0101011101
1101101011
```

A particular character of the alphabet is then equated with particular subsets of ones and zeros. Thus the following stimuli might be M's:

Figure 2	Figure 3
11100111	10100101
11011011	10011001
11000011	10000001
11000011	10000001

Consequently the goal for the learning system is to distinguish various letters of the alphabet which could appear on the grid in different positions, sizes, orientations, and styles. Cast in these terms, human recognition of patterns may be viewed as the ability to recognize given instances of the same character, each instance of which may differ widely from the others with respect to either position, size, orientation, and style.

As an exercise in AI successful pattern-recognition (with respect to given characters of the alphabet) would consist in emulation of the results of exercising this ability. As an exercise in CS, a successful pattern-recognition programme would simulate the *process* by which that ability was exercised.

The aims of AI are to devise mechanical means for executing tasks which hitherto required the actions of intelligent agents. There need be no attempt to simulate whatever intelligent process or procedure was used by human beings if it is possible to bring about the same results in other ways. Since the aims of AI are essentially practical, replication of human processes or procedures would be happily sacrificed for speed and efficiency. If there are ways of translating faster and more efficiently from Russian to English than those ways used by intelligent agents, so much the better. The goal is not to imitate the mind but to imitate what the mind can do. CS, on the other hand, is directed towards modeling the mind. The goal is to simulate the mental processes at work in human thought and action.

To follow Herbert Simon, J. C. Shaw, and Allen Newell, we can let a simulation of an alleged mental process be a computer programme the flow chart of which is (generally) constructed on the basis of observations (verbal reports, marks on paper, and so on) of intelligent behavior such as playing chess or checkers, proving theorems, and the like. The programme when run on the computer can be instructed to print a trace of its move by move activity which may then be compared to a putative description of the process.

As we shall see, a large number of as yet unsolved problems arise in trying to assess the theoretical importance of this tactic. But if we suppose the programme for the simulation is written in Information Processing Language —V (IPL-V), a language which works with lists and lists of lists of symbols, then the general theoretical situation may be depicted as follows:

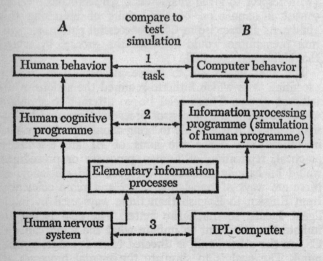

#1

where, at the moment, for reasons some of which will be discussed later, detailed comparison between the human- and machine-system insofar as there are any, exist for the most part at the task level (1). Hence the solid-line arrow which indicates that at least some comparisons can be made. The broken-line arrows 2 and 3 are meant to depict the general paucity of comparisons between items at that level in columns A and B. This lack is partly due to the fact that it is not yet known whether human beings can be accurately described as behaving in accord with pro- grammes, or how these might be depicted, etc: It is hoped, however, that task-level comparisons can be re- fined, properly assessed, that deeper comparisons will eventually be forthcoming at other levels (2 and 3), and that suggestive analogues to the mechanisms and processes known to be sufficient for producing certain machine out- puts will be discovered for human outputs.[2]

What I wish first to focus on, however, are some prob- lems in epistemology which have recently been para- phrased as problems in computer programming. For the extent of our failure to solve these problems (under either phrasing) probably represents the extent to which we fail to understand understanding.

III

PATTERN-RECOGNITION, IMPLICIT RECOGNITION, FAMILY RESEMBLANCES, RELEVANT PROJECTION CAPACITIES, AND THE CURSE OF CONTEXT

I shall begin with another claim of Sayre's. He writes:

> Yet we have argued that few would be able to say ex- actly what features of a given letter make it that letter and no other. If it were otherwise, the simulation of letter recognition would pose no serious problems of a conceptual nature. This points to the conclusion that

[2] For a further discussion of #1, see my "Cybernetics and Mind- Body Problems," *Inquiry*, 12, 1969, pp. 406–19.

there is no set of shape or topological characteristics of a given letter which might serve to distinguish definitely between inscriptions of that letter or other letters or marks which represent no letter at all. (p. 98)

He defines "invariant" as "the characteristic or set of characteristics which distinguishes a given class of individuals from all other classes, and the possession of which qualifies an individual for membership in that class."

With respect to Sayre's first point I would only emphasize that nothing very important follows from the fact, if it is a fact, that human beings are able to recognize items as belonging to a certain type without explicit awareness of an invariant shape or topological feature or set of such features. For this would leave open the question of whether human beings are in some sense implicitly aware of such invariants and rely upon them in their pattern-recognition competences. This is not to suggest, however, that invariant shape and topological features are made use of; it is only intended as an objection to the supposition that if they are, they must, at the moment of utilization, be available to our consciousness. (Compare: the sense in which a child has been said to know—recognize—sentences as grammatical without being able to articulate the criteria by which he does this.)

But the problem we sidle up to in all this is *the* central problem of pattern-recognition. That is, the problem which arises when one actually tries to enumerate characteristics (implicitly operative or otherwise) of objects belonging to a certain class in a way that permits variation and novelty amongst members within that class and at the same time excludes obvious non-members from that class. For example, it is natural to presume that an adequate account of our ability to recognize the written character "M" would explain why and how certain characteristics of M's enable us to see both m and M *as* M's. What Sayre believes is that there will be no shape or

topological characteristic(s) which is (are) both necessary and sufficient for a letter to belong to a certain class.
In the case, say, of the letter "A" there will be no single
visual feature or small set of visual features such as an
apex or bar position which will be common to all instances of A's. Sometimes the A may lack an apex, sometimes the bar (e.g., in lower-case a's). Sometimes the bar
may be close to the top of the letter, sometimes not, etc.

The overlap between pattern-recognition problems and
various philosophical perplexities should be obvious.

We all know Wittgenstein claimed that we classify
things or objects together not on the basis of noticing
that the objects of a similar kind satisfy a certain fixed set
of necessary and sufficient conditions, but on the basis of
perceived similarities amongst them for which he coined
the phrase "family resemblances." He asked what it is, for
example, for something to be a game. And told us to reflect on the fantastic variety of things we range together
under the description "is a game." In his *Philosophical
Investigations* he wrote:

> 67. I can think of no better expression to characterize
> these similarities than "family resemblances"; for the
> various resemblances between members of a family:
> build, features, color of eyes, gait, temperament, etc.,
> etc. overlap and criss-cross in the same way.—And I
> shall say: "games" form a family.

He goes on to provide a further illustration of why we
would call something (in this case a number) a certain
kind of thing rather than another. He asks:

> Why do we call something a "number"? Well, per-
> haps because it has a—direct—relationship with several
> things that have hitherto been called numbers; and this
> can be said to give it an indirect relationship to other
> things we call the same name. And we extend our con-
> cept of numbers as in spinning a thread we twist fibre
> on fibre. And the strength of the thread does not reside

in the fact that some one fibre runs through the whole length, but in the overlapping of many fibres.

But if someone wished to say: "There is something common to all these constructions—namely the disjunction of all their common properties"—I should reply: "Now you are only playing with words. One might as well say: 'Something runs through the whole thread—namely the continuous overlapping of those fibres.'"

With respect to Wittgenstein's remarks, however, it is hard to suppress the uneasy feeling that they leave us playing with metaphors. Instead of an alternative theory to replace the discredited one we are told that we group things under a common description (say, "is a game" or "is a number") on the basis of family resemblances. But how is this really very different from saying we do in fact recognize a variety of things or objects as being of a certain sort on the basis of their resemblance one to another? To point this out is not to provide an account or explanation of anything; it is simply to point to that which is in need of an account or explanation. It is, in effect, to point to the need of a theory of pattern-recognition.

For this reason I find it curious that Hubert Dreyfus in his robot-baiting *Rand* monograph (P-3244) "Alchemy and Artificial Intelligence" should cite Wittgenstein's doctrine as a kind of counter-example to current pattern-recognition programmes. He seems to treat the notion of "family resemblances" as if it were hooked to an obvious fact of perceptual experience; and as if by mentioning this fact we were treated to some sort of understanding of an unmechanizable phenomenon. But surely the notion is a problematic and semi-technical one to be introduced, if at all, as an acknowledgement that we have a competence for generalization which we do not yet begin to understand. Such acknowledgement hardly qualifies as explanation.

It is little advance over previous theories to be told, as Dreyfus tells us, that

> Recognition of a member of a "family" is made possible
> not by a list of traits, but by seeing the case in ques-
> tion in terms of its similarity to a paradigm (i.e., a
> typical case). (p. 44)

For we are not told what "seeing the case in question in
terms of its similarity to a paradigm" amounts to. There
is, so far as I know, only one clear construal of "recognition based on use of a paradigm." But this, ironically,
would be wholly alien to the sort of explanation which I
know would satisfy Dreyfus. The construal, which I don't
attribute to Dreyfus, amounts to viewing "use of a paradigm" as a template-matching procedure whereby the
letter "A," say, relative to some grid is digitized and used
as a paradigm to be superimposed on whatever character
is presented to the machine for consideration. A certain
degree of "fit" will then be necessary (and sufficient) for
the machine to output "is an 'A.'" Obviously this only
brings us back to another disconcerting encounter with
an insufficient and unnecessary set of allegedly necessary
and sufficient conditions the inadequacy of which the notion of "family resemblances" was introduced to remedy.
That such a template procedure is deficient can be seen
in the manner by which letters smaller or larger than the
template would be easily missed. For example, consider

where either the shaded A or the unshaded A could be viewed as the template and the other as the character-token it fails to "recognize" as an A.

There exist a variety of ways in which the sample may be magnified or reduced, etc., and hence made more susceptible to the template. But as Selfridge and Neisser point out:

> Such a procedure is still inadequate. What it does is to compare shapes rather successfully. But letters are a good deal more than mere shapes. Even when a sample has been converted to standard size, position and orientation, it may match a wrong template more closely than it matches the right one.[3]

In brief, I find Dreyfus' notion of "similarity to a paradigm" either intelligible (construed as "matching a template"), but clearly defective as an explanation of recognition competence, or as mysterious as recognition competence itself. (Compare: Chomsky's celebrated criticism of the Skinnerian use of the notion, "stimulus generalization.")

Wittgenstein's underdeveloped doctrine of family resemblances leaves us bereft of any account of what might be called "perceptual projection"—the ability which human beings have to recognize, on the basis of a finite number of experiences, a potentially infinite number of new and varied objects which they have never encountered before, as all being of a certain specified kind.

Here I should like to extend, without mishap, I believe, the use which the word "projection" has in Chomsky's work in grammar, and Ziff's and Katz and Fodor's (and Katz and Postal's) work in semantics.

What these writers call "the projection problem" is roughly synonymous with the problem of formulating the rules underlying what may be conveniently viewed as our

[3] "Pattern Recognition by Machine" in Feigenbaum and Feldman, p. 243.

syntactic-semantic pattern-recognition competence. I tend to view pattern-recognition (and production) as the general case and regard any phenomenon involving learning or skill as special instances of it.

And I think that even rather monorail skills such as learning to ride a bicycle can be seen as comprised of projective capacities: i.e., capacities which enable us on the basis of an exposure to a finite number of trials on a finite number of bicycles to acquire the ability to ride a potentially infinite variety of bicycles in an indefinite variety of ways ("Look, Ma, 28-inch wheels and no hands!", etc.). Were this hunch to prove accurate, it would probably have the side effect of bringing Ryle's cases of "knowing how" under the same general descriptions as his cases of "knowing that." But this is a topic which I can't explore here.

Very roughly, wherever we find a phenomenon which requires for our comprehension of it the formulation of and solution to a projection problem, the problem of "how to go on," we have a phenomenon involving pattern-recognition, and *vice versa*.

Wittgenstein, of course, was not consciously addressing himself to problems in pattern-recognition. He was, I believe, in effect attempting to answer questions left unresolved after years of philosophical haggling over the nature of so-called "real definitions" (the essence or defining properties of given things or substances). The interesting aspect of this cluster of problems is that what is wrapped up in any solution to them seems roughly equivalent to whatever it is that would constitute a solution to recognition problems. In other words, if we were able to explain how it is we come to recognize something as being a certain sort of thing, we would also be able to explain what it is for a certain sort of thing to belong to one class of objects rather than another. In this connection it is hard to decide if one should rejoice in the potential "psychologizing away" of a metaphysical problem, or despair in the expectation that problems analogous to the hoary metaphysical ones will reassert themselves in the context of simulation psychology.

To return to those remarks of Sayre's quoted at the beginning of this section, however, I would agree that it seems highly unlikely that any powerful *simulation* of human pattern-recognition capacities could be devised primarily in terms of rules which were sensitive only to shape and topological features.

Though obvious to some it may be useful to recount just why reliance on such features is so unsatisfactory. This is so for the unsimple reason that human recognition does occur within a context which very often plays a crucial role in determining how something is recognized as being a certain sort of thing. So it seems strategically necessary to take such features into account at the very outset.

For example, given the second letter in CATS AND DOGS it hardly matters whether the apex is closed, since the context will disperse all doubt as to whether an open apex A were an H or not an A. Here it is obvious that our ability to recognize an ambiguous inscription as being an A and not an H is partially determined by context. The importance of this example is not that it shows that the closed apex is not a necessary feature of A's, but that it shows that contextual features enter into the set of conditions sufficient for distinguishing A's from other letters in general. More emphatically, trying to decide whether an H-A-shaped inscription with either an open apex or converging sides is an A or an H in isolation is obviously an idle decision, since there is clearly no right choice to be made. Such decisions would have the flavor of real choices only if made against a background of real alternatives. In isolation an H-A-shaped inscription which could be construed as having either an open apex or merging sides *is neither* an A nor an H; it is simply an H-A-shaped inscription. To ask "But which, really, is it?" is like asking what the "deep structure" analysis is of a token of "Flying planes can be dangerous" when that token is produced by a parrot, or found written by the wind in the sand. So too for the following inscription:

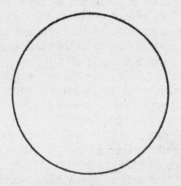

Is it an "o" as in cod? or a zero as in $1.00? How could we decide to opt for either of these descriptions? Why not say it is o-shaped or zero-shaped, or shaped *like* an o, or shaped *like* a zero? Suppose a cloud drifts over our head in that shape. Is it the letter "O" written in fluff? (Here I shall brush aside the clever rejoinder that what it really is is an inscription for illustrating the inappropriateness of the foregoing questions.)

Compare: a farmer might use a rock from his field for a doorstop and we might recognize it as such on the basis of how it looked. But imagine trying to decide whether a given rock is a doorstop apart from the context in which it is one. ("See this rock?" [pointing to a rock on the coffee table], "Well, is it or isn't it my doorstop?")

But once the contextual determinants are brought into the open—not that they had to be—there they are, always leering over our shoulder—it seems plain that the recognition of even simple characters will (often) depend on other levels of recognition abilities such as syntactic and semantic ones. For example, if we recognize the second to the last letter in the sentence "The cow chews cud" as an almost closed u, and not as a somewhat open o, it will no doubt be because of what we know about the meaning of the word "cud" and the meaning of the word "cod" (as well as what we know about the eating habits of cows). If successful "disambiguation" of letter script generally depends on, say, semantic abilities, then it would be unreasonable to seek a general explanation of letter recognition ability distinct from an overall theory of language-learning capacities. This should be emphasized since recognition programmes for individual letters have sometimes been discussed as if they were of interest apart from a general theory of linguistic capacities.

It may be distressing as well as exhilarating to a character-recognition theorist to find that problems in semantic interpretation crop up in connection with the recognition of seemingly simple characters. It's exhilarating in that the problem of constructing simple character-recognition programmes turns out to be a much deeper problem than it was at first believed to be. For it may at first have seemed that letters were a kind of minimal linguistic unit—building blocks of words, etc.—and that it would be easiest to devise a recognition programme for them, and then, hopefully, build up from there. What we soon find, however, is that recognition or interpretation at any one level of linguistic description (letter, phonemes, word, sentence, discourse) is a partial function of how we can construe the units at other levels. Or, as I would prefer to put it: disambiguation problems occur for every level of linguistic description and, in fact, for levels of non-linguistic behavior as well. (Compare: having observed a man's movements, we ask "Is he in pain or only pretending?") There is, thus, no "easiest level" as such for which to devise a pattern-recognition programme.

Unfortunately attempts to mechanize the process by which disambiguation takes place have been notoriously unsuccessful. As Oettinger has remarked:

The major problems of selecting an appropriate correspondent for a Source Word on the basis of context remains unsolved, as does the related one of establishing a unique syntactic structure for a sentence that human readers find unambiguous.

The major obstacle is that there is still no precise account of how one could build into a programme the fantastically varied background knowledge (e.g., that cows don't eat fish) which human speaker-hearers bring to a communication-situation, and which enable them in fairly systematic and facile ways to interpret correctly each other's utterances, even though considerable novelty may attend both the syntactic, semantic, and situational or pragmatic features of the remark which is interpreted.

Even Benjamin White, who is otherwise optimistic, writes:

None of these computer recognition programmes, for example, has tackled the problem of segmentation. In every case, it is assumed that there is but one letter, one vowel, one pattern in the computer to be recognized. No attempt is made to isolate the spoken vowel in a stream of connected speech, nor to isolate a single letter in cursive script.[4]

That disambiguation occurs at all linguistic levels, and that human beings systematically "bring it off" at all levels, indicates that a "projection problem" could be formulated for each level. Any fully integrated theory of linguistic and non-linguistic behavioral descriptions would attempt to formulate projection rules for each level of competence and explain each level's interactions with the other.

But I now wish to shift my attention from problems involved in simulating what may be seen as essentially sapient aspects of the mind to methodological problems

[4] "Studies in Perception," in Borko, *Computer Applications in the Behavioral Sciences*, p. 298.

indigenous to CS studies themselves as they are frequently conceived. And in section V I shall turn to the still different problems involved in modeling so-called sentient aspects of mentality.

PROTOCOLS, INTROSPECTION, AND BEHAVIORISM

A protocol is simply a subject's report of what he is doing while working through a problem presented to him by the CS experimenter. This record then forms the basis upon which the computer programme (say in IPL-V) is constructed. In short one interrogates the subject, then finds a suitable basic process or complex routine in the programming language to reflect what the subject reports himself as doing. These are strung together in an appropriate fashion and thus an entire programme for the problem-solving process is obtained. (The experimenter may, however, have to use his own discretion in substituting routines for what he takes to be gaps in the subject's reporting.)

Allen Newell and H. A. Simon in their study "GPS, A Program That Simulates Human Thought" (Feigenbaum and Feldman, pp. 279–93) provided a human subject with a problem as follows:

$$(R \supset {\sim}P) \cdot ({\sim}R \supset Q) \quad \Big| \quad {\sim}({\sim}Q \cdot P)$$

The subject was not told that this is a problem in elementary symbolic logic. He was only informed that he had twelve rules (described for him by the experimenter) for manipulating expressions containing letters connected by "dots" (·), "wedges" (V), "horseshoes" (⊃), and "tildes" (~) which were to stand respectively for "and," "or," "implies," "not." The subject was given practice in ap-

plying the rules, but prior to the experiment he had
worked on only one other problem of that sort. The experimenter informed him that he should try to obtain the
upper right corner expression from the expression in the
upper left corner using his twelve rules. At any time the
subject was able to request that the experimenter apply
one of the rules to an expression that was already on the
blackboard. Whenever the transformation was acceptable,
the experimenter would write down the new expression
in the left-hand column with the name of the rule in the
right-hand column beside it. The subject was asked to
talk aloud as he worked. The record of this, the protocol
for the first part of this particular experiment, is provided below:

Well, looking at the left-hand side of the equation,
first we want to eliminate one of the sides by using
Rule 8. It appears too complicated to work with first.
Now—no,—no, I can't do that because I will be elimi-
nating either the Q or the P in that total expression.
I won't do that at first. Now I'm looking for a way to
get rid of the horseshoe inside the two brackets that
appear on the left and right sides of the equation. And
I don't see. Yeh. If you can apply rule 6 to both sides
of the equations, from there I'm going to see if I can
apply rule 7.
Experimenter writes: 2. $(\sim R \vee \sim P) \cdot (R \vee Q)$
I can almost apply Rule 7, but one R needs a tilde, so
I'll have to look for another rule. I'm going to see if
I can change that R to a tilde R. As a matter of fact;
I should have used Rule 6 on only the left-hand side
of the equation. So, use Rule 6, but only on the left-
hand side.
Experimenter writes: 3. $(\sim R \vee \sim P) \cdot (\sim R \supset Q)$
Now I'll apply rule 7 as it is expressed. Both—excuse
me, excuse me, it can't be done because of the horse-
shoe. So—now I'm looking—scanning the rules here for
a second, and seeing if I can change the R to a knot,

a knot R, or a dash R in the second equation, but I don't see any way of doing it. (Sigh) I'm just sort of lost for a second.

Here the only rule we need concern ourselves with in order to understand the above phase of the subject's behavior is R6. $A \supset B \leftrightarrow \sim A \vee B$. In the first instance the subject applied R6 to both the left and right of $(R \supset \sim P) \cdot (\sim R \supset Q)$, and then changed his mind and applied it only to the left. Here, however, I am not interested in the actual character of the subject's derivation but only in the way in which the simulation of the subject's mental processes was thought by Newell and Simon to be made possible through the use of protocols. The use of protocols is not regarded as a necessary feature of computer simulation studies. Thus to show that the use of protocols was methodologically unsound would not show that CS studies were unsound *simpliciter*. Nevertheless, willingness to use the protocol method is indicative of certain preconceptions about mentality on the part of researchers working in CS, and it is this preconception which I wish to flush from cover.

The following questions can be asked of the protocol technique: What sort of data do the protocols make available to us? Do we *infer* from the presence of certain protocols that certain thought processes are taking place in the subject? If so, can we then somehow discover that the protocols are accurate indicators of the subject's "cognitive processes" which are, after all, that which is supposedly being simulated? Suppose one answers the just-raised question by claiming that the protocols are not a *basis* from which to infer certain cognitive processes, but are instead identical with the cognitive processes being simulated. As we shall see, this stance towards protocols is sometimes taken. Then, apart from the implausibility of the identification, we are faced with the question of what it is about protocols which needs to be explained. That is, protocols constitute a phenomenon which we generally understand in the sense that simply by understanding the language in the sense of being able to use it, we see what a person is up to. We might ask someone "What are you doing?" and he might reply "I'm looking to see if this symbol matches any of these." We then say "Oh I see." and we do! Given an appropriate computer language we can, of course, define a routine which instructs the machine to compare symbols until it finds a match. But what do we gain by this? What further illumination should we expect from constructing a computer programme which in some loose sense simply duplicates that behavior? It might be assumed that the "payoff" would come *only* after the processes *underlying* the computer's behavior could be shown to be analogous to the process (as yet unknown) underlying the human's protocol behavior. But this is often not assumed, and there is thought to be a theoretical-explanatory payoff simply in the construction of a programme the trace of which is roughly isomorphic to a string of human protocols. It is this that I do not understand.

If, on the other hand, the protocols are not taken to be identical with the cognitive process being simulated, but are taken to be representative of some other "inner" processes which are (possibly) nonverbal, aren't we face to face with classical introspectionism and its attendant methodological difficulties? I do not mean to suggest that these difficulties are insurmountable, but only that they should be acknowledged and dealt with.

Julian Feldman argues that the problems of introspectionism do not arise.[5] In support of his claim that "the thinking aloud" procedure is not to be confused with introspection, he cites the following passage from K. Duncker's *On Problem Solving:*[6]

This instruction, *"Think aloud"* is not identical with the instruction to introspect which has been common

[5] In Borko: "Computer Simulation of Cognitive Processes."
[6] *Psychological Monographs,* 58 (No. 270), 1945, p. 2.

in experiments on thought-processes. While the introspecter makes himself as thinking, the object of his attention, the subject who is thinking aloud remains immediately directed to the problem, so to speak, allowing his activity to become verbal. When someone, while thinking, says to himself, "One ought to see if this isn't ———," or, "It would be nice if one could show that ———," one would hardly call this introspection; yet in such remarks something is revealed."

Of course something is revealed. What is revealed is what the person is up to. It is not surprising that a person can often tell us what he's doing, what his plans are, etc. And, of course, the criticisms of introspective methods in psychology could not show, were never meant to show, that we can never really tell what people are up to by asking them. The question remains, what would be gained by simply simulating such tellings with a computer programme?

Newell and Simon are not unaware of the introspection issue. They write:

It is now proposed that the protocol of Fig. II constitutes data about human behavior that are to be explained by a psychological theory. But what are we to make of this. Are we back to the introspection of the Würzburgers? And how are we to extract information from the behavior of a single subject when we have not defined the operational measures we wish to consider?

Their answer to this question is as follows:

There is little difficulty in viewing this situation through behavioristic eyes. The verbal utterances of the subject are as much behavior as would be his arm movements or galvanic skin responses. The subject was not introspecting; he was simply emitting a continuous stream of verbal behavior while solving the problem-solver that explains the salient features of this stream of behavior.[7]

First note that protocols are initially said to constitute data *about* human behavior. Since Watson, "behavior" has been such an elastic sort of term that it is difficult to tell what it is being stretched to include or when it will snap back and sting our fingers. But here, at least, the protocols are viewed as data which are *about* something else. One paragraph later, however, protocols are treated *as* the behavior which is to be studied. This forces the question: "What is meant by 'explain'?" and "What is meant by 'the salient features of this stream of behavior'?" In the above characterization it seems that "the salient features of the stream of behavior" will by definition turn out to be those features of the problem solving which contribute to the derivation. But once cognitive processes have been assimilated to features of this kind, it is again unclear what is supposed to be explained. The assumed utility of simulating this behavior becomes suspect. The question is, is this what we are to understand by a programme which simulates human thought?

A more detailed account of what Newell and Simon consider a good theory of a subject's thinking processes is contained in the following (Feigenbaum and Feldman):

> We may then conceive of an intelligent program that manipulates symbols in the same way that our subject does—by taking as inputs the symbolic logic expressions, and producing as outputs a sequence of rule applications that coincides with the subject's. If we observed this program in operation, it would be considering various rules and evaluating various expressions, the same sorts of things we see expressed in the protocol of the subject. If the fit of such a program were close enough to the overt behavior of our human subject—

[7] Feigenbaum and Feldman, *op. cit.*, pp. 281–83.

i.e., to the protocol—then it would constitute a good theory of the subject's problem-solving.

And:

> Conceptually the matter is perfectly straightforward. A program prescribes in abstract terms (expressed in some programming language) how a set of symbols in a memory is to be transformed through time. It is completely analogous to a set of difference equations that prescribes the transformation of a set of numbers through time. Given enough information about an individual, a program could be written that would describe the symbolic behavior of that individual. Each individual would be described by a different program, and those aspects of human problem-solving that are not idiosyncratic would emerge as the common structure and content of the programs of many individuals.[8]

What I find important in the above passages is that the following conflations have taken place. Cognitive processes become identified with problem-solving behavior, problem-solving behavior becomes identified with verbal protocols, and a set of descriptions of the protocols from which a computer simulation programme can be constructed becomes identified with a theory of human thinking in general. Thus, the role of programme writing becomes that of enabling us to make generalizations concerning the sorts of strategies, maneuvers, and so on which human beings make in trying to solve certain kinds of problems. These generalizations are then treated as explanations of human thinking. This needs to be looked into.

First of all, it is not clear how the programme writing provides us with an analytic aid in formulating generalizations about the human behavior. Why not simply generalize about the protocols themselves? But more pointedly one can ask why we should assimilate the thought proc-

[8] Feigenbaum and Feldman, *op. cit.*, pp. 283-84.

esses involved in human problem behavior to the actual behavioral outputs of the human being (here either protocols, or jottings on paper [see Figure 3], and so on). If this were an appropriate assimilation what then would be the significance of searching for generalizations concerning any other levels but 1 (in diagram #1)? Although the computer's behavior may in some sense be "explained" in terms of a programme constructed out of certain basic processes we need more reason than this to support the view that an explanation of a human being's behavior in terms of some programme will be forthcoming. For we don't know if there is a comparable programme. That analogous human outputs may be described in such a manner that it is possible on the basis of their descriptions to construct a programme which when run on a machine produces similar outputs, is not to show that human outputs are the results of carrying out certain programme instructions. If I observe a design in the sand formed by the wind and tides it may be possible to describe the design in such a way that instructions in the form of a programme for a computer can be based on my description so that the machine will etch a design in the sand. This does not show that the wind and tides were programmed to make a design on the sand.

In the context of CS theory, it is little exaggeration to say that a clear description of the problem-solving behavior and its salient features is supposed to be a theory of the behavior. But this is rather like saying a theory of a spider's web-weaving abilities is just a clear description of how most spiders make a web by moving in this direction and then that direction and so on. This leaves unanswered any questions concerning the capacities which might underlie the behavior, whether the behavior was learned and if so, how, whether it was instinctual, or what-not. In just this way Simon and Newell's account neglects any attempt to explain the capacities underlying the behavior, what a human programme would actually look like, the role and nature of non-articulated thoughts, beliefs, and so on. Unless one is a more radical Rylean than Ryle and identifies the doing of a problem with the making of marks on paper or the audible utterances accompanying the attempt to solve the problem, one is faced with the question as to how the non-verbal features of mental processes should be explained. It is this feature of human problem-solving which computer-simulation work as conceived above fails to touch.

v

PROGRAMME-RECEPTIVE AND PROGRAMME-RESISTANT ASPECTS
OF MENTALITY

It should be obvious that most of the foregoing examples of mental phenomena for which CS programmes have been devised fall into the rough (and ready) category of problem-solving. At least this is clearly true of theorem-proving, chess-playing, etc. and unclearly true of other varieties of pattern-recognition. But it should be equally obvious that there exist a number of mental aspects of human beings which are not like this. For example, to have a pain, or to feel anxious, or to desire something, though all aspects of our mental life, seem to be quite different from anything resembling a problem-solving process or problem-solving behavior. They are instead, it appears, prime examples of non-problem-solving non-behavior. Surely they are *related* to problem-solving processes and the interplay between the two is important: For example, unless we had certain needs, desires, capacities for feeling, etc., we would not have certain problems, and would never exhibit a certain range of problem-solving. However, these same needs, desires, etc. are *not* problem-solving behavior in their own right.

So the question arises as to whether the non-problem-solving non-behavioral aspects of the mind are themselves susceptible to being simulated in the sense that theorem-proving or pattern-recognition processes are. I shall call this question the *simulatability question* for these aspects of mentality—i.e., the question of whether, given *current* CS programming techniques, it even makes sense to try to devise a simulation of such phenomena *using just those techniques.*

My short answer to this question is that there is a variety of mental phenomena which includes the having of pains and after-images, feeling anxious, being bored, etc., which are not receptive to being simulated in the sense that, say, theorem-proving is. And so I shall label them programme-resistant aspects of the mind. Insofar as such phenomena could be appropriated by a computer, it would not be a matter of writing routines which utilized current capacities (primarily of symbol-manipulating kinds). Instead, were we to devise analogues for these aspects of mentality it would have to be by making radical additions to the current stock of basic capacities which in turn determine the sorts of programmes which are possible. An imperfect, but useful, comparison: there is little point in trying to extend programming techniques so that a machine will print its programme trace in red ink unless already built into the machine are capacities for such printing. To provide the machine with new basic capacities is not a matter of devising routines, although once such capacities are present there is an obvious point to writing a programme which includes the instruction "print programme trace in red ink." So, too, with respect to whatever capacities might enable a machine to simulate the having of a pain, feeling, after-image, etc. Once the capacity for having an after-image or a feeling were provided, the instruction "describe your after-image" would have a point—but not before.

In what immediately follows then, I shall sketch what I think the distinction between programme-receptive and programme-resistant aspects of mentality consists in. I am not confident that I have coherently formulated a workable set of criteria for distinguishing between these two general aspects of the mind, but I do think that a workable set will be forthcoming and that the current proposals are at least aimed in the right direction.

1. Programme-receptive aspects of the mental are task oriented; programme-resistant aspects are not. In being task oriented they lend themselves to a cluster of characterizations quite inapplicable to programme-resistant aspects. A programme-receptive aspect is associated with *both* a process *and* the result of a process. (E.g., "What was he doing?" "Proving theorems." "How do you know?" "Here are the proofs." *or* "He went through such-and-such a process.") Thus in the case of theorem-provings, say, there is both a process—whatever may be involved in attempting to prove a theorem—and the result of this process which may or may not constitute a proof. And the term "theorem-proving" may be used, somewhat ambiguously, to refer to either or even both. In contrast to this, programme-resistant features of the mental do not lend themselves to this division. There is not, for example, an end result and a process leading to that result in the case of having an after-image, or feeling pain or feeling anxiety. Having an after-image may be the result of some other process (having concentrated on a bright light in a certain manner, etc.). But the process of which the having of an after-image is a result does not fall under the description "the having of an after-image." That phrase is not ambiguous as regards "process" or "end result" in the way that "theorem-proving" is. One might attempt to wrangle an end result out of such phenomena by contending that the end result in the case of having an after image *is* just the having of the after image. But this would not preserve the *distinction* between process and result. It would be a conflation within which the distinction I have sketched would disappear.

2. A second criterion flows naturally from the first. Given that programme-receptive mental features are associated with end results, they are often associated as well with the notions of success and failure. Processes designed to bring about certain end-results may or may not

bring them about. Hence a given process may be appraised or evaluated in terms of whether it achieves what it was designed to do. The aim of a theorem-proving process is to arrive at a proof. It may or may not be successful, may or may not achieve the goal, etc. In contrast to this, pains, emotions, and other programme-resistant mental aspects are not done more or less well. This for the simple reason that they are not the sorts of things which are done. They are things we have. Hence they are not things which are done more or less well. Even though we do not, generally, like being in pain, being in pain is not thereby unsuccessful in itself. Nor is the having of an after-image, etc. Of course, whether we are in pain may itself be a reason for saying that something we were doing was not successful. But the pain is neither successful nor unsuccessful, is not associated in this way with achievement or failure. But theorem-proving is so associated, as are other problem-solving activities. Note: I need not insist that every programme-receptive feature of mentality be associated with the notion of achievement or failure. Rather what I would contend is that *no* programme-resistant mental aspect is so associated.

3. Programme-receptive features of mentality are what I shall call "protocol-possible" phenomena, whereas programme-resistant features are not. Recall the account in the preceding section of how a subject engaged in theorem-proving may be asked to report on what he is doing while he attempts to arrive at a derivation. Remarks such as "I'm trying to see if I can move this outside the parenthesis" or "I would like to shift the horseshoe around so that this set of symbols is over here," etc., are then used as a partial basis upon which to construct the routines in a suitable computer language which when executed will provide a TRACE of moves which are then compared with the moves made by the human subject. In short, one derives a set of verbal reports, and then seeks to define analogous routines in the computer language. Whether or not the resultant simulations be

deemed successful, what seems unquestionable is that
the protocols do provide a fund of data which at least
permit the construction of routines in a computer language. But they only do this for programme-receptive
phenomena. In sharp contrast to this in the case of
programme-resistant phenomena, since there are neither
tasks nor sub-tasks to remark upon, the initial specification of what one is doing—someone saying "I am having
an after-image"—and the follow-up characterization of
how one is doing it, or what one is doing in doing it,
could at best be a paraphrase. Strictly speaking we have
already seen that one isn't *doing* anything. But let us suppress this for the moment. Even if in some surrealist way
one could say "What I was *doing* was having an after-
image," there would still be a very interesting difference
between this sort of doing and the sort of thing we do
when we prove theorems, play checkers, etc. The difference is this: in the latter case there is a series of subtasks
which the activity consists in. But in the case of having
an after-image, there is nothing *we* do in having it. When
asked what we are doing *in* having the after-image there
is nothing to say, except, perhaps, to paraphrase what we
have already said: for example, "Well, my having of the
after-image consists in my seeing this thing" or "I'm confronted by this blue shape," etc. That is, we say slightly
differently what we have already said. But in the case
of proving a theorem, to specify subtasks is not to paraphrase what one has said in saying he is proving a
theorem; it is instead to analyze it.

The above distinctions between programme-receptive
and programme-resistant aspects of the mental should be
of interest for a variety of reasons. If well-drawn it follows that it would be inappropriate to suppose that all
aspects of mentality could be simulated in the same fashion. If all aspects are mechanizable, only some—sapient
features—are mechanizable through programming. I find
it unfortunate that in virtually all philosophical articles
on minds and machines published in recent years, the no-

tion of being modelled by machine has been equated with
the notion of being programmable. It may well be that
sentient aspects of the mind are not beyond the pale of
mechanistic modelling. It seems utterly unlikely, however,
that such modelling could come about through developments in programming or software. Instead we should expect it to transpire through innovations in hardware. At
this point the area of research known as bio-simulation
takes on far greater importance than CS. But that presents a new tangle of issues we can't try to unravel here.

This may seem obvious once it is mentioned, but it has
not always been noted even within the context of CS
research. For example, in the book *Computer Simulation of Personality* (Tompkins and Messick) there is an
attempt to extend the techniques of problem-solving
simulation to the area of human affect—emotion, feelings,
neuroses, etc. The desire to incorporate an analogue of
emotion, feelings, etc. into a simulation programme for
cognitive processes is understandable and laudable. As
Herbert Simon points out in his highly provocative article
"Motivational and Emotional Controls of Cognition,"

> Since in actual human behavior motive and emotion
> are major influences on the course of cognitive be-
> havior, a general theory of thinking and problem solv-
> ing must incorporate such influences. (p. 24)

But Simon's own attempt to achieve the incorporation
by introducing an interruption system to which he likens
emotional behavior seems to me to fail. And this is because it is an attempt to assimilate an essentially programme-resistant aspect of the mind to programme-receptive features. Even if we view Simon's attempt as an
attempt to simulate the *effects* of emotion and not emotion itself, it is obvious that emotions may accompany and
influence our ordinary problem-solving activities without
in any sense interrupting them, and that such activities
may be interrupted without emotion being in any sense
the cause. But more important, emotion is different from

its effects, and since such effects may be brought about through a variety of non-emotional causes, we do not produce an interesting simulation of emotion nor incorporate it into a problem-solving situation simply by producing analogues of such effects.

Much more certainly needs to be said about the sorts of problems Simon is attempting to deal with as well as about the preceding issues. But it certainly doesn't need to be said here.

BIBLIOGRAPHY (Of major items quoted or frequently mentioned)

BORKO, HAROLD, ed., *Computer Applications in the Behavioral Sciences* (Englewood Cliffs, 1962).

DREYFUS, HUBERT L., *Alchemy and Artificial Intelligence* (Santa Monica, 1965).

FEIGENBAUM, EDWARD A. and JULIAN FELDMAN, eds., *Computers and Thought* (New York, 1963).

LUCE, DUNCAN R., ROBERT R. BUSH, and EUGENE GALANTER, eds., *Handbook of Mathematical Psychology*, Vol. I (New York, 1963).

REITMAN, WALTER, *Cognition and Thought* (New York, 1966).

SAYRE, KENNETH M., *Recognition: A Study in the Philosophy of Artificial Intelligence* (Notre Dame, 1965).

SIMON, HERBERT, "Motivational and Emotional Controls of Cognition," *Psychological Review*, Vol. 74, No. 1, pp. 29–39, 1967.

TOMKINS, SILVAN S. and SAMUEL MESSICK, eds., *Computer Simulation of Personality* (New York, 1963).

NOTES ON RYLE'S PLATO

G. E. L. OWEN

In 1939 Gilbert Ryle broached his apparently inexhaustible cask of new thoughts on Plato. He argued in a paper and a book-review in *Mind* that the *Parmenides* was "an early essay in the theory of types."[1] He found the same interests active in the *Theaetetus* and *Sophist*, other late dialogues which have philosophical and dramatic ties with the *Parmenides*. A year or so earlier, in "Categories," he had paid Aristotle a modified compliment, but his Aristotle was in essentials one of those already established in the literature. He has been understood to say that in those days it looked as though Aristotle had been, for the time at any rate, pretty well surveyed while Plato still called for exploration. But there is more than that to the interest that brings him so often back to Plato. In his studies of the late dialogues it became almost an alliance. Here are some comments, inadequate thanks for the illumination and excitement that have resulted. They centre in Ryle's discussion of the dialogue which Russell in *The Principles of Mathematics* called "perhaps the best collection of antinomies ever made."[2]

Russell's description of the *Parmenides*, like the diagnosis I quoted from Ryle, was evidently meant for the sec-

[1] The paper, but not the review of Cornford's *Plato and Parmenides*, was reprinted with an Afterword (1963) in *Studies in Plato's Metaphysics*, ed. R. E. Allen (1965), and page-references to this and other papers prefaced by "SPM" will be to this collection.

[2] *Principles*, p. 355. He also (p. 357) accepted Plato's argument from the proliferation of unity and being discussed in the last pages of this paper as a proof of an infinite class, but gave this up with apparent regret in the *Introduction to Mathematical Philosophy*, pp. 202–3, as conflicting with the theory of types.

ond and last part of the dialogue (137c–66c).[3] Certainly there are unsolved paradoxes enough in the first part. Zeno's are merely sketched for Socrates to disparage, but they are followed by the embarrassments in which Parmenides entraps Socrates when he tries to spell out his theory of Forms. But the systematic collection of antinomies on a large scale begins with the exercise in dialectic that Parmenides carries out in the second part. And it is immensely systematic. Many commentators from antiquity on have flagged after the early stages and offered correspondingly lop-sided interpretations. Ryle was not among them, and I imagine I have his sympathy for the obvious counter-move I must try later: drawing a map of the argument. But maps can be one-sided in other ways.

Broadly, the deductions in this part of the dialogue fall into four groups or stages, I–IV, and each stage into two movements, A and B. (For brevity I use these headings rather than Ryle's: Plato of course used none. So IA starts at 137c, IB at 142b, IIA at 157b, IIB at 159b, IIIA at 160b, IIIB at 163b, IVA at 164b, and IVB at 165e.) One movement in each stage (the "positive" movement) professes to prove, and the other (the "negative") professes to disprove, both members of various pairs of antithetical predicates of one and the same subject. In I and III the subject of the antinomies is ἕν or τὸ ἕν, "One" or "the One" or "Unity" according to the predilection of translators: I am inclined to prefer either of the first two versions for a reason that Ryle gives for preferring the third, viz. that Parmenides has undertaken to speak of one of Socrates' Forms, but pending comment I shall use them indifferently. In II and IV the subject of the paradoxes is everything other than One or Unity.

The first two stages are represented as starting from one hypothesis and the other two as starting from the contradictory of that hypothesis. Assuming that Plato does

[3] "The dialogue": Ryle has recently (e.g., *SPM*, p. 144) come to think the *Parmenides* a patchwork of parts from different dates. On this see the Additional Note.

not, as some think, equivocate on this point, his hypothesis in I and II is that One *is* and in III and IV that One *is not:* for the present, with a caveat, I shall follow Ryle here and write the easier English "exists" and "does not exist." The caveat is that some of the arguments (notably in IIIA, 162a–b) turn on the fact that Greek has only one verb at this date for "be" and "exist." And this need not make for bad philosophy: it is part of Plato's *tour de force* in the *Sophist* to isolate a number of puzzles which for us cluster about non-existence, without marking off an "existential" sense of the verb.[4]

Plato allows two small anomalies in his scheme. The first stage has an appendix (IC, 155e–57b) on the paradoxes of instantaneous change. And in the first but not in the later stages the negative movement precedes the positive. The reason for the later ordering is no doubt mere economy: once the subject of a negative movement is shown generally incapable of carrying predicates, it is enough to refer back to the positive antinomies for all the pairs of laboriously established predicates that are now denied it. The reason for starting with the negative movement in I is probably connected, on the other hand, with some broader functions that Plato means to assign to the dialogue. Dramatically he seems to place it at the head of a group containing the *Theaetetus, Sophist,* and *Statesman* (as well as perhaps the *Cratylus* and *Philebus*),[5] and as an introduction to that group it might be expected to play two roles: that of marking where previous theories are suspect or superseded, and that of broaching a set of problems with which its successors will be concerned. At any rate these two tasks seem to be

---

[4] Cf. M. Frede, "Prädikation und Existenzaussage" (*Hypomnemata*, 1967), and my "Plato on Not-being" in *Plato*, ed. G. Vlastos (Doubleday, 1970).

[5] The dramatic sequence of *Theaetetus, Sophist,* and *Statesman* is fixed (*Theaet.* 210d, *Soph.* 216a–b, *Ptcs.* 257a–b); the place of the *Parmenides* in the sequence is suggested, less certainly, by *Theaetetus* 183e–84a.

carried out, with some overlapping, by its first and second parts respectively; the overlap is inevitable since the new problems are largely the result of pressing dissatisfactions with the old theories. So the deductions of the second part begin with a negative movement because the general effect of that movement is to show the bankruptcy of one way of dealing with unity which had been characteristic of the theory of Forms brought up by Socrates in the first part (129a–e; cf. *Rep.* 525e). Just as a dyer's sample of vermilion might be a piece of cloth having that and no other colour, so it had been thought that in a higher world unity could be represented by a Form so paradigmatically unitary as to have no sort of plurality in it at all. The notion was helped by identifying the Form with the number 1 (*Rep.* 525e). How can 1 be another number of anything? but then how can it even be defined by any conjunction of properties? The question belongs to the lumber-room of philosophy partly because the movement IA was, *inter alia*, the necessary clearing-operation.

It is this network of deductions that was designed, in Ryle's view, to show by *reductio ad absurdum* part of the difference between two sorts of concept. In the nature of the case Plato could not have had labels for them; in Ryle's labelling they are the "formal" concepts, such as unity and existence, and "proper" or "specific and generic" concepts such as squareness and largeness. "When we treat a formal concept as if it were a non-formal or proper concept, we are committing a breach of 'logical syntax.' But what shows us that we are doing this? The deductive derivation of absurdities and contradictions does, and nothing else can. Russell's proof that, in his code-symbolism, ϕ cannot be a value of x in the propositional function ϕx is only another exercise in the same genre as Plato's proof that 'Unity' cannot go into the gap in the sentence-frame '. . . exists' or '. . . does not exist.'"

The logical apparatus of Ryle's discussion is recognizably that of "Categories" and some of his post-war writings. The logical forms which interest philosophers are ascribed to propositions (and not, as in an earlier paper, to "facts"), and concepts are assigned to different types which answer broadly to different roles in the formation of propositions: formal concepts "are not subject or predicate terms of propositions but rather the modes of combining terms" (itself an echo of Russell). One and perhaps the main job of philosophers is to expose forms of speech that, without falling into blatant nonsense, misrepresent the logical powers of the concepts they employ. As a statement of grammar, " 'Unity' cannot go into the gap in the sentence-frame '. . . exists' or '. . . does not exist' " would be false. Ryle takes it to be a statement of "logical syntax" proved by Plato. He does not of course think that Plato argues in the formal mode. So what does he take the proof to consist in?

Here there are two points at which one would like him to have said more.

First, he speaks more than once of both the hypothesis "Unity exists" and its contradictory as *entailing* the families of contradictions that they severally breed. As an analogy he cites Russell's use of the so-called Vicious Circle paradoxes to show that "$\phi(\phi\hat{x})$" is ill-formed. But he does not, of course, offer to show that Plato's antinomies follow from their first premises as directly as those which Russell collected to argue the need for a theory of types. On Ryle's own survey of the *Parmenides* there seem to be many other premises and assumptions intervening in the plot. The reader is left to wonder whether these interventions are systematic or perhaps just random—as they might be expected to be, for example, on Robinson's thesis that Plato "is genuinely failing to notice the extra premises as such."[6] But the answer, I think, is that they are systematic. They are so arranged that the conflicts between them are the nerve of Plato's argument. If I can

[6] *Plato's Earlier Dialectic*, ed. 2 (1953), p. 274.

establish this, there will be closer analogies to Plato's strategy to be found in the classes of puzzle that Ryle discusses in "Dilemmas."

More particularly, unity is a paragon of a formal concept and Parmenides picks out One or Unity as the subject of his hypotheses. So once more the alerted reader might hope to be shown just where and why the antinomies come from miscasting unity in a non-formal role— even if other paradoxes can be seen to come from a comparable miscasting of other concepts. But the comments with which Ryle intersperses his summary of the argument play coy to this expectation too. He is ready to suggest that the starting-point of the argument in IA is illegitimate because "Unity exists" and "Unity is unitary" are both "bogus sentences." But the reason he notices for rejecting the first sentence is that it couples "exists" with what is supposed to be a proper name, so this is a mistake about "exist" compounded with another about abstract nouns. (Thereafter, particularly on IIIA–B, he notices similar misuses of "exist" as "signifying a quality, relation, dimension, or state, etc.") The reason he suggests for calling the second sentence bogus is that it treats a universal as one of its own instances. (But if unity *were* a universal, would it not have to be one of that odd subset that instantiate themselves? Russell still thought so in *Principles*. Back to this later.) His only other detailed comment on the mistreatment of unity is: "We may suspect that the argument [of IA] presupposes that unity is a quality." So it does indeed: as I have said, it argues as though unity could preclude plurality as one colour precludes others. Still, extracting paradoxes from the miscasting of a non-quality as a quality is not enough to show (or show awareness) that it is a formal concept in Ryle's sense. The same miscasting was possible with any of that favoured set of incomplete predicates which seem to have provoked Plato to invent Forms as quasi-ostensive samples for them because the world, understandably, offers no such samples. The set, as any reader

of the *Phaedo* and *Republic* V–VII and the first part of
the *Parmenides* well knows, is a logical mixed bag including *large, heavy, equal, double, hard, just,* and *beautiful*
and their contraries and cognates as well as *one* and *many*
and *similar* and *dissimilar.* And the miscasting not only
could be but surely had been made. The Forms answering
to these predicates seem to have had, among their other
duties, that of being just those privileged (and logically
impossible) samples in which the attributes behave as
qualities.[7] When Socrates at *Parm.* 129b6–c3 says he will
be astonished if the Form of unity can be shown to be
plural or the Form of plurality shown to be unitary, he is
arguing from the same assumptions as when he lays it
down in *Phaedo* 102d6–103a2 that neither the Form of
largeness nor even its proxy largeness in the individual
can be or become small. Parmenides wrings a paradox
from the latter claim in *Parm.* 131c–e, and most of IA
together with the start of IB can be taken as addressed
to the former. There is nothing in this, central as it is to
Plato's emancipation from old confusions, to show a recognition that unity must be handled quite differently
from those overt or covert relatives and grade-concepts
that fill up his list.

Is this to say that Ryle has no evidence for his thesis?
Of course not. There are arguments, perhaps too obvious
for him to have singled out, that seem designed to show
the absurdity of treating Socrates' oneness as another
property co-ordinate with his pallor or smallness. The two
chief candidates will be interviewed later. Still it will be a
question how far they can be read as proofs, even in a
suitably philosophical sense of "proof." That Plato is at
grips with the logic of formal concepts here and in other
late dialogues seems to me certain, and this certainty was
established by Ryle. But an interest in proving the necessary distinctions does not seem to lie central to the strategy of the *Parmenides.* As I shall represent it, the method

[7] SPM, pp. 303–8.

that Plato explores with such enthusiasm is tailored not to the constructing of proofs but to the setting and sharpening of problems, and problems of a characteristically philosophical stamp. It is the first systematic exercise in the logic of aporematic and not demonstrative argument.

We shall get no further in this direction without the map I promised at the start. Here it is, as accurate as I can make it on this scale but with no claim to completeness.[8] It will help to fill Ryle's silence on the first point, for it tries to mark out, and locate conflicts between, the (or a representative majority of the) cardinal theses on which Plato's antinomies turn. I number the key-assumptions as Plato introduces them, trying to confine myself to those he expressly recognizes; though I have sometimes allowed myself a more general and abstract formulation when he cites only the particular application, and in doing so used forms not available to him. But in using letters in a way which had not yet become part of logic I preserve his ambiguities: on occasion "S is P" will cover identities as well as predications, and there are no type-restrictions on the terms. To mark one of those conflicts between theses which seem to me to be the nerve of his argument, I shall put the sign "#" before the reference to some thesis which rejects or otherwise undermines the thesis under discussion.

Finally, to avoid encumbering the map, I relegate to a note the definitions and divisions that are introduced and not subsequently challenged in the argument.[9]

[8] In an earlier version it has been refined and enlarged in theses by David Bostock and Malcolm Schofield, and I print it partly in the hope that it will prompt further efforts in the same field.

[9] In IA he defines "whole" (137c, cf. *Theaetetus* 205a, Aristotle, *Phys.* 207a9–10); "round" (137e, cf. *Epistles* vii 342b and Euclid's improvement in *Elements* i def. xv); "straight" (137e, cf. Aristotle, *Top.* 148b27 and contrast Euclid, i def. iv); "like" and "unlike" (139e, 140a, and thereafter unchallenged, cf. 147c; but see *Protagoras* 331d–e, *Philebus* 13d); "equal" and "unequal" (140b–c, designed to cover incommensurables); "coeval" (140e). IB takes these definitions over and adds one of "contact" (148e, adopted and reshaped

I. IF ONE EXISTS, WHAT CAN BE SAID OF IT?

IA (137c–42a) is negative in its conclusions. In addition
to the definitions mentioned,[9] its deductions depend
primarily on nine premisses.

(1) 137c: *The One is one and not many* [# the opening
argument of IB and, for a reason to be given directly,
(15)]. From this it is deduced that the One cannot have
parts or members or be a whole.

> (Very likely (1) depends on a confusion between the
> identifying and predicative uses of "S is P": One is not
> the same as Many and so is not many of anything. Let
> us call this the I/P confusion. It is surely one source of
> the so-called "self-predication assumption" which char-
> acterizes the theory of Forms both in earlier dialogues
> and particularly in Socrates' account of the theory in
> *Parm.* 128e–30a. It will be challenged by the schema
> in (15), which distinguishes identity from participa-
> tion, but the effect of (15) will in turn be spoilt by
> (16).)

(2) 137d: *The limits or extremities of anything are parts
of that thing* [#(11)]. From this, together with the last
conclusion, stem the proofs that the One cannot have
limits, shape, or position.

---

by Aristotle, *Phys.* 226b18–27b2). IC defines "combination" and
"dispersion," "assimilation" and its opposite, and "increase," "diminution," and "equalization" (156b). In addition, from IA on Plato
assumes the equation between having a location and being contained
in something which is standard in Greek philosophy (138a, cf. Zeno
B 5, Gorgias B 3, and Aristotle's analysis in *Physics* IV 1–5). As
for divisions, IA distinguishes "shape" into "round" and "straight"
(to which IB, 145b, adds "mixed"), and "change" (*kinesis*) into
"change of quality" and "motion" (138b–c, cf. *Theaet.* 181d: there
is an illegitimate conversion of one of the disjuncts in IIIA, 162e,
and IIIB, 163e, though previously the division was given correctly
in IIIA, 162d).

(Throughout the deductions, save for those concerned
with progress and regression in time, mathematical interests are obvious. Recall that the Form of unity had
among its other duties that of representing the cardinal
number 1. Here the geometrical application to points is
evident, and Aristotle makes it explicit in *Phys.*
212b24–25 (cf. 209a7–13). Arguing that points cannot
have a location because they cannot have a perimeter
is part of Plato's "war against points" (Aristotle, *Met.*
992a19–22).)

(3) 139e–40a and ?138c, 139c: *If anything has more
than one character or attribute these pluralize the thing*
—or, as it is put in IB, 142d, they are *parts or members*
of the thing. The attributes in question are unrestricted
in type: they include unity, identity, existence, in fact
anything distinguishable by the criteria in (4) below.

(A minor question is when this premiss is introduced.
It does not occur explicitly until 139e–40a. But some
think that from it, together with the conclusion given
under (1), stem the proofs that the One cannot (a)
change in quality or even (b) be identical with, (c)
differ from or be (d) like or (e) unlike itself or anything else. On the other hand, and by way of showing
how tentative this mapwork must be in detail, it is
arguable that (a), and (b) and (c) with their derivative (e), depend only on the I/P confusion: thus (a)
anything changing character is taken to lose its identity
(138c), and (b,c) whatever is (identical with) One is
not (not even predicatively) anything else, such as
same or different (139c–d). But (d) is expressly represented as depending on (3) and so, in retrospect, are
(b) and (c) (139e–40a). This still leaves (a) as dependent on the I/P confusion. In any event the argument for (b) imports a criterion of non-identity that
finds an echo in IIB and IIIA and *Sophist* 255a–c:)

(4) 139d: *If the statement that S is P differs in truth-value* (or, in the form in which it is assumed in IB, 142b–c, *differs in sense*) *from the statement that S is Q, then P is different from Q.* (Note the extension of this in IIIA, 160c: if the statement that S is P differs in sense from the statement that T is P, even when "P" stands for "non-existent," then S is a different thing from T. All such assumptions seem to be applications of the general view of words as names which appears in (17), but Plato does not draw the connection.) From the conclusions already listed under (3) it is further argued that the One is not equal or unequal to anything and that it has no temporal attributes.

(5) 138d: *Changes* (more strictly, *movements to a place*) *take time: to describe S as becoming P is to describe something temporally intermediate between an initial and a final state* [# the argument under (22), which trades on the possibility of describing the initial and final states as "p" and "not-p" or vice versa]. From the conclusions listed under (2) it is argued that the One cannot move in one place, and then from (1) and (5) it is shown that the One cannot change place either.

(The character of one of the negative movements is becoming clear. Again Aristotle makes the application to geometrical points explicit, at *Phys.* 240b8–41a6.)

(6) 141b: *If* (*when*) *X is becoming different from Y, it cannot be the case that Y is different from X: otherwise X would already be different from Y and not merely becoming so.* Hence it is argued that, if X is becoming older than itself, it is also becoming younger than itself. But from the conclusions under (3) and (4) the One can have neither this temporal property nor that of remaining coeval with itself; hence it does not exist in time.

(Formally (6) is an argument, but I give it as a premiss. The implicit but unexpressed premiss is

(6*) *If S is becoming P it cannot yet be P*
and this is challenged by (19) in the parallel context in
IB.)

(7) 141d–e: *What exists exists in time* (more exactly,
*Whatever is or becomes, is or becomes at some time past
present or future*). From this and the conclusions under
(6) it is argued that the One does not exist (more exactly,
is not in any way, is not *anything*).

(8) 141e: *If S is P, then S is or exists.* (Cited here in
the particular form "If the One is one, the One is," but in
its general form the premiss recurs in IIIA, 161e, and
IIIB, 163e, and it is challenged by IIIA in an argument
based on the considerations under (4).) From this and
the conclusion under (7) it follows that the One is not one
(or not One).

(It is worth remark that even this premiss, like its
predecessor, does not prove Plato's recognition of a
separate existential sense of the verb "to be." Arguably,
the logic of (8) appeared to him nearer to that of "If
Smith lies to one person, Smith lies.")

(9) 142a: *What does not exist can have nothing related
to it* [# the argument under IIIA]. From this and the
conclusion under (7) it follows that the One cannot be
named and that there can be neither speech nor knowledge, perception nor idea of it at all.

IB (142b–55e) is positive, and its deductions depend
primarily on premisses (10)–(20) together with some
from IA, viz. (1), (3), (4), (5), (6), (7), (8), and the
converse of (9). Two of these inherited premisses, (1)
and (6), are challenged in the same movement. The
opening arguments have no fresh premisses:

142b–43a: By (4), if the One exists its existence is not

the same as its unity; hence, by (3), unity and existence
are pluralizing parts of the one [#(1)]. But the same is
true of each part in turn. (Here, in ascribing unity to each
part, the argument seems to anticipate premiss (10); and
in ascribing existence to whatever is unitary it seems to
rely on (8).) Hence the One is a whole with infinite parts,
and unity and existence are infinitely distributed.

143a–44a: Furthermore, if the One and its existence
are differentiable they exhibit difference, which (seemingly by reliance on (4) again) is distinct from either of
them. The sums and multiples of these three generate all
numbers.

(10) 144c: *What is not one is nothing at all* (more
strictly, *if a part were not one part it would be nothing*)
[#(23)]. From this it is argued that any part of a
plurality is one, that anything divisible is divisible into
some number of parts, and generally that any number is
a number of units.

(Here starts one of the trains of paradox which show
the anomalous behaviour of unity as judged by that of
squareness or heaviness. The opening arguments of IB,
and the premiss (10) which they import, claim that we
cannot "abstract from" the unity or existence of a
subject because unity and existence must always be reimported in talking of whatever parts or members are
left. In giving a thing's properties we cannot systematically discount unity as we can systematically discount
shape or weight. This is what (23) will try to challenge.)

(11) 144e–45a: *A whole contains, and so limits, its parts*
[#(2), #(13)]. From this and the conclusions under (9)
and (10) it is argued that the One is limited as well as
unlimited.

(Here comes another trouble over unity, the unity of
any limited set. The effect of (11) is to upset (2) by

making the limit or limiting factor external to, and
not part of, what is limited. Trouble is coming with
(13).)

(12) 145b: *If X is limited X has spatial extremities.*
Hence the One has shape.

(For the importing of spatial terms cf. (14) and its
temporal analogue in (7).)

(13) 145c: *If X has parts X is identical with the aggregate of those parts* [#(11)]. From the conjunction of
(11) and (13) come the proofs that the One, qua parts,
is contained in itself, qua whole; and also (reversing the
roles) that it is not contained in itself. From this in turn
flow many of the later conclusions, as that it is in contact
with itself and that it is both larger and smaller than
itself.

(Premisses (11) and (13) say, respectively, that the
whole is an extra element over and above its parts, and
that it is nothing more than the parts. In the analysis
of syllables in *Theaetetus* 203e–5a these possibilities are
given as an exhaustive disjunction and not, as here, as a
conjunction. The disjunction is in turn superseded in
the *Sophist* 252e–53c, on which more below, and Aristotle puts the moral in its simplest form in *Met.*
1041b11–27: a syllable is a whole which is neither a
heap of elements nor an extra element.)

(14) 145e: *What exists must be somewhere,* sc. (the
standard treatment of location in Greek philosophy)
must be in something. From this and the conclusions
under (13) it is argued that the One must be both in itself
and in another; and that, qua "in itself," it is always "in
the same," and qua "in another," it is always "in something different." From this, by way of a flagrant fallacy
of relations, it is deduced that the One is static and moving and, later, that it is different from itself.

(The fallacy is that "in the same," which began by meaning "in the same thing as itself," is tacitly reconstrued as meaning "in the same thing as that in which it previously was"; and "in another" is successively construed as meaning "in something other than itself," "in something other than that in which it previously was," and "in something other than that in which it now is." Nor does Plato stop labouring the fallacy here, and this becomes a test-case for those who think him oblivious to all the component fallacies in the argument. The same misuse of "same" and "other," together with the I/P confusion, provides the later argument that nothing can be different from anything; and it was a comparable fallacy in IA that engendered confusions over "getting older than oneself" and "staying coeval with oneself." In the *Sophist* 259c–d Plato is severe on those who commit the fallacy and produce superficial paradoxes by failing to complete the predicates "same" and "other.")

(15) 146b: *Anything is related to anything in one of three ways: (a) by identity or (b) by difference or (c) as part to whole or whole to part.*

(The part-whole relation is exemplified in the sequel by "partaking of unity" or, what comes to the same, "being in a way (i.e., for present purposes predicatively) one" (147a). So here identity seems to be distinguished from predication. But the effect is spoilt by (16) which reimports, for negations at least, the I/P confusion.)

(16) 147a: *What is not one is related to One by (b) and not by (a) or (c).* Hence things that are not one have no unity of any sort [#(10)]; and from this, together with the conclusions under (10), they are argued to have no number at all.

(The argument is that being not-X excludes being X in any way whatever: the negation is construed as deny-

ing that the subject is X both in the identifying and
in the predicative sense of the words. So here is the I/P
confusion again; it is cleared up in the *Sophist* 256a–b,
but here Plato forces the issue by the challenge that is
coming in IIA. Meantime the present argument is reinforced at 147a by an appeal to (1), which reappears
yet once more at 148e–49a.)

(17) 147d: *Words are names, and to repeat a word is to
name the same thing twice.* Here "words" (*onomata*)
covers at least all those general terms for which Plato
had postulated Forms: thus it is argued that, in "A is
different from B and B is different from A," the two occurrences of "different" name a thing that A and B have
in common, and thus their difference makes them alike.
(The most general Greek expression for "word" also
means "name," but (17) is not just a muddle reflecting this fact. It embodies the logical or semantic atomism which had shown itself in earlier writings and
which probably underlies the assumptions in (4). Ryle
has often argued, I think rightly, that Plato manages to
recognize this linguistic model and reject it; later I
shall suggest that the decisive rejection takes place
when the *Sophist* moves beyond the disjunction of
(11) and (13). Meantime the view in its simplest form
faces the puzzle set by IIIA and IIIB jointly: even non-
existing things can apparently be mentioned and distinguished from others.)

(18) 150a–d: *Smallness is small, largeness is large, etc.*
(In detail: if smallness were itself equal to or larger than
anything, it would be *"doing the jobs of largeness and
equality, and not its own"*; and if there were no smallness
in anything else, "there would be nothing small *except
smallness."*) This is put to proving that nothing but largeness can exhibit largeness, nothing but smallness smallness, etc.

(Here, explicitly and even flamboyantly introduced, is the "self-predication" assumption which some believe that Plato was unable to recognize as a premiss of some paradoxes in the first part of the dialogue, including the notorious Third Man (132a–b). He applies it here to the very concept—largeness—which had been exploited in the Third Man, and uses it to produce still more outrageous consequences. Even if Aristotle had not recorded for us the Academy's recognition and formulation of the assumption it would take some determination to think of Plato as still reduced to "honest perplexity" by his inability to see that largeness cannot be a large thing.)

It is now deduced from (7) that the One exists in time, and from (6) and the conclusion under it that the One is getting not only older but younger than itself.

(19) 152c–d: *If X is becoming Y, then at any "present time" in the process X is (and not: is becoming) Y* [#(6), and esp. #(6*)]. The premiss is formulated quite generally and then applied to "becoming older" (152c6–d4): if the One is growing older then at any present time it is older. (Unluckily but idiomatically this is expanded into "older than itself," and used to argue that the One is also younger than itself, but this extra fallacy of relations does not affect the main point of the conflict between (19) and (6*): see the comment below.) Subsequently, by an extension of (5) to cases of coming-into-existence, it is argued that the One is both older and younger, and neither older nor younger, than the others. And further paradoxes are wrung from the idea of becoming relatively and asymptotically older and younger.

(Premiss (19) is plausible when applied to "X is in the process of becoming older (or taller)"; (6*) is plausible when applied to "X is in the process of becoming an octogenarian (or six feet tall)." In *Philebus* 23c–27c Plato brings out part of the difference between these two sorts of filling, saying that the second but not the

first sets a terminus to the becoming. Aristotle profited
from Plato's distinction in his own account of *kinesis*
and *energeia*. I take Plato to be pressing the need for
such a distinction by setting up (19) as a challenge to
(6), and the distinction once grasped is lethal to the
simple dichotomy of "being" and "becoming" that
Plato had inherited. Roughly, becoming is incompatible with being in (6) and entails being in (19): everything depends on the question, "Becoming *what?*")

(20) 155d: *What exists has (or can have) other things
related to it.* By this converse of (9), the One can be
named and spoken of and there can be knowledge, perception, and thought of it.

IC (155e–57b) is a joint appendix to IA and IB, using
some conclusions from each but dropping others. It
adopts those given under (1), (8), and the opening arguments of IB, but tacitly drops that under (7) on which
the conclusion under (8) depends.

(21) 155e: *If S is both P and not P it is P at one
time and not P at another.* From this together with the
various contradictions listed for the One, it is argued that
the One undergoes various forms of change from P to
not-P or vice versa.

(Here, by another I/P confusion, being both P and
not-P is construed as a matter of existence and non-
existence. On these terms (21) can be invoked to evade
all contradictions, including that on which (24) will
depend.)

(22) 156c: *There is no time in which S can be neither P
nor not-P.* Hence any change, construed as a transition
from P to not-P or vice versa, takes no time: it occurs at
"the instant."

(Premiss (21) depends on the law of contradiction, (22) on the law of excluded middle; but the excluded middle seems not to apply to descriptions of "the instant.")

II. IF ONE EXISTS, WHAT CAN BE SAID OF EVERYTHING ELSE?

IIA (157b–59b) is positive. It depends chiefly on premiss (23), together with (10), (15) and the converse of (1) (which thus foreseeably becomes an equation). But the inherited premiss (10) is challenged in the same movement.

157b: Things other than the One are not the One (and in this sense are called "not one," cf. 158c). So, by an appeal to the converse of (1), they must be distinguished from the One itself by forming a whole containing parts or members; and by (10) and the conclusions under it, each part must have unity by "partaking in the One."

(Here it seems initially that the argument wants to cut loose from the restrictive interpretation of "not one" given in (16). That interpretation reimported the I/P confusion into negation by pretending that the options given under (b) and (c) in (15) were mutually exclusive. Here, things other than the One are carefully said to be "not *the* One" before this phrase is replaced in 158c by "not one." Vain hope. The next move in the argument rejects (10) and the conclusions under it, and the puzzle is restored.)

(23) 158c: *If anything is related to the One by neither the first nor the third of the options under (15)*—i.e., neither is nor even exhibits unity—*it must be mere unlimited plurality* [#(10)]. Now considered in themselves ("at the time they are starting to partake of the One," or "abstracted in thought") the things other than the One answer to this condition and hence are bare plurality. In this way they are unlimited as well as (in virtue of the

unity that accrues to them) limited; and from these contraries all others are made to flow.

(See the comment under (10). (23) and its dependent arguments propose an answer to the question "What can be said of anything in abstraction from its unity?" as though this had the logic of "What was he before he became a greengrocer?" or "What sort of thing is it, apart from its shape?" (10) claimed in effect that the abstraction is impossible; and in particular, the hopeful answer that what is left is a kind of bare plurality runs against the conclusion under (10) that any plurality is a plurality of units, a conclusion repeated in IIB.)

IIB (159b–60b) is negative and relies wholly on premisses already introduced. The One and the things other than the One form an exhaustive disjunction. By the conclusion under (1) it is argued that the two camps cannot be related by (c) in the schema at (15), and evidently they cannot be related by (a) either; so the other things are isolated from all unity. If IIA were right, quite a lot could still be said of them. But IIB reverts to the conclusion under (10), that any plurality is a plurality of units; so these things other than the One are not plural either [#(23)]. They have neither number nor limit nor any enumerable properties whatever.

III. IF ONE DOES NOT EXIST, WHAT CAN BE SAID OF IT?

IIIA (160b–63b) is positive and relies on premisses already introduced or, in the case of (4) and (8), on more or less questionable extensions of them. By the extension of (4) noted under that premiss, it is argued that even a non-existent One can be known and mentioned and distinguished from other things; hence it has various properties and stands in various relations. Yet, by (8), if it does not exist it must lack properties and relations, from which it follows that it cannot have equality with anything; and hence, by a fallacy of negation which underlay another argument in IB (150d), it is deduced to be unequal to anything.

(The fallacy is the assumption that if something lacks a given predicate it must have some other of a family of incompatible predicates which includes the first. Perhaps the double use of "not," to signify both bare negation and this loaded variety, is acknowledged in *Theaetetus* 183b—though not, I think, in *Sophist* 257b.)

But now, by an extension of (8), the One must exist if only to *be* non-existent. From its existence and non-existence are deduced its mutability and other characteristics.

(But the detail of the argument makes it clear how far Plato is here from saying unambiguously that S must exist in order to have non-existence. Otherwise he would also be claiming that S must be non-existent qua *not being* non-existent. "To be" and "not to be" are run in harness here as in the *Sophist*, and that dialogue tackles its problems about not-being without giving up either the hard-won subject-predicate model for statements or the treatment of ". . . is . . ." and ". . . is not . . ." as a two-place predicate.)

IIIB (163b–64b) is negative and relies on premiss (24), together with (9).

(24) 163c: *What does not exist cannot also "in some sense exist"* [≠ the general argument of IIIA]. Hence, by (9), nothing can be said or known, etc., of the One.

(A beneficial truth about existence? But in the Greek the factotum verb "to be" is still in play. So Plato may be calling attention once more to a misuse of negation that began in (16) and will still exercise him in the *Sophist*: the assumption that what is not X, in some sense or respect, is not X at all. He may just be anxious to discredit the notion that *not to be* is *not to be any-thing*.)

IV. IF ONE DOES NOT EXIST, WHAT CAN BE SAID OF EVERYTHING ELSE?

IVA (164b–65e) is positive and relies on premisses already introduced together with the relational fallacy described under (14).

If the others are other, by (9) they cannot be other than the One; so they are other than each other. But if so they must be supposed, or must seem, to have plurality and hence, by the conclusion given under (10), they must be deemed to have number, unity, and the dimensional properties inferred from these in IB.

(IVA reinforces IIIA, arguing that even if the One does not exist it must figure in discourse and conjecture, however mistaken. IVB, like IIIB, replies by an appeal to premiss (9).)

IVB (165e–66a) is negative and relies wholly on premisses previously introduced. By (10) and the conclusions given there, any plurality is a class of units; and by (15) and the conclusions drawn from it in IIA any unit must partake in the One. But by (9) this connexion is now impossible, nor can the One be introduced in any connexion whatever. So nothing can be said of the others at all; hence nothing exists.

Now for some morals. Two negative conclusions will help clear the way for the positive.

Sometimes the antinomies have been diagnosed as an exercise in ambiguity. The key-hypotheses ἓν εἰ ἔστιν and ἓν εἰ μὴ ἔστιν have been thought to vary in sense between any two antithetical movements, and for a given movement the sense is to be gathered from the supporting premisses. But one thing our map shows is that the premisses which supposedly fix the sense for one movement commonly turn up in its twin as well. And some of them are both used and challenged in the same movement.[10] Again, the antinomies are sometimes branded as a professional lampoon or a school primer of fallacies. But the map makes it easier to see how often the premisses are the very assumptions which Plato puts to serious work in other dialogues of his maturity.[11]

Ryle rejected such attempts to diminish the seriousness of the work. But since a budget of unresolved paradoxes cannot be meant to expound positive doctrine, he saved the work's seriousness by reading it as a direct *reductio ad absurdum* of both one hypothesis and its contradictory —a project nearer to Kant's paradoxes than Russell's. It might be replied that in the *Sophist* Plato still seems content to have formal concepts as the subject of such hypotheses; but more recently Ryle has proposed a very late date for the second part of the *Parmenides* which would avoid this objection.[12] Even so, the map seems to show Plato far less single-minded than such a *reductio* would make him. And in particular it shows that throughout the deductions he recurs to one favourite strategem,

[10] The premiss (1) is used in IA and IB (and their appendix IC), and again in IIA and IIB. (3), (4), (5), (6), and (7) are used in IA and IB, and (2) after its entry in IA is implicitly subsumed under (13) of IB. (8) is used in IA and IB and again in IIIA and IIIB. (9) is used in IVA and IVB, and its use in IA is echoed by its converse in IB. (10) is used in IIA and IIB and again in IVA and IVB. (15) is used in IIA and IIB. Premisses both used and challenged in the same movement are (1) in IB, (6) in IB, (10) in IB and again IIA, (11) and (13) and (16) in IB. And (5), which is used in IA and IB, is challenged in their appendix IC.

[11] The premiss (1) is used in *Soph.* 245a and (2) in *Soph.* 244e. (3) is used, implicitly at any rate in *Theaet.* 157b–c, 209c; (4) in *Soph.* 255a–c; (6), or the unexpressed (6*) given under it, in *Tim.* 27d–28e, with which cf. *Theaet.* 182c–83b and *Soph.* 248a; (8) in *Soph.* 255e–56a, cf. 256e; (9) in *Soph.* 237c–39b; the disjunction of (11) and (13) in *Theaet.* 203e–5a; (18) in the "self-predicational" treatment of the Forms criticized in *Parm.* 131c–32b and later (cf. 134b6–7); (20) in *Soph.* 238a, and (24) in *Soph.* 239b.

[12] See the Additional Note, p. 358 f.

that of setting up a conflict between a pair of premisses or between one premiss and a thesis derived from others. And these various conflicts do most to generate the major contradictions between and within movements and stages of the argument; and they are serious. They set, without solving, problems that exercise Plato in other late dialogues.

Here are examples: I believe a more detailed map would show others. (i) The confusion between identity-statements and predications which had beset the earlier metaphysics is brought out, with especial reference to negations, by the conflict between (16) and the argument drawn from (10) in IB and IIA, and teased out in the *Sophist* (250 ff. and esp. 256a–b). (ii) Puzzles which we for some purposes can, as Plato could not, label as puzzles of non-existence, and which are taken up and transformed in *Sophist* 237b–63d, are set here by confronting (9) with the extension of (4) used in IIIA. (iii) The veteran assumption that "being" and "becoming" mark two different states characterizing different worlds (an assumption which the *Timaeus* appears to be trying to modify from within, without ever finally breaking the shell) is called in question by the conflict between (6) and (19), a conflict that Plato stresses by connecting it with the particular notion of "growing older"; and the conflict and the dichotomy are sufficiently demolished by the distinction in the *Philebus* noticed under (19). (iv) The conflict between (10) and (23) is another example of the same strategy: I reserve it for a later page. (v) An abstract puzzle about the relation of a whole to its parts is set by the juxtaposition of (11) and (13). In a more concrete version (but one which is said to have quite general application, *Theaet.* 204a2–3) these same premisses reappear as a disjunction in the *Theaetetus* argument to which I referred under (13). It is worth-while following this train of argument a little further into familiar territory, for it marks Plato's emancipation from the atomism noticed under (17) and, what is more to my purpose, it shows how the *Parmenides* sets without solving problems which Plato elsewhere offers to solve.

The *Theaetetus* (201d ff.) and the *Sophist* (253a, 261d) use Plato's favourite analogy of letters and syllables to illustrate the complexity of whatever can be known and explained, and therewith the complexity of what must be said to explain it. In the *Theaetetus* (202e–6b) Socrates tries to argue this complexity away. He urges that a syllable is either just the letters that compose it or a separate single entity produced by their juxtaposition; so knowing a syllable is either just knowing each letter or knowing the new incomposite, and either way the knowledge is just of simple objects and not of complexes. After all, he pursues, the whole business of learning letters is the effort to pick out each one by itself (206a). But when the *Sophist* takes up the analogy (252e–53a) it points out that a syllable is (not an aggregate of pieces and not an extra piece, but) a nexus of constituents of different types fitted together in certain ways; and the knowledge of letters exercised in spelling is not just an ability to tell the letters apart but the knowledge of how they can be legitimately combined and how, in virtue of their different powers of combination, they differ in type. The *Philebus* (18c) points one moral: no letter can be learnt in isolation from the rest. And the *Sophist* argues that it is like this with our knowledge of the "forms" or concepts which give our words meaning, and with our knowledge of the words themselves: they too cannot be learnt in isolation, they too are marked off by their powers of combination into different types (253a, 261d). Speaking is not stringing nouns together, and learning to speak is not, as the *Cratylus* had implied, a piecemeal business of correlating atoms of the world with atoms of language. This is a familiar enough train of argument;[13] my excuse

[13] There is no space to discuss Ryle's attractive suggestion (*Phil. Rev.* lxix, 1960, pp. 431–51, answered by D. Gallop, *Phil. Rev.* lxxii, 1963, pp. 364–76) that when Plato speaks of letters he means not the separate written characters but the "abstractable noise-differences"

for recalling it here is that the quandary from which it sets out in the *Theaetetus* is typically set as a conflict of theses in the *Parmenides*.

Anyone who stresses, as I have, the plurality of philosophical interests that Plato engineers into these paradoxes must ask why he tries to give some unity to the business by the architectural scheme I sketched earlier. Here is part at least of a reply. At the start of the antinomies (135d–36c) Parmenides promises that the ensuing exercise in dialectic will be an application and extension of Zeno's methods. And Zeno's hand can surely be seen in the deductions from one hypothesis, the fresh starts in the trains of argument, the consequent clusters of contradictions or seeming contradictions. But what of the extension of the argument from one hypothesis to its contradictory, and from the subject of the hypothesis to everything else; and above all what of those conflicts between theses that I have made the focal points of the enterprise?

The Zeno we need is, of course, Plato's Zeno: a defender of Parmenides who wrote one book consisting wholly of arguments against plurality (*Parm.* 127e–28e). Whether Plato's interpretation was accurate is immaterial here and undecidable anyway. Some years ago I proposed a scheme which would allow the extant arguments of Zeno to be grouped into such a book.[14]

Plato does not think Zeno proved his case and does not represent himself as taking over a method of proof. To use an anachronism, it is not the shape of the vault but the use of the buttresses that he means to acknowledge and adopt. To begin with he has seen that Zeno, arguing

which cannot be produced separately. Even if Plato means to be understood phonetically, the analogy of notes and chords that he conjoins with that of letters and syllables (*Theaet.* 206a–b, *Soph.* 253a–b, *Phil.* 17a–c) suggests that he does not have Ryle's moral in mind.

[14] See *Proceedings of the Aristotelian Society*, 1958, pp. 199–222.

against all those who naïvely suppose the world to contain a plurality of things, proceeds by offering his opponents options. Either the kind of division that produces the alleged plurality is of a sort to end after a finite number of steps or it can be continued for an infinite number, and then on this second option either it reaches some limiting indivisibles or it can never be finished; and Zeno professes to wring an absurdity from each of these possibilities. If this is so (and I am taking my old scheme as a working assumption), such a method of trying the alternatives explains not only the variations that Plato plays on his hypothesis but other devices he adopts in the later dialogues, such as the use of logical division that he defends in the *Philebus*: division prevents hasty generalizations about a class from some unrepresentative subset.

But his acknowledgment to Zeno goes deeper than this. Zeno seems often to overpress his paradoxes by joining in one conclusion the consequences of more than one option—as when he says that the members of a plurality must be "so small as to have no magnitude yet so large as to be boundless." Yet these conjunctions are not arbitrary, just because each of the conflicting options is (or is made by Zeno to seem) plausible in its own right. Suppose *per impossibile* that the division of any magnitude is pushed as far as it will theoretically go, then the end-products can have no magnitude (else divisions can still be made) yet must have some magnitude if the thing divided is not to vanish into nil components; and from this he goes on to extract the conjunction already quoted. Similarly—there is a copybook example in the paradox noticed under (v) of the previous section—Plato manufactures contradictions both within and between the movements of his argument by treating both parties to one of his conflicts as forming one logical conjunction, just as at the end of the dialogue (166c) he collects all the preceding inimical conclusions into one contradiction. The training in dialectic that he acknowledges to

Zeno, and illustrates in his own antinomies, is a training in the presentation of conflicts between theses each of which seems cogent in its own right. He neither adopts nor proposes any general training in the resolving of such conflicts.

Still, even if proofs are not Plato's central interest in the *Parmenides*, does he not incidentally manage to prove some differences between unity (and therewith all numbers, according to the arguments under (10)) and common properties such as size and colour?

1. Surely this is the moral of the collision between (10) and (23). He seems to be pointing to that logical indispensability that he claims for unity in the *Philebus*: its character of being presupposed by all forms and subjects of discourse (15d4–8, 16c9, 19b6). He does it by exploring the embarrassments we run into if we try to describe any subject or congeries of subjects that has no unity and cannot be resolved into parts having any, something that happens not to be or contain one of anything at all. He proceeds as though this were a project as straightforward as describing a subject that lacks some shape or size; and then he proposes an answer that, in the fashion of the dialogue, is made to seem unavoidable under (23) and impossible under (10).

Yet here too the conflict is plainer than the moral to be drawn from it. For one thing, it is not clear that his argument allows him to mark off unity from, say, relative size and weight. The question he professes to answer under (23) is, What can be generally true of things which are coming to have but do not yet have any unity? (Cf. 158b5–9.) But consider the predicate "large," which he takes to be typically applicable to whatever is larger than something else (not necessarily larger than a standard object or than the average of some class). A comparable puzzle seems to arise if we ask, What can be true of something which is coming to have but does not yet have any largeness? For the answer seems to be that it cannot then have any size at all, yet the question implies that it is of a type to have some size or other. Let us look for an argument that does force a distinction between "large" and "one," that diverse pair that had for so long rubbed shoulders in the theory of Forms.

2. Given a certain view of Plato's grasp of the issues, there is a brace of arguments that seem to force just this distinction. And they are evidence of that distribution of duties between the two parts of the dialogue that I suggested earlier. It is in the first part that, in the view of many including Ryle, Plato brings out a fallacy that had pervaded his earlier statements of the theory of Forms. He had, in Ryle's words, spoken as though universals could be instances of themselves; and he now proves, by ascribing largeness to itself, that to credit anything with both functions generates a regress, in this case a regress of largenesses that turns the supposedly single Form into an unlimited class (*Parm.* 132a–b). Notice that the regress does not depend on mistreating largeness as a quality: it is equally effective whether or not the relational nature of the attribute is recognized. That Plato was able to isolate the mistake which lies at the root of this and other troubles in the context is, I think, put beyond question by premiss (18) and the arguments under it: I refer to my note there.

Now there is a comparable regress in the second part of the dialogue, making use this time of the "ingredience" model of predication that appears in premiss (3); and it seems designed to show the recalcitrant behaviour of such putative properties as unity and being. In IB (142b–43a) Plato argues that if unity is a part or property of something (in this case, the One) it is *one* of the thing's parts and there *is* such a part; and the same is true of the thing's being. So both unity and being have the parts or properties of unity and being, which in turn have both parts, and so *ad infinitum*. But suppose Plato to have recognized the point of his first regress, namely that the common run of a thing's properties are not to be assigned to themselves; then here is a dilemma. Either he must say that unity and being cannot be component properties of anything on the same terms as its colour and size, or he must rule that unity cannot be said to be unitary or being to be. But the second alternative will not readmit them as component properties of anything, for Plato is ready to argue that any component is *one* part and there *is* such a part. He seems to be marking off the sort of concept—identity and similarity and some others as well as unity and being—that will appear as "common" in *Theaetetus* 185c4–d3 and as the ubiquitous vowel-connectives of *Sophist* 253a4–6, c1–3, concepts which must be reintroduced in describing their own behaviour as in talking about anything else (e.g., 255d9–e6, 257a1–5).

Does this settle the question? Only for those who take Plato to have come to grasp the difference between largeness and anything large, and for those others who think him incapable at any time of that confusion. There are some who still think he never saw the distinction, and the review of their reasons would take us far outside the *Parmenides*. Their Plato is a grimmer and more baffled man than Ryle's, and more baffled on these issues than Plato's immediate colleagues and successors.

What positive conclusions Plato wants to be drawn from his nexus of conflicting arguments is perhaps, like the song the Sirens sang, a question not beyond all conjecture. It seems to me more conjectural than the programme I have ascribed to him. But whether he is trying a prentice hand at a highly sophisticated kind of proof, or constructing a frame within which to set and tie together puzzles about a remarkable family of very abstract concepts, Ryle's chief point is made. These are the concepts and the problems with which Plato will so often be concerned henceforth, and Ryle was the first to turn the eyes of Plato's modern readers in this direction.

Additional note. Recently Ryle has come to believe that the two parts of the *Parmenides* must have been written at different times and without the initial intention of combining them in one dialogue. For "while Part I is in Oratio Obliqua, Part II, apart from one initial 'he said' [sc. 137c4], is in Oratio Recta" (*SPM*, p. 145). Let us tease this out. First, the words ascribed to the disputants are given throughout in direct speech. Secondly, the report of the conversation in which these quoted words occur is put in the mouth of Cephalus, who was unluckily not present at it; so Plato makes him give it in the form "Antiphon told me that Pythodorus told him that Socrates said . . ." But of course Plato can't keep this up even in the first Part: over and again there is a straightforward "Socrates (or Zeno or Parmenides) said . . ." (ἔφη used of one of these characters at least 13 times, in addition to 3 εἶπεν which of course may be a misreporting of an original εἰπεῖν). Moreover, as in the *Republic* and other dialogues, there are stretches of dialogue without an intervening "he said" (e.g., 134a6–d3), and these come most naturally when the argument is being jabbed ahead and broken only by words of assent. Once the interlocutor fades into total insignificance, in Part II, the "he said"s equally drop out of sight. But, thirdly, Ryle has a special thesis in view. Most of the dialogues, including the parts of the *Parmenides*, were in his eyes written with a view to dramatic presentation. So the first part could be assigned to one actor reading "Cephalus" while the second asked to be distributed between "Parmenides" and "Aristotle," and two different dramatic dates would be involved. This general thesis of Ryle's I shall not discuss; but the imagination labours at the thought that the second part, with its unremitting complexities and its cowed interlocutor, was designed to be absorbed and enjoyed at one or more dramatic readings. This new twist to the suggestion that the thing was planned as an academic joke comes implausibly from the man who argued best for its total seriousness. In any event it was Plato who patched it together for his own purposes, and those purposes I have been trying to make clear.

IN DEFENCE OF PLATONIC DIVISION

JOHN ACKRILL

1. Expositors of Plato have sometimes identified Plato's later dialectic with *diairesis*, the method of division recommended and exemplified in well known parts of the *Phaedrus, Sophist, Politicus,* and *Philebus*. In his *Mind* paper of 1939 (reprinted in R. E. Allen's *Studies in Plato's Metaphysics*), and again in the chapter on Dialectic in *Plato's Progress*, Professor Ryle has made scathing remarks about this "method," and has drawn a sharp contrast between it and genuine dialectic or philosophy: the construction of Linnaeus-type genus-species trees has nothing to do with the philosophical activity of hard reasoning which leads to truths about the powers and interrelations of topic-neutral concepts. While allowing that Plato may on occasion have attached some (improper) importance to division Ryle holds that the philosopher who wrote the central part of the *Sophist* and the *Parmenides* could not (then, or seriously, or for long) have supposed division to be a significant part or instrument of philosophy.

I think that Ryle has exaggerated the contrast between Platonic division and genuine dialectic or philosophy—both in Plato's thought and in fact—, and I want to mitigate the sharpness of his contrast by suggesting a more generous interpretation of division. I shall not attempt a close study of the relevant texts, but I shall try to say enough to show that it is bad history of ideas to write Platonic division off as a minor aberration, and that a less severe appraisal of it may discover in it material worthy of a philosopher's consideration.

2. A brief survey of four dialogues will serve to make clear what difficulties stand in the way of one who seeks to ex-

cise division from the serious development of Plato's thought.

Phaedrus. Socrates' speeches have been dominated by the necessity to define love and to distinguish different varieties of irrationality or madness; at 265c Socrates says that, whatever may have been light-hearted in the speeches, two procedures were used which deserve serious attention. "The first is that in which we bring a dispersed plurality under a single form, seeing it all together; the purpose being to define so-and-so, and thus to make plain whatever may be chosen as the topic for exposition. For example, take the definition given just now of love: whether it was right or wrong, at all events it was that which enabled our discourse to achieve lucidity and consistency. [The second procedure] is the reverse of the other, whereby we are enabled to divide into forms, following the objective articulation; we are not to attempt to hack off parts like a clumsy butcher, but to take example from our two recent speeches" (265de, Hackforth's translation). After giving a (not quite accurate) account of how in those speeches the single form of madness or irrationality had been divided, Socrates continues: "Believe me, Phaedrus, I am myself a lover of these divisions and collections, that I may gain the power to speak and to think; and whenever I deem another man able to discern an objective unity and plurality, I follow 'in his footsteps where he leadeth as a god.' Furthermore—whether I am right or wrong in doing so, God alone knows—it is those that have this ability whom for the present I call dialecticians."

Ryle does not deny that the natural interpretation of this passage makes Plato assimilate division to dialectic (like Ryle I omit special reference to the reverse operation, "collection"). But he argues—using arguments to be examined below—that certain considerations "require us to suppose that in the *Phaedrus* he means but omits to say explicitly that division is only a preparation for dialectic" (P.P. 141). The last sentence in the *Phaedrus*

passage quoted above certainly allows us some leeway, and
if Ryle had suggested that Plato felt some qualms about
identifying division with dialectic one would not have to
disagree. But it is surely unplausible to say that the writer
of that warm testimonial to collection and division really
meant that they are only "a preparation for dialectic"—
a philosophically quite unrewarding propaedeutic for
eighteen-year-olds, a Pass Mods. subject for freshmen. Nor
can the testimonial be treated as a rather silly aside: the
account of division picks up points about the method and
motive of Socrates' earlier speeches, and is echoed in later
discussions of "scientific rhetoric" at 270–71.

Sophist. This dialogue "consists queerly of a stretch of
highly abstract and sophisticated philosophical reasoning
sandwiched between some division-operations which presuppose no philosophical sophistication whatsoever"
(P.P. 139). It is difficult to dissent from this verdict, but
the queerness demands explanation. Why did Plato make
up this "clumsily assembled sandwich"? The sharper one
draws the contrast between division and genuine philosophy the more baffling the problem. That Plato did not
find the contrast so sharp is shown by a passage (which
Ryle refers to) within the central, sophisticated section.
For having brought out the need for a "science" to determine which forms (or "kinds") blend with one another and which do not, and to detect any all-pervasive
forms that serve to connect or disconnect others, the
Eleatic stranger continues: "And what name shall we give
to this science? . . . Have we stumbled unawares upon
the free man's knowledge and, in seeking for the Sophist,
chanced to find the philosopher first? *Theaetetus:* How
do you mean? *Stranger:* Dividing according to Kinds,
not taking the same Form for a different one or a different one for the same—is not that the business of Dialectic? . . . And the man who can do that discerns
clearly *one* Form everywhere extended through many,
where each one lies apart, and *many* Forms, different
from one another, embraced from without by one Form;

and again *one* Form connected in a unity through many wholes, and *many* Forms, entirely marked off apart. That means knowing how to distinguish, Kind by Kind, in what ways the several Kinds can or cannot combine" (253ce, Cornford's translation). The stranger then repeats that this is dialectic and its practitioner is the philosopher.

Ryle says that it is "tempting, though not compulsory, to infer that Plato thought that the task of constructing kind-ladders was not only a propaedeutic to the philosopher's or dialectician's task; it was a part of it or else the whole of it" (P.P. 140). Rather it is compulsory, however unwelcome, to infer that Plato saw at least a close connection between division and the philosophical task of mapping the interrelations of concepts. Perhaps he was quite wrong to think so; in this case we have to recognise and try to understand his mistake. Perhaps, however, we load the dice unfairly against him if we give the most trivial possible interpretation of his "division" and the most limited and rarefied interpretation of "dialectic" or "philosophy."

Politicus. Like the *Sophist* this dialogue contains numerous division-operations and explicit recommendation of the procedure of division. There is little hard argument of the kind so excitingly exemplified in the central part of the *Sophist.* Ryle concludes that the *Politicus* was designed for beginners only (P.P. 285), "for the special benefit of the philosophically innocent novices who were at that moment getting their freshmen's training in the ABC of thinking" (P.P. 139). It is easy to share Ryle's evident distaste for "this weary dialogue"; it is less easy to brush aside as he does the evidence that when Plato wrote it he attached great importance to division as an essential instrument or part of dialectic. Ryle writes: "Dialectic is alluded to only twice, at 285d and 287a, and then only in the Stranger's explanation of the preparatory role of the intellectual exercises that he is giving" (P.P. 139). This is a rather misleading comment. It suggests that the Stranger contrasts dialectic with the kind of operations of division and definition he is engaged in, and that (like Ryle) he regards such operations as merely preliminary to the quite different tasks of dialectic proper. In fact, however, the Stranger contrasts simple division-operations on easy concepts with more difficult ones; and the implication is not that dialectic has nothing to do with division, but that it has very much to do with it. Nor are the two "allusions" to dialectic mere passing allusions: they are embedded in long theoretical discussions of procedure.

The thought that his trivial and lengthy divisions, culminating in a definition of weaving, may be criticised as excessive leads the Stranger to distinguish two types of measurement. One is concerned with the relative length or magnitude, etc., of different things, the other is concerned with whether a thing is *too* long or large, etc., with reference to a certain standard. Having made this division of measurement into two "parts," the Stranger develops a generalised criticism of those who fail to follow correct procedure. "Because they are not accustomed to conduct their enquiries by dividing into sorts, they straight off jumble these very different things together, thinking them similar; and then again they do the opposite, dividing other things but not into their parts. Whenever one starts by perceiving the common nature of the many things, one ought not to give up until one has seen in it all the differences that constitute sorts. Whenever, on the other hand, one has seen the multifarious differences in pluralities, one ought not to be able to be discouraged and stop until one has brought all the related things within one similarity and confined them all within the being of some kind" (285ab). The Stranger now turns to the motive and purpose of the discussion of the statesman and of the attempt to define weaving. A pupil learning to spell a given word is not so much interested in how to spell that particular word as in increasing his proficiency in orthography in general. "Now

what of our present question about the statesman? Has
it been raised for its own sake, or rather so that we may
become better dialecticians about everything? Clearly the
latter. No man of sense would want to chase after a definition of weaving for its own sake. But what most people,
I think, fail to realise is this: some of the things there
are have sensible likenesses, easy to recognise, and these
can be indicated without difficulty when anyone wishes
in reply to a request for a *logos* of such a thing to avoid
trouble and indicate them easily without a *logos*. But the
greatest and most important things have no images fash-
ioned with clarity for men; to content the enquirer's mind
there is nothing to show which can be fitted to a sense-
perception so as to give adequate satisfaction. This is why
we must practise the ability to give and receive a *logos* of
each thing. The incorporeals, the finest and greatest of
things, are clearly shown only by a *logos* and in no other
way; and it is for the sake of them that all our present
discussions are taking place. Practice in anything is easier
with relatively minor examples than with more important
ones" (285d–86b).

There is room for discussion as to the precise contrast
Plato intends between forms or concepts which can be
illustrated by sensible instances and those which can only
be made clear in a definition. One thing, however, is obvious. The notion of practising on easy cases like weaving in order to acquire greater skill to handle other cases
would be entirely out of place unless the envisaged operations on or about the difficult concepts were taken to
be similar in kind to those we practise on easy ones; and
these are indisputably division-operations. Again, when
the Stranger says that we study the particular case not
out of special interest in it, but in order to increase our
capacity to do dialectic about anything, he certainly implies that exercises in the general dialectical skill we seek
will be of the same kind as the particular exercises we
do to acquire the skill. Thus the fact that there is only
one explicit reference to dialectic in the section 284e–86b

does not prevent us drawing from the whole section the clear conclusion that dialectic is or at least essentially involves division.

The other use of the term "dialectic" (287a) is embedded in a context which leads to the same conclusion. The stranger says that if our discussion is criticised for being terribly long we shall defend ourselves by referring to its purpose, and we shall try to show that, even if it is very long, it is not *too* long—judged by the standard of what is appropriate for our purpose. We are not out to give pleasure or, primarily, to get a quick answer to the particular question before us. What we value most is "the method itself, which consists in the ability to divide into sorts." A discourse will be acceptable, however long, if it "makes its hearer better able to find things out." It is no good for a critic to complain that our discussion is long. He must show that if it had been shorter it would have done more "to make its participants good at dialectic and at finding out how to make clear in a *logos* the things there are" (286b–87a).

The method of division is here identified with skill at dialectic and with getting clear about "the things there are." These are alternative ways of describing the ulterior object of our particular discussion. Thus the whole section from 284e to 287a assimilates division to dialectic, and in doing so offers to justify the tedious divisions in the surrounding parts of the dialogue. So however tedious or even pointless we may find these divisions we cannot say that Plato thought them unrelated to genuine dialectic or philosophy. Nor can we say that he thought them related to dialectic merely as elementary formal logic is related to philosophical investigations. He clearly takes the operations of dialectic in general to be the same in kind as the division-operations he himself conducts. If these are preparations for more important and difficult operations they are so not in the way in which cleaning saucepans is a preparation for making cakes, but in the

way in which making scones is a preparation for making
cakes and other more elaborate confections.

Philebus. Ryle says that "in the *Phaedrus*, the *Politicus*
and, debatably, the *Philebus* Plato seems closely to connect the task of dialectic with the tasks of Definition and
especially Division" (P.P. 135). He does not explain his
"debatably" or revert to the *Philebus* in connection with
his thesis that division is a philosophically worthless procedure that plays no part in dialectic. It is true that, as
in the *Politicus*, there are only two explicit references to
the practice of dialectic. But, as in the *Politicus*, consideration of the contexts forces the conclusion that Plato
is advancing a method of division as characteristic of
dialectic, which is itself identified as the noblest science
of all, which seeks truth about unchanging realities.

Socrates outlines a method which, he says, is easy to
describe but very difficult to practise. He says he has
always been a lover of this method, though it has often
eluded him and left him desolate and perplexed. "We
ought, whatever it be that we are dealing with, to assume
a single form and search for it, for we shall find it there
contained; then if we have laid hold of that, we must go
on from one form to look for two, if the case admits of
there being two, otherwise for three or some other number of forms: and we must do the same again with each
of the "ones" thus reached, until we come to see not
merely that the one that we started with is a one and an
unlimited many, but also just how many it is" (16d,
Hackforth's translation). This is the method the gods
have given us "for enquiring and learning and teaching
one another." The careful use of this method and the
noticing of all the forms intermediate between the original one and the unlimited plurality is what distinguishes
the dialectical from the eristic mode of discussion (16b–
17b).

The examples Socrates proceeds to give are interestingly different from others so far mentioned: the division of language into its elements is not a simple case of

genus-species articulation. This however need not prevent our insisting against Ryle that Plato is here recommending some sort of division-procedure as of the highest importance. Moreover there is appeal to it later in the dialogue, when the participants come to examine pleasure on the one hand and knowledge on the other. That the method just explained is to be applied to these is explicitly stated at 18e, 19b, and 20a; and, though the task is postponed, the detailed discussion of pleasure and knowledge from 31b to 59c takes the form of an analysis of each into its different types. One can indeed contrast the official statement of the method with the loose structure of the later discussion. But Plato evidently regards the latter as somehow exemplifying the former.

The other reference to dialectic is at 57e, where Socrates picks it out as the truest, most accurate, and purest form of knowledge. Its objects are the truest entities, unchanging and divine. Socrates allows that a man needs more than this knowledge in order to live. "Imagine a man who understands what justice itself is, and can give a *logos* conformable to his knowledge, and who moreover has a like understanding of all the other things there are. Will such a man be adequately possessed of knowledge, if he can give the *logos* of the divine circle and divine sphere themselves, but knows nothing of these human spheres and circles of ours?" (62a). Evidently not. But the important point for us is that the kind of knowledge here attributed to the dialectician is knowledge of what so-and-so is, expressed in the appropriate *logos* of the thing. While there is here no reference to division, the assimilation of dialectic to definition is clear, and the inference that the way to get the desired definitions is the method recommended earlier in the dialogue is an obvious one. *That* is how the gods told us to conduct our investigations and to learn and to teach one another; understanding of the essential nature of each form is the objective and outcome.

This cursory survey is, I hope, sufficient to establish the

following points. (a) In all these dialogues Plato regards
division as the method of dialectic, which is itself directed to clarifying the nature of forms of all kinds. The
differences between different accounts and examples of
division are of great interest and importance, but not for
present purposes, since we are concerned with a broad
contrast between two general views of dialectic. In all
the dialogues considered, dialectic is explicitly associated
with some kind of division procedure; in none is it identified with the type of argument about topic-neutral concepts that Ryle exclusively commends. (b) The references
to division in these dialogues cannot be dismissed as
obiter dicta representing temporary silliness, or as the result of a senile patching together of passages originally
distinct. For they are not just passing allusions: they are
closely integrated into the whole flow and argument of
each dialogue. (c) Instead of arguing that the writer of
these dialogues was a good philosopher and could not
therefore seriously have proposed to do philosophy by
the method of division, we must ask: since the writer of
these dialogues was a good philosopher, and did seriously
recommend division, is there perhaps some way of understanding his recommendation which will make it seem
perfectly reasonable? We may need to allow that he waxed
over-enthusiastic about a certain approach he thought important, and that he exaggerated its utility or role in philosophy (including his own philosophy); but the mass of
evidence requires that we should try to find some element of serious philosophical worth in the method Ryle
so firmly rejects.

3. Some of Ryle's reasons for rejecting the Method of
Division as useless for the resolution of any serious philosophical problem are contained in the following passages.
"First of all it can only be applied to concepts of the
genus-species or determinable-determinate sort, and it is
not concepts of this sort that in general, if ever, engender
philosophical problems. And, next, most generic concepts
do not subdivide into just two polarly opposed species;

usually there are numerous species of a genus or sub-species of a species. And the question whether a sort divides into two or seventeen sub-sorts is, in general, a purely empirical question. So nearly any case of a philosopher's operation by division could be upset by the subsequent empirical discovery of sorts lying on neither side of the philosopher's boundary lines. And, finally, there is room for almost any amount of arbitrariness in the selection from the ladders of sorts *en route* for the definition of a given concept. . . . There are many tolerable and no perfect ways of defining most of the sort-concepts that we employ" (*Mind* 1939, p. 322, reprinted in R. E. Allen: *Studies in Plato's Metaphysics*, pp. 141–42), "A chain of *summa genera, genera, species, sub-species* and *varieties* is not itself a chain of premises and conclusions. But what is more, it cannot in general be deductively established or established by *reductio ad absurdum*. The work of a Linnaeus cannot be done *a priori*. How could Plato who knew exactly what question-answer arguments were really like bring himself to say, if he did say, that the philosophically valuable results of such arguments are kind-ladders?" (P.P. 136).

In this section I propose to consider these points in turn, and first the objection that most generic concepts do not subdivide dichotomously. Ryle half-withdraws this complaint in *Plato's Progress*, but he still says that Plato "is tempted to treat this articulation as being necessarily dichotomous, though he prudently resists this temptation some of the time" (p. 135). There is in fact abundant evidence that Platonic division into kinds is not, and is not thought of as being, necessarily dichotomous. In the *Philebus* passage already quoted, Plato recommends looking for a division into two, "if the case admits of there being two, otherwise for three or some other number" (16d). None of the subsequent examples is dichotomous, nor does the later discussion of types of pleasure and knowledge seek dichotomous kind-ladders. The *Phaedrus* account stresses the crucial importance of following the *natural* articulation of the item under examination (265e); and though the illustrative description of the division of madness refers to left-hand and right-hand lines of division, the actual practice followed was not dichotomous (e.g. 238a–c, 244–45). Later on (270c) Socrates says that the way to think about the nature of anything is to ask whether it is simple or multiform, and, if it is multiform, to enumerate the forms. The principle is then applied to types of speech and types of soul, in which discussion there is no suggestion of dichotomous division. The Stranger's recommendation of division in the *Politicus* makes no reference to dichotomy, and it is immediately followed by an enquiry into kinds of productive skill which is explicitly non-dichotomous. "It is difficult to cut them into two. . . . So since we cannot bisect, let us divide them as we should carve a sacrificial victim into limbs. For we ought always to cut into the number as near as possible to two." (287c) The metaphor of the natural carving of a joint is that of the *Phaedrus*; the principle of minimising the cuts is that of the *Philebus*.

It is not difficult to understand why Plato should advise the enquirer to try for two or very few cuts at each stage: a slapdash division into a lot of species will very probably cause important similarities and groupings to escape notice. The advice is however subordinate to the basic requirement that divisions must correspond to the natural or real structure of the subject-matter. That Plato's practice is not in general dichotomous has been sufficiently indicated above. That it is dichotomous in large parts of the *Sophist* and *Politicus* is not surprising. For he is not here seeking to bring to light the structure of a whole genus, but to achieve a definition of a particular species. For this purpose the important thing is at each stage to hit on the *relevant* sub-genus of the superior genus; the irrelevant sub-genus can be thrown away—and it doesn't *matter* if here are some other (irrelevant) sub-genera we have not mentioned.

Ryle complains that the method of division is not a

method of demonstration or argument, and that since it is an empirical question into how many sub-sorts a sort divides, division cannot be done *a priori*. To take these points as showing that Plato's advocacy and practice of division have nothing to do with real philosophy is to take a narrow view of both philosophy and division. A reasonably sympathetic interpretation of the latter will see in it a method aimed either at defining a specific term or at clarifying and analysing a general concept. Of course the steps by which a definition is reached or tested are not deductive—as Aristotle was often to insist; and of course the recognition that (say) "enjoyment" covers many diverse types, and the bringing to light of the diversity, are not exercises in pure *a priori* thought. Yet both these projects seem capable of being distinctly and importantly philosophical. Certainly Aristotle gave much fruitful attention to both, and his efforts in these directions are as much admired as his efforts to clear up problems involving topic-neutral concepts.

That one of the aims of Platonic division was to get a clear and correct definition of particular terms hardly needs proof. Introducing his divisions in the *Sophist* the visitor remarks that the use of the same name does not prove that people have the same "thing" in mind, so it is always desirable to make clear by a definition the meaning of the term (218bc). The same point in the *Phaedrus*: "If anyone means to deliberate successfully about anything, there is one thing he must do at the outset: he must know what he is deliberating about; otherwise he is bound to go utterly astray. Now most people fail to realise that they don't know what this or that really is: consequently when they start discussing something, they dispense with any agreed definition, assuming that they know the thing; then later on they naturally find, to their cost, that they agree neither with each other nor with themselves. . . . So we ought to agree upon a definition of love which shows its nature and its effects, so that we may have it before our minds as something to refer to

while we discuss whether love is beneficial or injurious"
(237b–d). Interest in the "what is it?" question and the
search for definition are of course as characteristic of
earlier Socratic dialogues as of these later dialogues; and
indeed most of the vocabulary used in later expositions
of methodology is already found casually employed
in earlier dialogues. It is not of present concern to ask
how far the later expositions reflect or modify earlier practice, or even how useful they are as guides to reaching
good definitions. What is clear (and relevant) is that
Plato sees the definition of terms as one of the aims of
division, and that from Socrates to Aristotle such definition—elucidating the meaning of interesting terms—is
regarded as an important task of philosophy. No doubt
not all terms are of interest to the philosopher, and no
doubt there are important types of definition or elucidation which Platonic division does not cater for. But it
would seem altogether too restrictive to exclude from
philosophy the attempts so many philosophers have made
to clarify particular concepts—even though such attempts
are not exercises in deductive reasoning and cannot be
conducted *a priori*.

Often, though, Platonic division is concerned not to
elucidate a particular term but to illuminate a whole area,
to lay bare the structure of some "genus." A hostile characterisation of the method can make it seem very silly:
what philosopher spends his time constructing kind-ladders? Consideration of the diverse examples of the
method permits a more generous construal. Distinguishing different kinds of types of so-and-so need not be (if
the so-and-so is well chosen) a philosophically barren
activity; and distinguishing the different senses of a word
(though not of course any word) can surely be a significant philosophical achievement. Certainly Aristotle (not
to mention Ryle) devotes much effort to these tasks. It
may be admitted that neither Plato nor Aristotle is absolutely clear about the difference between distinguishing types of X and distinguishing senses of "X" (nor

indeed is the difference always easy to maintain). But either activity can be philosophically rewarding; and it is difficult to deny that Platonic division concerns itself with such activities.

Some of the passages already referred to show that Plato regards himself as applying division in such non-futile exercises as: distinguishing purely quantitative measurement from measurement against a norm or standard; mapping the complexities of the concept of enjoyment; recognising the diversity of types of *techne* (a word that covers crafts, arts, and sciences); and investigating the forms that irrationality or "madness" can take. No doubt these actual exercises—and many others that could be added—fall short of the complete and systematic analysis of a general concept which the *Philebus* account recommends us to seek. But they are essays in that direction, fragmentary contributions towards the full understanding the philosopher seeks. Though argument is often involved in establishing conceptual distinctions, these are not themselves conclusions of deductive reasoning; they demand insight and produce clarification—visual metaphors that abound in Plato's accounts of and efforts in division. That they cannot be conducted *a priori* does not mean that they are a matter for empirical research as opposed to philosophical reflection. Ryle's sweeping dismissal of Plato's hopes for division and his tries at it amounts to a denial that conceptual analysis is a proper part of the philosopher's task.

How important was Platonic division in advancing the study of ambiguity? Only two small points can here be made. First, the terms "division" and "divide" repeatedly turn up in reports of the work of the sophist Prodicus, who was noted for his interest in drawing verbal distinctions. Socrates very often refers to him, and several times professes himself his pupil (e.g. *Meno* 96d, *Protag.* 341a, *Charm.* 163d). Some of his distinctions find important echoes in Plato and Aristotle, for example that between "wish" and "desire" (*Protag.* 340a) and that between different types of enjoyment (*Protag.* 337c). At *Phaedrus* 267b Socrates attributes to him the recognition that what is required in speeches is not that they be long or short, but that they be of the right length—the distinction generalised by Plato in the *Politicus*. If Zeno is the father of the method of reasoning found in the *Parmenides*, Prodicus with his concern for the precise meanings of words and the drawing of distinctions is surely an important precursor of Platonic division. Secondly, a word about Aristotle. He reaches new sophistication in the study of ambiguity, and is rightly praised for noticing and exploiting the fact that different uses of a word may be overlapping or interrelated in various ways, and that one use or sense may be primary and others secondary or parasitic. Many of Plato's divisions exhibit such features, and it would be surprising if they were not part of the material and impetus for Aristotle's enquiries. Among the divisions I have in mind are those in which one side is defined by reference to what is genuine or real or original or pure or perfect, while the other side is defined by reference to the bogus, the apparent, the imitative, the impure, the defective (for example, *Sophist* 236, 265–66, *Politicus* 293, *Philebus* 55–57).

Ryle complains that the method of division can only be applied to concepts of the genus-species or determinable-determinate sort, and that such concepts do not normally engender philosophical problems. Dialectic proper, on the other hand, as practised in the central part of the *Sophist* and in the *Parmenides*, is concerned to resolve *aporiai* (puzzles) by investigating the topic-neutral concepts which are "the hinges on which turn both confutations and philosophical discoveries" (P.P. 144).

The complaint that Platonic division cannot get to work on philosophically interesting concepts could be made even by one who resisted Ryle's too narrow view of dialectic or philosophy as the attempt to solve *aporiai* through logical enquiries about topic-neutral concepts. But the complaint depends upon a strikingly unsympathetic construal of Plato's theory and practice of division. Consider, for example, Ryle's remarks on page 140 of *Plato's Progress*. He has over several pages been making scathing comments on the philosophical inutility of constructing kind-ladders after the manner of Linnaeus. He contrasts it unfavourably with the Stranger's exploration in the middle of the *Sophist* of the mutual dependences and independences of the Greatest Kinds (like Existence, Identity, Otherness), an exploration that does not yield one kind-ladder, however short. "For the Greatest Kinds are not related to one another as genus to species or as species to co-species." Ryle continues: "Even to render 'γένη' by 'kinds,' and *a fortiori* by 'classes,' is to prejudice the interpretation of the Stranger's operations. *Existence, identity* and *otherness* are not sorts or sets of things, embracing subsorts or subsets of things." I do not want to claim that this bit of the *Sophist* is an exercise in division (and it is not immediately germane to enquire how Plato thought it was related to division, as the evidence quoted above shows that he did); I am only claiming *an* important place for division in Plato's thought and practice (and in philosophy). The point I draw attention to is that Ryle rejects as prejudicial the translation of γένη as "kinds" in the passage he admires, because the items under investigation are evidently not sorts or sets of things. Yet his talk about the passages he does not admire gains much of its effect by its use of a hard-edged terminology which attaches to Platonic division all the scholastic precision and philosophical futility of a traditional genus-species tree. Might one not adopt a more sympathetic approach? It is not only in the arguments about existence, etc., that the terms γένη and εἴδη do not carry the fixed associations of "genus" and "species." They are regularly used, before and after Plato, in a much freer way; and Plato himself, conspicuously untied by technical terms, constantly uses them interchangeably. That

Platonic division has something to do with dividing will not be denied. But what sort of dividing Plato takes it to cover, and what sorts of terms are capable of being divided, can be determined only by consideration of all the texts. The outcome of such consideration is not, I suggest, that Platonic division is to be rejected as a very narrowly defined procedure of no philosophical interest. The appropriate criticism is quite the reverse. Platonic division covers a variety of types of analysis and gets applied to a variety of types of term. No less than the word "analysis" itself, which has been a modern slogan in philosophy, "division" is dangerously imprecise but philosophically suggestive. Commendation of it is not a brief stupidity or senility on Plato's part, for it represents a continuing stand in his philosophical activity—and also in Aristotle's. Aristotle does indeed have, as Plato does not, a rather closely worked out account of strict genus-species kind-ladders. But he continually speaks of divisions and of kinds and sorts ("genera" and "species") in contexts where nobody supposes that he is, or thinks he is, doing the work of a Linnaeus. When he speaks of his categories as "divisions" of being, or distinguishes movement, alteration, and growth as different "sorts" of change, nobody complains that he is performing absurd Linnaean operations upon the concepts of being and change. May not Plato's efforts be accorded a like charity?

4. It is compatible with this defence of Platonic division to allow that his formal accounts of it are variously defective or even misleading, and to admit a contrast between the systematic and comprehensive procedure set up as an ideal and the fragments of useful analysis actually achieved. Let us grant too that something quite different is afoot in the examination of some topic-neutral concepts in the middle part of the *Sophist*. There is, however, the question how division is related (in fact or in Plato's mind) to the *Sophist* investigation. For Ryle there is an absolute contrast: division is futile,

the *Sophist* investigation is philosophy. No question arises as to how they are related, even though Plato himself clearly implies that they are. I think that the relation can be made out if, having adopted a more generous interpretation of division than Ryle's, we now give a rather wider scope to the enquiries made or advertised in the central part of the *Sophist*.

Plato does not say that the concepts to be investigated here are "the Greatest Kinds," only that they are *some* of the greatest kinds. He does not explain the term "greatest," but it will not be too risky to think with Ryle of formal or "common" concepts, bearing in mind such passages as *Theaetetus* 185–86 and *Parmenides* 136. This does not yet show that Plato in the *Sophist* takes dialectic or philosophy to consist in the exploration of "the mutual dependences and independences of the Greatest Kinds" (P.P. 142). Plato justifies selecting a few of the greatest kinds for investigation by saying: "we will not take all the forms, for fear of getting confused in such a multitude" (254c). Of course he has a positive reason for dwelling on the forms he does proceed to discuss. But the clear implication of his remark is that the full-scale study of the interrelations of forms would require study of all forms. This is indeed quite explicit in the account of dialectic at 253b–e, partly quoted above (p. 375). For the task of discovering "pervasive" forms which serve to "connect" or "divide" other forms is set alongside, and not contrasted with, the task of systematically determining the mutual concordances and discordances of forms in general. To put the point in a nutshell (and in non-Platonic idiom), the dialectician or philosopher is invited not only to examine such concepts as compatibility and entailment, but also to determine *what* compatibility and entailment relations hold among concepts in general. Ryle says that "dialectic, here equated with philosophy, is described at 253c–d as the science which discovers how the 'Greatest Kinds' are 'joined' with and 'disjoined' from one another" (P.P. 140). Rather it is described as the science which discovers how forms in general are related to one another *and* notices and studies the relational forms themselves. The dialectician will get clear the whole structure of the conceptual scheme he investigates, *and* be clear about the formal or structural concepts themselves.

Dialectic as the study of the interrelations of forms (not just "Greatest Kinds") still looks a good deal richer than division into kinds. But the gap is no longer unbridgeable and Plato's association of dividing by kinds with knowing how kinds can and cannot combine (*Sophist* 253de) is not unintelligible. Division certainly exhibits *some* important interrelationships of concepts and reveals *some* possibilities and impossibilities of combining. The discovery of *other* interrelationships, and the study of the relational concepts themselves, may easily be seen as natural extensions to the task of division. Plato need not feel, as clearly he does not feel, that in recognising additional requirements for an adequate understanding of "the world of forms" he is setting division aside as irrelevant.

5. I do not wish to claim too much for this brief attempt to rehabilitate Platonic division in face of Ryle's censures. It seems to me certain that Plato took division seriously, and that we should therefore give serious and sympathetic attention to it, seeking to extract from his theorising and practice something of philosophical significance. To say this is not to deny the outstanding excitement and importance of his investigations into topic-neutral concepts. And to oppose Ryle's verdict on division is not to deny the outstanding excitement and importance of his work on Plato in general, which has been a guide or a goad to so many of us over several decades.

VERBS AND THE IDENTITY OF ACTIONS—
A PHILOSOPHICAL EXERCISE IN THE
INTERPRETATION OF ARISTOTLE

TERRY PENNER

Aristotle in *Metaphysics* θ6 divides actions into two classes (which he calls *energeiai*, usually translated as "activities," and *kinēseis*, usually translated as "movements"), apparently primarily on the basis of the behaviour of the present and perfect tenses of the verb-phrases corresponding to these actions. According to a natural interpretation of this "tense test" (as I shall call it),[1] if we use "X" for the verb-phrase corresponding to the action, then X-ing is an *energeia* ("activity") just in case

"I am X-ing" entails "I have X-ed,"

e.g.,

"I am enjoying myself" entails "I have enjoyed myself"
"I am gazing at the statue" entails "I have gazed at the statue";

and X-ing is a *kinēsis* ("movement") just in case

"I am X-ing" entails "I have *not* X-ed,"

e.g.,

"I am learning" entails "I have not learned,"
"I am walking from the library to Nassau Hall" entails "I have not walked from the library to Nassau Hall."

Various qualifications have to be made at once. First, "I have enjoyed myself" must not be taken to imply (as it

[1] Cp. Zeno Vendler, "Verbs and Times," *Philosophical Review* (1957), 143–60, reprinted in revised form in Vendler's collection of essays, *Linguistics in Philosophy* (Ithaca: Cornell University Press, 1967). The crucial bit is quoted in J. L. Ackrill, "Aristotle's Distinction between *energeia* and *kinēsis*," in R. Bambrough (ed.), *New Essays in Plato and Aristotle* (New York: Humanities Press, 1965), 135–36. Cp. also Anthony Kenny, *Action, Emotion and Will* (New York: Humanities Press, 1963), Chapter 8.

can do, even in Greek)[2] that I have stopped enjoying
myself. (I will simply take it that it need not imply this,
as it need not in Greek.) Similarly for "I have gazed at
the statue." With "learn" and "walk from the library to
Nassau Hall," on the other hand, the perfect tense entails that I have stopped doing the action which was going on when the present tense truly applied. Second, the
perfect-tensed expressions in these examples ("I have
learned," etc.) should not be construed as frequentative
or as referring to past occasions of learning, etc., but
rather as referring to the very same action (of learning,
etc.) as that referred to in the present-tensed expressions
in the examples ("I am learning," etc.). Doubtless more
qualifications still need to be added to make the examples
right. But these will perhaps suffice for purposes of showing the possibility of our making such a distinction. I
shall in any case, later in the paper, be challenging this
exposition of the distinction in many important details
(including the translation of *energeia* as "activity": thus I

2 Aristotle worries over this point in *Topics* Z. 146b13 ff. The
Topics is generally taken to be an early work, and on the basis of
this passage I would guess that the *energeia-kinēsis* distinction had
not yet been developed. Another passage which I judge to be early
is *De Sophisticis Elenchis* 22, which contains an early and somewhat
puzzling version of the *energeia-kinēsis* distinction, in which the tense
test is connected with the active-passive distinction. The active-
passive distinction also occurs in this connexion in *De Anima* B5.
However the scope of this paper does not admit an exploration of
all passages in Aristotle relevant to the distinction. For the works of
Aristotle already mentioned, I use the following obvious abbrevia-
tions: *Met.*, *Top.*, *S.E.*, *De An.* I also use *E.N.* (for the *Nico-
machean Ethics*), *E.E.* (for the *Eudemian Ethics*), *Catg.* (for the
Categories), G&C (for the *Generation and Corruption*). For Ryle's
works I use *CM* (*Concept of Mind*), *D* (*Dilemmas*), *SME* ("Systematically Misleading Expressions"), *Catg.* ("Categories"), *P.A.*
("Philosophical Arguments"), *Pr. Ph.* ("Proofs in Philosophy"), *On
Forgetting* ("On forgetting the difference between right and wrong").
Of these I shall refer to *SME* and *Catg.* by means of the pagination
they have in the two volumes of A. Flew (ed.), *Logic and Language*. For further bibliographical detail on these works of Ryle, see
the bibliography of this collection.

shall continue to use the Greek words, *energeia* and *kinēsis*—"movement"—until, later in the paper, I establish the translation I favour for *energeia*). In an appendix to this paper I have given a new translation of Aristotle's actual words on the subject in *Met. θ6*, a translation which departs in a number of respects from standard translations.

It was Ryle who first showed analytical philosophers the gold mine there was in Aristotle for the topic of verbs and actions (as for many other topics). Further, it was he who introduced the present distinction into analytical philosophy. His distinction between task verbs and achievement verbs (*CM*, 149–53) is closely related to this distinction, and *Met. θ6* is explicitly invoked at *D*, 102, to claim that seeing and hearing, like enjoying, are not processes (*kinēseis*) and so cannot be experiences (cp. *CM*, 151–52); for I can say "I have seen it" as soon as I can say "I see it." And finally, Ryle refers to Aristotle in several discussions of pleasure, e.g., *D*, ch. 4 and *Pr. Ph.*, exploiting arguments of Aristotle in *E.N.* X.4 (the other main passage in Aristotle generally agreed to be a discussion of the *energeia-kinēsis* distinction), e.g., that "quickly" and "slowly" are appropriate to the latter but not to the former. I do not here discuss all the details of Ryle's distinction, but only those which are closest to parent passages in Aristotle. But it seems to me that Ryle's general approach to Aristotle is both very fruitful (here one thinks of the delightful *On Forgetting*) and remarkably like that of Aristotle himself to the same problems, though Ryle's is clothed in talk of "the logic of . . . ," "logical form," etc. Since Ryle's approach to the present distinction seems to me to be less that of an ordinary language philosopher and more that of a follower of Russell, it may be worth while to digress briefly to say what I take this approach to be.

The groundwork of *CM* may be seen in formation in the three powerful theoretical articles, *SME* (1931), *Catg.* (1937), and *PA* (1945). What we observe there is a conception of philosophy as a clearing away of certain confusions due to the misleading character of grammar. Thus "Jones is reprehensible" and "Unpunctuality is reprehensible" are grammatically parallel; but that they are not logically parallel can be seen from the fact that although if Jones is a certain man it follows that a certain man is reprehensible, it does not follow that if unpunctuality is a certain universal, a certain universal is reprehensible (*SME*, 20). What Ryle's programme was in more detail is nicely captured in the following two quotes from Wittgenstein:[3]

> All philosophy is "critique of language" . . . Russell's merit is to have shown that the apparent logical form of the proposition need not be its real form.
>
> (4.0031)

> In order to avoid these errors, we must employ a sign-language . . . which obeys the rules of *logical* grammar —of logical syntax. The conceptual symbolism of Frege and Russell is such a language which, however, still does not exclude all errors. . . .
>
> (3.325)

The idea is to use formal logic as the foundation—but only the foundation—for getting the logical form of a sentence right.[4] I say "only the foundation" since for

[3] L. Wittgenstein, *Tractatus Logico-Philosophicus* (tr. D. F. Pears and B. F. McGuinness, London: Routledge and Kegan Paul, 1961).
[4] Roughly, two sentences would have the same logical form if parities of reasoning suggested by their symbolic representations are preserved. There would be a single logical form for any given sentence if we could read off from a single symbolic representation all and only the deductive inferences justified from this sentence. The idea of a single logical form for any given sentence has come to seem unattainable. But the more limited idea of two sentences having the same logical form relative to just some inference-patterns—by each having at least some symbolic representations which preserve expected parities of reasoning—still seems useful. Ryle seems to me to throw more weight on the later idea in *SME*, and this emphasis becomes increasingly apparent in the later articles.

Ryle an expansion of the language of *PM* was almost certainly going to be needed—though Ryle himself has not offered any of the formal machinery himself. By expansion I mean a further exposure of the logical structure of propositions in the way in which "Everyone is as happy as everyone else" has successively more of its logical structure exposed in the following symbolizations:

p
$(\forall x)(Hx)$
$(\forall x)(\forall y)(Hxy)$

To take some Rylean examples, "Socrates is wise" and "Plato is wise" have the same logical form as "x is wise" (*PA*, 18); and "x is wise" has, presumably (*PA*, 10) the same logical form as "x is green," "x is merry"—let us say it has the "logical skeleton" (*PA*, 7, 8, cp. 18), "Φx." But antinomies and contradictions would arise if we substitute "large" or "three" for "wise" or "merry."[5] The sentence-factors ". . . is large" and ". . . is merry" are not of the same logical form (*SME*), have different logical powers (*PA*), are [the linguistic counterparts of proposition-factors] of different types or categories (*Catg.*). Thus the symbolism of *PM* must be re-deployed to set forth statements involving "large" (e.g., by talk of relations to a class) or involving numbers (e.g., by the use of quantifiers or by means of the Frege-Russell definition). But it is an open alternative that to get logical

[5] Ryle must have had in mind something like the following:
The musketeers are merry, so each of them is merry.
but not: The musketeers are three, so each of them is three. Accordingly, statements using number-adjectives have to be re-formulated: their grammatical form misleads us (see G. Frege, *The Foundations of Arithmetic* (tr. J. L. Austin, Oxford: Blackwell, 1950), sec. 29, cp. Pr. Ph., 155–56). What about "large"? "Mickey is a merry rodent" becomes "Mx & Rx," "Mickey is a merry animal" becomes "Mx & Ax." But then if "large" were construed in the same way as "merry," "Mickey is a large animal" would follow from "Mickey is a large rodent" and "Mickey is an animal"—for "Lx & Ax" follows from "(Lx & Rx) & Ax"—a clearly undesirable result.

types right, the symbolism of *PM* has to be expanded.[6]
Ryle has more recently suggested (e.g., in *D*, ch. 8) that
his concern is not with re-deploying or expanding the
symbolism of *PM*, but with a venture co-ordinate with
formal logic—informal logic. This emphasis is, however,
quite different from that found in the three articles we
are now discussing. One passage will do (but see also
Catg. 67–68, 77–78, 79–81):

> Every proposition has what will here be called certain
> "logical powers"; that is to say it is related to other
> propositions in discoverable logical relationships. . . .
> Further, for any logical powers possessed by a given
> proposition it is always possible to find or invent an
> indefinite range of other propositions which can be
> classed with it as having analogous logical powers. For
> the rules of logic are general. . . . Formal logicians
> learn to extract the logical skeletons of propositions
> in virtue of which these and any other propositions
> embodying the same skeletons can function as prem-
> isses or conclusions of parallel valid arguments.
>
> (PA, 7)

Talk, then, of pleasure and pain not going through the
same "logical hoops" (e.g., *D*, 60, 66, 109) or of "inference hoops" (*Pr. Ph.*, 156), for which Ryle uses arguments he draws from Aristotle, is in the same way talk
of the logical form of propositions. Ryle used Aristotle
for the purpose of discovering logical structure.

In this perspective, we can see that the problem with
verb phrases is to display logical parallelisms and non-
parallelisms which underlie the unity suggested by the
single classification "verb-phrase." To run is normally to
be engaged in running, but to know is not normally to
be engaged in knowing; indeed to suppose that to know
is to be engaged in some kind of mental doing is to have
a false picture of mind (*CM*, 116). To have a grasp on

[6] As in A. N. Prior's tense logics.

the logic of occurrence words like "run" and disposition words like "know" will save us from at least some false theories of the mind. In a similar way perhaps such a theory as Plato's, that pleasure is a replenishment of a bodily need, may be refuted, and the shortcomings of superficial statements of, and reactions to, hedonism and utilitarianism exposed. Such has been the main use to which Ryle has put Aristotle's *energeia-kinēsis* distinction (*Pr. Ph.*, 155; *D*, ch. 4). In Aristotle's terms, pleasure is an *energeia* (thus the class of *energeiai* includes more than actions), while replenishment of a need is a *kinēsis*; [but the classes of *energeiai* and *kinēseis* are mutually exclusive, therefore] pleasure is not a replenishment of a need.

Having given this very rough account of the *energeia-kinēsis* distinction, and of the way in which it has been introduced into analytical philosophy, I turn now to the main business of the paper. Most of it will be transacted by my replying to Professor J. L. Ackrill's aporetic attack (Bambrough, 121–41) on the treatments of this distinction given by Aristotle and by Ryle as interpreter of Aristotle. I shall argue that Ackrill's criticisms appear to have force against any Rylean interpretation of Aristotle's distinction because Ryle did not carry his concern for logical form far enough in this case, while Ackrill's criticisms themselves rest, some of them, on a mistake due to excessive attention to grammatical form (or as we nowadays have to call it, surface grammar).

The parts of Ackrill's attack which I shall be concerned with may be summarized in the following eight claims.

> (i) Ryle implies that Aristotle's *energeiai* were meant to be instantaneous, since they "declare termini": I look, and then, as soon as I see, I have seen, and just as soon as I win I have won. (*D*, 102: in *CM* Ryle had considered success verbs which go on for a time, e.g., "keeping in view"). Ackrill argues that, on the contrary,

energeiai are generally thought of as going on for a time. [On this point Ackrill is clearly right, as a glance at the examples in the translation in the appendix will show.][7]

(ii) When Aristotle says that we can say "I have seen" as soon as we can say "I am seeing," the point he really has in mind (Bambrough, 135) is that "I have seen" refers to a period of time preceding the moment to which "I see" refers. But this positively *excludes* the possibility that there be any instantaneous *energeiai*. (Whenever "I have seen" is true, "I am seeing" will have to have been true through some preceding period). [But Ackrill hesitates over Aristotle's puzzling implication that pleasure can occur in a "now" or instant, while *kinēseis* cannot (Bambrough, 130).]

(iii) Though "Aristotle's description of his *energeia-kinēsis* distinction seems to add up to a useful distinction, his treatment of examples is not in accordance with that distinction" (Bambrough, 134). In particular, a star *kinēsis* verb, "walk," satisfies the *energeia* criterion: "I am walking" entails "I have walked." (I use the present continuous since the Greek present tense is generally imperfective; the perfect is generally per-

---

[7] R. J. Hirst has offered the interesting suggestion that Ryle's mistake here was to misread *telos* at 1048b22 as "terminus" rather than "end" in the sense of "goal" (*The Problems of Perception* (New York: Macmillan, 1959), 132), and he himself interprets the *energeia-kinēsis* distinction in terms of the indefinite continuability of *energeiai*, unlike *kinēseis* which must stop when their built-in termini are reached. So too Ackrill, following Vendler. (On continuability, see further the translation below of the relevant part of *Met.* θ6, together with my note to 1048b27). Hirst's suggestion still seems to me too simple. I suspect Ryle was also influenced, especially in putting forth his two types of success verbs in CM, by Aristotle's claim that pleasure can be had "in a now (i.e., instant)" (see section III below), a claim which Ackrill rightly finds embarrassing on his interpretation (Bambrough, 130).

fective—a fact which will turn out not to have been obvious.)

(iv) An attempt of Aristotle's to rescue walking as a *kinēsis* (*E.N.* X.4, esp. 1174a31 ff.) by saying "the whence and the whither constitute the form" fails. Aristotle's claim is, in brief, that (whether or not "I am walking" entails "I have walked") whenever I am walking I am walking from A to Z, and "I am walking from A to Z" does *not* entail "I have walked from A to Z." Indeed it entails "I have *not* walked from A to Z." But then, by the same process as that by which Aristotle makes walking into a *kinēsis*, we can turn a star *energeia*, enjoying, into a *kinēsis*. For to enjoy is surely to enjoy something—let it be the ninth symphony. But "I am enjoying the ninth symphony" does not entail "I have enjoyed the ninth symphony"—I may be called away before the performance is over. The same applies to "I am enjoying hearing the ninth symphony." Thus a star example of a *kinēsis* is saved only at the expense of a star example of an *energeia*. The same fate is suffered by seeing: "I am seeing a movie" does not entail "I have seen the movie."[8]

8 Zeno Vendler, in the paper mentioned in n. 1, treats "walking" as an activity (*energeia*) word and "walking from A to Z" as an accomplishment (*kinēsis*) phrase (his actual examples are "running" and "running a mile," but I take it that this comes to the same thing). But having treated "seeing" as not in general an accomplishment (*kinēsis*) word, he goes on, at the very end of his paper, to treat "seeing *Carmen* on TV" as yielding a "queer accomplishment sense of *seeing*." This surely reflects an indecision as to whether he is treating verbs or verb-phrases. The same indecision may be observed in Kenny (*op. cit.*, 173) when he claims that the perfect-tensed "I have loved her for eight years" entails the present-tensed "I love her." I owe my notice of this indecision in discussions of the tense test to Donald Davidson.

(v) In *E.N.* X.3, Aristotle argues that pleasure cannot be a *kinēsis* or a *genesis* (a coming-to-be), and so cannot be a replenishment as Plato claimed, since all *kinēseis* are quick or slow or some other speed, whereas being pleased is not something one does or is quickly or slowly or at any speed. But the quickly-slowly test [as I shall call it] is not emphasized by Aristotle, so the basis of the distinction must be sought elsewhere, namely in the tense test.

(vi) Aristotle's definition of *kinēsis* at *Physics* Γ.1–2, which might have been expected to be of some help to us, is in fact no help since it appeals to one of two types of potentiality, namely "imperfect potentiality"—which is just a potentiality for a *kinēsis* as opposed to an *energeia*.

(vii) Aristotle's claim at 446b2 and 1174b12–13 that there is no coming-to-be of an *energeia* is not only of no help but also rather unfortunate since Aristotle holds that there is no coming-to-be of *kinēseis* either (*Phys.* 225b15 ff.).

(viii) In *Pr. Ph.* 155, Ryle praises Aristotle for his refutation of the Platonic theory of pleasure, and represents this refutation in the following way.

> If enjoying something were a process from state to state, it would follow that a person could have begun to enjoy something but been prevented from finishing, as a person can begin his dinner but be prevented from completing it. But, though a person may enjoy something for a short time or for a long time, he cannot have half an enjoyment. Enjoyments can be great or small, but not fractional. This demolishes Plato's assimilation of the concept of pleasure to the general type of concepts of process or transition.

This is an unacceptable exegesis of Aristotle's
point about adding specific descriptions of the
walk to the occurrence of the verb "walk" (mentioned in (iv) above). Nor is Ryle's use of such
words as "interrupt," "prevent from finishing,"
"complete," or "half" acceptable, those words
not being translations of any phrases Aristotle
uses.

In one form or another I shall be contesting all of
Ackrill's claims but the first. My line of attack may be
seen in connexion with claim (iv). Ackrill interprets Aristotle's point about the whence and whither constitut-
ing the form in such a way that the adding of "the ninth
symphony" to "I am enjoying . . ." is parallel to the adding of "from A to Z" to "I am walking . . ." Now one may
concede immediately that the additions are grammatically
parallel and would have seemed so to Aristotle (verb plus
accusative case). But it is quite another matter to suppose
that they are logically parallel, as Ackrill must surely do if
his objection is to have any force (he must, so to speak,
use the phrase "By parity of reasoning, . . ."). Now if
the locutions each refer to an action or something like
an action (pleasure, unlike most of the *energeiai* Aristotle
speaks of, is never taken by Aristotle to be an action),
then following Frege we should seek the conditions of
identity for these actions or whatever. To fully carry out
this search is beyond my powers; but I believe enough
can be said about necessary conditions of identity of
kinēseis to show that the two verb-plus-accusative phrases
are not logically parallel, but have only, as Frege would
say, the same grammatical form (*sprachlichen Form*).[9]
I shall argue that this move of asking for the criteria of
identity and not Ackrill's move (of supplying grammatical accusatives for the verbs "walk" and "enjoy"—or, in

[9] *Op. cit.*, sec. 29. On conditions of identity, see secs. 55 ff., esp.
56, 62.

the material mode, of speaking of the distance walked as parallel to the piece of music enjoyed) captures Aristotle's intentions in his remark "the whence and whither constitute the form." The word "form" (*eidos*) is an extremely important word in Aristotle's philosophy, and I shall argue that Aristotle saw the point about *eidos* as one not about objects in any ordinary, grammatically derived, sense, but about criteria of identity.

This task, ascertaining conditions of identity for actions, processes, etc., is one that Ryle (and just about everyone else) has persistently neglected. He has been willing to say that enjoying a walk is one process, not two; but he has not been willing to tell us how to count the processes that there are.[10] As we shall see, Aristotle does try to do this; and his attempt will prove satisfactory enough to block Ackrill's objection.

Having exploited the point about conditions of identity to explain how Ackrill misses the point of the addition of the words "from A to Z" to the words "I am walking"

[10] See Hampshire's review of *CM* in *Mind* (1950) [reprinted in this volume, pp. 17–44 (Eds.)]. Donald Davidson's "The Logic of Action Sentences" in N. Rescher (ed.) *The Logic of Decision and Action* (Pittsburgh: University of Pittsburgh Press, 1968) is, so far as I know, the first attempt to do this seriously for anything Aristotle would have called a non-substance—except for numbers, which have been much worked over. It will be obvious from p. 413 ff. of this paper that my debt to the writings of Davidson in finding, after much searching, what I think is an intuitive formulation of the importance of Aristotle's remark "the whence and whither constitute the form," and of its connexion with the quickly-slowly test, is very great. There is also a considerable debt, one which I owe in common with all serious students of Greek philosophy, to the writings of Anscombe and Geach on the identity of substances in Aristotle.

It might just be worth noticing here that the contrast of logical with grammatical form would not be entirely strange to Aristotle. In *S.E.* 22, already mentioned in connexion with the *energeia-kinēsis* distinction in n. 2, Aristotle discusses mistakes in reasoning due to the grammatical form (*schēma tēs lexeōs*) suggesting similarities that are not really there, e.g., between "flourishing" and "cutting." The famous "Third Man Argument," also expounded in *S.E.* 22, is considered by Aristotle to be another instance of this.

and "I have walked," I go on to show in succession how
this same point explains the applicability of "quickly"
and "slowly" to the things Aristotle calls *kinēseis* and not
to the things he calls *energeiai*, the locution "pleasure
can be had in a now," Aristotle's peculiar definition of
movement and finally his point that there is a coming-
to-be of *kinēseis* but not of *energeiai*. The villain of the
piece will prove to be *the state of motion,* which (at least
on certain very plausible Aristotelian assumptions) can
only be supposed to exist if one confuses *energeiai* and
kinēseis (sections II–IV); and some misunderstandings
about "instantaneous velocity," as well as an injustice to
Aristotle over his treatment of Zeno's Arrow Paradox,
will be cleared up (n. 18 and App. II). In the final section, I sketch some implications of making *energeiai* and
kinēseis mutually exclusive classes of actions: in particular the consequence that many things normally thought
to be single actions consist of a *kinēsis* and an *energeia.*
And something of Aristotle's conception of the "object
of pleasure" will emerge.

I

I speak first to Ackrill's claim that in "Everything
[that at any time is hearing] at the same time hears and
has heard,"

the "has heard" can be taken to refer to a period of
time preceding the moment to which the "hears" refers.
First let us say something that holds of both *kinēseis*
and *energeiai*. If a man *starts* to X at time *t* he cannot
be said to *be X-ing at t*; it is only at some moment later
than *t*, say *w*, that he can be said to be X-ing. Since
no two moments are contiguous there must be an in-
terval between *t* and *w*; and however short this period
(*t* to *w*), it is a period of X-ing preceding the moment
w at which the man is said to be X-ing. Thus as soon
as it is true to say "he is X-ing" it is true to say "he has

been X-ing." And Aristotle argues for all this at some
length in *Physics* VI. 5 and 6, claiming that there is
no absolutely first sub-period in a period of change or
movement, but that "everything that is in motion must
have been in motion before" (236b33).

(Bambrough, 126-27)

He then goes on to say that the difference between
energeiai and *kinēseis* is that with the latter we *cannot*
say with reference to the preceding period "He has X-ed,"
whereas with the former we *can* say with reference to the
preceding period "He has X-ed." The importance of this
talk of the preceding period is that it excludes (a) there
being a first moment of an *energeia*, and (b) there being
any *energeiai* which are instantaneous (so that Ryle cannot adduce "see" in the sense in which it characterizes the
successful outcome of looking, i.e., in the sense of "spot,"
as an *energeia* verb).

Now why has Ackrill gone into this "something that
holds of *energeiai* and *kinēseis* alike" before saying what
the difference is between them? It has been to show the
importance of talk of the preceding period for *energeiai*
as well as *kinēseis*. It has been to show that

(1) "He has X-ed" in the case of an *energeia* is, if true,
true *at* the relevant present moment *in virtue of* a
preceding period of X-ing,

just as we have with *kinēseis* both of the following:

(2) if a bit of X-ing is successfully completed at a certain moment, then "He has X-ed" is true *at* that
moment *in virtue of* the whole preceding period
of X-ing

(with which cp. 1174a20-21: "Every *kinēsis* is complete
whenever it produces what it was aiming at—[it is com-
plete] either in the whole time or in this [time, i.e., the
time at which it produces that at which it is aiming]"),
and also

(3) if a bit of X-ing is going on, then "He has been
X-ing" is true *at* that moment in virtue of the preceding period of X-ing.

Now it seems to me that (1) is clearly true for *energeiai*
if for "He has X-ed" we substitute the quite different
phrase, used in (3), "He has been X-ing." It may well be
that it is Ackrill's use of the latter locution (cp. in the
last two sentences of the quotation above "has been
X-ing," "have been in motion") that led him to assert
(1).[11] But as Ackrill certainly agrees, the words of Aristotle with which we are concerned are to be translated
"He has X-ed." But it is not clear that "He has X-ed"
cannot be true in virtue of the present moment (which
with *energeiai*, though not with *kinēseis*, can be a moment of X-ing), so that a preceding period of X-ing is
just not required. And whatever Aristotle means by
"pleasure can be had in a now (instant)" (1174b7-9),

[11] Ackrill, in company with Hardie and Gaye, mistranslates
236b33 as "must have been in motion before" (quotation above),
which means "must *have been moving* before." It should be the
quite different "must *have moved* before." The Greek perfect is almost always both perfective and present. At 222b7-11 (*ēdē bebadika*)
it appears as a non-frequentative past tense, but throughout the discussion of movement in *Phys* Z it is present and perfective, e.g.,
at 232a5 (*ekei bebadikos*), 232a11 and the interesting argument at
232a6-9 (cp. 240b30-241a6) where Aristotle invents the word
kinēma ("quantum jump"). Similarly, in the passage under consideration, 237a15 can only be read as present and perfective; and,
in the closely related passage that follows, the same is true at 237a18,
23. The temptation to translate the perfect of *kineisthai* as "has
been moving" instead of "has moved" is one of the bad effects of
using "motion" and its cognates when discussing Aristotle, instead
of "movement" and its cognates. (Another bad effect, talking of a
"state of motion," is discussed in the next section.) So the translation
"has been moving" is linguistically implausible. Had Aristotle wished
to say something requiring a past continuous tense, he would have
used the present tense (as he does at 237a18, 23, 232a11) or the
imperfect tense (as he does at 231b30, 232a1-2). "Must have moved
before" means: "It has moved" was true at each of a succession of
instants before now (237a3-11): and in each case it is a different
distance that has been moved.

and whether or not it entails that there are instantaneous
energeiai—I offer answers to both these questions in section III—it surely entails that with the *energeia pleasure*
"He has X-ed" [for the time being, read this as: "He has
enjoyed himself"] can be true in virtue of the present
moment. So Ackrill's position, being inconsistent with
this entailment, cannot be right.

What of Ackrill's suggestion that for Aristotle the argument that there is no first sub-period of change or
movement was meant to apply equally to *energeiai*?[12]
The first thing to notice is that the main argument at
236b32–237a35 (cp. 237b9–22, esp. 11, 15, 21) depends
upon a feature peculiar to *kinēseis*, namely that the
whence-to-whither is infinitely divisible. We can see this
in the employment of the propositions

(4) If I am moving a distance KM and am now at
point L, then I have moved a distance KL, and in
half of the time it took me to move the distance
KL I will have moved, if moving uniformly, a distance equal to ½KL

(236b34–36, extended indefinitely at 237a3–11, using
propositions about velocities of continuous movement
established in *Phys.* Z 1–2), and

(5) If at a certain instant I have changed [i.e., changed
a certain amount], then I am not at the starting
point (237a21–22); but then there must be an
intervening period of time, in half of which I have
changed another amount (237a26). So I was moving before.

[12] From 236a7 ff., there might seem to be a sense of "change"
in which "I am changing" entails "I have changed"; but it turns out
to be a special sense of the perfect only. What it comes to is "I
am changing [from A to B]" entails "I *have begun to change* [from
A to B]," which will scarcely yield an *energeia*-sense of "change."
(It might be just worth noting that in *Phys.* Z it is Aristotle's
practice to restrict *kinēsis* or "movement" to local movement and
to use *metabolē* or "change" to cover, in addition, changes in quality,
etc.).

Thus no matter what present moment we take, the period of time between the last moment at which one was at the starting point (terminus: 239a34–35) and the present moment is divisible; so there is no absolutely first sub-period of time during which I was moving and no first moment of time at which I have moved a certain distance. Thus Ackrill must fall back on those changes (*metabolai*) which "have to do with contraries and contradictories" (237b1–2, cp. 224b28–35, 236a35–b18) where the feature of infinite divisibility is not present, e.g., the change from white to grey. Here Aristotle is prepared to argue that there is no first moment of change solely on the basis of time (237a35–b9), in much the way Ackrill suggests for *energeiai*, like hearing. So the question arises whether we should extend the argument from such changes to the (distinct) class of *energeiai*. A careful look at the argument concerned with these kinds of changes will show that there is no reason to suppose Aristotle would have applied it in the same way to *energeiai*. The argument at 237a35–b9, on the most charitable interpretation, refers back (b3) not to the arguments involving infinite divisibility just mentioned, but to the full argument at 236a14–27, the essential part of which is this:

> If the thing in question is at rest in the time CA, and is supposed to have first changed in the time AD, then because it is at rest throughout CA it is at rest at A. But then if at D it has changed, AD cannot be indivisible, for then at the indivisible time AD it will both be at rest and have changed. But if AD is divisible, then it will have changed throughout AD. [So either way, if A is the last moment of rest, D cannot be the first moment at which it has changed.]

Notice two things. First, one of the premisses used, "it is at rest at moment A," is inconsistent with Aristotle's true doctrine that in a now or instant there can be neither movement nor rest (234a24–b9, 239a10–14, 14–22, cp. 239a23–b4; "I am moving" cannot be true at an instant, but only in a period of time, although "I have moved" can be true both at a time and for the whole period of the completed movement in question: 1174a20–21, 237a15). No wonder, then, that Aristotle paid more attention to the arguments involving infinite divisibility. (It is in fact not difficult to regard the two passages containing the present argument as rather tossed off by Aristotle. The carelessness is accounted for by Aristotle's confidence in the conclusion as established by the argument from infinite divisibility.) Second, if we ignore the arguments concerning infinite divisibility and consider just this argument, allowing (contrary to Aristotle's usual doctrine) sense to the idea of moments of rest and moments of movement, then the application of the law of non-contradiction in the argument above merely requires:

> not-both (there is a first moment of movement and there is a last moment of rest).

That is, it is purely arbitrary whether we say there is no first moment of movement or no last moment of rest. (The account of being at rest as being in the same state now as *before* may have been what swayed Aristotle here: 234b5–7, 239a15–16.) Thus if we were to apply the argument to *energeiai*, we could perfectly well have first moments of *energeiai* (as we have already seen is desirable), provided only that there is no last moment of our having the unactualized *hexis* (disposition), *aisthēsis* (sense faculty), or whatever.[13]

I conclude that there is no reason to suppose that the argument that there is no first moment (or sub-period) of movement or change was meant to apply to *energeiai*; and that if it did it would be inconsistent with other

[13] This is an adaptation of an argument I learned from G. E. L. Owen: see *"tithenai ta phainomena"* in J. Moravcsik (ed.), *Aristotle* (New York: Anchor Books, Doubleday, 1967) esp. 183–87, reprinted from S. Mansion (ed.), *Aristote et les Problèmes de Méthode* (Louvain: Symposium Aristotelicum, Publications Universitaires, 1961).

things Aristotle says (about pleasure being had in a now), as well as with the truth conditions for perfect-tensed *energeia* sentences. So talk of a preceding period being required for the truth of such sentences is unjustified. On the question of the time reference of the perfect tense, Ryle is right and Ackrill wrong.

II

We may turn now to Ackrill's objection (claim (iv)) that if "walk" is saved from being an *energeia* verb by adding "from A to B," the "whence" and "whither" which "constitute the form," we can, by the same token, make a paradigm *energeia* verb, "enjoy," a *kinēsis* verb by adding "the ninth symphony." The objection may be put in the material mode: if the distance one has walked is indeed different from, and only a part of, the distance one is walking, so also in the case of enjoying a performance of the ninth symphony, what one has enjoyed is different from, and only a part of, what one is enjoying.[14] To defeat the objection we must show how to interpret "the whence and whither constitute the form (*to pothen poi eidopoion*)" in such a way as to avoid the damaging parallel.

Now form (*eidos*) is an extremely important notion in Aristotle's philosophy, so before accepting arguments based upon the use Ackrill makes of it, it will be well to

[14] If I am right in my translation of *Met. θ*6 below, the problematic nature of this objection is simply accentuated: for according to that translation, the way in which *energeiai* and *kinēseis* are opposed to each other with respect to tense is, fully expressed, (not what was presented on p. 1, but): with *energeiai* it is the same thing that one simultaneously (*hama*) is X-ing and has X-ed, whereas with *kinēseis* it is a *different* thing that one simultaneously is X-ing and has X-ed; I am seeing (i.e., looking at) and have seen the statue, but I am walking the distance AB and have walked the different [and shorter] distance AA'. My way of dealing with Ackrill's apparent counter-examples (enjoying the ninth symphony, cp. seeing a movie) is expounded later in this section.

go into the question of how it might be being used in this argument. The word *"eidos"* is characteristically translated both as "form" and as "species." In many passages it is clear that there is no difference of meaning intended by Aristotle: see e.g., 1030a6–13, 1033b29–34a8, 1033b5–13, 31–32, 1038a5–6 with 19–20 and 25–26. This comes out very clearly in Aristotle's frequent use of "same in number (or *eidos* or genus)" and "one in number (or *eidos* or genus)": see e.g., 1016b32–33, 1054a33–35: for two things to be the same in number they must both have the same matter and be one in *eidos*. Callias and Socrates are (one and) the same in *eidos* ("same" is defined in terms of "one": 1054a29–b2) but not the same in number, this being established by a difference of matter (*Met.* Z8). This matter is potentially a *this* and is made actually a *this* by the presence of the *eidos* in the matter: thus the same *eidos* picks out two parcels of matter as two men (see 1042a27–31 and cp. *De An.* 412a6–9). So long as Socrates remains a man (*man* is Socrates' *eidos*), he remains the same in number in spite of any other changes. When a parcel of flesh and bones acquires the *eidos man*, a man comes-to-be. And when the flesh and bones which go to make up Socrates cease to be a man and become a corpse, Socrates no longer exists (*Catg.* 4a10–b19; *Phys.* 188b8–26, 190a31–b9; G&C 319b25–320a4, 321a23–29 with b23–24). The *eidos* of a substance, in short, gives us the criterion of identity for that substance.

Is this understanding of *eidos* applicable to non-substance categories as well? Surely not in the sense of *eidos* in which it marks off different *this*es by marking off different bits of matter? Aristotle certainly uses *eidos* for non-substance categories (e.g., *Phys.* 190b28; *Met.* Z7.1032b3–14, H5.1044b22–23), and even *eidos* and matter (e.g., *Met.* Λ4.1070b17–35, esp. 20, 21, 28, 33; *De An.* A1.403b2). And although he thinks movements are not *this*es (219b30), he is still prepared to discuss seriously the question of when they are one in number, one in *eidos*, and one in genus. (The senses of "one" and "same" would, according to *Met.* Δ6 and Γ2, be derivative from that in which these words apply to substances: cp. *Met.* Iota 1 and 2 and *Phys.* E4 with *Phys.* 220a7. It is interesting that in Iota 2 oneness of colour does *not* require oneness of substance.) These three types of oneness are discussed in connexion with movement in *Phys.* E4. Having said what it is for movements to be one in *eidos* or genus, Aristotle turns to the question what it is for a movement to be one in number:

> there are three things in terms of which we speak of movement, that which [is moving], that in which [it is moving] and the *when*. I mean that it is necessary that that which is moving be something, e.g., a man or gold, and that this be moving in something, e.g., in place or in affection, and when. For everything moves in a time.
>
> (227b23–26)

It is the *in which* with which the *eidos* is associated (227b29–30, 228a1–2) and this normally requires the same starting-point and end-point (224a21–b10, b29, 225a1 with 224b35–225a20, cp. 1033a24–28, 1069a36–1070a1), same path (this requirement is introduced at 227b14–20, apparently as a refinement on the previous requirement to deal with certain special cases: see also the splendidly dialectical 248a18–249a3), and same method (e.g., flying, walking: 249a17–18, *E.N.* 1174a31). Thus for a movement to be numerically one and the same, there must be the same method, the same thing changing, the same starting-point, the same end-point, the same path, the same starting-point of time, the same end-point of time.

Consider the following two conditions:

(i) start at the same place, end at the same place (same whence, same whither)

(ii) start at the same time, end at the same time.

(i) and (ii) are both necessary conditions of numerical identity in a local movement, and (i) is a necessary condition of sameness of *eidos* of a local movement. (Analogues to these conditions could be set up for such other Aristotelian examples of *kinēseis* as slimming, learning, housebuilding, etc.) These two conditions are singled out over and over again in Aristotle's subtle and detailed treatment of movement and continuity in *Phys.* Z (e.g., 235a14, 237a19–20, 239a23–24, 241a25–29, as well as 234b11, and 232b20, 236a30–31, b3–4, b10, 237a25, b23). Now, given that Aristotle explains such adjectives of speed as "quick," "slow," "equally fast" in terms of covering so much distance in so much time (218b13–20; also 232a20–21, *Phys.* Z 2 *passim*, esp. 232b20–23, 233b19–22), it will be obvious that any such movement must admit of some adjective of speed. More generally, any entity whose conditions of identity include (i) and (ii) or their analogues must admit of "quick," "slow," etc., and their analogues. This will enable us to show that *energeiai*, not admitting such adjectives, do not include both (i) and (ii) among their conditions of identity, and so enable us to evade the damaging parallel Ackrill sought to set up. I begin this task by once more (see n. 11 above) attacking the idea of a state of motion, and the use of the verb phrases "am in motion" and "have been in motion." For it will emerge that, on certain natural Aristotelian assumptions, there is no such thing as a state of motion, and that to suppose there is is just to confuse *energeiai* with *kinēseis*. (See also Appendix II.)

Consider the following objection:

There are two different things Aristotle might mean by "*kinēsis*." Take two reports of the same movement, one given in a past continuous tense, one in a past noncontinuous tense:

(a) He was moving to London.
(b) He moved to London.

(b) entails, while (a) does not, that he got to London. To (a) we can add "*at* time t," while to (b) only "*between* times t′ and t″ " seems appropriate. So surely there are two different questions Aristotle should be addressing himself to which he never sorts out—(a) what is it to be in a state of motion, and (b) what is it to carry out a movement. Is he not then guilty of a confusion in implying as he does that one account of movement will fit both kinds of inquiry?

In reply, we should notice that if Aristotle is guilty of a confusion here, it is a quite conscious running together of the two notions: thus at 231b25–28 Aristotle implies that there is movement over a certain distance if and only if there is a moving over that distance, and that if we say the movement is divisible in a certain way, we must say the moving is too. Second, it seems unfortunate in any case to seek from Aristotle a distinction between *being in a state of motion* and *carrying out a movement;* for since "I am in a state of motion" entails "I have been in a state of motion,"[15] it would make *kinēsis,* now taken as "motion," an *energeia,* and so would collapse the whole distinction Aristotle is interested in. But third, we can in any case show that "being in a state of motion," if it is to mean anything at all, must be taken to mean something like "completing a movement from some A to some B." For if we are indeed analysing the action expressed by ". . . is moving," then it is clear that the action in question must be quick or slow or some other speed (234a24–26). But we have seen above that Aristotle explains "quick" and "slow" as "going from some A to some B in a short (long) time." Hence, one cannot be in a state of motion at an instant without fulfilling the criteria laid down for carrying out movements. (Aristotle's argument at 234a24–31 that in a now or instant nothing can be moving—in a now nothing can be at rest either, as he argues at 234a31–b9—

---

[15] Here the present tense is not a present continuous. But I take it that this is inessential. (English idiom might equally have called for "I am having a state of motion.") In the next paragraph we leave grammar (surface grammar anyway) and turn to logical considerations.

is merely a more complex use of this third argument.)
This third point constitutes a justification for doing without the *being in a state of motion* referred to in the objection. What Aristotle is really interested in is something
which is neither quite the notion (a) of the objection
(expressed with a continuous tense) nor the notion (b)
(expressed with a non-continuous tense). He is interested
in something like: *what it is to be carrying out a movement from A to B.* (I say "something like" because here
too one has to watch out for the state of *being in process
of moving from A to B* which is once again a *being in a
state of motion.*) But the third point also shows how the
quickly-slowly test for the *energeia-kinēsis* distinction,
given at *E.N.* X.3, is connected with the whence and the
whither. It is not just that one *can* supply a verbal complement—"from Oxford to London"—with "I am walking": it is that a verbal complement *must* be supplied if
we are to get statements about movements into proper
logical form. That is to say, "I am walking" is at best an
incomplete description of any given case of walking,
given Aristotle's claim that there is moving if and only if
there is a movement (and cp. Aristotle's argument that
movement over an infinite distance is impossible since
there is no end-point of the movement: *Phys.* 241a26 ff.):
we should always have "For some A and some B, I am
walking fom A to B."

The logic of the situation may perhaps be clarified by
the following device. Talk about conditions of identity
inevitably suggests talk of quantification and of objects:
that of which "Φ" is true is *the same thing as* that of
which "Ψ" is true, so there is some object x such that
(that same) x is Φ and (that same) x is Ψ.[16] "I am walk-

[16] It may be felt that talk of "same" does not require quantification, since if *a* does the same thing as *b* does, namely to Φ, all
we need say is "Φa & Φb." However, this works only if there is a
"namely" clause. It is just those cases where there is not a "namely"
clause which make trouble for the nominalist—see Nelson Goodman's
contortions over "same number" in *The Structure of Appearance*
(New York: Bobbs Merrill, 1966), ch. 2, sec. 3.

ing," in the case considered, refers not just to me, but also to my walking. Thus we will say:[17]

(6) $(\exists x)$ (I am doing x & x is a walking & x is from Oxford to London & x is between t′ and t″).

Thus "I am walking" will in this case pick out the same movement as "I am walking from Oxford to London" does. The last two clauses in (6), since they give necessary conditions of identity of the action, must be present if we are to specify which walking is in question. (Cp. also what I was forced to say on p. 394 above about the examples of the tense test: "the perfect-tensed expressions . . . should . . . be construed as . . . referring to *the very same action . . . as* that referred to in the present-tensed expressions. . . .") Their presence together in the specification of what it is I am doing explains why "quickly" and "slowly" apply equally to both:

I am walking
I am walking from Oxford to London.[18]

[17] That I break the formula up in this way, rather than writing simply

$(\exists x)$ (I am doing x & x is a walking from Oxford to London between t′ and t″)

is a result of Davidson's reply (*op. cit.*) to Kenny on "variable polyadicity." In brief, we wish to be able to infer "I am walking" or "I am walking from Oxford to London" from "I am walking from Oxford to London between t′ and t″." This cannot be done with the formula just written down, at least in ordinary predicate logic, whereas it can with the formula in the text. For the point made in the text, that in order to use "that same x" we have to have the same whence and whither, the formula just written down might seem sufficient. But there is an obvious motivation—the one Davidson gives—for having one clause for each necessary condition of identity we are interested in.

[18] It is a corollary of this analysis that adverbs and adjectives like "quickly" and "quick" are incomplete not just relative to the mover or type of movement (cp. "a quick dachshund," "a slow gallop")— as Davidson notices (*op. cit.*, 82)—but also relative to the distance involved in the movement to which the verb of movement refers. Both "He was walking quickly" and "He was walking slowly" can therefore be appropriate to 12:01 if in normal circumstances a normal adult covered continuously relatively little ground between 11:00 and

It remains to show that "I am enjoying the ninth symphony" does not in the same way refer simply to me and to my enjoyment, where the enjoyment has as its object a "whence and whither." This can be shown by simply applying the quickly-slowly test. We have

---

1:00, yet between 12:00 and 12:02 covered relatively a lot of ground. Which sentence one *utters* will depend, among other things, upon how much one knows about the movement and what one's interests are. But the truth-conditions of "He was walking quickly (slowly)" are adjusted according to which of these two movements one is referring to. This corollary seems to me intuitively plausible, and I take it to be confirmation of the analysis I am offering. Also intuitively plausible is the way this gives just the right degree of arbitrariness to the counting of movements and to the selecting of starting-points and end-points of movements: movements and submovements, like sets and subsets, are not so very different.

There will be those who think it just obvious that in the example in question "He was walking quickly" is true, and "He was walking slowly" is false, and perhaps instantaneous velocity will be invoked and contrasted with average velocity to the detriment of the latter. But of course instantaneous velocity is only a special kind of average velocity (not because a limit must be the same kind of thing as the elements of the sequence in terms of which it is defined, but simply because it is hard to see how we could make intelligible to ourselves the point of using this particular limit without treating the sequence in question as a sequence of average velocities). In any case, I am inclined to think that the plausibility of favouring instantaneous velocity rests upon the accidental fact that most movements we are interested in have relatively regular acceleration curves. For consider the following thought-experiment. One half of all humans turn out when walking to move very irregularly when their progress is observed at a micro level. Their progress exhibits sudden bursts of extreme speed which last for a period of time quite imperceptible to the naked eye. So on the whole they appear to move just as quickly or slowly as the other half of humans, as witnessed by their similar records at races of the ordinary kind. I think that in this case we should, for either half of humanity (and regardless of the fact that some of them may have an incredibly high instantaneous velocity), give the same answer to the question "Is he moving quickly or slowly?" asked at 12:01 in an ordinary non-scientific context. The result of the thought-experiment is, then, that those who insist that in the original case the person is walking quickly are relying not on instantaneous velocity, but on a relatively small movement carried out within some specious present including 12:01. (The same holds for the jerky walking movement of a person with a game leg.)

I am walking from A to B quickly
I am walking quickly

but not (using "*" for the rejection of a sentence as un-grammatical):

*I am enjoying (myself) quickly
*I am enjoying the ninth symphony quickly
*I am seeing the movie quickly.

If the last two make any sense at all, it is not because the enjoying or the seeing go quickly but because the symphony or movie go quickly.[19] A natural move here is to suggest that in such a case "quickly" modifies a suppressed *kinēsis* verb going with "movie" or "symphony." I do not know whether an examination of this suggestion from the point of view of transformational grammar would support these Aristotelian intuitions about these peculiar sentences.[20] But from a logical point of view we might have something like:

(7) $(\exists x)(\exists y)(x \neq y$ & I am doing x & y is being done & x is an enjoying & y is a ϕ-ing & of(x,y) & y is from the first chord to the last chord & y is between t' and t'')

where "ϕ-ing" is a dummy *kinēsis* word, and "of(,)" stands for the relation between my enjoying and the ninth symphony.

[19] This suggestion is due to Rogers Albritton.

[20] T. C. Potts, "States, Performances and Activities" in *Proceedings of the Aristotelian Society*, Supplementary Volume for 1965, 79–80, makes a beginning along the lines suggested in the text. The whole article, which I came across only after having completed this part of the paper, makes use of suggestions contained in the early theory of transformational grammar. The conclusions I have come to, which are rather different from those of Potts, are based primarily on logical considerations, except for my conjecture of a suppressed verb with "enjoying the ninth symphony." I am told these questions have not yet been extensively investigated by transformational grammarians.

I employ "of(,)" to distinguish enjoyment of the ninth symphony from enjoyment which simply accompanies the ninth symphony—e.g., enjoying chocolates when the orchestra is bad (cp. *E.N.* 1175b12–13). I employ "ϕ-ing" to make clear that "the ninth symphony" in "I am enjoying the ninth symphony" refers not to an orchestral score, nor to Beethoven's creation, but to an individual performance.[21] Hence "the ninth symphony" yields, in the formula giving the analysis, a *kinēsis* predicate, ". . . is a ϕ-ing," and therefore, among others, both a whence-whither predicate, ". . . is from the first chord to the last chord," and a time predicate, ". . . is between t' and t''." These three sentence-frames, taken together, would yield the pre-analytic predicate ". . . is of the ninth symphony" giving the apparent object of the enjoyment. This explains the half-sense we spoke of getting out of "enjoying the ninth symphony quickly"—the "quickly" is attracted to the "y" variable in the formula (as the last two clauses of the formula make clear) since it does not go with the "x" variable, which represents the grammatically dominant verb of the sentence. And it is this failure of "quickly" to go with the "x" variable, which explains why "enjoying the ninth symphony quickly" seems ungrammatical.

What we can say, in summary, is this. Having shown that the use of "quickly" and "slowly" for movements

---

[21] I use "ϕ-ing" rather than "performance" or "playing" because the latter expressions suggest a number of distinctions which are simply irrelevant to the present point. For example, consider the sentences:

a) I enjoyed the ninth symphony when it was played here last week.

b) I enjoyed that performance (though I generally find the ninth a bore).

c) I enjoyed the playing of the ninth (the players had such fun).

d) I enjoyed the ninth last week, even though it wasn't performed very well (its greatness can transcend a poor performance).

This rationale for the use of "ϕ-ing," which is an improvement over one offered in an earlier draft of the paper, is due to suggestions of Gareth B. Matthews.

follows directly from the criteria of identity for movements, we can contrapose and say that since "enjoying a
symphony" and "seeing a movie" do not accept "quickly"
and "slowly" in the required way, what these phrases refer to is not simply a single movement in each case, but
rather two actions or action-like entities, one of which,
enjoying (or *seeing*) is not a movement, and one of
which is a movement. Enjoying and seeing aren't "going
anywhere," though the movie and the symphony are. And
the latter fact explains the half-sense we can make out of
"I am seeing the movie quickly." But the conditions of
identity of seeing and enjoying will not include starting-
point and end-point. I have attempted to make this, and
other points, clear by the use I have made of the quantificational formulas (6) and (7).[22]

Putting together all the above passages, we get the
following conclusions. The quickly-slowly test can be jus-

22 Important confirmation of this analysis, at least so far as concerns *kinēseis*, may be found in *Phys.* Z1,231b28–232a20. This valuable passage contains the tense test for *kinēseis* in terms of a strictly
temporal sense of *hama* ("simultaneously," "at the same time") a
characterization of local movement in terms of the whence and
whither (231b29), and connects speed with distance (surely here
connected in Aristotle's mind with the whence and whither) and time
(232a20–21). Aristotle is never very explicit about the connexion
of passages elsewhere with his main exposition of the *energeia-kinēsis*
distinction in *Met. θ*6. But no one has ever doubted that the treatment of pleasure on *E.N.* X.4 was thought by Aristotle to be an
important use and, in the case of *walking*, explanation (the whence
and whither), of that distinction. The passages I have been citing
throughout this section seem to me to show that he also thought of
the distinction as fitting together with other things he says, e.g., in
the *Physics* (see 1174b3). It seems to me that this must be equally
true of *E.N.* X.3 (with the quickly-slowly test) as of *E.N.* X.4, even
though Aristotle is no more explicit in the former than in the latter
passage about the connexion with the distinction as expounded in
*Met. θ*6. (In fact the language in which the quickly-slowly test is
set forth in *E.N.* X.3 is loaded with the terminology of the distinction
as it appears in *Met. θ*6: *teleion* vs. *ateleis* (1173a29–30), *kinēsis*
(1173a31, cp. *kinēsis & genesis* at a30, with 1174b5–10), *energein*
(1173b3) and the example of *walking* (b1).)

tified in terms of the criteria of identity of movements, it being the point of Aristotle's reference to *form* in his discussion of walking to introduce the idea of criteria of identity. And as the quickly-slowly test turns out to be a consequence of the fact that actions to whose expressions "quickly" and "slowly" apply include the whence and whither, so too the tense test, properly interpreted, is such a consequence. Instead of one or other of these tests being the "basis" of this distinction, we have a basic distinction, various aspects of which (speed and degree of completeness respectively) turn up in these tests. These conclusions represent my reply to Ackrill's claims numbered (iii) to (v) above.

Before concluding this section, however, four philosophical matters must be briefly mentioned. First, my use of quantificational formulas has relied mainly on the features of identity and countability of what is quantified over: I have tried to avoid taking a stand on the nature of the referring involved in quantifying, e.g., on whether or not this referring commits me to the existence of what I refer to.[23]

Second, I am assuming that such quantificational formulas as (6) are extensional, as is implied by my taking it that every case of walking is a case of walking from some A to some B. (Consider the case where I am mistaken as to the identity of the point to which I am walking.) Thus, if the movements of humans are actions, they need not be voluntary actions, since we would not expect to treat voluntary actions extensionally. Indeed, for Aristotle there are involuntary, as well as voluntary, *praxeis*: see E.N. 1109b30 ff. And Aristotle's analysis would apply equally to the movements of inanimate objects.

---

[23] Aristotle insists both upon speaking of "one and the same quality" (city, movement, etc.) and upon reducing all uses of "one," "same," and "be (exist)" to the uses of these words for substances (perhaps in ways that could not be accepted by one who holds a Quinean theory of ontological commitment).

Third, in quantifying over *energeiai* in (7), I went further than was necessary for purposes of rebutting Ackrill's claims, and it may be urged that an adverbial analysis could have been given of enjoying, seeing, etc., without giving up the arguments against Ackrill. Of course how high one rates avoidance of quantification over *energeia* very much depends on one's theory of referring. But even if the Quinean theory seems the natural one to adopt, there are reasons for exploring the view that does quantify over *energeiai*, e.g.,

  (i) We have already found it necessary, in expounding the tense test, to speak of the perfect-tensed verbs as referring to *the very same event as* the present-tensed verb. So in using the tense test we commit ourselves to referring to *energeiai*.

 (ii) Aristotle in *Met. θ*6 certainly speaks of *energeiai* as if we referred to them co-ordinately with movements, as if *energeiai* and *kinēseis* formed mutually exclusive classes of actions.

(iii) Aristotle (unlike Ryle and Quine) probably thought that acts of thinking and seeing were just as much among the events that took place in the world as acts of running, slimming, etc.; and if they did so without a whence and whither being in any way associated with them, so much the better (see n. 40 below).

(iv) Exploration of the ontologically inflationary view should be a stage towards evaluating the wisdom of pursuing in the philosophy of mind the ontological economy that (again not too distantly from Quine) Ryle has consistently advocated ("one process, not two").

Fourth, some *energeiai*, e.g., some cases of enjoying,[24]

[24] Currently, analytical philosophers seem to divide pleasure or enjoyment into the three cases, the pleasure of pleasurable sensations, the enjoying of things one does, and being pleased that something

involve intentional contexts and will, at best, complicate some of our arguments. Thus although it seems perfectly defensible to say that if I am walking, I am walking from some A to some B, it is doubtful whether one should say that if I am enjoying walking I am enjoying walking from some A to some B—especially if, as Ryle claims, enjoying doing something is attending to doing something in a certain way ("pleasure is a species of attention"). In particular, the argument

> —movements always have predicates of a certain kind (speed-predicates) and *energeiai* never have such predicates, so what has a movement-predicate true of it cannot have an *energeia*-predicate true of it—

involves a suspect use of Leibniz's Law if the *energeia*-predicate brings in an intentional context: if an *energeia*-predicate is false of an event under one description, it may nevertheless be true of it under another description. So certain cases of enjoying, for example, may be contingently identical with certain movements. It is not clear to me that Aristotle can get around this objection. (In practice Aristotle seems to me to be somewhat less aware than Plato of the need for caution where intentional contexts are involved.) But of course Aristotle's line on *kineseis* and *energeiai* will still be worth examining if there are some *energeiai* which can properly be given an extensional treatment. In section V, where I examine some of the philosophical implications of having these two mutually exclusive classes of actions, I work on the assumption that there are such *energeiai*.

---

is the case. The last case (first adumbrated in Plato's discussion of false anticipatory pleasures in the *Philebus*, but more or less disregarded by Aristotle in *E.N.*) certainly seems to involve intentional contexts; and the second case at least sometimes does (see S. Marc Cohen's question "What is the object of enjoyment of the man who enjoys running up the stairs thinking he is charging San Juan Hill?" [*Philosophical Review*, 1969, 388]).

III

To lend support to the interpretation offered in the preceding section, I now try to show how the interpretation helps to clear up Aristotle's puzzling remark in *E.N.* X.4 that it is not possible to be moving "not in a time," whereas this *is* possible for pleasure, since the pleasure had in a now is a whole. "Surely," one is inclined to say, "enjoyment or being pleased can't take place at a point in time without taking some time? How can there be a pleasure at precisely 12:01:00, and no pleasure on either side of 12:01:00, however close?" One attempt to alleviate puzzlement has been to say that one is pleased *for* a certain time, whereas one builds a house *in* a certain time (Kenny, 176 n). However, I think the correct explanation can be brought out by considering Aristotle's proof at 234a24–31 (cp. a31–b9) that in (or at) a now ("instant," "moment": I shall use these two words interchangeably for a durationless point of time) nothing can be moving (as nothing can be at rest), essentially by arguing that if anything is moving it must be moving quickly, slowly, or at some other speed (see also 231b25–28: something is moving if and only if there is a movement from A to B). This latter argument (from *moving* to *moving at some speed*), which seems to me correct and has never, so far as I know, been challenged,[25] proceeds directly from the two necessary conditions of identity for movements singled out in section II, distance and time-period. A body can move at a certain speed only by covering certain distances in certain periods of time. Thus nothing can be moving at any speed in (or at) an instant; so nothing can be moving in (or at) an instant.

To this it might be objected that *at* the instant in

[25] It has been as close to analytic as anything may be that if I am moving I am moving at some speed. I make no predictions about the development of scientific conceptions of speed or movement.

question the object *is* covering some distance during a period of time. But this would only give us a sense for "moving quickly" for the period of time in question, and not for instants within that period. After all, every instant can be considered as "in" indefinitely many periods. And, in the same way, with sequences of nested periods, we get a sense of "moving quickly" only for the sequences. So the argument stands, in spite of its apparent consequences for the science of dynamics and its (apparently) real consequences for the history of dynamics— *acceleration*, and hence *force*, and (what is crucial for purposes of evaluating Aristotelian dynamics, as Professor Owen has pointed out in the article criticized in Appendix II below) *the force required to initiate movement*, require the notion of velocity at an instant.

We can now see that what Aristotle is saying, when he asserts that pleasure can be had in a now, is that while moving cannot be taking place in a now—if there is to be moving in a now there will have to be a movement from some A to some B in the now—pleasure *can* take place in a now since the conditions of identity for pleasures are not given in terms of any "A" or "B."

[I have pictured Aristotle in the last few paragraphs saying equally "there is no movement in a now" and "there is no movement at a now." He has been praised for the former and criticized for the latter, especially in connexion with Zeno's Arrow Paradox. In Appendix II I argue that Aristotle is more nearly right in thinking there was no difference between moving in a now and moving at a now, and indeed that to draw this distinction is to tempt one into talk of the state of motion.]

Thus "pleasure can be had in a now" does not entail that there are any instantaneous *energeiai*. If Ryle was relying on this passage (n. 7 above) in attributing this view to Aristotle, he was mistaken. On the other hand, we have seen in section I that Ackrill has now shown that the tense test entails that there are *no* instantaneous *energeiai*. Nor can Ackrill claim on the basis of 1048b26–29 in *Met. θ6*, translated in Appendix I, that all *energeiai* are continuable; for this parenthetical point is made only about the *energeia living* (see also my note *ad loc.*). For my own part, I believe that Aristotle thought all his examples of *energeiai* went on through time. But nothing he says, so far as I know, entails either the truth or the falsity of that belief.

Section II will also help us with Aristotle's troublesome and much ridiculed[26] definition of movement as the *entelecheia* of the potential *qua* potential. As Ackrill apparently agrees (Bambrough, 139), the word *energeia* is, in this context and for present purposes, used interchangeably with the word *entelecheia* (translated by Ross as "realization"). However *energeia* has here a broader meaning than that in which it is contrasted with *kinēsis*: for *kinēsis* turns out to be definable as a certain kind of *energeia*.

Of this definition, Ackrill remarks that although it looks as if it is *not* speaking of the *energeia* of a certain type of potentiality (an imperfect potentiality), but rather of the actualization (*energeia*) of a potentiality in a certain way (namely *qua* potential), it turns out that there are, after all, two types of potentiality, potentiality for a *kinēsis* (so that *kinēsis* = *energeia* of an imperfect potentiality, i.e., of a potential *qua* potential) and potentiality for an *energeia*. Hence the definition is of no help for purposes of clarifying the *energeia-kinēsis* distinction since the definition itself presupposes the distinction. So apparently what happens in the definition is that the "*qua* potential" marks off one kind of potentiality, potentiality for a *kinēsis*, from the other kind.

[26] E.g., by Descartes, near the end of *Regulae* XII, in E. S. Haldane and G. R. T. Ross (eds.), *The Philosophical Works of Descartes* (Cambridge: Cambridge University Press, 1911), Vol. I, and Locke in *An Essay Concerning Human Understanding* (New York: Dover, 1959), III, iv, 8–10.

Section II above will allow us to show that this account is mistaken.

We may begin with Ross's account of the definition (in his commentary on the *Physics apud* Γ1)[27] which Ackrill endorses and offers in support of his own account:

> An aggregate of bricks, stones etc., may be regarded (1) as so many bricks, stones etc., (2) as potentially a house, (3) as potentially being in course of being fashioned into a house. The movement of building is the realization not (1) of the materials as these materials (they are, previously to the movement of building, already actually those materials), nor (2) of their potentiality of being a house (the *house* is the realization of this), but (3) of their potentiality of being fashioned into a house. Similarly every movement is a realization-of-a-potentiality which is a stage on the way to a further realization of potentiality and only exists while the further potentiality is not yet actualized. Hence it is imperfect (b32) and, though in a sense an *energeia*, is distinct from an *energeia* in the narrower sense in which "*energeia*," implies that no element of potentiality is present at all.

The first thing to notice here is that it is not clear what Ross intends by (3). If we take it as first introduced, then it is a potentiality for an *energeia* as opposed to *kinēsis*—

> "These bricks are in course of being fashioned into a house" entails "These bricks have been in course of being fashioned into a house"

—rather unfortunate in a definition of *kinēsis*; and in addition, in order to get a definition of movement out of what Ross says, we should have to have

> the actualization (*energeia*: broader meaning) of the potential$_3$ qua potential$_2$,

[27] W. D. Ross (ed.), *Aristotle's Physics* (Oxford: Clarendon Press, 1926).

since there can be nothing incomplete about an actualization of the potential$_3$ (if the potential$_3$ were actualized at all, it would, on this interpretation, have to be actualized completely at any time), while "actualization of the potential$_2$ qua potential$_2$," taken literally, appears to pick out the incomplete house. So it is probably more charitable to take (3) as it appears the second time in the above quotation, not in accordance with its first appearance but, in Ackrill's way, so that

"These bricks are being built into a house" entails "These bricks have *not* been built into a house."

Then of course we get the circularity in the definition that Ackrill mentioned. It will be well to look afresh at what Aristotle tells us about his definition.

In the extremely important preface (200b26–201a9) to the definition of movement, as well as in the postscript at 201b24–35, he has explained in a general way that his idea in the definition is that movement is what intervenes between something potentially having a predicate of a certain category and the same thing actually having it (the whence and the whither!). Thus we have alteration for the category of quality, growth and diminution for the category of quantity, locomotion for the category of place and coming-to-be for the category of substance (cp. 201a9–16 with the preface and postscript, as well as with 225b5–9, for these identifications). When the thing in question has the predicate potentially, it has the privation of what it has when it has the predicate actually (201a5, b26, b34). This, I think, shows clearly that the potency in question is of type (2): in the case of coming-to-be, for example, the privation is the formless collection of bricks and stones, and the actual substance is the formed house (cp. 201a5 with 190b1–191a3, 193b18–21).

But having the general idea of what Aristotle wants to get across, and knowing which potency and which actualization are in question in the definition does not yet explain the syntax of "the *entelecheia* of the potential *qua* potential." Aristotle himself is none too good at explaining how the different parts of his definition go to explain the idea he wants to get across. At 201b10 we see the problem:

"For either the housebuilding or the house is the *energeia.*"

Here we need a word to translate *"energeia"* which can cover either the process of building a house or the product of that process, the house. "Actualization," which is process-product ambiguous,[28] will do the trick where neither "actuality." (= product) nor "activity" (= process), the two standard translations of *"energeia"* will do. (Translators have served the philosophical public badly here in translating *"energeia"* now "actuality," now "activity"—and usually without comment).[29] What is potential here is the matter, the bricks and stones which are potentially a house. And the point of *"qua* potential" when added to "the actualization of the potential" is simply to make clear which actualization is in ques-

[28] For an interesting discussion of the process-product ambiguity, see Vendler's "Effects, Results and Consequences" in R. J. Butler (ed.), *Analytical Philosophy* (Oxford: Basil Blackwell, 1962), Vol. I, reprinted in the collection mentioned in n. 1. The replies by Bromberger and Dray in Butler (Vol. I) and by Shorter (Vol. II, 1965) are also worth consulting.

[29] The translator's task has not been made easier by the fact that *energeia* is also sometimes used to cover both kinds of actualiz*ings* —actualizations in the technical sense (i.e., as opposed to movements) and actualizations of the potential *qua* potential. Again in *Met.* θ8, esp. 1050a21–b3, *energeia* is being used to cover *energeia* in the technical sense *as well as* the product of a movement (except for 1050a31–34, which a21–23 shows us we should discount: Aristotle's real view there is that *energeia* is cognate with *ergon,* "work" and *telos,* "end," used as in *Met.* θ6). Thus, there are at least four different uses of *energeia* (of which the last, incidentally explains the sense in which *eidos,* form, is *energeia:* it is both terminus and end of the movement of coming-to-be for a substance). It is noteworthy that Aristotle is able in all of the passages I have mentioned to get across the technical distinction we are interested in —in different terminology in each case!

tion, the house or the housebuilding. Once the house has been built the only actualization we have on our hands is the thing actualized, the house (the housebuilding is all over); but *before* the house has been built, i.e., while the matter is still only potentially a house, if there is any actualization at all, it is the actualizing, the housebuilding (the house doesn't exist yet). Hence movement is that actualization of the potential which exists *while* the potential still exists. (Perhaps we should say "while the potential still exists *as such*, on the grounds that it would be true *per accidens* to say that the potential exists even when it is fully actualized, since the thing that *was* potential exists. If we take this line, the *"qua"* will do two jobs: the one just mentioned is a natural one for *"qua"* to do, and might explain why we have *"qua"* instead of some blatantly temporal word, while the first job, deputizing for "while," is less natural, but has strong textual support: see 201b6-7, 11–12).

According to this account there is only one type of potency involved, the one that Ross says is not involved, a type to be explained (as in the paragraph before last) in terms of the whence and whither. So far from it being "potency" that has two readings in the passage, it is *energeia*, or as I shall henceforward call it, "actualization," that has two readings—and it is the function of the *qua* clause to make clear which of these two readings it has. Accordingly, the definition is doing neither what Ackrill says it is doing (speaking of the actualization of one of two types of potency) nor what he says it *looks* as if it is doing (for it's not a case of singling out a certain way of actualiz*ing*, but of singling out a certain kind of actualiz*ation*).

I conclude that the considerations of the preceding section throw light on the definition of movement, and in so doing confirm the interpretation in that section. "The whence and the whither constitute the form" explains not only the two tests of the preceding section

(involving speed and degree of completeness) but also
the dictum "pleasure can be had in a now," as well as the
definition of movement.

Before passing on to the next section, however, I
should like to dwell briefly on the fact that Aristotle
comes out all right on the definition of movement in
spite of the fact that he apparently did not realize the
way in which *"energeia"* and *"entelecheia"* are ambiguous; for although he gives semantic analyses of a large
number of philosophically important terms at various
points in the corpus, but especially in *Met.Δ*, including
a semantic analysis of *"energeia"*'s bedfellow *"dunamis,"*
he never does this for *"energeia."* In fact earlier in *Met.*
*θ*6, Aristotle has implied that one has to see the various
uses of *"energeia"* by analogy and by the use of induction
("one shouldn't seek a definition of everything":
1048a35 ff.). Underlying Aristotle's unawareness that
energeia is process-product ambiguous may be a deeper
fact about the Greek language which I present only as a
conjecture. This is the relative poverty in Greek of
process-product ambiguous words. Greek verb-nominali-
zations—unlike English ones ending in ". . . ing,"
". . . ation," and a number of philosophy's most crucial
words, "statement," "thought," "idea," "perception,"
"sensation," "conception" (cp. "concept")[30]—tend
clearly to distinguish process and product. Thus we have
praxis and *pragma*, *poiēsis* and *poiēma*, *tmēsis* and
tmēma, *noēsis* and *noēma*, *to legein* and *to legomenon*,
aisthēsis and *aisthanomenon* (cp. *aisthēton*). I do not,
of course, claim that Greek words with endings which are
regularly process endings cannot turn up as product words
(cp. *rhēsis* and *hupothesis*), nor that process-product ambiguous words do not turn up elsewhere in Greek philosophy (see my treatment of *doxa*, "belief" or "judg-

[30] See G. E. Moore's "The Refutation of Idealism" in *Philosophical Studies* (London: Routledge and Kegan Paul, 1922), p. 19, for
an early recognition of the importance of the ambiguity of some of
these words.

ment" as opposed to *doxazein* and to *doxazomenon* in
"False Anticipatory Pleasures: *Philebus* 36c3–41a6," forthcoming in *Phronesis*), but only that ambiguities are rare
enough in Greek in general and in philosophical contexts
in particular to have escaped the attention of even so
wary a philosopher as Aristotle. We should not be surprised, then, at Aristotle's stammering over his definition
at 201b27 ff., or at the verbal contradictions in his references to the definition of movement (at *De An.* 431a6–7,
movement is the *actualization of the incomplete* while at
Physics 257b8–9, movement is the *incomplete actualization* of the movable).[31] Aristotle knew what alternatives
the phrase "*qua* potential" marked off, but he had no account of how the phrase did this. The account of how it
does this must exploit a linguistic distinction of which he
was apparently unaware.[32]

IV

Claim (vii) of those attributed to Ackrill attacks Aristotle's apparent claim at 1174b9–14 that movements are
distinguished from pleasure and seeing by the fact that

[31] It is true that at 201b31–33 Aristotle explains the incompleteness of the actualization (*energeia*) in terms of the *potential* being
incomplete. If this was what was meant at 257b8–9, the contradiction would be *purely* verbal, and both passages just mentioned in
the text might seem to give the account Ackrill wants. Apart from
the fact that I have already established (as I hope) the superiority
of a quite different view for the whole discussion in which 201b31–
33 is embedded, I am cheered by the fact that the *entelecheia* with
which the incompleteness of the *entelecheia* is contrasted at 257n7–8
appears to be (though no doubt this is debatable) what would be
predicted on my view, the whither (a place, a quality, a form: b8, 9,
10), as it is on either side of the talk of incompleteness at 201b31–
33 (see esp. b26–30 and a33–35). The talk of incompleteness was a
theoretical whistling in the dark of something he understood quite
well in practice.

[32] After I had finished my account of Aristotle's definition of
movement, my attention was drawn to a very full and rather different
discussion of this definition by Aryeh Kozman in *Phronesis* (forthcoming). I have been unable to consider it here.

there is no coming-to-be of pleasure or of seeing. Aristotle says:

> From these considerations too it is clear that those who say pleasure is a movement or a coming-to-be do not speak well: these [i.e., movements and comings-to-be] are not said of all things, but of things that are divisible into parts and are not wholes. For there is no coming-to-be of seeing or of a point or of a unit (and none of these things *is* a movement or a coming-to-be); but nor is there of pleasure. For it is a kind of whole.

Ackrill comments:

> Unfortunately it is hard to understand why Aristotle thinks it worth pointing this out in connection with the distinction between *energeiai* and *kinēseis,* for he holds that there is no coming into being of *kinēseis* either. The point is stated and argued in *Phys.* E.2.
>
> (Bambrough, 137)

Since Aristotle places some emphasis on the class of things that "are and are not without coming-to-be or passing-away" (hearing at 446b2 ff., touching and moving "as some say" at 280b6 ff.—the "some" had better not include Aristotle, given the passage just quoted—points, units, and even forms (*eidē*) at 1044b21–22, 1043b15, cp. 1033b5), we may hope that there is some explanation for this apparent contradiction. A closer look at *Phys.* E.2 shows that such an explanation is indeed possible.

Aristotle is in this passage interested less in questions about the origin of change (is there a first moment or sub-period of change, etc.?) than in the ontological priority of substance (cp. *Phys.* Γ1.200b32–201a3): the only things which may *strictly* be said to change or come-to-be are subjects, usually substances. But it is therefore perfectly possible that we be able to speak of a change of a change *in a non-strict way.* To put the point of my remarks in another way, we should not infer directly from the denial of a change of a change that Aristotle would have denied that there could be a concept of acceleration;[33] he would only have insisted that such a concept be constructed without conceding to velocity the same ontological privileges as the moving object. We can perhaps illustrate this by means of the following parable. A certain language is devised to reflect what ordinary language does not, the ontological priority of the things we choose to call substances,[34] let us call it "canonical notation." Then the message of *Phys.* E.2 is that "canonical notation" will not allow us to speak of the coming-to-be of either *energeiai* or *kinēseis*. Nevertheless, there may be in ordinary language (or in some other language, call it "unreduced notation") the means for saying that there are comings-to-be of *kinēseis*, but not of *energeiai*. Thus ordinary language (or unreduced notation) will reflect the ontological differences between *energeia* and *kinēsis* where "canonical notation" does not: though undoubtedly the ontological differences will show up in some difference in the translation into "canonical notation" if it is to be truly a canonical notation. Let us see how this suggestion works.

What could this coming-to-be of a movement be? Surely we should expect there to be no process of change from

[33] "Notoriously, Aristotelian dynamics failed to deal adequately with acceleration." (Owen, at p. 221 of the article discussed in Appendix II below.) Owen does not make the claim rebutted in the text.

[34] I say "things we choose to call substances" rather than "substances" because although in *Met.* Z1, Aristotle sets out the ontological priority of substance according to his own doctrine of the categories, he is making a more limited point about ontological reduction—some beings may exist only if certain other beings exist (see *E.E.* A8.1217b11–16), and only if the sense in which the first beings exist is semantically derivative from the sense in which the other beings exist. This can be seen from the fact that in *Met.* Z2 he takes it to be an open question as to whether stars, numbers, or Platonic Forms are substances. This point applies *mutatis mutandis* to being a "this." Neglect of it can lead to premature rejection of many of Aristotle's anti-Platonic arguments.

rest to movement. The first thing to notice about this at-first-sight insuperable objection is that the objection invites Aristotle to interpret "movement" as "state of motion"—a move I have already castigated as (at least) un-Aristotelian. So Aristotle is not committed to denying that there is no coming-to-be of the state of motion in any interesting sense of "deny," since the state of motion is, for him, an *Unding*. What then *is* Aristotle committed to when he asserts that there is a coming-to-be of the *telos* of the movement (cp. 1174a19–21, 27–29)? The coming-to-be of the complete movement, like the coming-to-be of the complete temple, must be by steps. But a pleasure (which is complete at any time) or a point or a unit or one of those actions which are *energeiai*, does not come into existence by a series of steps.

If this is right, then Aristotle's point about coming-to-be can be made clear in terms of Ryle's remarks about pleasure in *Pr. Ph.* (quoted on p. 402 above). Let us say that there are two senses of "come-to-be," "begin," and "stop," but that pleasures can come-to-be, begin, and stop in only one of those senses. The sense in which one can begin to be pleased is not one for which we can supply the contrasting locutions "is prevented from finishing," "is interrupted," "has half an enjoyment." Such locutions can be supplied only where we have an action for which it is already laid down what is to count as middle and end of that action, e.g., housebuilding. Again, to have stopped being pleased is not to have finished in the sense that either there was nothing left to do (cp. 1048b26–29) or in the sense that if he had stopped a little earlier he would have been interrupted and so not finished. And finally, the sense in which pleasure can come-to-be matches the above senses in which one can begin to be pleased and can stop being pleased, but not those which contrast with "is prevented from finishing," "is interrupted," "has half an enjoyment." Pleasure is and is not without a process of coming-to-be—the Aristotelian equivalent of "Now you see it, now you don't."

Ackrill rightly remarks (Bambrough, 134) that these contrasting locutions are not translations of any phrases in Aristotle's text. But it should be clear by now that without these locutions it might not be clear to the reader of Aristotle what the sense is in which enjoyment comes into existence or begins to exist, and what the sense is in which it does neither of these things (contrast 1175a21 with 1175a5). Aristotle in fact marks the sense in which pleasure comes into existence not only by talking of "is and is not without coming-to-be . . . ," but also by his subtle use of Greek tenses[35] at 1173a34–b2:

> one can *get pleased* (*hēsthēnai*) quickly as one can get angry quickly; but one cannot *be pleased* quickly . . . , whereas one can be walking, be growing, etc., quickly.

To translate "*hēsthēnai*" as "become pleased" as is most often done (e.g., by Ross, followed by Ackrill) is just to fail to mark these distinctions which I claim Ryle has correctly extracted from Aristotle's point about coming-to-be.

These remarks constitute my reply to Ackrill's claim (vii), and they are also a sort of reply to his claim (viii). Ryle's remarks, I have suggested, are more illuminatingly construed as directed toward Aristotle's point about coming-to-be than as directed to the passage Ackrill supposes they are directed to.

I have already construed the tense-test and the quickly-slowly test as consequences of "The whence and whither constitute the form" for the proper description of different aspects of the two types of action, etc. The same may now be said of the coming-to-be point. Consider now the following complaint made by Ackrill.

> The obvious candidates for things *of* which there is a coming into being . . . would be products of processes of making or terminal states following processes of

---

[35] *Phys.* Z8 is a veritable feast of the subtle use of tenses and verb forms: see esp. 238b23–26, 239a3–5, 10–14.

change. But such products or states are relevant to the distinction between *energeiai* and *kinēseis* only in so far as *kinēseis* are processes *leading to* such products or states, that is, are (in a broad sense) comings-into-being, while *energeiai* are not. But this is simply to repeat the point Aristotle has already made, that *energeiai* are not themselves comings-into-being or *kinēseis*.

This complaint is to be met by conceding that the coming-to-be point is indeed not making a new distinction, but is an alternative description of the same distinction, this time considering the aspect of coming into existence ("comes-to-be") instead of either speed ("quickly," "slowly") or degree of completeness (present and perfect tenses of verbs). It is as much or as little a new point as those expressed with the adverbs and verb-forms mentioned. This completes my examination of Ackrill's claims.

V

The philosophical theses attributed to Aristotle in section II now require some qualification and elaboration. The theory of action and of enjoying actions which will emerge (though only sketchily) will at some points be very close to the text, while at others it may appear to be at best a drawing out of Aristotelian assumptions. I carry out this elaboration by means of answers to a series of questions and objections, and will work on the basis of the assumptions of mutual exclusiveness, extensionality, etc., set out at the end of section II. The first question raises a problem about the identity of actions, and the other questions are directed to the notion of "object of enjoyment" with which Aristotle is working.

"First, your requirement of the mutual exclusiveness of the classes of movements and actualizations, though it no longer runs into the troubles Ackrill's apparent counter-example might seem to make for it (a given action of walking from A to B seemed, under the description 'walking,' to be an actualization, while under the description 'walking from A to B' it seemed to be a movement), still meets troublesome cases. For consider 'I am Ψ-ing,' where to Ψ is to exercise one's physical faculties for the sheer animal joy of so doing. Under this might come playing tennis just because one loves to be active and to be in the sun, yawning-and-stretching or just walking for the sheer physical joy of it. (I distinguish this last case from walking for exercize, for this suggests that there are certain more or less standard distances to be covered). Now with some reservations,[36] it seems to me that in such cases 'I am Ψ-ing' entails 'I have Ψ-ed'; what one is doing is what one has done. But in Ψ-ing I might be walking to New York, hence the same action would be both a movement and an actualization, thus destroying once again the mutual exclusiveness you have said Aristotle wants between the classes of movements and actualizations."

Aristotle, I claim, would have accepted that in the case in question there are two actions or action-like entities involved, an actualization (Ψ-ing) and a movement (walking)—an inside and an outside, so to speak, of what is commonly called "the action" (but the inside is not necessarily anything mental).[37] In general, if there is a

[36] For example, it may be that a certain amount of ground has to be covered before I can be said to be Ψ-ing, say one step. But even here it might be said that, of course, one has to warm up a bit before the actual Ψ-ing begins.

[37] The use of "exercize" in "exercize one's faculties" (as explained) corresponds to certain uses of words like *chrēsthai* and *ergon*. Already in the *Protrepticus*, before he has a movements-actualizations distinction (see the use of *kinēsis* at fr. 14 (Ross), and cp. n. 2 above), Aristotle is employing the word *chrēsis* and its cognates to indicate the superiority of actualizations to dispositions (fr. 14) and the pointlessness of products of makings—which are of course *kinēseis* in the technical sense opposed to actualizations—if one cannot *use* these products (fr. 5 with fr. 6). The *ergon* ("work") of an action will in some cases be the action itself, in some cases a product of the action (the product may be a substance, a quality, a quantity, or a place). Where *ergon* and *chrēsis* coincide, there we

natural faculty involved in some movement I carry out,
then whether I intend to or not,[38] I am both (a) exercizing the faculty and (b) carrying out the associated
movement, the latter quickly or slowly, the former not.
And one cannot make an informed choice of the one
without the other. Thus what we would usually think of
as a single action turns out to be two action-like entities.
If, as I claim, Aristotle was willing to pay this price,[39]
he has ensured the mutual exclusiveness of the classes
of movements and actualizations.[40]

---

have an actualization in the technical sense. Where they do not, we
have a movement. Thus *chrēsis* corresponds to the use of *energeia*
for "actualizings" noted above at n. 25. With both *chrēsis* and
energeia in this use, we may compare *praxis* which is sometimes used
for *poiēseis* (makings, which include, for example, the actions of
doctors in bringing about a state of health in a patient) and sometimes contrasted with them. See esp. *E.N.* 1139b1–4, 1140a5–6,
b6–7, where Aristotle argues in the fashion noted for the *Protrepticus*
the superiority of *praxis* to *poiēsis*.

[38] The irrelevance of intention to Aristotle's theory of action
emerges in the fact that one may fail to know the *hou heneka* (the
"that for the sake of which") or *telos* ("end") of one's action:
see *E.N.* 1135b14–16, 1111a5, *Phys.* 196b35–36, cp. 21–22. But we
still await a full account of Aristotle's theory of goals.

[39] Just how high a price is involved depends upon the answers to
a number of questions I have tried, as far as possible, to steer clear
of in this paper (see the last few pages of section II). It might be
noted, however, that in the philosophy of mathematics, slightly
analogously, there is a price to be paid for the definition of number,
namely, quantification over both objects and sets of objects.

[40] It can be seen immediately that this "two entity" theory goes
well with Aristotle's preference for the life of contemplation over the
life of moral virtue or liberality, or over political life: the life of contemplation requires fewer of the necessaries (read: fewer of the things
necessary *for carrying out the movements associated with* the exercizing of the virtues in question—1177a27–b1, 1178a23–1179a32).
And there is no associated product of the action (read: no product
of any associated movement there might be—1177b1–27). It also
accords with the preference for the pleasures of contemplation over
the bodily pleasures, since the latter are exercizes of the healthy or
satisfied part only (1152b35–36, 1154b18–20, 30–31, cp. 1173b9–
15) as the deficient part is acted on and a movement in it carried
out to completion (*kinēseis* and *geneseis*: 1152b32–33 with 28,

"Well, here is another objection. Although your use of (7)

(7) $(\exists x)(\exists y)(x \neq y$ & I am doing x & y is being done & x is an enjoying & y is a Φ-ing & of (x,y) & x is from the first chord to the last chord & y is between t' and t''),

above, is sufficient to show that 'I am enjoying' entails 'I have enjoyed' even where the enjoyment in question

anaplēroumenēs: 1153a4, *agomenōn*: 1153a12, *oude meta geneseōs pasai*: 1153a9–10, pleasures of movement: 1154a13–18, 26–29).

We can go further, and show that Aristotle held a "two entity" theory of bodily sensations one enjoys (takes pleasure in, gets pleasure from). Bodily pleasures which result from an actualization or activity (*energeia*) of the healthy part, cannot be had without an associated movement in the deficient part. But the actualization of the healthy part is *not identical with* the restorative process in the deficient part (1153a9–10: no pleasure is a movement, and *only some* are associated with movements). In Book VII (which includes all the above references concerning bodily pleasure except 1173b9–15), at 1153b9–12 (with a10–11, 14), Aristotle identifies the actualization of the healthy part ("actualization of a disposition in accordance with nature") with the pleasure. [Notice that the sense in which the actualization of the healthy part (= the pleasure) is an actualization is clearly not the broad sense in which *kinēseis* are actualizations of a sort (n. 29 above), but the sense we require, that in which it is opposed to *kinēsis* (1153a9–12: notice also *chrōmenōn*, cognate with *chrēsis*, *telos* and cp. *eis tēn teleiōsin agomenōn tēn phusin* with *De An.* 417b16: *tēn epi' tas hexeis kai tēn phusin*. The latter occurs in a passage which I claim, though I have not the space to show it, is also about the *energeia-kinēsis* distinction.)] The identification is probably made partly for reasons of ontological parsimony (cp. Ryle's "one process, not two"), partly for phenomenological reasons (cp. VII.1153a6–7, 20–23, X.1175a21–b28, b35). In the later Book X, Aristotle says that pleasure accompanies the actualization in such an intimate way that there is some dispute over whether pleasure and the actualization are the same (1175b33, cp. 1174b23–1175a3). But he decides that, because it would be odd in the case of enjoying seeing (thinking) to say that the pleasure of seeing (thinking) *was* the seeing (thinking), he should *not* say that a pleasure and the actualization enjoyed are identical. But in both books bodily pleasures involve both a movement and an actualization. So I take it that Aristotle held a "two entity" view of "having a bodily sensation" in these cases.

is the enjoyment of the ninth symphony (an analogous formula doing the same job for 'I am seeing a movie'), still your new translation of *Met.* θ6.1048b32–34

> 'It is a different [distance AB over which] one is moving and [AA' over which] one has moved [something]. Whereas one has seen and is seeing (is thinking and has thought) the same thing.'

threatens to raise Ackrill's difficulty in a few form. What is that. same thing that I simultaneously am seeing and have seen in the case of seeing a movie?"

A disastrous misstep here would be to say that since seeing and enjoying are "complete at any time" and can take place "in a now" (*E.N.* 1174a14–19, b14), therefore the objects of seeing and enjoying at any instant will themselves have to be instantaneous. For since Aristotle holds (justifiably, I have argued) that in a moment there is neither movement nor rest, there will be no instants of movements to be the objects of enjoying or seeing; so the only objects of instants of seeing or enjoying would have to be instants of actualizations—these new actualizations presumably being interpolated between the seeing and enjoying on the one hand and the movements seen and enjoyed on the other hand. But then, as Ryle would be swift to point out, another actualization would be needed between the new actualization and the movement—and so on to infinity.[41] (This logical point is of course quite without prejudice to the question of whether or not enjoying the ninth symphony involves a further actualization, e.g., an activity of some kind of the agent. Thus if I am to be said to be enjoying someone else's activities, there may still have to be an activity of my own integral to my enjoyment, e.g., observing the other person's activities—whether or not it is correct to *say* that what I am enjoying is observing the other person's activities (see n. 21 above). I give reasons below for thinking Aristotle does believe there is a further actualization in the case of

[41] I am indebted here to Fred Dretske and Peter Unger.

enjoying. But there would be no reason to think there was an extra actualization involved in "seeing a movie" besides the actualization seeing and the movement implicit in "movie.")

How then are we to face the difficulty? In n. 14 above, I glossed the passage causing us difficulty by speaking of it being different distances I simultaneously am moving and have moved, but the same *statue* (say) that I simultaneously am seeing and have seen. This suggests the simplest explanation of the present remark—that Aristotle has here simply forgotten about cases of seeing where "seeing" takes as its grammatical object a whence-whither expression like "movie."[42] If Aristotle has forgotten about such cases, then we seem to have two alternatives. One is to say that he would not have known how to react to such cases (this would undoubtedly be Ackrill's view). The other alternative is to say that he would have denied that seeing a movie, as seeing, was different from seeing a statue—or, less question-beggingly, that it was, as seeing, less "complete at any time." Now it must be admitted that this latter alternative turns away from the question of 1048b32–34, "Is what one simultaneously is X-ing and has X-ed different or the same?" to the question of completeness (b23, 29–30). These questions of course converge for a verb phrase like "see a statue" or a verb like "move"; and I believe it is because of *moving*, investigated with such care in *Phys.* EZ that Aristotle brings up the former (basically grammatical) point here. But that the former is nevertheless the subordinate question, and that it may legitimately be turned away from, appears not only from the structure of the passage in question, but also when we reflect on certain grammatical matters. (i) There is no obvious grammatical object or complement for such movement verbs as "convalesce," "housebuild" (b25, 31). (ii) Many actualization verbs do

not take grammatical complements of any kind, e.g.,
"live," "live· well," "be happy" (b25–27). But the crucial
point which must be decided is whether (iii) the whence-
whither point in *E.N.* X.4 is to be taken as an attempt to
rescue the tense test by supplying a grammatical object. I
have in sec. II given what I take to be conclusive reasons
for answering this question in the negative. To the arguments there may be added (what G. E. L. Owen has remarked) that the Greek word Aristotle uses for enjoyment
has no perfect tense. Aristotle is very little given to purely
syntactical points.[43] His concern in using the perfect
tense is with completeness. In the *Top.* Z passage mentioned in n. 2 he makes clear that he understands use of
the perfect tense to entail completeness (which he there
thinks may entail having stopped); but the lack of ̇a perfect tense does not prevent him from extending the point
to the completeness of enjoyings.[44]

Thus if we retain the new translation of b30–34, the
new form of Ackrill's objection has to be met by saying
that "it is the same thing that one is seeing and has seen"
is not *meant* to be generalized to all *energeiai;* and that
"it is a different distance one is moving and has moved,"
where it is fully explained, is extendable to all movements,
including those which do not take natural grammatical
complements, and is to be understood in terms of completeness and the necessary conditions of identity of these
movements—as in sec. II above. Thus in seeing a movie,
the seeing, like the enjoying in enjoying the ninth symphony, is complete at any time, it "free-wheels" along
with the running of the movie—sight being a natural

---

[43] This is why explanation of his position on movements lends
itself much better to the kind of Davidsonian semantical analysis
which I have suggested in sec. II than to analyses of the Vendler-
Ackrill type which are so far syntactical as scarcely to raise questions
of the identity and countability of the movements and actualizations signalized by the verbs or verb phrases in question.

[44] *energēkenai* and *pepausthai hēdomenoi:* contrast 1048b26–27
where Aristotle holds that use of the perfect entails having stopped
only in the case of movements.

faculty one exercises *for its own sake* and regardless of the consequences (see *E.N.* 1174a5, 1096b17). (Actually, seeing a movie or a tragedy probably also involves exercizing one's aesthetic or mimetic capacities, skills, etc., as well as one's purely visual faculties.)

"You have recently taken to speaking also in terms of *completeness* as well as identity. What is this completeness? It seems we have a completeness with a temporal dimension (for movements: see 1174a20–21) and a completeness which is instantaneous (for actualizations: the actualizing is complete at every instant of a continuous period of actualizing). How is this to be explained?"

In a general way, Aristotle makes it clear that talk of completeness goes together with talk of *eidos* at *Met.* 1021b14–23. But better for our purposes is the connexion between being complete (*teleios*) and having a goal (*telos*) which was certainly in Aristotle's mind in connexion with this distinction (see esp. *Met.* θ6.1048b22, *E.N.* X.4.1174a20–21, 25–26). For to say "I am running a mile" or "They are playing the ninth symphony" (referring to movements) is to say that the actions are incomplete: there is more running and more playing to be done for the actions to be complete. But to say "I am enjoying the ninth symphony" is not to say that the enjoying is incomplete. The enjoyment is complete at any time, since —this is surely Aristotle's thought here—*one is as close to achieving one's goal (telos) in enjoying at one moment as at any other moment*—and one does not get the goal more quickly by having the symphony played more quickly.

"But now you are suggesting that playing a symphony quickly is quickly achieving the goal of playing the symphony, which is in general false. The rule 'For movements, to be X-ing quickly is to be quickly achieving the goal of X-ing' carries some plausibility for many of Aristotle's standard examples of movement (e.g., *slimming, housebuilding, convalescing, learning*), but it does not for *all* actions which can be done quickly or slowly, as our present example clearly shows."

Here the "two entity" theory may help us out. According to it we should say that besides the movement of going from the first chord to the last chord, there is the exercizing of one's musical skills, talents, etc. The latter is not done quickly or slowly, whereas the former is done quickly or slowly. Similarly, cases of walking will, to a greater or less degree, also be cases of Ψ-ing. One can play the symphony quickly because there is a movement which unavoidably accompanies this kind of actualization of one's musical skills, etc.; but so doing is not in general quickly achieving the "goal of playing the symphony" since the goal of exercizing one's musical skills, etc., may only be attainable when one plays the symphony at a certain speed. Similar remarks apply to playing tennis, enjoyable cases of learning, etc.[45] In each case there are two actions, or two action-like entities, the one not to be had, perhaps, without the other. ("Goal" here is used in an Aristotelian way—one need not be aware of what the goal of one's action is, see n. 38 above.) Other cases will be more like pure actualizations, others more like pure movements.

This view of the completeness of certain actions or action-like entities may be supported by looking at Aristotle's theory of enjoyable activities and pleasurable sensations. For in *E.N.* X.4–5, Aristotle implies that the only things enjoyed are *energeiai*: every pleasure "completes" an *energeia* (1174b31–33) to which it is "germane" (1175a29–b24). Now by *energeia* here I think Aristotle means actualization as opposed to movement.[46] But

---

[45] On this theory, as on the Vendler-Ackrill theory, there is an explanation of why it is harder to play tennis quickly than to play a quick game of tennis or to play a game of tennis quickly. For on this theory the first locution is more suggestive of *chrēsis*, of an exercize of one's faculties.

[46] I have not the space here to rebut the reply that Aristotle is not here using *energeia* in the technical sense (see n. 28 above). But if pleasure is complete at any time, is a supervenient end to

I do not think he means that the only things that can be said colloquially to be enjoyed are such actualizations. For in the case of bodily pleasures he speaks of "enjoying (taking pleasure in) the replenishment" (*hē-desthai tēi anaplērōsei*: 1173b15, cp. 1154b26–29). Similarly, Aristotle speaks of the enjoyment of the lover of housebuilding (1175a34–35) even though housebuilding is a paradigm case of a movement (1174a20).[47] So what the pleasure is "germane to," what the pleasure "completes," is an actualization and not a movement even where the grammatical object of the verb "enjoy" in the sentence describing the pleasure refers to a movement. In any case we should have expected this result from the facts that Aristotle construes pleasure in an activity along the same lines as pleasure in a sensation and that Aristotle demonstrably holds a "two entity" theory of pleasurable sensations (n. 40 above). Thus if the only things to which pleasures are germane, the only things which pleasures complete, are actualizations, then most so-called actions (those which can be enjoyed and which can be quick or slow) will consist of two entities—a movement and an actualization. (Attributing to Aristotle such a bizarre theory of action does make me somewhat uneasy. On the other hand some of the bizarreness would be removed if

the *energeia* it completes (1174b31–33), and is so intimate to that *energeia* as to be almost indistinguishable from it (1175b32–33), the *energeia* itself will surely be complete at any time. The pleasure would therefore seem to be the pleasure of an actualization of some capacity, tendency, skill, or whatever of the agent.

[47] It is the exercizing of the housebuilder's art, and not the movement of housebuilding which makes the so-called action of housebuilding comparable to thinking at *De An.* 417b9. (Notice also *eis hauto hē epidosis kai eis entelecheian* at 417b6–7 with *epididoasin eis to oikeon ergon, chairontes autōi* at *E.N.* 1175a34–35). The "two entity" theory also explains why at 417a21–b16, *learning* appears on *both sides* of the distinction Aristotle is interested in: at 417a31–32 it is an ordinary kind of alteration by contrast with contemplation which is "either not an alteration at all or an alteration only in a special way," whereas at 417b12–15, learning is "either not an alteration at all or an alteration only in a special way"!

we were not committed to the ontological implications
Quine says are carried by the considerations of identity
and countability on which I have been insisting primarily
[see p. 422, as well as nn. 23, 39 above, and, for possible
extensions of the analysis, n. 53 below].)

So in the case of "enjoying housebuilding" we have the
movement progressing to its terminus at a certain speed,
and the enjoyment flowing equably along (to mis-apply,
comparably, a famous mis-description), as does the exercizing of the skills with which the movement is associated
and to which the pleasure is germane.

By way of summary, my suggestions as to Aristotle's
analyses of different cases of pleasure may become clearer
in the following formulations. In Book VII, we have for
"I am having a pleasant bodily sensation":[48]

(8) $(\exists x)(\exists y)(\exists u)$(I am doing x & x is an enjoying
& u is a replenishing of the deficient part of me & u
is from A to Z & u is between t' and t'' & y is an exercizing of the healthy part of me in accordance
with a natural faculty or disposition & x $=$ y &
associated (y,u))

For the pleasures of contemplation we should expect:

(9) $(\exists x)(\exists y)$(I am doing x & I am doing y & x is
an enjoying & y is a contemplating & x $=$ y)

As n. 40 will make clear, this becomes altered in Book X
to something like the following:

(10) $(\exists x)(\exists y)$(I am doing x & I am doing y & x
is an enjoying & y is a contemplating &
germane(x,y) & x $\neq$ y).

[48] See n. 40 for some argumentation on various features of this
analysis. Replenishment may be thought of as the Platonic (and
thence Aristotelian) equivalent for homeostatic, physiological processes with which bodily pleasures are correlated (? or identical). See
Plato, *Philebus* 31b ff. For "association," see *meta* at 1153a9, geni-
tive absolute constructions at 1153a3, 4, 12 and *sumbainein* at
1154b18; and in Book X see 1173b12–13.

And for bodily pleasures in Book X we get, by making
appropriate adjustments to (8):[49]

(11) $(\exists x)(\exists y)(\exists u)$(I am doing x & x is an enjoying & u is a replenishing of the deficient part
of me & u is from A to Z & u is between t′ and t″
& y is an actualizing of the healthy part of me in
accordance with the sense of touch &
germane(x,y) & associated (y,u) & x ≠ y).

Finally, for "I am enjoying housebuilding," we get:

(12) $(\exists x)(\exists y)(\exists u)$(I am doing x & x is an enjoying & I am doing u & u is a housebuilding & u is
from shapelessness to shaped house & u is between t′ and t″ & I am doing y & y is an exercizing of my housebuilding skills & germane(x,y) &
associated (y,u) & x ≠ y).

An incidental benefit of this deploying of (8) to (12)
may now be noted. If (12) can be established as the
analysis of, as we say, enjoying movements one *performs*,
and (11) as the analysis of movements one *suffers*, then
there will have been little likelihood of Aristotle confusing
the enjoying of activities with the having of pleasant sensations, of his confusing enjoying the activity of smelling
roses with enjoying the smell of roses.[50] Urmson's (at
first sight plausible) charge itself makes the confusion
that this section—and indeed the whole paper—has been

[49] I have incorporated into (11) the point, plausibly urged by
Urmson, that Aristotle thinks of the bodily pleasures as exercizes of
the sense of touch. See J. O. Urmson, "Aristotle on Pleasure" in
Moravcsik, *op. cit.*, 325–27, citing E.N. 1117b23–18b8, *De An.*
414b6–11.
[50] As is claimed by Urmson, *ibid.*, 326–31. Urmson also appears
to claim that the only *energeiai* that are enjoyed are those of sensing
and thinking, a view which certainly has a good deal of support (see
e.g., *Rhet.* A11, E.N. IX.9). But even apart from the pleasures of
housebuilding and writing (1175b18–19), Aristotle could surely not
have forgotten the pleasures of actualizing the virtues in virtuous acts
(see e.g., E.N. I.7–8, esp. 1099a7–21).

trying to clear up in the interpretation and philosophical discussion of Aristotle, namely, supposing that what Aristotle might colloquially call the "object of pleasure" is what he thought the pleasure was directly related to in the way suggested by the surface grammar of the sentences we employ to describe enjoyments.

CONCLUSION

In hoc libello I have argued that the energeia-kinēsis distinction should be understood by seeing what Aristotle means when he says in connexion with walking that the whence and whither constitute the form. This I do by invoking the conditions of identity of movements, thus, in one direction anyway, going a step further than Ryle has gone in his fruitful application of the logical form—grammatical form distinction to the philosophy of mind. Once this is done, Ackrill's apparent counter-example to Aristotle's distinction ("I am enjoying the ninth symphony" does not entail "I have enjoyed the ninth symphony") can be seen itself to rest upon a mistake about logical form. The conditions of identity of movements also prove to explain a number of otherwise puzzling features of Aristotelian doctrine, in particular:

(i) the connexion of the quickly-slowly test with the tense test (sec. II);

(ii) how Aristotle fails to consider the state of motion, it being an Unding (sec. II);

(iii) how pleasure can be had in a now (sec. III);

(iv) Aristotle's definition of movement and the trouble he has explaining it (sec. III: here I conjectured that some of the difficulty Aristotle has arises from the philosophical insignificance of the process-product ambiguity in Greek, and that the contrast with English in this respect explains some of the difficulty interpreters have had in seeing what Aristotle is getting at in his definition);

(v) Aristotle's claim that there is no coming-to-be of *energeiai* and yet that there is of *kinēsis*, thereby apparently contradicting things he says in *Phys.* E2 (sec. IV).

In addition, I have argued that the following attacks on Aristotle (or, in the first case, a Rylean interpretation of Aristotle) fail:

(a) Ackrill's claim that "I have seen" for Aristotle means "There is a time before the present instant during which 'I am seeing' was true of me" (sec. I);

(b) the claim of Owen that Aristotle mishandled Zeno's Arrow Paradox, and the claim common to Owen and Vlastos that Aristotle confused "in an instant" with "at an instant" (Appendix II);

(c) Urmson's claim that Aristotle assimilated the pleasure of pleasurable sensations to the pleasure of enjoyable activities (sec. V, near the end).

In section V, I have tried to tie together some philosophical and exegetical loose ends of the first four sections. Suppressing my Rylean intuitions, I have presented a "two-entity" theory of most actions, according to which each such action has both an inside, an *energeia* of some natural disposition (or etc.) and an outside, a movement.[51] I found this theory useful in explaining the following:

[51] One's Rylean intuitions suffer less with the addition of enjoyment as a third entity. For when Aristotle distinguishes enjoyment from the actualization to which it is germane, he says virtually what Ryle says in support of his view that the enjoyment of an activity and the activity itself are one thing and not two (*Pl.*, in Gustafson, 201; cp. also the very frequent "separate clockability" argument). The denial of the identity of the enjoyment with the actualization to which it is germane may seem, upon reflection, insufficient to justify also quantifying over pleasures. My doing so here has been mainly a matter of convenience. I shall not investigate here the possibility of re-casting (8)–(12) in Ryle's adverbial manner.

(A) why certain actions which can be done quickly or
slowly are not such that we can say of them that
doing them quickly is achieving quickly the goal of
doing the actions;

(B) Aristotle's notion of pleasure being "germane to"
and "completing" an actualization.

The "two-entity" theory also shows us how to meet a
difficulty about learning in *De An.* B5 (n. 42), and over-
comes the objections of Potts (*op. cit.*, 73) and Ackrill
(Bambrough, 140–41) to supposing the passage is not
about the movements-actualizations distinction. I have
been able only to sketch this "two-entity" theory and its
pedigree; such an elaborate and far-reaching theory will
have a great many implications I cannot claim to have
examined here or at all. But the presence of such a theory
in Aristotle nevertheless seemed worth trying to establish.

With this much by way of apology, I must leave the
theory in its present rude state. I must even suppress my
inclination to add a section on the significance of the
energeia-kinēsis distinction for Aristotle's ethical theories
(esp. in connexion with determining what Ryle would
call the "logical type" of candidates for the supreme good)
and for Aristotle's ethical methods (esp. in connexion
with the large place given to examination of the virtues—
here note especially *E.E.* B1.1219b26, 33 and *E.N.*
1097b22–98a18—and cp. the defining of "life" and "soul"
in *De An.* B1–3 ff. in terms of potencies had by the entities for whom the definitions were being given), or for
Aristotle's aesthetics[52] although I think in both cases[53]
that the significance is very great.[54]

[52] The Aristotelian theory I have presented in this paper lends
some support to, and is supported by Humphrey House's account of
plot, character, and catharsis in *Aristotle's Poetics* (revised with a
preface by Colin Hardie, London: Rupert Hart-Davies, 1965), Chapters 5, 7, 8.

[53] There are consequences elsewhere, e.g., with the distinction between *acts* and *events*. Consider, for example, our intuition that we
want "The door opened" to follow from "The key opened the door,"

and this to follow from "I opened the door with a key." An Aristotelian "two-entity" theorist would say immediately that we can isolate easily that *movement*—the door opening—referred to in each of these sentences; moreover on an appropriate reading of "association" (which I have left undefined in this paper), the notion of agency can be interpreted as the bringing about of a certain movement (or the prevention of a certain possible movement) by *the actualization of certain powers, skills, etc.* In that way "I opened the door with a key" would refer both to the actualization involved and to the movement involved (as well as to the instrument) while the other two sentences refer only to the movement or to the movement and the instrument. The implication relations mentioned then follow directly. The difference between my raising my arm and my arm rising will be accounted for in a similar way.

54 Among innumerable debts to friends, colleagues, and students, I should like to single out Richard E. Grandy, Gareth B. Matthews, S. Marc Cohen, J. L. Ackrill, Gilbert Harman, and Alexander Nehamas (all of whom were good enough to read earlier drafts of this paper), the Hammond Society at Johns Hopkins University (who heard an even earlier draft and asked many helpful questions), as well as Gregory Vlastos, David J. Furley, Donald Davidson, S. Wheeler III, Thomas Robertson, and George Pitcher. There are also antique debts to discussions years ago in Oxford with Ackrill, Owen, and Ryle. None of the above can be held to endorse any of this final draft, though in my view they have all contributed in one way or another to such value as it has.

Met. θ6. **1048b18** Since (i) none of the actions of which there is a terminus is an end, but [all] are of the class of things which are means to an end,[1] e.g., slimming, and [since] with these[2] when someone is [for example] slimming, he is in movement[3] in this way, that for the sake of which the movement takes place not yet obtaining, these are not actions, or at least not complete actions. **22** For none of them is an end.[4] But (ii) that in which the end inheres *is* an action. E.g., one is seeing [and has seen] [[simultaneously]],[5] is understanding [and has understood], is thinking and has thought; whereas (i) it is not the case that one [simultaneously] is learning and has learned, is getting better [i.e., convalescing] and has got better [i.e., all better]. One *is* (ii) living well and has lived well, is happy and has been happy [[simultaneously]]."

26   If this were not the case, [the action] would have to stop at some [specific] time, as when one is

---

[1] I.e., the end in question is acquired only when the action is completed.

[2] *Auta*: referring back to the class mentioned, and forward to *tauta*, with the example squashed in between. The singular *praxis* for "actions" is awkward but not unparalleled (e.g., 1035a16, 992b7); and "body" must be understood as the object of the transitive verb for "slim." Ross supposes that *auta* stands for "the parts of the body," and translates "the bodily parts themselves, when one is making them thin, are in movement in this way." The text of the first seven lines of this passage is very corrupt, and there is general agreement that, in this first sentence, at least three corrections have to be made, e.g., [*tou ischnainein*] *he ischnasia* [*auto*] . . . *huparchonton*. . . . But both Ross's and my translations are awkward, and perhaps yet more corrections are required. Fortunately, the general sense is relatively uncontroversial.

[3] Or: "in a movement."

[4] End: *telos*: Complete: *teleios*.

[5] "Simultaneously" in b23, 25 translates *hama*, a plausible emendation for the senseless *alla*, ("but"). There are genuine *hama*'s at b30, 33, as well as at *De Sensu* 44b62.

slimming. But this is not so in the case we are
considering—where one is living and has lived.[6]

29 We should call [type (1)] *movements*, [type (ii)]
actualizations. Every movement is incomplete—slimming,
learning, walking, housebuilding—these are movements
and incomplete.

A A′ B For it is not the case that simultaneously one
is walking [from A to B] and has walked [from A to B],
is housebuilding and has housebuilt [= has built a
house], is coming-to-be [something] and has come-to-be
[that same thing], is being moved and has been moved

---

[6] This point, that movements are not continuable beyond their
termini while actualizations are in general continuable beyond any
given fixed point, has been held (e.g., by Hirst, *op. cit.*, 132, and by
Ackrill, following Vendler) to be the main point Aristotle is making
in this chapter. However, it seems to me that the chapter's tense-
criterion and its emphasis on *incompleteness* (fully explained at
1048b29–34, properly understood) show the continuability point to
be merely a desirable consequence of Aristotle's criterion as dealing
with movements *before* they reach their termini.

[7] I have added grammatical complements in this sentence entirely
without textual warrant because it makes the clear sense of the passage emerge. It is *some same thing* (distance, object which some
matter is coming-to-be, etc.) with respect to which each case of
coming-to-be, walking, and being moved is carried out. That this is
the sense of the passage becomes clear from Aristotle's emphatic
use of "but it is a different thing . . ." in the next lines. Moreover,
without the grammatical complements, Aristotle's remarks will be
false for walking and being moved, pretty clearly false for coming-
to-be (they would only be true if "has come-to-be" meant "has
changed" in the sense "has begun to change"—see n. 12 above) and
even perhaps for housebuilding (it's only by making it the same
house that is in question for "I am housebuilding" and "I have
housebuilt" that one can ensure that it is not the case that these
two locutions are simultaneously true of me).

Notice that the grammatical complements are of different grammatical types: "from A to B" is accusative, and "something" and
"that same thing" are nominative. In the paper I talk sometimes of
criteria of identity, sometimes of "true object" of the verb.

Ross translates the passage differently: "But what is being moved
is different from what has been moved, and what is moving from
what has moved. But it is the same thing that at the same time has
seen and is seeing." That the correlatives "different" and "same"

[the same distance];[7] rather it is a different [distance, AB, over which] one is moving and [AA' over which] one has moved [something]. Whereas one has seen and is seeing (is thinking and has thought) simultaneously the same thing.

34 By actualization, then, I mean something of this latter kind, by *movement* something of the former kind. Let's take it as clear, then, from these and suchlike considerations, what *that which is actually* is and what it's like.

APPENDIX II: A NOTE ON ARISTOTLE'S TREATMENT OF ZENO'S ARROW PARADOX

The arguments given at the beginning of section III are inconsistent with some of those developed by G. E. L. Owen in his treatment of Zeno's Arrow Paradox ("Zeno and the Mathematicians," *Proceedings of the Aristotelian Society* (1957-68), esp. 215-22). Owen argues that Aristotle's claim that in a moment that is neither movement nor rest, which Aristotle develops against one of Zeno's premisses, represents a "failure to come to grips with" that premiss, and leads Aristotle to attack the other premiss of Zeno's argument which is "wholly respectable." Owen argues that the claim in question represents a "surrender to Zeno," that Aristotle in making this claim thereby accepts the (not false but) absurd picture of the flying arrow "bottled up in a piece of time that fits it too closely to allow any movement." My arguments, on the other hand, support Aristotle's handling of the premisses in question. Let us see how this is so.

Owen suggests, quite rightly in my view, that the premisses Aristotle is considering in his presentation of Zeno's

---

are *objects*, not subjects of the verbs in question, seems to me to be strongly suggested by S.E. 178a9 ff. The use of the direct object for distances moved over is frequent in *Phys.* Z, as is the claim that the distance one *is moving* is different from the distance one *has moved* (e.g., 231b28-232a1, 237a25-28, 28-35). The difficulties over "seeing" are discussed in Sec. V of the paper.

argument at 239b5–9, b30–33 (cp. a23–b4) are (a) in each moment of its flight the arrow must be stationary, since evidently it has no time to move, and (b) what is true of it at each moment is true of it throughout the whole period. Aristotle *corrects* (a) to read "in any moment of its flight the arrow is neither moving nor at rest," and *attacks* (b) on the grounds that the period of the arrow's flight is not made up of the instants of that flight. Owen, on the other hand, holds that (b) is correct, and Aristotle should have attacked (a) by saying that in (or at) each moment of the flight the arrow is moving—not perhaps in the primary sense of "is moving," but in a perfectly acceptable sense of "is moving" which is derivative from the primary sense (used with periods of time) and sanctioned by usage. "We rule that, when and only when it is correct to say 'X was moving throughout the period *p*,' it is also correct to say 'X was moving at any moment *t* in *p*.'" This rule of Owen's may be bolstered (as it has been by Owen in classes at Oxford) by an appeal to the distinction between "moving *in* an instant" and "moving *at* an instant," conceding to Aristotle that it is senseless to speak of "moving *in* an instant," but denying that it is senseless to speak of "moving *at* an instant," to which sense can and must be given" (G. Vlastos, "A Note on Zeno's Arrow," *Phronesis* (1966), p. 14n35). Vlastos argues that Aristotle "completely failed to grasp this distinction," and cites, relevantly enough, the inconsistency at 236a15 ff. noted in the next to last paragraph of section I above. However I have argued there that this argument is not the main argument that Aristotle is interested in in that context and that it is indeed quite peripheral; that is to say, I think we should regard the inconsistency at 236a15 ff. in the way we did in section I, as a slip, as a lapsing from his true view according to which there can be no movement and no rest *either in a now or at a now*. In other words, I do not think that Aristotle would be discomfited by having the distinction of "in" and "at" brought to his attention (he uses both words, e.g., *en* at 235b31, 237a20–24, 239b5, 263b17 ff., and *kata* at 220a5, 237a15, 239a35 and—of a stretch of time—at 239a31). He would simply deny that either of the two arguments adduced by Owen establish that one can be moving at an instant in *any* sense of "move." Let us consider these two arguments, which are quite distinct.

First Owen's rule for establishing a derivative sense of "move." This, Aristotle would say, confuses movement with the state of motion, a step castigated in section II, and so falls afoul of the *energeia-kinēsis* distinction. This can be seen in the dialogue Owen imagines between Zeno and Aristotle. Owen has Zeno saying to Aristotle's attack on (b) that if *at any moment* of the afternoon I am asleep, then I am asleep *throughout* the afternoon; and he has Aristotle reply (in effect) that for Zeno's reply to be correct, we should have to substitute "at any period, however small" for "at any moment." Aristotle, however, would surely have replied that by both the quickly-slowly test and the tense test, sleeping is an *energeia,* and there is therefore absolutely nothing wrong with saying someone was asleep at a certain instant. The substitution in question is therefore quite unnecessary. "Zeno" has simply misunderstood Aristotle's doctrine. Aristotle has no *general* presumption against saying that if X was Φ-ing throughout a period *p,* then at any moment *t* during *p* he was Φ-ing. It is just that this cannot be said with movement, or, more generally, with *kinēseis.* If we were right above that for any case of moving there is a movement, and therefore a distance and a period of time—and just this is required if every case of moving is to be a case of moving at some speed—then that at which (or in which) one is moving is just that period and not the instant. (The mistake here is a particularly insidious one, for it is tempting to indicate a point on a graph—cp. Owen, 219—or the position at an instant of a speedometer needle, and say "You see, it is moving at this point in time." But these very cases are cases that require speed. So the above argument applies with full force.)

The second argument for a derivative sense of "move" in which one is moving at an instant is that from the differential calculus and the limit of a sequence of ratios of distances to periods of time. Now Aristotle can perfectly well grant that this yields us a (derivative!) sense of "instantaneous velocity" and so a secondary sense of "moving at an instant"; but this is perfectly irrelevant to Aristotle's reply to Zeno. This secondary sense of "moving at an instant" does not show that there is any sense of "move" in which one is moving at an instant; if anything, it shows that there are secondary senses of "instantaneous" or "at an instant" (cp. the use of "now" for a specious present or for almost any period around the present instant, a use Aristotle comes close to at 222a20–24). But Zeno cannot be employing any such secondary sense of "at an instant" in this Aristotelian version of the Arrow Paradox. The differential calculus is irrelevant to the paradox. And, *contra* Vlastos (pp. 13–14 with nn. 32, 35) there is no failure of insight on Aristotle's part on the distinction between physical and semantic reasons for the truth of "there is neither movement nor rest in a now." Aristotle's arguments require no sophistication relevant to the paradox.

The burden of my reply to Owen's charge that Aristotle "mishandled" the Arrow Paradox can be brought out by considering a slightly different formulation of the paradox which Zeno could have employed against Owen had Owen denied (a) by asserting that it was in *another sense* of "at an instant" *true* that the arrow was moving at an instant:

(a′) At a moment no distance is traversed; and
(b) what is true at each moment of a period is true throughout the whole period; so
(c) throughout the whole period no distance is traversed,

insisting of course that he is employing the ordinary sense of "at a moment." (This formulation in fact catches precisely the cash-value of Aristotle's reply to (a) that "in a moment there can be neither movement nor rest": that it does so is missed, I think, because of the failure to see the implications of Aristotle's claim that there is moving if and only if there is a movement). Here Zeno's premiss (b) requires us (improperly, as Aristotle observes) to add up moments in order to get a period, to regard a period as "composed of nows." For only this addition of distances traversed yields us the total distance traversed. The correct reply to this formulation of the paradox is that for *kinēseis* we have to substitute "in any sub-period, however small" for "at any moment" in (a) or (a'), making them false. Here Aristotle seems to me to be right, Owen wrong.

Owen's commitment to accepting (b), even in this context, may be surfacing in his imaginary dialogue between Zeno and Aristotle where to Aristotle's correction of (a) to "in a moment there can be neither moving nor rest" he has Zeno replying (at 218) that, by premiss (b), the arrow will be neither moving nor at rest, "and as a paradox that will do." If, as *appears* to be the case, Owen is here endorsing Zeno's reply, then he will hardly be able to object to the reformulation of the paradox in the pre-ceding paragraph. In fact Zeno's reply would have been correct for an *energeia*. But for a *kinēsis* it is incorrect. Thus Owen's charge of mishandling appears to rest upon a failure to observe the *energeia-kinēsis* distinction.

CHRONOLOGICAL LIST OF PUBLISHED WRITINGS 1927-1968 OF GILBERT RYLE[1]

1927

Critical Notice of Roman Ingarden, *Essentiale Fragen. Mind*, Vol. XXXVI, pp. 366–70.

1929

Critical Notice of Martin Heidegger, *Sein und Zeit. Mind*, Vol. XXXVIII, pp. 355–70.

"Negation," *Proc. Arist. Soc.*, Supp. Vol. IX, pp. 80–96. (Symposium with J. D. Mabbott and H. H. Price.)

1930

"Are There Propositions?" *Proc. Arist. Soc.*, Vol. XXX, 1929–30, pp. 91–126.

Editor's Foreword to Proceedings of the Seventh International Congress of Philosophy held at Oxford, England, September 1–6, 1930, Oxford University Press, p. vi.

1931

"Mr. Ryle on Propositions, Rejoinder," *Mind*, Vol. XL, pp. 330–34. (A reply to R. Robinson in the same volume.)

1932

"Systematically Misleading Expressions," *Proc. Arist. Soc.*, Vol. XXXII, 1931–32, pp. 139–70. Reprinted in Antony Flew (ed.), *Logic and Language, First Series*, Blackwell, 1951.

"Phenomenology," *Proc. Arist. Soc.*, Supp. Vol. XI, pp. 68–83. (Symposium with H. A. Hodges and H. B. Acton.)

Review of A. Wolf, *Textbook of Logic; Philosophy*, Vol. VII, pp. 96–97.

[1] The editors are grateful to Gilbert Ryle for his assistance in preparing this bibliography.

Review of Ralph Eaton, *General Logic*; *Philosophy*, Vol.
VII, pp. 235–39.

1933

"Imaginary Objects," *Proc. Arist. Soc.*, Supp. Vol. XII,
pp. 18–43. (Symposium with R. B. Braithwaite and
G. E. Moore.)

"'About'," *Analysis*, Vol. 1, 1933–34, pp. 10–12.

"Locke on the Human Understanding," *John Locke Ter-
centenary Addresses*, Christ Church, Oxford; Oxford University Press, pp. 15–38.

Review of J. N. Findlay, *Meinong's Theory of Objects*;
Oxford Magazine, Vol. LII, 1933–34, pp. 118–20.

Review of B. M. Laing, *David Hume*; *Philosophy*, Vol.
VIII, pp. 220–25.

1935

"Internal Relations," *Proc. Arist. Soc.*, Supp. Vol. XIV,
pp. 154–72. (Symposium with A. J. Ayer.)

"Mr. Collingwood and the Ontological Argument," *Mind*,
Vol. XLIV, pp. 137–51.

1936

"Unverifiability by Me," *Analysis*, Vol. IV, 1936–37, pp.
1–11.

Review of Bent Schultzer, *Transcendence and the Logical
Difficulties of Transcendence*, *Philosophy*, Vol. XI,
pp. 234–39.

1937

"Induction and Hypothesis," *Proc. Arist. Soc.*, Supp. Vol.
XVI, pp. 36–62. (Symposium with Margaret Mac-
Donald.)

"Taking Sides in Philosophy," *Philosophy*, Vol. XII, pp.
317–32.

"Back to the Ontological Argument," *Mind*, Vol. XLVI,
pp. 53–57. (Reply to E. E. Harris, "Mr. Ryle and
the Ontological Argument," *Mind*, Vol. XLV,
pp. 474–80.)

1938

"Categories," *Proc. Arist. Soc.*, Vol. XXXVIII, 1937–38,
pp. 189–206. Reprinted in Antony Flew (ed.),
Logic and Language, Second Series, Blackwell,
1959.
Welcoming speech to the 4th International Congress for
Unified Science, *Erkenntnis*, Vol. VII, pp. 303–6.

1939

"Plato's Parmenides," *Mind*, Vol. XLVIII, pp. 129–51 and
302–25. Reprinted in R. E. Allen (ed.), *Studies
in Plato's Metaphysics*, Routledge & Kegan Paul,
1965.
Review of Karl Britton, *Communication*; *Philosophy*, Vol.
XIV, pp. 366–70.
Review of F. M. Cornford, *Plato and Parmenides*, *Mind*,
Vol. XLVIII, pp. 536–43.

1940

"Conscience and Moral Convictions," *Analysis*, Vol. VII,
pp. 31–39. Reprinted in Margaret MacDonald
(ed.), *Philosophy and Analysis*, Blackwell, 1954.
Review of W. M. Urban, *Language and Reality*; *Philosophy*, Vol. XV, pp. 202–4.
Review of Brand Blanshard, *The Nature of Thought*; *Philosophy*, Vol. XV, pp. 324–29.

1945

"Philosophical Arguments," Inaugural Lecture as Wayn-
flete Professor of Metaphysical Philosophy; Oxford
University Press, 20 pp. Reprinted in A. J. Ayer
(ed.), *Logical Positivism*, The Free Press, Glencoe,
Illinois.
"Knowing How and Knowing That," *Proc. Arist. Soc.*,
Vol. XLVI, 1945–46, pp. 1–16.

1946

"Why are the Calculuses of Logic and Arithmetic Ap-
plicable to Reality?" *Proc. Arist. Soc.*, Supp. Vol.
XX, pp. 20–29. (Symposium with C. Lewy and
K. Popper.)

Review of Marvin Farber, *The Foundations of Phenomenology; Philosophy*, Vol. XXI, pp. 263–69.

1947
Review of Karl Popper, *The Open Society and Its Enemies; Mind*, Vol. LVI, pp. 167–72.

1949
The Concept of Mind, Hutchinson's University Library, 334 pp. Italian translation by F. Rossi Landi, *Lo Spirito come Comportamento*, Einaudi, Turin, 1955. Spanish translation by Eduardo Rabossi, *El Concepto de lo Mental*, Editorial Paidós, Buenos Aires, 1968. German translation by Kurt Baier, *Der Begriff des Geistes*, Philipp Reclam Jun., Stuttgart, 1969.

Discussion of Rudolf Carnap, *Meaning and Necessity; Philosophy*, Vol. XXIV, pp. 69–76.

1950
" 'If,' 'So' and 'Because,' " Contribution to Max Black (ed.), *Philosophical Analysis*, Cornell University Press, pp. 323–40.

"The Physical Basis of Mind," A Symposium with Lord Samuel and A. J. Ayer in Peter Laslett (ed.), *The Physical Basis of Mind*, Blackwell, pp. 75–79. Reprinted in Antony Flew (ed.), *Body, Mind and Death*, Macmillan, 1964.

"Logic and Professor Anderson," *The Australasian Journal of Philosophy*, Vol. XXVIII, pp. 137–53.

Review of M. H. Carré, *Phases of Thought in England; Philosophy*, Vol. XXV, pp. 181–83.

1951
"Heterologicality," *Analysis*, Vol. XI, 1950–51, pp. 61–69. Reprinted in Margaret MacDonald (ed.), *Philosophy and Analysis*, Blackwell, 1954.

"Thinking and Language," *Proc. Arist. Soc.*, Supp. Vol. XXV, pp. 65–82. (Symposium with Iris Murdoch and A. C. Lloyd.)

"Feelings," *The Philosophical Quarterly*, Vol. 1, pp. 193–205. Reprinted in William Elton (ed.), *Aesthetics and Language*, Blackwell, 1954.

"The Verification Principle," *Revue Internationale de Philosophie*, Vol. V, pp. 243–50.

"Ludwig Wittgenstein," *Analysis*, Vol. XII, 1951–52, pp. 1–9. Reprinted in Irving Copi and Robert Beard (eds.), *Essays on Wittgenstein's Tractatus*, Routledge & Kegan Paul, 1966.

1952

Review of J. Wisdom, *Other Minds*; *The Listener*, Vol. LXIV, p. 953.

"Graduate Work in Philosophy at Oxford," *Universities Quarterly*, Vol. VI, pp. 380–83.

1953

"Thinking," *Acta Psychologica*, Vol. IX, pp. 189–96.

"Ordinary Language," *Philosophical Review*, Vol. LXII, pp. 167–86. Reprinted in Charles Caton (ed.), *Philosophy and Ordinary Language*, University of Illinois Press, 1963.

1954

Dilemmas, The Tarner Lectures, Cambridge University Press, 129 pp. Italian translation by Enrico Mistretta, "Dilemmi," Ubaldini, Rome, 1968.

"Proofs in Philosophy," *Revue Internationale de Philosophie*, Vol. VIII, pp. 150–57, and contributions to discussion pp. 158–69.

"Pleasure," *Proc. Arist. Soc.*, Supp. Vol. XXVIII, pp. 135–46. (Symposium with W. B. Gallie.) Reprinted in Donald Gustafson (ed.), *Essays in Philosophical Psychology*, Anchor Books, 1964.

Review of *L'enseignement de la philosophie* (Publications Unesco, Paris, 1953). *Universities Quarterly*, Vol. VIII, pp. 293–95.

1956

"Sensation," Contribution to H. D. Lewis (ed.), *Contemporary British Philosophy, Third Series*, Allen &

Unwin, pp. 427–43. Reprinted in R. J. Swartz (ed.), *Perceiving, Sensing and Knowing*, Anchor Books, 1965.

"Hume," Contribution to M. Merleau-Ponty (ed.), *Les Philosophes Célèbres*, Editions de l'art, Lucien Mazenod, Paris, pp. 206–9.

Introduction to *The Revolution in Philosophy*, Macmillan, pp. 1–11. (An introduction written specially for the book which consists otherwise of previously broadcast talks by A. J. Ayer and others.)

1957

"The Theory of Meaning," Contribution to C. A. Mace (ed.), *British Philosophy in Mid Century*, Allen and Unwin, pp. 239–64. Reprinted in Charles Caton (ed.), *Philosophy and Ordinary Language*, University of Illinois Press, 1963.

"Predicting and Inferring," Contribution to *Observation and Interpretation in the Philosophy of Physics*, Proceedings of the Colston Research Society Symposium, Vol. IX, University of Bristol, pp. 165–70.

Final discussion with Mary Warnock & A. M. Quinton. Contribution to D. F. Pears (ed.), *The Nature of Metaphysics*, Macmillan, pp. 142–64. (A series of talks originally broadcast in the Third Programme of the B.B.C. in 1955.)

Review of Ludwig Wittgenstein, *Remarks on the Foundations of Mathematics; Scientific American*, Vol. CXVII, pp. 251–59. (A general survey of Wittgenstein's work.)

1958

"On Forgetting the Difference Between Right and Wrong," Contribution to A. I. Melden (ed.), *Essays in Moral Philosophy*, University of Washington Press, pp. 147–59.

"A Puzzling Element in the Notion of Thinking," *Proceedings of the British Academy*, Vol. XLIV, Oxford University Press, pp. 129–44. Reprinted in Dudley Bailey (ed.), *Essays in Rhetoric*, Oxford

University Press, 1965, and in P. F. Strawson (ed.), *Studies in the Philosophy of Thought and Action*, Oxford University Press, 1968.

Reply to J. Garelli, "La notion de possibilité dans l'analyse logique de l'esprit de Gilbert Ryle," *Revue de Metaphysique et de Morale*, Vol. LXIII, pp. 126–27.

"T. D. Weldon (Obituary)," *The Oxford Magazine*, Vol. LXXVI, 1957–58, pp. 527–28.

1960

"Letters and Syllables in Plato," *Philosophical Review*, Vol. LXIX, pp. 431–51.

"Epistemology," article in J. O. Urmson (ed.), *The Concise Encyclopaedia of Western Philosophy and Philosophers*, Hutchinson, pp. 128–35.

Comment on Mr. Achinstein's Paper, *Analysis*, Vol. XXI, 1960–61, pp. 9–11.

Review of Richard Wollheim, *F. H. Bradley; The Spectator*, Vol. CCIV, p. 81.

1961

"Use, Usage and Meaning," *Proc. Arist. Soc.*, Supp. Vol. XXXV, pp. 223–30. (Symposium with J. N. Findlay.) Reprinted in G. H. R. Parkinson (ed.), *The Theory of Meaning*, Oxford University Press, 1968.

1962

"A Rational Animal," *Auguste Comte Memorial Lecture*, University of London, Athlone Press, 25 pp.

"Abstractions," *Dialogue* (Canadian Philosophical Review), Vol. 1, pp. 5–16.

"Thinking Thoughts and Having Concepts," *Logique et Analyse*, No. 20 (*Thinking & Meaning*, Entretiens d'Oxford, Organisées par l'Institut Internationale de Philosophie, Septembre, 1962), pp. 156–71.

"La Phénoménologie Contre *The Concept of Mind*"; La Philosophie Analytique, *Cahiers de Royaumont Philosophie*, No. IV, Les Editions de Minuit, Paris, 1962, pp. 65–84.

1963

Review of G. E. Moore, *Commonplace Book 1919–53*. *New Statesman*, Vol. LXV, pp. 85–86.

1965

"The Timaeus Locrus," *Phronesis*, Vol. X, pp. 174–90.
"Dialectic in the Academy," Contribution to R. Bambrough (ed.), *New Essays on Plato and Aristotle*, Routledge & Kegan Paul, pp. 39–68.

1966

Plato's Progress, Cambridge University Press, 311 pp.
"Jane Austen and the Moralists," *The Oxford Review*, No. 1, pp. 5–18. Reprinted in B. C. Southam (ed.), *Critical Essays on Jane Austen*, Routledge & Kegan Paul, 1968.
Review of Stuart Hampshire, *Freedom of the Individual*; *New Statesman*, Vol. LXXI, p. 52.

1967

"Plato," article in Paul Edwards (ed.), *The Encyclopaedia of Philosophy*, Macmillan and Free Press, Vol. VI, pp. 314–33.
"John Locke," *Crítica Revista Hispano Americana de Filosofía*, Mexico, Vol. 1, pp. 3–16.
"Teaching and Training," Contribution to R. S. Peters (ed.), *The Concept of Education*, Routledge & Kegan Paul, pp. 105–19.

1968

"Dialectic in the Academy," Contribution to *Aristotelian Dialectic*, Proceedings of the third Symposium Aristotelicum, Oxford University Press, pp. 69–79.
"Thinking and Reflecting," Contribution to G. N. A. Vesey (ed.), *The Human Agent*, Royal Institute of Philosophy Lectures, Vol. 1, 1966–67, pp. 210–26.
"The Thinking of Thoughts," University of Saskatchewan, *University Lectures*, No. 18, 20 pp.

NOTES ON CONTRIBUTORS

John L. Ackrill is Professor of the History of Philosophy at Oxford University and Fellow of Brasenose College, Oxford.

John L. Austin was White's Professor of Moral Philosophy at Oxford University and Fellow of Corpus Christi College from 1952 until his death in 1960.

A. J. Ayer is Wykeham Professor of Logic at Oxford University.

D. G. Brown is Professor of Philosophy at the University of British Columbia.

Keith Gunderson is Associate Professor of Philosophy at the University of Minnesota and Research Fellow, Minnesota Center for Philosophy of Science.

Stuart Hampshire is Professor of Philosophy at Princeton University.

G. B. Matthews is Professor of Philosophy at the University of Massachusetts.

G. E. L. Owen is Professor of Philosophy and the Classics at Harvard University.

Terry Penner is Assistant Professor of Philosophy at Princeton University.

Anthony Quinton is Fellow of New College, Oxford.

Gilbert Ryle was Waynflete Professor of Metaphysical Philosophy and Fellow of Magdalen College, Oxford, from 1945 to 1968.

J. M. Shorter is Fellow of Lincoln College, Oxford.

F. N. Sibley is Professor of Philosophy at the University of Lancaster.

J. J. C. Smart is Professor of Philosophy at the University of Adelaide.

P. F. Strawson is Waynflete Professor of Metaphysical Philosophy and Fellow of Magdalen College, Oxford.

J. O. Urmson is Fellow of Corpus Christi College, Oxford.

G. J. Warnock is Fellow of Magdalen College, Oxford.

NEW STUDIES IN ETHICS

Edited by W. D. Hudson

This major series of monographs has been planned to cover the whole range of ethical theory from the Greek philosophers to the latest developments in contemporary philosophy. Each study is complete in itself, and the series provides a unique treatment of the main philosophical problems in ethics.

"The writers of the *New Studies in Ethics* are all somewhat iconoclastic; no cows are sacred. They are seeking to stimulate really fresh discussion in clear precise English."—A. C. Adcock, *Hibbert Journal*

Other titles in preparation